D[...]
Advocate

*Godfroy Langlois
and the politics of Liberal Progressivism
in Laurier's Quebec*

WITHDRAWN

Other fine books from the same publisher:

The Traitor and The Jew, by Esther Delisle
Zen & the Art of Post-Modern Canada, by Stephen Schecter
The Last Cod Fish, by Pol Chantraine
Seven Fateful Challenges for Canada, by Deborah Coyne
*A Canadian Myth: Quebec, between Canada and the
Illusion of Utopia*, by William Johnson
Economics in Crisis, by Louis-Philippe Rochon
Dead-End Democracy, by Yves Leclerc
Voltaire's Man in America, by Jean-Paul de Lagrave
Judaism: From the Religious to the Secular, by A.J. Arnold

Canadian Cataloguing in Publication Data

Dutil, Patrice A., 1960-

Devil's Advocate : Godfroy Langlois and the politics of Liberal
Progressivism in Laurier's Quebec
Includes bibliographical references and index

ISBN 1-895854-31-8

1. Langlois, Godfroy, 1866-1928. 2. Quebec (Province) -
Politics and government - 1867- . 3. Legislators - Quebec (Province) - Biography. 4. Journalists - Quebec (Province) - Biography. I. Title

PN4913.L36D87 1994   070.92   C94-941305-4

To receive our current catalogue and be kept on our mailing list
for announcements of new titles, send your name and address to:

*Robert Davies Publishing,
P.O. Box 702, Outremont, Quebec, Canada H2V 4N6*

Patrice Dutil

Devil's Advocate

*Godfroy Langlois
and the politics of Liberal Progressivism
in Laurier's Quebec*

ROBERT DAVIES PUBLISHING
MONTREAL-TORONTO

Copyright © 1994, Patrice Dutil
ISBN 1-895854-31-8

This book may be ordered in Canada from

General Distribution Services,
☎1-800-387-0141 / 1-800-387-0172 FAX 1-416-445-5967.
In the U.S.A., Toll-free 1-800-805-1083

Or from the publisher, (514)481-2440, FAX (514)481-9973.

The publisher takes this opportunity to thank the
Canada Council and the *Ministère de la Culture du Québec*
for their continuing support.

Table of Contents

For Maha,
Nicole, Natalie and Isabelle

Preface

The book you are about to read is described by the publisher as the biography of a talented and colourful person, the journalist and politician, Godfroy Langlois (1866-1928). At the centre of violent storms of controversy throughout his lengthy career, this extraordinary man was vilified by the priests of his time, condemned by his Archbishop, and run out of the newspaper which he directed and of the political party in which he played an important role. But this book is in fact far more than a simple biography.

Langlois, it is true, is at the heart of the matter here. But to my mind, he is but a pretext for a larger undertaking, a vast mural which brings alive the federal, provincial and municipal political world of Montreal at the turn of the century. The story of Godfroy Langlois has inspired Patrice Dutil to turn out an astonishing gallery of portraits: Wilfrid Laurier, Israël Tarte, Archbishop Bruchési, Honoré Beaugrand, Lomer Gouin and dozens of other contemporaries parade here, in the rich textures of their historical truth, exposed under a sharp and penetrating light.

The thread that connects them and allows the reader to follow this churning, fast-paced narrative is the history of a wing of Laurier's Liberal party: the *vieux rouges* of the 19th century and their 20th century heirs, the radicals and progressives of pre-1914 Quebec.

Godfroy Langlois himself was a notorious Freemason, a resolute anti-catholic and anti-clerical. As such, he is a perfect symbol of the extremist radical tendency in Quebec's political class. Successively editor-in-chief of the Montreal newspapers *La Patrie*, *Le Canada* and *Le Pays*, Langlois also represented the Montreal riding of Saint Louis in the Legislative Assembly, and was a vitriolic critic of the province's educational system and of the intrusion

of the clergy into the temporal world. He described himself as the spiritual heir not only of Louis-Joseph Papineau,
but also of the famous anti-clerical *Institut canadien*, holding sharply radical views directly inspired by the Parisian
Parti radical.

If you are among those for whom, like myself, the name
Honoré Beaugrand meant nothing more than a Montreal
subway station, for whom Lomer Gouin seemed to be no
more than a carbon copy of his father-in-law Honoré
Mercier; if you knew nothing of Simon-Napoléon Parent
and Félix-Gabriel Marchand; if the "Préfontaine clique"
has no relation in your mind to the street in East-end
Montreal bearing that name, then this book will be for
you, as it was for me, a revelation. Just as if you believed
until now that the problems of obligatory and free public
schooling and the standardisation of textbooks only go
back to the Duplessis era, or thought that *Cité libre* was
the first to raise the problem of clericalism in Quebec.

In short, Patrice Dutil's seminal work is destined to refresh
our understanding of Canadian and Quebec turn-of-the century politics and of the decisive influence that Montreal
municipal politics had on the governments in Ottawa and
Quebec City. Insofar as the number of our contemporaries
who suffer from short memory syndrome is considerable
(some might even diagnose general amnesia), this work will
have no shortage of readers.

They won't be disappointed. The book, in its original
form, was a doctoral thesis presented at York University. Be
reassured, however: while *Devil's Advocate* has all the qualities of an outstanding academic work (widely-researched,
with precision in its affirmations, numerous references and
true perspectives), it displays none of the well-known faults
from which such works often suffer. This is a story told
without complacency or self-satisfaction, free of intellectual-
ist jargon, a heady tale recounted at full throttle in a simple
and clear way.

I trust that you will glean from its reading as much pleasure and knowledge that I gained myself.

Gérard Pelletier

Gérard Pelletier, a former editor-in-chief of Montreal daily newspaper *La Presse*, has also served Canada as Secretary of State and Ambassador to France.

ACKNOWLEDGEMENTS

Long in the making, this book is the result of the support of many people; too many of whom have not been sufficiently thanked.

The research for this book took place in numerous archives and libraries in Quebec City, Montreal, Ottawa and Toronto. In all cities, the archivists were invaluable guides to various collections. Three of them, however, were particularly helpful and I want to make sure they see how much I appreciate their efforts: Madame Monique Montbriand of the Archives de la Chancellerie de l'Archevêché de Montreal; Madame Françoise Telmosse at the CEGEP Lionel-Groulx in Ste. Thérèse; and the many kind people at the York University Interlibrary loans department, who always did their utmost on my behalf. I was able to make use of two private archives. I am grateful to Ms. Anne Bourassa for the permission to quote excerpts from Henri Bourassa's correspondence. Mr. Godfroy Marin allowed me full and free access to his small collection of his grandfather's papers. I am very grateful to him for entertaining my questions and for relating to me what he remembered hearing of the Godfroy Langlois "legend." Mr. Marin also introduced me to Mme Corinne Maillet, whose father, Dr. Gaston Maillet, was a close associate of Godfroy Langlois. Ms. Maillet knew Godfroy Langlois late in his life, and I spent a memorable afternoon in her study exchanging impressions, debating thoughts and confirming hunches.

Naturally, the book bears the imprint of a great deal of the scholarly insight I was able to take advantage of while researching and writing. I want to thank two academics: Pierre Trépanier at the Université de Montréal, who first brought the mystery of Godfroy Langlois to my attention, and Ramsay Cook who directed the Ph.D. thesis that is at the core of this book. Other scholars, notably William Irvine at Glendon College, Michael Behiels of the University of Ottawa and A.I. Silver of the University of Toronto, read parts of the original manuscript and offered helpful suggestions. Needless to say that while I am happy to acknowledge the contributions of these individuals, I remain solely responsible for the errors and the interpretations in this work.

I am duty-bound to thank Ms. Joy Manson, editor the *Journal of Canadian Studies* for permission to use parts of a 1993 article I published in that journal. As well, I must thank the University of Toronto Press for permission to reuse parts of an article I published in the *Canadian Historical Review* in 1988. It is a real pleasure to also acknowledge the support, enthusiasm and energy of Robert Davies. I am gravely indebted to his contribution to the world of ideas.

Finally, it is the support of my parents, my in-laws and my family, through thick and thin, that accounts for the completion of this book. To Maha, who has lived with Godfroy Langlois as long as I have, this book is dedicated.

Toronto, August 1, 1994

INTRODUCTION

> *"[In defining radicalism]*
> *in Canada*
> *It's our journalists*
> *who have counted."*
>
> —*Frank Underhill, 1960*[1]

I T WAS A PLEASANT AFTERNOON, late in the spring, one
of the last springs of the nineteenth century. After a day
of boating amongst the Thousand Islands, ten men gathered around a park bench and commemorated their day with
a group picture. They wore nifty caps, sported exotic mus-
taches, and except for one man (the cabinet minister) seemed
relaxed as they smiled at the camera. Standing among them
waiting for the photographer's flash was Charles A. Geoffrion, Minister without Portfolio in Wilfrid Laurier's cabinet. He was flanked on one side by Senator Joseph-Philippe
Casgrain and by Norman W. Trenholme, who was about to
be named judge in Montreal. On the other side was J.A.C.
Madore, the M.P. for Hochelaga, and J.A. Drouin, the Vice-
President of the Club National. Léger Meunier, a typographer, sat in the grass. Standing in the middle was Godfroy
Langlois, the editor-in-chief of the Liberal Party's French
daily in Montreal, *La Patrie*. The others, identified as "Senecal", "Talibert" and "Archer" have altogether escaped historical records. Who were these men, and why did they choose
each other's company on that memorable day of boating?[2]

I found this picture buried in a small private collection of
Godfroy Langlois's papers; one of only a few photographs
that were kept by the family. What was its significance?
There are no clear answers, but there are clues. Was this a
meeting of Freemasons? Godfroy Langlois and Léger Me-

unier had both been founding members of the Montreal lodge of the Grand-Orient de France in April 1896.[3] Two of the men were high ranking Liberal politicians in Ottawa. Six of the nine men were known members of the Montreal Liberal party organization. Was this indeed simply a meeting of the Liberal party?

The main clue to the story might be Godfroy Langlois himself. In his own time, he was identified variously as "Lucifer's direct representative", "a burn out ", "a threat to the nation", "the helm of a movement," "a dangerous man" and "a national shame" and certainly provided a contentious target as a "radical" politician. His name has been forgotten, effectively buried in the conservative Quebec of the 1920s and 1930s that wanted to make sure he was forgotten. His grandson and namesake, Godfroy Marin, encountered his grandfather's reputation in the mid-1930s, when he was a schoolboy at Brébeuf. His teacher, a priest, asked him to stay after class one afternoon. The priest quietly indicated that they would pray together for the boy had "bad blood" since his grandfather had been an "enemy of the church and of the Holy Father." Langlois's name has seldom been raised by any history of the day, save perhaps a few footnotes, if anything. There are no streets named after him; no schools, CEGEPS or subway stations bear his name in Montreal. His memory has never been invoked by the Liberal party; his presence was always understandably overshadowed in this golden day of Liberalism by the name and reputation of the pride of Quebec: Sir Wilfrid Laurier. But this neglect, I would argue, has significantly warped our understanding of the Liberal party under Laurier. More importantly, this neglect has also forced unfortunate categorizations on the evolution of ideologies in Quebec.

Godfroy Langlois was a key player in the Liberal party of Quebec as chief editor of its major newspapers in Montreal from 1895 to 1910. In this capacity, he defined what I call "Liberal progressivism": an ideology of reform, blended from an essence of traditional Quebec *rouge* attitudes, a reaction against the excesses of capitalism, a strong sense of national pride mixed with an equally strong distrust of nationalists, and a remarkable interpretation of the radical ideologies that raged in the Third French Republic. He chose the symbols of Liberal progressivism, elaborated its argumentation and gave this system of thought credibility. He picked the issues, set the agenda for debate and often played a major role in organizing the necessary political machinery to get things done. This journalist, to borrow Underhill's phrase, counted in the formulation of radical ideology in Canada. People eventually came to debate the nature of Liberal progressivism in Quebec, and consistently illustrated their views by comparing themselves to Langlois.

Ideology played a very significant role in the politics of Godfroy Langlois. The tendency to dismiss the importance of politics and of ideologies other than nationalism in Quebec during the years 1867-1936 has had a great impact on the study of the politics of reform. Much work has been done on the *rouges* and on the Institut Canadien, two associations held as exemplars of French Canadian ideologies of reform, but it was agreed that these manifestations of the politics of reform had disappeared without leaving a trace long before the turn of the century, even if historians could not agree on a specific date.[4] Students of Quebec history were therefore left to imagine the evolution of Quebec's politics, particularly those of the Liberal Party in Quebec (which was dominant in that period) in an ideological vacuum. Laurier's "Liberal Quebec" is practically interpreted as ideologically homogeneous, totally bereft of factionalism, let alone radicalism.[5] Through a study of the politics and passions of Godfroy Langlois, this book aims to show that the impulse of reform did not die from the blows *rougisme* suffered at the hands of the church and of the conservative-minded leadership of the Liberal party in the years of Laurier. Indeed, reform politics — *rouge* politics — played a key role in the evolution of the Liberal party in those years.

But ideology was not the only game in town. If Langlois represented a standard in the Liberal progressivism "movement," he never acted alone. Personally popular, he consistently found political friends. Clearly, the fact that he was allowed to work in the high ideological offices of the Liberal press bears testimony to his clout and to his support. As Liberal progressivism evolved, sometimes winning political battles, sometimes losing support, Langlois constituted a common thread to the many campaigns. He provides for us today, as he did for his contemporaries, a reference point to a critical moment in the evolution of reformist thought and reformist politics in Quebec at the turn of the century. He is a point of entry that leads to a more comprehensive understanding of many historical problems: confusions on the nature of leadership, on the presence of party infighting at the national, provincial and municipal levels, and on the rise of a distinctly French-Quebec form of progressivism.

A few words on the structure of the book. It is my firm belief that an "ideology" cannot be firmly grasped unless the politics that express it, or fail to express it, are understood. Attempts to define ideologies by simply referring to a few newspapers, a method used *ad nauseam*, are grossly inefficient: they help, naturally, but only reveal marginal tendencies. My understandings of ideology go beyond the confines of a newspaper column or of public speeches; an ideology will not be fully understood unless its praxis is defined. I have found clues to defining the ideology of Liberal progressivism in newspapers and also in private archives, but most of all I have sought to measure the words of their leaders against their actions. I discovered that municipal politics were a particularly fertile ground for the study of what ideologies actually meant once played out in the political arena. Many "reformers", including some Liberal progressives, were willing spokesmen for the values of a progressive liberalism, but proved to be far less open to change once given the harness of the state. Municipal politics provided an environment that prompted many to change, or to prove, their colours. The same, of course, can be said of provincial and national politicians. Reflecting on some of the events covered in this book, Dominique Monet, a leading nationalist spokesman, told Wilfrid Laurier in 1905 that he hoped historians reviewing the political life at the turn of the century would avoid the "politics of intrigue".[6] This book, it will be candidly said, ignores Monet's advice completely and is very concerned with political intrigue, the itchy underbelly of give-and-take political bargaining, because it had a significant impact on the expression of political ideologies. The power mongers, the influence peddlers, the arm twisters, those who saw politics as a noble calling that could bring about change as well as those who saw it as an instrument for personal advancement and as a brake on change, paraded daily before Langlois's editorial desk. They were part of his life, and he, as an *engagé* intellectual, assimilated them both. Political intrigues show how ideologies really *work*.

Yet, for the sake of clarity, the civic politics were kept separate from provincial politics as much as possible although the two arenas shared the same players. Similarly, "ideological" developments were treated separately from "political" decisions not because they were disconnected (they emphatically were not), but because each aspect of the politics of Liberal progressivism required individual attention. I thus opted to divide this study of Langlois's work into three chronological sections, each one dealing "synchronically" with the various aspects of the rise, the triumphs and the failings of Liberal progressivism in Quebec.

Part I traces the formative stages of Godfroy Langlois's career against the backdrop of Liberal politics in *fin-de-siècle* Quebec. Part II focuses on the elaboration of Liberal progressivism. Radical *rouge* thinking is observed here as it grapples with the urban problems of Montreal and launches an attack on the conservative forces of the Liberal party in this city and matures slowly to a state I identify as Liberal progressivism. Part III scrutinizes the various dimensions of the decline of Liberal progressivism in the wake of Lomer Gouin's ascent to power. As Langlois reacted to the failures of the Lomer Gouin administration and radicalized his understanding of Liberal progressivism, many of his former associates rejected his politics. Shifting coalitions and ideological contradictions as well as leadership changes isolated Langlois further from mainstream Liberalism, both at the municipal and provincial levels.

In the end, this book seeks to understand what brought together Godfroy Langlois and those nine boaters I referred to at the outset. Other people made their way in and out of their circle, but they and so many others formed a consistent, if anonymous, core of Liberal political opinion. This is the story of their associations, of that moment regrettably frozen in time.

(Notice to reader: French-language quotations have been translated to English in most cases, to make the text more fluid.)

Notes

1. Underhill and P.W. Fox, *The Radical Tradition: A Second View of Canadian History* (Script of "Explorations", CBC Television, June 8 and 15, 1960).

2. This picture is in the Godfroy Langlois Papers, private collection, file P1.

3. Roger Le Moine, *Deux Loges montréalaises du Grand Orient de France* (Les Presses de l'Université d'Ottawa, 1991), p. 12.

4. For instance, Jean-Paul Bernard, the most important historian of the French Canadian rouge movement of the nineteenth century, argued that radicalism fatally exhausted itself in the Confederation debates of 1866 and 1867 and was dealt a lethal blow when the church denounced the Institut canadien in 1869. See his *Les Rouges: libéralisme, national-isme et anticléricalisme au milieu du XIXe siècle* (Montreal, 1971), conclusion. Yves-François Zoltvany, on the other hand, perceived that the post-Confederation years were a difficult and trying period for the *rouges*, but insisted that radical thought still played a role until 1874, even if "le rougisme, à toutes fins pratiques, est chose du passé" by the time the Liberals under Joly attained power in 1878. See his "Les libéraux du Québec, leur parti et leur pensée, 1867-1875" (M.A. thesis, Université de Montréal, 1961), p. iv. Marcel Caya was also unconvinced by the results of Bernard's autopsy. Seeing the fate of radical rougisme

decided by a generational struggle between the old wing (the *vieux rouges*) and a new style of activist politicians like Mercier and Laurier, Caya perceived some life in the radical movement after 1878 and placed its death near 1886, when most of the radicals finally rallied behind Mercier's *Parti national*. See "La formation du parti libéral au Québec, 1867-1887" (Ph.D. thesis, York University, 1981). After that, according to the conventional wisdom, radical doctrine declined rapidly into oblivion so that by the end of the nineteenth century, it is nothing but a "socially marginal" and "silent" movement. See Fernand Dumont, "Quelques réflexions d'ensemble" in Fernand Dumont (ed.) *Idéologies au Canada français, 1850-1900* (Québec, 1971), p. 9.

5. See H.B. Neatby, *Laurier and a Liberal Quebec* (Toronto, 1973)

6. Public Archives of Canada, Wilfrid Laurier Papers, C821, Monet to Laurier, 22 mars 1905.

CHAPTER I

NEW INSPIRATIONS

THE SMILING YOUNG MAN was fulfilling a dream he had cherished for years. While he carefully measured his steps down the picturesque Pont d'Iena, his round face gently caressed by the sweet August breezes of Paris, Godfroy Langlois's spirit soared. Paris, like its young Canadian visitor, was celebrating the centennial of the French Revolution in 1889. As the engineering of the Eiffel Tower proudly demonstrated, France was modernizing. Electricity illuminated the town's lamps for the first time, making Paris a true city of lights. Godfroy Langlois simply loved France, and his admiration for its people, its writers, and its political culture was only reinforced by the modern dynamism of the era of the impressionist painters, of the Boulanger "affair" and of radical politics. As he posed in François Mulnier's esteemed photography studio in the boulevard des Italiens, he probably knew he had found enough inspiration in the triumphs of the Third French Republic to last him a lifetime.

In many ways, the wayward young man was retracing the steps of many of the older French Canadian radicals. Papineau, Dessaulles, Buies, Fréchette, Beaugrand had all studied or spent extended sojourns in France, and had been deeply impressed by various currents of French thought.[1] Honoré Beaugrand, a leading radical, had exclaimed on the eve of Sarah Bernhardt's much celebrated arrival in Montreal in 1880: "Notre pensée se résume en quatre mots: l'amour de la

France."[2] But when Langlois left Canada late in the summer of 1889, it seemed as though radicalism had lost its certainties in Quebec. Honoré Mercier had rallied the Liberal troops behind him with his eloquent rhetoric and his many promises. Radicalism, unable to legitimate its existence in the face of such a champion, seemed obsolete. Even crusty "old radicals" like Louis Fréchette and Rodolphe Laflamme now seemed to have finally accepted the vision of a tempered nationalist liberalism.

Indeed, French Canadian radicalism appeared to be in perpetual crisis during the nineteenth century, a distinct loser in the politics of identity. Always the prey of disputes and political factionalism, it lost its meaning at different times to different partisans. At first, to be a *rouge* was to be a member of *L'Avenir*'s founding editorial board in 1847. In 1849, it signified that one had broken with Louis-Hyppolite Lafontaine's increasingly conservative inclinations and had followed Louis-Joseph Papineau and the embryonic *Parti démocratique*. It meant that one had signed the annexation manifesto, or at least had supported it. It also meant that one attended the sessions of the Institut Canadien, supposedly in order to imbibe the ideas of France's more radical, sometimes anticlerical, thinkers.[3]

Those fragile certainties proved incapable of withstanding political winds. By 1851, *l'Avenir* had been judged as too radical by the *rouges* themselves and only few of them actually supported it. In that year, a small number of supposedly radical Institut Canadien members even tried to have it removed from their club's shelves! It was in this context that *Le Pays*, a publication whose mandate it was to rid Liberalism of its anticlerical hues, was born. But even it was successful only in part, and the undying *rougisme* of some of its editors was only suppressed temporarily by Antoine-Aimé Dorion when he bought the newspaper in 1858. For its part, the supposedly radical Institut Canadien hardly enjoyed a solid and consistent constituency. It suffered massive losses in membership throughout the late 1840s and 1850s, and by the

1860s the leaders of this emaciated organization of about 300 were actively lobbying the church for recognition as an association which was not antithetical to the Holy See's interests.

The project of Confederation animated *rougisme* for a time, winning it a slew of adherents who opposed a deeper association with the English colonies, but who cared little for the core anticlerical beliefs of those few individuals who still professed an uncompromised vision. Following Confederation, a number of these new *rouges* worked with moderate Liberals to transform the party so as to disassociate it unequivocally from past reputations. In 1872, many of the former *rouges* worked with Honoré Mercier to forge the *Parti national*, but had failed to convince a majority of Liberals of the necessity of giving the Liberal party a new name. Having failed at that task, Mercier worked ceaselessly throughout the late 1870s and 1880s to convince both the *rouges* and the moderate Liberals that the Liberal party needed a complete overhaul in order to appeal to the electorate. Mercier cajoled the *rouges* with promises of educational reform. In 1875 he wondered aloud "if the time has not come or if the time will not soon be here when the guardians of children will be punished if they remain indifferent to their education."[4] A year later, he had been even more unequivocal: "The state can and must intervene to ensure that this obligation [to attend school] is realized," he told the *Club national*. "I consider the importance of mandatory education to have been demonstrated and that it is the state's power to execute it."[5]

Mercier's campaign to exorcise *rouge* ghosts was given resounding support in 1877, when Wilfrid Laurier hammered the final nails in the *rouge* coffin in his brilliant Quebec City speech on a Liberalism that had turned its back on its *rouge* origins. Laurier wanted to show that radicalism was nothing but an infantile stage in the evolution of French-Canadian liberalism, that the platforms of l'*Avenir* had advocated "a complete revolution of the province," which was "absurd and impossible." Like many occasional *rouges*, Laurier wanted to see the Church accept Liberalism. He argued that Liberals aspired not to a "social" liberalism or even a "catholic" liberalism, but to a political liberalism fashioned after the British model. The Catholic church had nothing to fear: According to Laurier, French-Canadian Liberals were unlike European liberals, who were not "liberals" but "revolutionaries" who "in their principles," were "so extravagant that they aim at nothing less than the destruction of modern society." "With these men," Laurier proudly announced, "we have nothing in common."[6]

Mercier's promise found sympathetic ears, and gradually his idea of a *Parti national* gathered steam. The purification effort failed but was quickly renewed when Mercier assumed the leadership of the Liberal Party in 1883 and worked to realize, this time successfully, another *Parti national*. A new publication, *Le Temps*, was established in Montreal in 1883 to propagate the *Parti national* gospel and old radicals such as Rodolphe Laflamme, Louis-Honoré Fréchette and L.O. David gave it credibility by submitting articles. In November of that year, a meeting of the *Club national de Montréal* was convened to put together a programme for the new political incarnation. Universal suffrage and "national independence" were nailed into the platform, but more important for the old *rouges* was the inclusion of a demand for "obligatory instruction."[7]

Not all *rouges* were able to tolerate what was to be nothing but a political marriage of convenience. Philippe-Auguste Choquette, a young Montmagny organizer, earned his first public recognition by publicly refusing to collaborate because "the Liberal party is the true national party," thereby refusing to recognize Mercier's strategy. George Washington Stephens, a Montreal member of the Legislative Assembly, was equally opposed.[8] But they proved to be the exceptions. Mercier's cause was greatly improved with his brilliant victory in the provincial election of 1886. Even Joseph Doutre, the bitter radical who had removed himself from politics in the early 1870s, supported Mercier. The leaders of the *Association libérale de Montréal,* which had been formed in February 1883 to fight "conservative infiltration", also decided to join with the Mercieristes. Even Honoré Beaugrand, the uncompromising editor of the Liberal *La Patrie,* conceded that he could live with Mercier (especially if *Le Temps* was pulled out of production). Frédérique-Liguory Béique, another founding member of the *Association libérale de Montréal,* became the new Premier's personal secretary. Joseph Robidoux, also an ALM veteran and Charles Langelier, both known for the *rouges* sympathies, became Ministers in the first *Parti national* cabinet. Mercier seemed to enjoy the support of a range of Liberals, including the best known *rouges,* at least for the first two years of his mandate. Mercier had been triumphant: The meaning of *rougisme* had by now been lost on most people, except those few who made it their life's work to oppose it. But before long, even the labels given to *rougisme* by its enemies no longer held much validity.

Godfroy Langlois, not yet twenty-three years old as he walked the streets of Paris, accepted the ideological situation of French Canadian radicalism as it presented itself to him. As an avid student of history, he had come to nurture a fondness for the radical ideals and for the legendary pugnaciousness of the Institut Canadien and often dreamed of a revival of the spirited old politics. He was not alone in caressing that dream. He gave himself the mission not just to simply recover lost ideals. As France had changed since the days of Papineau's stay in the 1840s, so had Quebec. New conditions demanded new solutions, and it was not in the old issues of Dessaulles's *l'Avenir* that Langlois sought new ideals, but in the French Republic he so lovingly explored in 1889. Of the 32 million tourists who visited Paris in that festive year, many came from the shores of the St-Lawrence. Like Rémi Tremblay, a journalist friend who also visited the exposition, Langlois undoubtedly visited the various monuments and museums of the city,[9] and lingered on the *grands boulevards* now made famous by Henri de Toulouse-Lautrec's etchings. He left Paris sometime in September "bringing home memories that will be eternal."[10] Feeling worldly, Godfroy Langlois was ready to take his place in the Liberal party and in French Canada's bourgeois press.

Godfroy Langlois was born in a prominent Ste-Scholastique family on December 26, 1866, and was quickly indoctrinated into the family politics by the time he could stand at one of the elder's knee. His father, Joseph Langlois, was a merchant of considerable importance in the village while his uncle, Charles Langlois, ran a successful wholesale merchandising business in Montreal. Joseph Langlois was the son of one of the pioneers of Ste-Scholastique and had not wasted any time in affirming his presence on the local political scene. He became a municipal counsellor in 1862 and would not relinquish his place until 1910, when a fatal illness forced his retirement. He was elected mayor of Ste-Scholastique for the first time in 1890 and would only leave that office fifteen years later. The chief merchant of Ste-Scholastique was obviously an able politician with a knack for survival: he was an avid Liberal in an area that doggedly voted Conservative until the mid 1890s.[11]

Joseph Langlois married three times and fathered five children. Three of the children were borne by his first wife, Olympe Clément: Corinne, the eldest; Henri, and Godfroy. Another two daughters, Gabrielle and Marie Stéphanie, eventually followed.[12] Born in a relatively affluent family, Godfroy Langlois received an education consistent with the aspirations of Quebec's bourgeoisie. After elementary school in the village, he was enrolled at the Collège Ste-Thérèse in the fall of 1881 with two other boys from Ste-Scholastique. He was taught by Jules Graton, a young deacon, and immediately made his mark on the school's record books. For the academic year 1881-1882, Langlois placed third overall in his class and garnered a few distinctions. He placed third in Latin and in English, placed fourth in religion, and received honourable mentions in French, Greek and geography.

Unfortunately, the young teenager's performance was not sustained. The following year, he only placed second in Latin and won honourable mentions in only Greek, geography and English. In 1883-1884, Langlois's performance deteriorated further, as he won no honours at all.[13] For reasons that are unclear, Langlois was evidently not inspired by his schooling and left the institution after his disastrous third year. When prompted to remember his sojourn at the Collège Ste-Thérèse, he first recalled the bad food and the misguided educational programme. Launching a crusade against the *collèges classiques* in 1893, Langlois bitterly denounced his *alma mater*. "In your institution," he wrote in an open letter to the director of the college,

> students are bored to death every day for six years learning their Latin versions and their Latin themes, for four years learning Greek versions and then again three years learning Latin verses. The French language has always been treated as a secondary thing at Ste-Thérèse, so much so that I have seen young people from this institution fail their exams in the liberal professions because there were so many grammatical errors in their manuscripts. I know [...] young people [...] who, after having spent eight years in your college, cannot write a narration or a letter without at least making a half-dozen mistakes. And those former students are not imbeciles![14]

The young journalist's acrimonious criticisms of the school did not extend to all the staff. His teacher in those three years, Jules Graton, was eventually ordained priest, and remained a lifelong friend. Langlois left Ste-Thérèse in June 1884 and was enrolled in the Collège de St-Laurent, situated not far from Montreal's northern fringes at the time. This institution was administered by the Ste-Croix order and offered a more modern curriculum in comparison with Ste-Thérèse. English, for instance, had a privileged place in the school as many Franco-Americans were educated there.

Business studies were also the object of serious attention in this school's curriculum.[15]

Langlois studied at St-Laurent for three years. Excelling in his studies, he graduated as gold medalist of his class in June 1887 and always kept fond memories of this institution. "I spent some very good years there [...] such things are not forgotten," he told his old friend and teacher, abbé Elias Vanier, some forty years later. Regardless of the many charges of anti-clericalism and anti-catholicism levelled against him over the years, Langlois never lost contact with his *alma mater* and its religious instructors. "I may have been suspect in the eyes of some, in those days long ago when I battled in parliament and in the newspapers," he confided to abbé Vanier, "but I have nonetheless remained an old and faithful friend of your institution."[16] As in all things, there came a time to leave and in September 1887, at age 20, Langlois enrolled at Laval University's Montreal Law School.

It is difficult to gauge with what confidence Langlois moved to Montreal. He was not particularly handsome. Short of stature (he measured just over five feet), he was already slightly corpulent. His clear blue eyes were partly hidden behind *pince-nez* spectacles uncomfortably perched on the bridge of his nose. As soon as he could grow it, he had worn a mustache, and sported a tuft of beard below his bottom lip. Indeed, his pictures reveal a reserved, piercing look that almost seemed to betray a certain bitterness. Still, his cherubic features and the ironic smile that played across his thin lips could not entirely support that grave look in his eyes. By all accounts, Langlois's charming good nature and generous sense of humour were never overwhelmed by his taxing endeavours.

Young Langlois read voraciously and, as a distraction, dabbled in music. He enjoyed singing, making good use of a not unpleasant, rather high-pitched tenor voice.[17] He also played the piano, and often displayed his musical talents at political gatherings.[18] Langlois's first love was always reading, however, and the political history of numerous countries captivated him. Perhaps frustrated by the fact that few shared his interests, Langlois was often heard demanding that modern history play a greater role in the curricula of elementary and secondary schools, and rarely failed to invoke some historical circumstance in his public speeches.

His main concern in the fall of 1887, however, was the study of law and at the time of his arrival, Montreal was an exciting place to be for a young man. Strongly shaken by the Riel affair and the cholera epidemic of 1885, Montreal's ambiance had been inexorably transformed in the year immediately preceding Langlois's freshman year at university. Honoré Beaugrand, the unrepentant radical, had been elected mayor in 1886. The city's face was changing rapidly. Ste-Catherine street was becoming the commercial center of the city as the department stores brought their locations closer to the latin quarter. Morgan's, Birk's, Ogilvy's and countless others seemed to underscore the strong English presence in Montreal that perhaps contributed to the feverish sense of patriotism Langlois and his classmates felt in those days.

Langlois did not stay long in the narrow halls of Laval. Bored by the academic approach to law, perhaps, he chose to pursue his legal studies as an apprentice, and became a clerk in the prestigious Raymond Préfontaine-Eugène Lafontaine law practice. That Langlois was accepted in this notable firm was indication of the early promise his career already showed. Eugène Lafontaine basked in the prestige of being part of a great "patriote" family, had been a federal member of Parliament for Napierville, but was now concentrating his efforts on his law practice. Raymond Préfontaine was also deeply involved in Liberal politics. A student of Antoine-Aimé Dorion, he had been a federal member of Parliament for the riding of Chambly, but was now more actively involved in municipal affairs. In 1883, he had been elected Mayor of Hochelaga and had successfully orchestrated his city's fusion with Montreal the following year. In 1884, he was elected alderman and would sit in Montreal's Municipal

Council for almost twenty years. He had supported Honoré Beaugrand's bid for the mayoralty in 1886 and had contributed significantly to the activities of the "Comité Riel" in that same year.

Préfontaine always considered himself a radical *rouge*, even though his actions were often at odds with that evolving definition. While he had long associated himself with *rouge* names like Dorion and Beaugrand, he seemed to distance himself from the rhetoric of political purity as the 1880s wore on. By the late 1880s, his presence in the Montreal City Council became associated with political corruption. Langlois, for one, who had carefully chosen the Lafontaine-Préfontaine legal office because of its obvious *rouge* connections, was quickly disenchanted with Préfontaine's brand of politics and quit after a few months. He moved to Rodolphe Laflamme's firm.

The dashing and debonair Rodolphe Laflamme was a brilliant and unorthodox member of Montreal's legal community, and had made himself a splendid reputation for recruiting some of the Liberal party's best young talent. Wilfrid Laurier, the future Prime Minister of Canada; Arthur Buies, one of Quebec's best journalists; Louis Riel, who would lead the North Western rebellion; Lomer Gouin, future Premier of Quebec, to name but a few, had sharpened their legal understanding while working with Laflamme. Their mentor was an impressive personality, a sharp wit, and an enduring friend. He was born in Montreal in 1827 and educated at the Collège de St-Sulpice and at McGill University. At the age of 17, he had taken part in the founding of the Institut Canadien, and he had become president of the organization by the time he was 20 years old. Laflamme worked at *l'Avenir*, and his influence never failed to guide the radical tendencies of the Institut Canadien. Many saw him as aloof, easily given to making his legal arguments in cold, laboured logic. Unmarried, Laflamme enjoyed an uncharacteristically free life. "He had numerous horses and dogs," remembered his friend and fellow-traveller Laurent-

Olivier David, "frequented the clubs of the English aristoc-
racy, and easily yielded to fancy tastes and the most capri-
cious whims."[19] Laflamme grew wealthy through his law
practice, often pleading the causes of the rich seigneurs, but
made room in his work to help those less capable of paying
his high fees.

The most famous was the Guibord case. Joseph Guibord,
a member of the Institut Canadien, had indicated in his final
will that he wished to be buried in the cemetery plot he
owned in the Côte-des-Neiges cemetery. The local *fabrique*
authorities refused this wish to his widow, arguing that
Guibord's membership in an organization hostile to church
interests disqualified his request. It may have appeared odd
to see an inveterate high society advocate like Laflamme
argue the case of the widow of a deceased stenographer like
Joseph Guibord, but in his own time, Laflamme embodied
the most unrepentant free thinking in the Liberal party, and
he saw this case as a test of the church's authority.[20]

The Guibord case lasted over four years, and seemed to
erode Laflamme's radical verve. The case was complicated,
the politics associated with it were even more complex and
last but not least burdensome was the sheer irony of the
whole argument. Guibord, after all, did not consider that
membership in the Institut Canadien compromised his rights
as a Catholic to be buried in a Catholic cemetery. It was more
than the validity of Guibord's case that was on trial, it
seemed. *Rougisme* itself was being tested. Through the many
attempts to reach a compromise, the exhausting case carried
itself through numerous appeals, and by the time the courts
finally found in the Guibord widow's favour in 1874,
Laflamme seemed to have lost the fire of his early days. He
had found time to be elected to Parliament in 1872, and in
1874 had resigned his own membership in the Institut Canadien, reportedly so as to symbolize his orthodoxy and thus
ensure his reelection in the Montreal riding of Jacques-Cartier. He retained his seat during the 1874 election and in 1876
was asked to join Alexander Mackenzie's cabinet first as

Minister of Inland Revenue and then as Minister of Justice. "Laflamme has suddenly become very pious," noted the Prime Minister half-jokingly in 1877.[21] Indeed, Laflamme became a good example of what was continually compromising the definition of the *rouge* movement in the 1870s and 1880s. He gradually came to recognize Honoré Mercier's brand of moderate Liberalism and there always lingered a doubt regarding Laflamme's own philosophical convictions. He lived and died, according to Laurent-Olivier David, as a devout Catholic.[22]

Laflamme's days of glory were well behind him when young Godfroy Langlois knocked on his door, and his mindset at the time of Langlois's clerkship is difficult to assess. Laflamme's combination of high ideals, renewed religiosity, and bitter cynicism nonetheless had an impact on Langlois. When prompted by industrialist H.J. Morgan who was writing a book on the leading citizens of Montreal, Langlois admitted that "M. Laflamme was for me a very good friend and a wise counselor."[23] Langlois's debt to Laflamme proved to be considerable indeed. First, Laflamme told Langlois he was wasting his time studying law and the young protégé would heed that bit of advice very quickly. But Langlois's debt to Laflamme was greater than for the professional advice he received. It was while he worked alongside Laflamme that Langlois learned that the *rouge* brand of radicalism, as it stood in 1889, would not survive. It was while studying in Laflamme's office that Langlois also became a member of the *Club National,* and it was there that he witnessed the first signs of the rapidly decaying *rouge* consensus on the Mercier regime.

That uneasy consensus of *rouges* and *castors,* of Liberals and Conservatives, around Mercier began to crack in 1889 when Ernest Pacaud automatically wrote in the April 22 edition of *l'Electeur* that all Liberals were united in supporting Mercier. Calixte Lebeuf, a thirty-nine year old lawyer and President of the *Club National* leaped on Pacaud's contention. "Are you serious when you write that the partisans of

Mr. Mercier are united?" he insisted. The impetuous Lebeuf did not spare his words as he related that many former "Liberals" thought Mercier's cabinet was staffed with incompetents, and outright accused Pacaud and Mercier of enriching themselves with government money. "There are no principles, no honesty, no promises kept, no honour," Lebeuf exclaimed.[24] "The liberals, the real ones, the honest ones are disgusted [...] they are organizing; they do not want war, they would even rather save the government in spite of itself, but they have resolved to save the Liberal party and its great and honourable traditions, even if the government should perish!"[25]

Lebeuf's diagnosis of the political sickness that had gripped the *Parti national* rested on Mercier himself and on his entourage. "Mercier must escape the *castor* lock, and show himself to be more liberal. We don't consider him to be liberal; we even know that deep down, his ideas are anti-liberal; but he must remember that it was the liberals that made him what he is and that carried him there." Lebeuf's harshest words were for those he considered to be the new cancer that was eating away at the "old principles", and who were leading the *Parti national* in an anti-Liberal direction. Pacaud was himself singled out as specifically bad for the Liberal cause as were two powerful Liberal members who were now Montreal aldermen: Raymond Préfontaine and Cléophas Beausoleil.

Lebeuf's letter seemed to resuscitate radicalism; to bring it back from the deliberate confusions of Mercier's agile political maneuvering. With Lebeuf, *rougisme* seemed literally to twitch back to life and was already searching out its enemies. Lebeuf's own final words were indicative of a renewed sense of power. "The day we want to remove him [Mercier] from his pedestal," Lebeuf warned, "he will come down faster than when he came up."[26] Lebeuf penned his acrid letter on *Club National de Montréal* letterhead, but it was clear that he was not speaking for the executive committee or for the membership at large. Lomer Gouin, the club's Vice-President and

Mercier's son-in-law, was unimpressed by Lebeuf's threats. The attitude of Rodolphe Lemieux, the Club Secretary, was not clear. The last member on the club executive was young Godfroy Langlois, who held the post of Secretary-Archivist. He said nothing publicly, but witnessed, and learned, as events unfolded.

A noisy meeting was called on May 8 to discuss the Lebeuf letter. The "old Liberals", who had once embodied the irreverent *rouge* philosophies and tendencies but who had been politically seduced by Mercier, supported Lebeuf, and wanted to see his declaration given the full support of the *Club National*. Honoré Beaugrand, the editor and owner of *La Patrie*, for example, argued furiously in favour of Lebeuf. Facing the "old Liberals" were strong Mercier supporters: Lomer Gouin, Raymond Préfontaine and Raoul Dandurand, who argued against Lebeuf.[27] The motion was defeated and in October of that year Lebeuf resigned his position as President of the club. He was replaced by Lomer Gouin. Langlois took off to Paris.

Some of Langlois's ideas had begun to congeal by then. The trip to Paris came at a time when Langlois needed a chance to reflect upon Mercier's direction of the *Parti national*. He had witnessed a schism created by those who wanted the party to be more radical in its practices and in its policies and less concerned with electoral gain, but had yet to formulate publicly his own response.

*

*   *

In this light, it would be difficult to exaggerate the importance of the French Third Republic on the evolution of Langlois's approach to radicalism. France attracted him like a magnet, and it was not a mere coincidence that he chose France as the destination of his first travels. As a student, he studied the French past with a voracious appetite, he observed its politics with a keen interest, cherished many of its ideals, and admired the articulateness of the widely-differing French politicians. The radicals in France clearly captivated him and with good reason: French liberalism, the traditional fountain of radicalism, had undergone many transformations since the 1840s, when the first generation of *rouges* had travelled to France. For the young Langlois, France was the ideal laboratory of liberalisms; a workshop of ideologies whose teachings could be brought to the shores of the St-Lawrence.

In France, where no "Liberal party" existed formally, it was the "radicals" who developed liberalism into an ideology willing to tailor its basic principles to the exacting requirements of a modernizing society. There was a precocious conviction that laissez-faire liberalism had left in its wake too many victims, but that all the same, that philosophy deserved to be maintained and updated. Perhaps because of this adherence to vague principles, it has always proven difficult to understand all the tenets of radicalism as a comprehensive, consistent whole. Contradictions abounded and ideals often lost their cogency when applied to practical situations. In this ideological context filled with inconsistencies, French radicals thrived. Repressed, denied communications, they evolved a certain posture, a certain attitude, certain values and symbols more than they developed a formal "ideology."

French liberalism, in fact, was wont to define itself as a function of its enemy. When embodied by Voltaire during the eighteenth century, it presented itself as an opponent to the privilege and arbitrariness of the elite. In the nineteenth century, it interpreted itself in opposition to the concept of monarchy and the privileges of the few. As it faced the contradictions wrought by the liberal economic systems which created quite un-liberal capitalist privilege, some adherents to the ideology sought new answers. It was clear with the industrial revolutions that liberal economies were forcing liberals into a crisis of self-examination.[28] Equality, many came to recognize, was now not simply a matter of law, but one of social justice.

Responding to this, many radicals came to argue that the only way to create equality was through better use of the school system and through the exploitation of the state's resources. The established system of privileged institutions, of restricted access to knowledge, worked against the ideal of an enlightened population. In 1869, comprehensive school reform was enshrined in Léon Gambetta's "Belleville" programme. The radical's main demands revolved around individual liberties and would endure with only slight modifications as the "radical" manifesto. Gambetta demanded, among other things, universal suffrage, constitutional changes, total freedom of the press and total freedom of association. He also demanded the separation of church and state and mandatory, free, and neutral education at the primary and secondary levels. Just as importantly, Gambetta demanded economic reforms. "The economic reforms that can bring about social change and political transformation must be sought out and studied in the name of justice and social equality," Gambetta professed. "Once generalized and applied, this principle can remove social antagonisms and bring about our objective: Liberty, Equality, Fraternity."[29]

A year later, France was invaded by Germany and was eventually defeated. The loss at Sedan cost the captured Bonaparte all his credibility and the Second Empire crumbled. Radicals of various sorts emerged with the founding of the Third Republic, eager to put into practice a programme that had been clandestinely hammered out for over twenty years. Jules Ferry formulated a renewed platform of educational reform. "Neither the right to work, nor the right to vote, that is to contribute to the formation of the state's rights, are therefore subject to the privileges of birth," he declared in 1870. "These are the heritage of each man in this world. But there is still one of those inequalities inherited at birth: educational inequality. This is the problem of our century...."[30]

With the 1880s, the "Radicals" met with great electoral success and became prey to factionalism. Disagreements over the means required to meet an agreed end rocked the radical boat and many decided to abandon ship. Some followed Gambetta, others followed the more exacting demands of Georges Clemenceau's "Radical Socialists". Disagreement ran so deep that there would not exist in France a radical party until 1901, leaving individual "radicals" to defend the amorphous principles. Each had his own ideas regarding the ultimate goals and means of radicalism, but few voiced them as forcefully or as coherently as Clemenceau. Inspired by an Comteian positivism, he personified the reconsideration of dominant laissez-faire liberalism in the latter half of the nineteenth century. Throughout the 1880s, he struggled for the rights of workers against big business as well as for judicial, penal and constitutional reform.

As the name *radical* implied, Clemenceau wanted to attack the "root causes" of France's social problems. His ideology was a mixture of radical tactics and moderate goals but stemmed from liberal principles and philosophies. He demanded justice for the worker, but never advocated revolution, especially not violent upheavals. He was in favour of educational reform, the separation of church and state, but abhorred the idea that the state should assume all authority. Radical socialism in general argued for a much more active state role in the economy in order to assure, as Clemenceau often put it, that "the individual could realize his potential."[31]

Clemenceau's call for state regulation, not state ownership, influenced many policy proposals. His parliamentary group proposed bills dealing with unemployment and accident insurance, old-age pensions, industrial safety, limitation of hours, regulation of night work, factory inspection, child labour and compulsory arbitration in industrial disputes.[32] The Clemenceau group's demand for an increased role for the state emanated from their economic and social blueprints. Seeking to achieve social peace through peaceful means, they put their faith in the rule of law and in the regulatory powers of the state. The state, in other words, was called upon to

administer the social contract. As one of their best chroni-
clers observed, a sizeable element of the radicals of Clemenceau's ilk "sought continually to lead France in the
direction of the welfare state".[33]

To the French radicals, the issue was not the concentration
of wealth, but its misuse. Here the state could play a role.
Radicals advocated that the state assume some role in the
economy. The utilities, for instance, could be owned and
operated by municipalities. Similarly, the railroad system
had to be nationalized. The same could be said about the
banks and the mines. Turning to social problems, French
radicals also called for state involvement. They urged state
intervention "so that liberty does not remain a word devoid
of sense. In place of laissez-faire ... we demand that the state
intervene to protect the poor, women, children, to provide
all citizens with the means to develop their faculties and
defend their rights." [34]

In the field of social legislation left-wing radicals were
particularly concerned with income security and work
safety. Most of them strongly supported compulsory and
industry-wide schemes designed to protect all workers
against unforeseen tragedies. Government, they argued,
owed assistance to those in distress. Similarly, they advocated
old-age pensions so as to protect the aged worker. "Protect"
was a key word for them. Indeed, it is important to note that
while most radicals fervently argued in favour of social
equality, few of them were willing to demand a truly socialist
platform of the kind Karl Marx and his French apostles
envisaged.

Radicals supported the working man's cause, and worked
assiduously to legalize and protect unions. Most of them
"considered labor organizations a necessary part of the inte-
gral democracy they desired," noted historian Léo
Loubère.[35] Because democracy's meaning was extended to
include industrial relations, radicals saw unions as acceptable
representatives of the working class. Only then could strikes
be avoided, as workers and management faced off in the

neutral terrain of a strictly regulated sport. Many radicals demanded state-imposed arbitration so as to quickly resolve disputes and avoid strikes, and many of them demanded that this arbitration be made compulsory.[36]

The demands for state involvement in economic and social realms in the name of equality, however, should not be construed as the unalloyed essence of philosophical radicalism as it evolved in the last decades of the nineteenth century. Interwoven, and, indeed, at the root of the radical philosophical orientation was a deep respect for the role of the individual in forging his own destiny. Even the most rabid radical-socialists of the last twenty five years of the nineteenth century (Clemenceau is again a case in point) never lost the opportunity to justify their actions in the name of the individual. As such, it was visibly far more liberal than socialist. For most radicals, civil, juridical, and material equalities were sought in order to emancipate the individual first, not a class. Equality would emanate from a common standpoint from where each individual could rise according to his abilities and desires.[37]

The question of the individual played a cardinal role in defining radical policies towards education. Because education had traditionally been subject to the church's hegemony, many radicals were anticlerical, some were openly linked to the Freemasonry. Education — a personal, intimate undertaking — was perceived by liberals as the panacea that would cure all of France's economic and social ills, and, not least, free the individuals. "At the heart of the program for social education lay the conviction that education provided the means for the disenchanted to acquire a material stake in society," wrote one historian of the Third Republic as he paraphrased radical doctrines. "Instruction is useful, skills coupled with an indoctrination into acceptable social values would equip the proletarian or the marginal farmer with the tools by which he would become a property owner. Thus perforce integrated into the bourgeois world, or at least at its edges on unequal terms, the worker no longer would find himself at war with that world. He would become its ardent defender."[38]

The radicals made a convincing case and educational policy has been equated in the minds of many with the Third Republic's finest successes. In 1882 Jules Ferry introduced a series of laws that made elementary education mandatory for all children under 13 years. Equally, education was to be free and non-denominational. Indeed, the educational laws exemplified the true nature of radical philosophy in the Third Republic. At stake was state involvement in an area traditionally reserved for the Church. Also at stake was the survival of the individual, of all individuals. Most radicals were ready to prepare the individual for the struggle for life by giving him an education and ensuring that his evolution was not hamstrung by arbitrary laws and regulations. Their firm belief that the rule of law, and not ownership of property, would engender progress in society clearly demarcated them from the socialists. Clemenceau again said it best: "I affirm that the policy of a democracy is to emancipate the least enlightened group, in the fastest manner possible, by the group that has the advantage of education and insight."[39] If Clemenceau's words in 1884 defined the political ideals of the radicals of France at the end of the nineteenth century, they also inspired the likes of Godfroy Langlois.

*

*　　*

Following the *Club National* dispute and his trip to Europe in the late summer and early fall, Langlois took Laflamme's advice to abandon the study of law and to pursue a career in journalism. "Disposition," he later recalled, "pushed me towards that profession."[40] His head full of "radical" dreams and ambitions inspired by his mentor Rodolphe Laflamme, Langlois immediately set himself to work to begin his journalistic career with the organization of a publication called *Le Clairon*. Fruit of the collaboration of four young men that included J.G. de la Durantaye, Ephrem Taillefer, Ernest Tellier and Godfroy Langlois, *Le Clairon* saw the light of day for the first time on December 7, 1889.

In appearance, *Le Clairon* was very much a nineteenth century newspaper. With few lengthy articles, it really never lived up to its promise of becoming a literary weekly, but it did fulfill its other intention of becoming a political newspaper. While the news was briefly reported, it was injected with generous editorial comment. Already, Langlois's rhetoric was recognizable in the stinging sarcasm of his by-line "Coups de plume". "A travers le monde," another of Langlois's regular contributions, reflected the young journalist's interest in world affairs.[41]

If management experience was lacking at *Le Clairon*, ambition certainly was not in short supply. "Above and beyond our personal interests are a love of country and a desire to see it prosper, we will work assiduously to defend the principles we cherish and hope to see realized for the greater good of our people," the editors announced in their opening editorial.[42] The "principles" alluded to were developed only cryptically. Like most, if not all *rouges*, they approved of Wilfrid Laurier as well as of Honoré Mercier. Still, it was clear that even the most diplomatic language could not hide the fact that *Le Clairon*, echoing the views of Calixte Lebeuf, insisted on seeing the *Parti national* uphold "liberal" principles.

The Lebeuf affair of the Spring of 1889 had an impact on the pages of *Le Clairon*. Lomer Gouin, Lebeuf's successor as President of the *Club National,* contributed a significant article to *Le Clairon*, setting out both the precision and the general confusion of his political thinking. A true political chameleon, Gouin practised with an almost religious fervor the politics of wavering from right to left to right again. Born in Grondines in 1862, Gouin studied law under Conservative John Abbott. He then moved to study with the radical Liberal Rodolphe Laflamme, before becoming, for a brief time, Laflamme's law partner. In 1888 he moved into the circle of the Quebec Prime Minister by marrying Honoré Mercier's daughter, Eliza. Mercier had a powerful impact on him, and like his mentor, Gouin would graciously move from radical, leftist rhetoric to very practical, rather conservative actions. Gouin, four years older than Langlois, seemed already caught between his philosophical ideals and the political considerations brought about by his marriage. For whatever reasons, it was always difficult to ascertain where Gouin stood on political principles. "Silent, taciturn, eternally introverted, he did not reveal his thoughts to anyone, not even his most intimate friends," wrote Raoul Dandurand of Gouin.[43] Gouin's goal, as ever, was to help conciliate the various factions, and the piece he published in *Le Clairon* manifested a measured response designed to heal the wounds of the Lebeuf affair. His objective was to demonstrate that radical *rougisme* still had an important role to play in the *Parti national.*

Gouin argued that the label a political party used was insignificant. What mattered, according to him, were not words, but actions. "For us, convinced partisans of the political idea of liberalism," he wrote, "we have never believed that it was necessary nor sufficient to call ourselves liberal in order to be so, and it always occurred to us that a sincerely national government could be nothing other than a true and liberal government."[44]

Gouin was obviously defending his father-in-law Mercier in light of Lebeuf's vicious accusations, but was very careful not to alienate the "radicals". Pointing to England as an example, he argued that liberalism on the British Isles was nothing but a synonym for hypocrisy, while in France, where no "liberal" party existed, liberal ideas were widely current. "We are liberals," he concluded, "we hold to the liberal idea, but we do not see a difference between the words liberal and national."[45] It is doubtful that Gouin's superficial debate of semantics convinced any radicals, but, ironically perhaps, he had succeeded in at least identifying himself as one individual who was interested in participating in their debates.

As *Le Clairon* progressed over the early months of 1890, it was abundantly clear that Langlois was playing a greater role in determining the editorial content of the newspaper. He authored all the important articles, especially the ones that deliberately sought controversy. Already, the young man manifested his desire to revise the radical *rougisme* of yesteryear and infuse the members of the *Parti national* with the modern ideas that roamed France. As such, he was far more a disciple of Lebeuf than a partisan of Gouin's views. Indeed, Langlois repeatedly argued that the Liberals of 1890 were not radical enough: "There are still some *rouges* who are not afraid to have convictions and that are proud and honest enough to have the courage of their convictions. There are still some liberals, we are of their number, and will always be."[46]

Langlois did not believe Gouin's argument that liberalism and nationalism naturally went together. He saw the *Parti national* experiment as a temporary situation wrought by particular circumstances. "For a number of years liberal policies were secondary to national ones because there were demands for which a struggle was necessary and because there was a revenge to be organized," he wrote, confident that Liberal principles would again have an upper hand.[47] The Riel experience still fresh in his mind, Langlois harked back to the old *rouges* slogans, even declaring himself opposed to Confederation and for years advocating annexation to the United States. The Manitoba Schools Question only inflamed those passions. "If you give yourself the right to attack our liberties and to put us in chains in certain provinces where you are the majority," Langlois threatened English Canada, "we who are the masters in Quebec can allow ourselves to retaliate. At certain times, we would be right to become more despotic so as to teach you, as you have taught us, how hard it is to be the subjects of tyranny."[48]

Despite its promises to avoid controversy, *Le Clairon* confronted nearly all of Quebec's institutions, and did not spare the church. In March 1890, Langlois launched a crusade against the tithe. His aim was not to abolish it, he argued, but to make it more equitable. He used the question as a pretext to lambaste the church, forcing his readers to compare him to the best of the *anciens rouges* : "Our clergy", he wrote "has been king on our shores and it does not like, anymore today than it did yesterday, to see its flock remove itself from its influence; it has made the people simple-minded and obsequious and the French Canadian priest has never been used to audacity or to movements that did not augment his influence."[49]

"We have the courage to say out loud what other people think deep down," Langlois was already writing often, "it is to say that our province is retarded in the way it deals with the clergy, and that the tithe is an eminently unjust institution."[50] With that kind of rhetoric, *Le Clairon* quickly attracted attention and was quickly labeled as dangerously radical. But the paper could not sustain itself. *Le Clairon* was taken off the newsstands in March 1890 after only four months of publication, unable to make its way in Montreal's saturated newspaper market. [51]

The intrepid foursome was thrown out of work, but had no reason to despair. Tellier and Taillefer started a law practice and both Durantaye and Langlois were hired by *La Patrie*, the French Liberal organ in Montreal. Evidently, Honoré Beaugrand's curiosity had been piqued by Langlois's outspoken editorial comments — many of which were directed at *La Patrie* itself— and he offered him a job as city editor, probably to replace Rémi Tremblay, who left *La Patrie* temporarily following disagreements over the daily's "attitude".[52]

Applying his poetic call for a renaissance, Langlois was awakened to the new realities of *rougisme*, hoping to find for it the necessary room for a regeneration and a reorientation. He was responding to his new world, along with many others who were seeking new winds to capture in their tattered radical sails.

Notes

1. On Langlois's trip see *Le Clairon*, 7 décembre 1889. The picture taken in François Mulnier's studio is in the privately-held Langlois Papers, file P1. On the significance of Paris in French Canadian thought, see Serge Jaumain, "Paris devant l'opinion canadienne-française: les récits de voyages entre 1820 et 1914" *RHAF*, 38, 4, printemps 1985. On the mood of Paris, see Charles Rearick, *Pleasures of the Belle Epoque* (Yale, 1985); Roger Shattuck, *The Banquet Years* (New York, 1968).

2. *La Patrie*, 8 septembre 1880. Cited in P. St-Arnaud, "La Patrie, 1879-1880", *in* Fernand Dumont (ed.) *Idéologies au Canada-français, 1850-1900* (Québec, 1971), p. 222.

3. See N.S. Robertson, "The Institut canadien: An essay in Cultural History", (M.A. thesis, University of Western Ontario, 1965).

4. *Courrier de Ste-Hyacinthe*, 6 novembre 1875. Cited in Victrice Lessard, "L'instruction obligatoire dans la province de Québec de 1875 à 1943" (Ph.D. thesis, Université d'Ottawa, 1962), p.13.

5. *La Vérité*, 24 février 1883. Cited in Lessard, op.cit., p. 16. See also J.O. Pelland (ed.) *Biographie, discours et conférence de l'honorable Honoré Mercier* (Montreal, 1890) pp. 603-604. See also L.A. Rivet, *Honoré Mercier, Patriote et homme d'État* (Montreal, n.d.) pp. 114-127.

6. The 1877 speech is contained in Ulric Bathe, *Wilfrid Laurier on the Platform, 1871-1900* (Quebec, 1900). See page 67.

7. *La Patrie*, 12 novembre 1883. Cited in Caya thesis, op.cit., Appendix C.

8. Caya thesis, p. 485.

9. See Rémi Tremblay, *Pierre qui Roule* (Montreal, 1923), p. 207.

10. *Le Clairon*, 7 décembre 1889.

11. *l'Echo des Deux-Montagnes*, 25 février 1892.

12. See Joseph Langlois's obituary in *La Presse*, 23 mai 1910; See also Langlois Papers, file A, Joseph Langlois's testament, 27 mai 1909 and file P1, early family photographs.

13. CEGEP Lionel-Groulx, Ste-Thérèse-de-Blainville, *Annalles térésiennes*, 1881-82, 1882-83, 1883-84.

14. La Liberté, 30 mars 1893

15. See Léo Morin, "Historique du Collège de St-Laurent" in *Enseignement Secondaire au Canada*, vol XIII, janvier 1934. See also Claude Galarneau, *Les collèges classiques au Canada-français* (Montreal, 1978)

16. Langlois Papers, File C, Langlois to abbé Vanier, 10 juin 1925.

17. *Le Progrès* (Windsor, Ontario), n.d. (January 1900?) Newspaper clipping in Langlois Papers, Scrapbook A, p. 14.
18. To cite but one example, Langlois played at Louis-Philippe Brodeur's banquet in 1906. See *La Presse*, 19 juin 1906.
19. L.O. David, *Mélanges historiques et littéraires* (Montreal, 1917), p. 52.
20. On the Guibord Affair, see Lovell C. Clark, *The Guibord Affair* (Toronto, 1971). See also a discussion of the impact of the Guibord Affair on *rouge* politics in Patrice Dutil, "The Politics of Progressivism in Quebec: Godfroy Langlois and the Liberal Party, 1889-1914" (Ph.D. thesis, York University, 1987), chapter 1.
21. Cited in T.A. Burke, "Mackenzie and his cabinet, 1873-1878" *CHR*, XLI, March 1960. p. 146.
22. L.O. David, *Mes contemporains* (Montreal, 1894), p. 118.
23. PAC, H.J. Morgan Papers, Langlois to Morgan, n.d. (late 1894).
24. PAC, Honoré Mercier Papers, Vol.1, C. Lebeuf to E. Pacaud, 23 avril 1889.
25. *Ibid.*
26. *Ibid.*
27. Marcel Hamelin, "Introduction" in Marcel Hamelin (ed.) *Les mémoires du Sénateur Raoul Dandurand* (Ottawa, 1967), p.2. Robert Rumilly based his account on a lost "procès-verbal". See his *Honoré Mercier et son temps* (Montreal, 1935), p. 85.
28. On the impact of the capitalist economy on liberalism, see Guido de Ruggiero, *History of European Liberalism* (Boston, 1927), Part IV, chapter 6.
29. Cited in Georges Lefranc, *Les gauches en France* (Paris, 1973), pp. 289-290.
30. *Ibidem*, p. 148.
31. Jack D. Ellis, *The Early Life of Georges Clemenceau* (Lawrence, 1980), p. xi.
32. *Ibidem*, p. 97.
33. Léo Loubère, "The French Left-wing Radicals: Their Economic and Social Program since 1870" *AJES*, 26, 1, April 1967, p. 189.
34. *Ibidem*, p. 194.
35. Léo Loubère, The French Left-wing Radicals, their Views on Trade Unionism, 1870-1898" *IRSH*, 7, 1962, p. 205. See also his "Left-wing Radicals, Strikes and the Military, 1880-1907" *FHS*, vol. 3, Spring 1963.
36. Léo Loubère, "Les radicaux d'extrême-gauche en France et les rapports entres patrons et ouvriers, 1871, 1900" *RHES*, 42, 1964.
37. A good discussion of radical individualism is in Jean-Thomas Nordmann, *La France radicale* (Paris, 1976) pp. 13-16. For Clemenceau's individualist streak, see Ellis, *op.cit.*, pp.93-94.

38. Sanford Elwitt, *The Making of the Third Republic* (Baton Rouge, 1975), p. 197.

39. Jean-Thomas Nordmann, *Histoire des radicaux* (Paris, 1974), p. 92.

40. H.J. Morgan Papers, Langlois to Morgan, n.d. (late 1894)

41. The longest article to appear in the paper, an examination of political affairs in Italy, was signed by Langlois. See *Le Clairon*, 21 décembre 1889.

42. *Le Clairon*, 7 décembre 1889.

43. Marcel Hamelin (ed.) *Les mémoires du Sénateur Raoul Dandurand* (Ottawa, 1967), p. 116.

44. *Le Clairon*, 14 décembre, 1889.

45. *Ibidem*.

46. *Ibidem*.

47. *Ibidem*.

48. *Le Clairon*, 7 décembre 1889.

49. *Ibidem*, 15 mars 1890.

50. *Ibidem*, 8 février 1890.

51. Paul Rutherford, *Making of the Canadian Media* (Toronto, 1978), p. 50.

52. Rémi Tremblay, op.cit., p. 208.

CHAPTER II

YOUNG PROVOCATEUR

Musettes, éveillons nos coeurs endormis,
Aux champs, ces fleurs ont des senteurs
nouvelles.
Partout on entend des frôlements d'ailes.
Et des bruits d'amour tombent
des vieux nids.
— Godfroy Langlois, 1890[1]

BARELY OUT OF SCHOOL, fresh from a trip to France and emboldened by three months of *effronterie* journalism, Godfroy Langlois reported to work at Honoré Beaugrand's *La Patrie*. It was difficult to resist the influence of the mercurial character that was the 42 year old Honoré Beaugrand. Devilishly cultured, a self-proclaimed "libéral très avancé" and a "francmaçon très avancé", dashing in appearance with his angular facial features, piercing eyes, and overgrown mustache, Beaugrand was an overbearing character that had already lived too many lives. Born in Lanoraie in 1848, he had attended the Collège de St-Viateur and seemed destined to live out his life along the lines of the average middle-class French Canadian, but chose differently. Attracted by the military regimen, Beaugrand enrolled in the newly inaugurated Ecole militaire de Montréal in the winter of 1865. He graduated that August (the science of war was quickly learned) and immediately set out for adventure. He was only seventeen years old when he joined the French expedition to Mexico that had been dispatched to rescue Maximilien. By all accounts, he fought gallantly and was later rewarded by the French Emperor for his bravery in the field of battle.[2]

In 1867, Beaugrand decided to visit the Europe he had defended instead of returning home. He spent two years in France, apparently absorbing anti-clerical thoughts,[3] then slowly made his way back to North America. He travelled to New Orleans and was hired at *l'Abeille*, Louisianna's main French-language publication. His stay was short as he returned to his beloved Mexico to work as a journalist until 1871. In that year, he decided to move closer to his native land and found work in Fall River, Massachusetts.

In Fall River, Beaugrand was exposed to the ideas of the local freemasonry. Four years after his arrival, he married Eliza Walker in Boston's Methodist Church. His daughter, born the following year, was not baptized as a catholic. In 1875, Beaugrand was named "master" of the local free-mason lodge. Fortified by his new title, he decided to strike out on his own in the journalistic world and founded *La République*. A year later, he moved the publication to St-Louis, where his anti-clerical rhetoric became noticeably virulent. In 1877, the St-Louis Episcopate denounced Beaugrand and the rejected journalist decided it was time to return to Canada after an eleven-year absence.

Beaugrand moved his family to Ottawa, where he immediately founded *Le Fédéral*. His publication lasted five months. In October of that year, Beaugrand arrived in Montreal and launched *Le Farceur*, a satirical political journal. *Le Farceur* scarcely survived longer than Beaugrand's earlier venture, as he leaped at the opportunity of directing the Liberal Party's debates. Indeed, *Le National*, the Liberal organ that had replaced *Le Pays* in 1871, was now going out of business. Having finished *Jeanne La Fileuse*, his novel about the French-Canadian emigration to the United States, Beaugrand launched *La Patrie* in February 1879. The party needed a paper to fill the void, and Beaugrand felt he could increase his own influence within the Liberal party as its editor.

La Patrie quickly became a point of assembly for the radicals still lingering in Quebec. Beaugrand quickly attracted Louis-Honoré Fréchette, Arthur Buies and Alphonse Lusignan, and the staff of the new publication wasted little time in setting their tone: "For the real liberals there are no compromises possible with the Conservative Party leaders," Beaugrand wrote in September 1879, barely two years after Laurier's famous speech. "We will stand our ground or we will fall, true to our principles and our policies, without sacrifice of our convictions."[4] It was not surprising to see Beaugrand lead the opposition against Mercier as the latter formed the *Parti national* in 1883. Though he would eventually be loyal to Mercier through most of the 1880s, Beaugrand would continue to argue that only a truly radical party, loyal to the convictions of the founding fathers of Liberalism, could succeed in attaining power, or, more importantly, in affecting reform. He ran on a progressive platform for the Mayoralty of Montreal and was elected in 1885. In his editorials, he upheld many of the old political platforms such as reciprocity with the United States, the abolition of the Senate and of the Legislative Council, sharp tax reductions, reform of the bureaucracy and new land sale policies. Above all, he sought reform in education, including mandatory school attendance.

Honoré Beaugrand dominated the political circles, the people, the ideas, and the inspirations into which Langlois moved during the spring of 1890. This was an environment that would shape his own perceptions of reality. Jean-Thomas Nordmann, a leading historian of radicalism in France, has argued that radicalism went beyond the sterile boundaries of political principle and was in fact a "political culture," a system of values and habits as well as a code of political ideas.[5] Debate, romance and controversy were the benchmarks of the history of French radicalism, and were not absent from the history of the French-Canadian variant. As Langlois joined *La Patrie*'s staff, he was exposed to a regenerating Liberal body of opinion. Undoubtedly, he was among those who gathered at Hector Berthelot's infamous Sunday night "ten o'clock gin" sessions. It had become a habit for the humorist Berthelot to assemble at his house most of Montreal's "advanced" thinkers. Beaugrand was there, of course. So was Marc Sauvalle of *Canada-Revue*, as well as Arthur Buies, Gonzalve Desaulniers and a score of journalists, poets, businessmen and artists.[6]

The ordered social life of the mid-nineteenth century radicals was giving way to the whims of a new generation. Where Dolly's and Gianelli's restaurants had been haunted by the Institut Canadien generation, and where the Hotel Richelieu had been a favourite meeting place for young "radicals" in the 1870s and 1880s,[7] Langlois was likely to follow his boss to the Grand Vatel. Raymond Préfontaine would be there, quietly nursing his whiskey-vermouth at the bar. His gang in tow, Beaugrand would meet with his old friend Fréchette, and maybe tease Prime Minister Honoré Mercier if he was in town. As one member of Beaugrand's clan remembered, "the good humour would reach its climax" when the latest trip to France was discussed or as a recent publication was dissected. Once the apéritif consumed at the Grand Vatel, the Beaugrand group would saunter to Victor Olivar's restaurant before paying a visit either to "Madame Duperrouzel" or to Pierre Cizol's rundown "Au pied de cochon." Some days, the troops would gather at the smoke-filled "Ricketts" on St-Vincent street for a slice of roast beef.[8] Langlois would later enjoy quite a reputation as a wine connoisseur and as a gourmet (and a *gourmand*). He probably would have traced his love of gastronomy to those early days eating beside the assiduous world-traveler Beaugrand, who made it a point of spending — and eating — most winters in France.

The point was that the *fine-gueule* Godfroy Langlois was not the only individual who wanted to revitalize the radical *rouge* tradition in the wake of Mercier's victory. Unmarried, he had time to spare to hobnob with Montreal's intellectual elite — hopping from tavern to restaurant, from hotel to hotel — in search of good political gossip as much a good food. The Hôtel St-Gabriel next to "Ricketts" on St-Vincent street, the Ottawa Hotel on St-Jacques street, the Cadillac, the Balmoral and most of all the Hotel Windsor and the Hotel Viger were mandatory hangouts for a young newspaperman eager to keep abreast of unfolding events.[9] Indeed, what Langlois absorbed from his readings and his studies under the supervision of Laflamme was confirmed and legitimized by the small coterie of "radicals" that surrounded him the newsrooms and bars of the early 1890s. One simply would not associate with Laflamme, Beaugrand, Fréchette and not absorb at least some of the ideals into which they breathed a spirited life. They were an intrinsic part of the early inspirations, and Langlois sponged their views and reviews with abandon.

There was also an element of romanticism. It was fundamental to radicalism in France and it certainly had its influence on Langlois mind. Like many young intellectuals of his day, Langlois was swept by the elegance of the Parnassian school of French poetry. Eager to emulate the likes of Paul Verlaine in a search for a "pure" poetry purged of the traditional narrative, countless young writers dabbled in the part of versification. As Langlois's only published poem amply demonstrated, this was art for art's sake: its purpose was to convey moods and subtle impressions. His *A ma musette*, part of a movement of poets that sought to emphasize states of mind rather than conceptual knowledge, was published in *Le Glaneur*, a short-lived literary journal. "It is without a doubt the organ of a small number of them [young people] who felt, as they entered life, the need for mutual admiration in order to hide their individual weaknesses," sarcastically wrote Arthur Buies in a decidedly uncharitable mood.[10] But Buies was not far off the mark. Langlois's poetic description of a walk in flowery gardens in search for new beginnings was not a great success.[11] Although he started and ended his poetry career with *Le Glaneur*'s first and only edition, Langlois was part of the irreverent first wave of talent that later coalesced into the Ecole Littéraire de Montréal and peaked with the work of young Emile Nelligan. Other journalists would persist and over the years many young radicals of Langlois's ilk came to dominate the "école". Gonzalve Desaulniers (a "voltairien de salon" according to historian Marcel Trudel[12]) and Gustave Comte, in particular, continued to combine "advanced" liberalism with poetry.[13]

If poetry was nothing but an excuse to get together with good friends for Langlois, politics seemed less and less a friendly game. Four years into his first term, Mercier called an election in June 1890. Campaigning on his record, the Premier was seeking a renewed mandate for his particular vision of Quebec and Canada. Langlois's relationship with Beaugrand would complicate the young man's already tenuous views of the *Parti national* as *La Patrie*'s publisher decided to reenter active politics to run against the governing party by presenting himself in opposition to Mercier's choice in the riding of St. Louis: Henri-Benjamin Rainville.

Beaugrand was putting in electoral terms what Lebeuf had denounced only a year earlier. Accusing Mercier of failing to fulfill the promises made to Liberals, Beaugrand also had harsh words for Rainville himself, who as alderman in Montreal, was widely suspected of corruption. The Beaugrand-Rainville fight easily captivated the attention of the Montreal press in this otherwise staid electoral contest, and for a while, it seemed as though things were going in Beaugrand's favour. Four days before the June 17 election, Mercier arrived in Montreal and lashed out against Beaugrand and Montreal's newly fanged "radicals". "I repeat that my government is a national government, and not a liberal government," he intoned, "I am a liberal, but let us be clear on the meaning of that word. I am a liberal in that I favour progress, but I am neither a radical nor a freemason."[14] Langlois's activities during the election were not highlighted by the press, but considering that he routinely dated this period as the beginnings of his political career,[15] it is safe to assume that he did participate in his boss's campaign. Notwithstanding the support he might have received from his newsroom, Beaugrand was not strong enough to defeat Rainville who won the riding by the slim margin of 11 votes.

Defeated but not vanquished, Beaugrand quickly succeeded in finding another cause that could potentially unite what was left of the radical constituency. Once again, the rallying symbol for Beaugrand was republican France and the political line which was followed followed closely the attitudes of the *radicaux* in France. In early October 1890, preparations were begun to organize festivities around a visit to Montreal by the heir to the French throne, the Comte de Paris. A meeting was called by the organizing committee. Uninvited, Honoré Beaugrand and Louis Fréchette hurried to the meeting anyway, and immediately set out to oppose the gestures. Fréchette argued loudly that it was a mistake to honour the "declared enemy" of the French republic and proposed this motion, which was seconded by Beaugrand:

> That notwithstanding the respect due to the Comte de Paris, we consider that it would be unacceptable for an official demonstration of support for him to take place in Montreal, considering that his official position as pretender to the French throne could be considered in France as an act of hostility towards the government of France.[16]

Beaugrand then threatened that if a demonstration were held in favour of the Comte de Paris, he would organize a counter-demonstration to show that "if there are monarchists in Montreal, there are also citizens who are proud to be republicans." Three people voted for the Beaugrand motion: Beaugrand himself, Fréchette, and a newcomer to the "radical" cause, Raoul Dandurand. Beaugrand took up the cause in *La Patrie*, and did not fail to identify various "nationalistes" with the monarchist cause. "Our readers are aware of the war waged against republican France in certain press quarters and in a certain coterie of 'officials'," he editorialized, "and holding a public reception to honour the official enemy of the republic would be an insult to history and would lead the world to believe that French Canada is only populated with reactionaries and enemies of liberal France."[17]

On October 20, a few of Beaugrand's friends gathered at *La Patrie*'s editorial desk to consider possible actions. Opting against a public demonstration, they decided that a cable be sent to the President of the French Republic, Sadi Carnot, to inform France that the heir to the throne was not unanimously welcomed on Canadian soil: "The undersigned, French-Canadians, in light of M. Le Comte de Paris's visit to Montreal, wish to present to you their most respectful regards and to reiterate their sympathies and their adhesion to the republican institutions France has freely given itself. Long live France! Long live the Republic!"[18] Fifty names were initially published below that telegram, including that of Rodolphe Laflamme, who headed the list, C.A. Geoffrion, Honoré Beaugrand, Louis Fréchette, Raoul Dandurand, Calixte Lebeuf, and Marc Sauvalle. On the 25th of October, almost two full pages of *La Patrie* were devoted to the signatures of the petition. Godfroy Langlois's name appeared near the bottom of the fourth column.

Beyond its very important symbolic significance, *La Patrie*'s campaign really amounted to little. The scheduled banquet took place and it was presided by that champion of moderate Liberalism, Louis-Amable Jetté. Where it did meet with some success was in shedding light on where radicalism was headed in Quebec. Although some of the former radical *rouges* still refused to follow Beaugrand's lead,[19] the latter met with the success that had eluded him for some time. The Comte de Paris affair was his political vengeance. One of the few unable to come to grips with Mercier's brand of liberalism, Beaugrand had alienated many people over the years. Marc Sauvalle and Rémi Tremblay, two of his star journalists, often resigned over political questions, only to return a few months later. Even Fréchette had quit Beaugrand in 1885 in order to join the pro-Mercier *l'Electeur* in Quebec City. The tide was now changing, and Fréchette instantly resigned his position when his boss Ernest Pacaud, the owner of *l'Electeur*, refused to support Beaugrand over the Comte de Paris issue. He would stay at *La Patrie* until 1896.[20] For their efforts in the affair, both Fréchette and Dandurand were given the cross of the French Legion of Honour. Beaugrand, for reasons unexplained, was not similarly decorated.

Beaugrand's search for an issue that would test the viability of French-Canadian radicalism was not the cause but a symptom of a growing trend. A year earlier, Godfroy Langlois had trumpeted a revival of sorts in his denunciation of the clergy published in *Le Clairon*. There were others. Aristide Filiatreault, for example, continued the demands of the old radicals. As Langlois launched *Le Clairon*, Filiatreault released the first edition of *Le Canada Artistique* in December 1889. He met with considerable success in recruiting contributors: Alphonse Lusignan, Honoré Beaugrand, Rémi Tremblay, Marc Sauvalle, Calixte Lebeuf, Gonzalve Desaulniers, Arthur Buies and Louis Fréchette. Despite its nominally narrow focus, its purpose closely paralleled that of *Le Clairon*. It called for educational improvements as well as local improvements in Montreal. *Le Canada Artistique*, like Langlois's publication, did not last long. It was scuttled in January 1891 and reborn as the more broadly-mandated *Canada-Revue*. If *Le Canada Artistique* defined its radical demands within its concerns with apolitical art, *Canada-Revue* was less subtle.[21]

Eager to address his native region in radical accents while still working in Montreal, Langlois had joined hands with lawyer J.D. Leduc, and launched *l'Echo des Deux-Montagnes* on November 6, 1890, eight months after *Le Clairon* had ceased publication. Langlois's liberalism flourished during the publication of *l'Echo des Deux-Montagnes*. His new review was not a departure from the style he had already made his at *Le Clairon* and his support of the "principles of 1837" found fertile ground in the issues of the day. In *l'Echo*, Langlois attempted to define the contours of his "radicalism" in more succinct terms. "The doctrine of *l'Echo* can be summarized in a simple sentence," he announced in July 1892, "to say out loud what people think deep down."[22]

More specific when tackling particular issues, Langlois's philosophy gradually took a more defined shape. Issues of educational reform, of clergy privileges, and of party politics continued to be discussed. "*L'Echo des Deux-Montagnes* is a Liberal paper," Langlois wrote in November 1892, "passionately Liberal, we are supporters of a great number of reforms such as reforms in education, reforms in the clergy, reforms in the magistrature, reforms in politics etc."[23]

Politically, despite its claim to being "passionately liberal", *l'Echo des Deux-Montagnes* supported Mercier and the *Parti national*. Swept by the tide of nationalism that flooded Quebec in the wake of the Riel hanging, Langlois had chosen to support the Mercier coalition in *l'Echo des Deux-Montagnes* because it was perceived as an efficient realization of the "great national movement of 1885."[24] Indeed, Langlois felt he was a part of that movement. He was virulently critical of Dalton McCarthy since the abolition of the separate schools in Manitoba. In 1892, when the Judicial Committee of the Privy Council announced that Manitoba was within its rights to abolish catholic schools, Langlois was livid:

> Let us open our eyes and observe what is happening. We are now at a point where we are no longer at home in Canada even though we are Canadians and there is but one valiant small corner on this Earth where we are not being trampled, its the province of Quebec. We are strong here because of our concentration and because we are a majority [...]
> The time has come to put an end to concessions and to make ourselves respected. From now on, we must be more French than we have ever been, we must speak French everywhere and always, we must only give to the English element what it has a right to in this province of Quebec. There must be a national awakening in all four corners of Papineau's province.[25]

Langlois's reaction to the Manitoba Schools question summarized his views of where Quebec liberalism had to be directed. In his call for a greater sense of nationalistic pride, he evoked the image of Papineau and of the fight of the 1837 rebels against British imperialism. The Manitoba Schools question helped to revive the notion that annexation to the United States was desirable. This idea, most popular in the 1840s but which still showed traces of life as late as the mid-1870s, had slowly been placed in limbo for almost twenty years. Another reason for the revival of the annexationist sentiment was the impact of the McKinley tariff imposed on Canadian products in response to Macdonald's National Policy. It was clear that the increasing protectionism of the two North American countries was having little beneficial effect on either economies. But Langlois went further in his calls for annexation to the United States. "It is certain that we have arrived at a time when radical changes must be made to Canadian life," he declared at a meeting of the *Club National* in December 1892. Rejecting the ideal of Canadian independence in the face of the American presence, Langlois openly advocated the forgotten notion of annexationism. "Independence in a country where our language and our schools have been abolished in New Brunswick and in Manitoba does not appeal to me."[26]

If the school crises fuelled Langlois's sense of nationalism, it also reinforced his sympathy for the radicalism of earlier days. It was in this uneasy context that *l'Echo des Deux-Montagnes* sparked debate on the erection of a monument to commemorate the rebellions of 1837. "The hour is right to build columns for those brave people who gave their lives for the conservation of our language and of our beliefs, as we experience a bitter, cruel time," Langlois wrote in 1891. "We have become the object of fanatical persecutions and the remembrance of our heroes would only warm our patriotism and revive our zeal."[27] Furthermore, Langlois did not fail to link his sense of nationalism with a distinct anticlericalism. "We need a monument to those who were persecuted to their graves by religion, to those who were denied forgiveness by the priests, even though they died for the country."[28]

Langlois pursued the anticlerical fight he had instigated at *Le Clairon*. "Our poor religion has served false pretexts and its ministers have acted as intellectual pirates to insult and to crush if possible those who had the courage to express their opinions frankly," observed Langlois. "Religion will remain eternal but its ministers will change and their ideas will certainly be more liberal."[29] Not surprisingly, Langlois wrote those remarks on July 14, the French national holiday. Part of his liberalism, in addition to the "principles of 1837" was the adoption of the "principles of 1789," a hodgepodge of ideas that summarized themselves as "the decree that men are born free and remain free and equal in law, that there no longer exists a nobility, no peerage, no hereditary distinctions, no class distinctions."[30] "For all those who have studied history objectively, the French revolution is a sacred work," Langlois insisted. "It is the era of modern freedom, it is a recognition of equality among men."[31]

Typically, Langlois highlighted the opposition to the church during the French revolution,[32] giving good cause for many of his critics to declare that he hated the church. Langlois, like most French-Canadian radicals of the nineteenth century, never gave real proof of it. "I belong to a catholic family, and I am a very moderate catholic," he confided privately in 1894.[33] What Langlois meant by the phrase "very moderate catholic" is open to speculation, but it was clear that the young man did not accept the church's historical authority without question. His attacks on the historical role of the clergy were pointed, especially when the subjects of privilege and education were broached. Langlois spared no words in demanding that education be taken out of the church's hands: "Lay education!—Another of those diabolical machines in which we are in favour because it is in the people's interest and because the state must spare no efforts in teaching and enlightening those who have been systematically plunged into illiteracy and ignorance."[34] Similarly, the *collège classique* was singled out as a weak link in the educational system of Quebec. Unlike his predecessors who had taken their cues from religious thinkers like LaMennais, Langlois was inspired by more positivistic doctrines. There was more at stake than church hegemony in Quebec, according to his interpretations. Gone were the old *rouge* demands that Liberals be allowed to speak as catholics. Liberals should speak on their own terms, regardless of what the church professed, Langlois argued. Social and economic problems had to be rectified because only they could guarantee a measure of individual freedom.

By so closely tracing the early steps of French liberals, by emulating them both in his diagnoses of what ailed the human condition and what could best cure it, Langlois was beginning to define a new philosophy in Quebec. His ideas of politics owed much of its impulse to the *rougisme* of his mentors, but was strongly permeated by the novel ideals of modern French radicalism. As such, his concept of Liberalism was French, and only slightly affected by British currents.[35]

Seeking to legitimize his early demands for a quiet revolution of mentalities in Quebec, Langlois often evoked the name of famous figures of the Third French Republic. "Gambetta, who preached the love of republicanism to his friends, said once that to know and love the republic, it is necessary to place it in the shoes of the peasants," Langlois noted in 1893. "Here we must do the same to make the cause of public education known and loved. For French-Canadians to have a measure of prestige, of influence, of value, they must be armed and be placed in a position to struggle forcefully."[36]

Langlois concluded at an early age that the reforms and ideals of the Third French Republic could be profitably adopted in Quebec. Already, the young journalist sought to redefine Liberalism. He succeeded in finding the weaknesses of the party ideology and applied himself to a search of new ideals. At stake was no longer the need to show that liberalism and Catholicism were compatible as his ideological ancestors tirelessly aimed to show, or that liberalism was devoid of any contentious philosophical meaning, as Wilfrid Laurier often argued. For Langlois, it was the individual's survival that was at stake in a depressed economy. Like many old radicals, he wanted to see educational reform in Quebec but grew to believe that progress would be measured only if education was made mandatory, free and secular. Only then could the individual be equipped to fight his struggle for life. And only then could the "nation" or the "race" thrive.

Honoré Mercier and the *Parti national* had posed many philosophical, political and psychological problems for the radicals. While he had advocated reforms of all kinds during the 1870s, Mercier himself had proven that he was unable to bring them to life while he governed. Still, many radicals had been convinced of his good intentions. Laflamme, Doutre, Béique and Langelier surrounded him so as to be close to power, suspecting that radical liberalism alone would never bring them to Quebec city. For most of them, the *Parti national* was a political tactic that could allow reforms to be implemented from the political "back door." Psychologically, the *Parti national* experience was also taxing because the impulse to criticize and make demands was always there, but repressed by political considerations. There were some sporadic outburst of radical anxieties during Mercier's administration such as the Lebeuf controversy described in the first chapter, but they were few, relatively weak, and always easily contained.

The situation changed dramatically when on December 16, 1891, Lieutenant-governor Angers asked for the Mercier government's resignation following the Baie des chaleurs scandal. As Calixte Lebeuf had predicted less than two years earlier, Ernest Pacaud was at fault. A bribe of $100,000 had apparently been given to him by a railway company allegedly to pay off some of the Premier's personal debts. In what soon became the "Anger Coup", Boucherville, the Conservative Party leader, was asked to form a government and immediately moved to dissolve the Legislative Assembly.

As Quebeckers prepared to vote for the second time in two years, *Parti national* potentates retired in droves, and those few who remained in the electoral ring denounced their leader. By 1892, Langlois was not the only journalist in Quebec demanding political and ideological change, nor was he alone in the party to reassess the merits of the *Parti national* experiment of the Liberal party. "I unequivocally repudiate Mr. Mercier," Joseph-Philippe Casgrain, a lifelong friend of Langlois, excitedly told the electors of the riding of l'Islet. "I am resolved to fight him and his entourage with the objective of bringing about a change in the system, radical and effective change, and to put an end to this system of compromises and of political pillaging of all sorts."[37] George Washington Stephens, never a fan of the *Parti national* concept, told the electors of the riding of Huntingdon that "if Mr. Mercier had followed the traditions of the Liberal party, he would have been one of the great benefactors of this country. He followed another path, and the entire governmental system has been stained by the fraudulent practices of men in which we invested our trust."[38] Casgrain similarly argued that Mercier was to blame for the corruption, in words that were eerie echoes of those spoken by Lebeuf. "It seems that Mr. Mercier had risen too far and too fast," he told his electors. "Once at the summit of power, he was blinded by excesses and awestruck by the honours, he became dizzy and he fell...."[39]

Godfroy Langlois's few actions were telling. He was already attracting notice as vice-president of the *Club National* by this time, but chose not to run for office under the *Parti national* banner. In Montreal Honoré Beaugrand again attempted to defeat Rainville in St-Louis, but both he and Casgrain in l'Islet were trounced by the Conservative candidate. Casgrain's tactic of lambasting his own leader almost worked, losing the contest by the slim margin of two votes. Mercier himself was elected with only a small plurality, but four of his ministers were defeated.

Removed from office less than two years into its second term, the *Parti national* had been dealt a fatal blow and left Liberalism in Quebec in a tailspin. Some saw hope. Charles Langelier later recalled that "the vote of the people [...] was not a repudiation of Liberalism, it was mostly a reaction. The Liberal party had been wiped out, but its principles were still there."[40] It is difficult to agree with Langelier's memories of a general optimism. The *Parti national* had worked hard to keep "liberal" programs out of the provincial debates and had put into effect none of the "principles" those who considered themselves true liberals believed in. The task of defining a new liberalism in a political culture steeped in conservative and nationalist rhetoric was easier to define than to carry out. Still, the emaciated parliamentary group was soon renamed "Liberal" and Félix-Gabriel Marchand, a veteran politician and Mercier partisan, was left with the difficult task of rebuilding the party. Many Liberals like Langlois were calling for a complete rejection of the politics of Joly, Mercier and Laurier and a return to the "old principles". Indeed, Langlois was almost drowned out by a sudden chorus of demands for reform and annexation to the United States.

Langlois, for his part, shared the optimism that the Liberal Party would rise like a phoenix from the *Parti national* ashes. His first attempts to define a political course for the new Liberal Party was hampered, however, by the church. Indeed, it took little time for the Archbishop of Montreal to react to Langlois's increasingly hostile critiques in the wake of the *Parti national* defeat, and on November 11, 1892, the church's position was made clear. Judging Langlois's *l'Echo des Deux-Montagnes* to have seriously injured the church, its disciplines and its priests, Monseigneur Edouard Fabre, the Archbishop of Montreal, prohibited its reading along with Aristide Filiatreault's *Canada-Revue*.

Langlois explained the interdiction in predictable terms. "Our language was too plain, our thoughts too free," he told H.J. Morgan. Langlois abided by the Archbishop's decision, but only in part. Unlike *Canada-Revue*, which enjoyed a staunch, urban and more anonymous readership, Langlois's patrons were largely rural, where reading habits could not easily be kept secret. While Filiatreault could afford to be cocky with the Archbishop, Langlois certainly was unable to imitate him and expect to retain his advertisers and readers. He and his partner J.D. Leduc ceased publication immediately and quickly moved to appeal the church's decision. Langlois and his partner, accompanied by Rémi Tremblay (who had again returned to *La Patrie*) visited Fabre in the Archdiocesan Palace in Montreal. They argued that their attacks were not against the church but rather against some of its individual members. Fabre apparently listened patiently, but was unimpressed.[41]"We ask all the good friends of *l'Echo des Deux-Montagnes* not to alarm themselves about the interdiction against our newspaper. We ask all those who intended to abandon our journal in accordance with the Ordinance to be patient and not to hasten to return their copies," wrote Langlois.[42] Despite his conservative readership, it was certainly not Langlois's intention to cease publication. "*L'Echo des Deux-Montagnes* is not dead," he told *La Presse*'s reporter. "Its editors will not capitulate. We have nothing to reproach ourselves with, and we do not regret one word of what we have written."[43]

Urged by his old friend and mentor Rodolphe Laflamme, Langlois resumed publication. To circumscribe the Archbishop's *ukase*, he started within a fortnight *La Liberté*, which was so similar to *l'Echo* that the traditional inaugural editorial was dispensed. The new publication was laid out as *l'Echo* had been, with the same number of pages, the same sponsors, and the same by-lines. There were two exceptions to this rule, however. Publication date was changed from Tuesday to Thursday and J.D. Leduc would abandon the newspaper a few months later. Langlois's attitude was unchanged. "We will continue the battle against Toryism, against retrogrades and against abuses," he promised, "we will struggle courageously so that the principles we consider just do triumph."[44] He did promise to moderate his attacks on the church, but as he told H.J. Morgan. "during the year 1893 [we] fought the whole year against the clergy of Two Mountains."[45] In fact, Langlois only spaced his critiques a little more. In March 1893, for instance, a certain Abbé Hétu was reported to have complained that Ste-Scholastique's parishioners were not generous enough in supporting their church. He apparently went so far as to say that neighbouring priests earned far more from notably poorer and less populous parishes. Langlois leaped at the provocation. "Here is a man who receives a stipend of at least eighteen hundred dollars," he argued. "He pays about a hundred dollars to his vicar, he has no family to raise, no children to educate, no taxes and no rent to pay and yet he must ask for more. What must the poor farmers who work like mercenaries every day and those poor workers who toil daily think?"[46]

The demands of the local priest and the depressed state of the economy forced Langlois to recognize that there existed in Canada a "rich man's politics" and he again accused the church of supporting the monied classes. "The clergy will always be conservative in outlook," he said, "because in its doctrine and in its temperament, the priesthood must protect the status quo [...] Mgr Fabre is a Tory and he will use his authority and his words to defend the present government."[47] "The country has been ruined by protectionism," Langlois declared in 1894 as he laid the blame squarely on some of Montreal's rich establishments. "The Drummonds, the Redpaths, the Ogilvies, the Galts have made themselves rich; they have horses and castles, they have millions and it is the poor unemployed who have made those fortunes who are now starving."[48]

It was a significant turn in Liberal rhetoric to perceive differences in class interests, and as such Langlois again demonstrated a departure from traditional confines of radical thought in Quebec. His experiences in Montreal had obviously taught him that some classes were exploited by others, and as the depression proved interminable, he spoke less of nationalism and even placed anticlericalism on the back-burner. Unlike his radical predecessors who were largely unconcerned by the ravaging economic and social effects of industrialization, Langlois already saw a *"retard"* in French Canada's ideological and economic evolution. Comparing

the French Canadian farmer to his Ontarian counterpart
(where political protest had found a voice in the Patrons of
Industry), Langlois even came to a startling conclusion. "The
agricultural people of Ontario," he wrote, "have come to
realize that, for a long time, they were being toyed with by
exploiters, monopolies and political maneuvering. But one
morning, they shook their apathy. Today they are a force to
be reckoned with." The French Canadian, Langlois observed,
was politically inactive in comparison with his Ontario
counterpart. "In the province of Quebec, our good farmers
are enveloped by indifference and lethargy and don't care as
to how things are done as long as the planet stays round and
continues to rotate. As a general rule, as long as the 'Canayen'
has read the *feuilleton*, the hangings, the sport page and other
idiocies, he has read it all."[49]

The solution to this poor sense of democracy, for Langlois,
was educational reform. "We are among those who firmly
believe that if we are to add prestige, influence, and value to
our people, we must ensure that it is vigorous and solid. Its
masses must be enlightened, they must know of the progress
being made and they must have the tools to compete."[50] In
sum, Langlois's dream was to witness a quiet revolution of
mentalities. "In a country such as ours where the population
is apathetic towards all things of the mind we must develop
everything that is vital in our people so as to struggle against
the invasion and the general devastation of the English,"
Langlois argued repeatedly, "we believe that the establishment of a mandatory system of education would be a
giant step in the road to reform."[51]

In his earlier writings, Langlois had restricted his demands
for educational reform to simple institutional changes, but
as the economic crisis approached a point where it seemed as
though it would be difficult for French Canada to emerge
from the morass, Langlois lost patience. "As a nation," he
declared as early as 1893, "we are today on the continent of
America in a sad state of inferiority."[52] Almost as if to find
solace in the triumphs of Republican France, Langlois pub-

lished his glowing obituary of Jules Ferry, France's father of educational reform, a few weeks after that terrible diagnosis.[53]

The young journalist's concern for educational reform was only a facet of the growing thesis that marked the last two years *La Liberté*. "We have fallen behind" gradually became a common refrain, hardly a patriotic call to pride and courage.[54] His work in the Ste-Scholastique publication was a telltale sign that he was finding difficulty in adapting the old radical ideals to the times in which he lived. He did not reject them, indeed, his call for a revival of the "principles of 1837" in the wake of the Manitoba School Question and for annexationism in light of the destructive effects of Macdonald's National Policy did manifest his admiration for the old radicals. Yet something was surely missing in the Liberal ideological equation for young Langlois. Anticlericalism still had relevance, but it was apparently clear to the journalist that the reason why the clergy was strong in Quebec lay in the fact that most politicians of both parties supported it and that the populace was weakened by its educational infirmities. His solution: State involvement in education where the teaching of all would be guaranteed by law. Similarly, there seemed to be little value in pressing for a nationalism when it was obvious that the French Canadian "nation" was divided unto itself, with one class exploiting the other.

Langlois wrote and edited *L'Echo* and later *La Liberté* on a part-time basis only. He continued to work with Beaugrand at *La Patrie* but accepted an offer to join *Le Monde* as assistant editor in December 1893. *Le Monde* had been purchased by a consortium of businessmen who were eager to reorient the traditionally ultramontane daily.[55] Genuinely loyal to its title under the new management, it was given an international mandate and held itself to the publication of news from around the globe and to refrain from *La Patrie*-style polemics. Its editorial comments were few and never harsh in tone, hardly in keeping with Langlois's style. The experience he lived at *Le Monde* in his administrative capacity, however, would prove to be an effective career decision.

The years from 1893 to 1895 were thus relatively quiet for Langlois as he worked at *Le Monde* and vented his spleen in *La Liberté*. Others were making radical noises. Aristide Filiatreault, the owner of the condemned *Canada-Revue* eventually ceased publication of that review in September 1894 and launched *Le Réveil*. He published *Au pays des ruines* and *Ruines cléricales* in 1893. The tract was reminiscent of the old radical diatribes, criticizing the church, highlighting its alleged moral corruption. L.O. David, hardly the rabid radical of earlier days, even published his contentious *Le clergé canadien, sa mission, son oeuvre* in 1896. Less vehement than Filiatreault in his philosophical criticism of the church, David did manifest some displeasure with the church's political influence, and lambasted the clergy for not supporting the 1837 rebellions. He called for improvements in the schools, in particular for a reduction of the time spent studying the classical languages. He even cited one of Langlois's articles in *Le Monde* calling for educational reform![56]

David was content to call on the clergy to remove itself from the political arena. "What we must deny to the clergy," wrote David, "is the right to ban from the church those men who want to exercise their rights as citizens and yet who want to remain catholics and patriots according to their good judgment and conscience."[57] Both Filiatreault and David's pamphlets were denounced by the church. Filiatreault typically remained indifferent to the condemnation, but David immediately withdrew its publication, much to the disgust of Honoré Beaugrand and the rest of the radicals.[58] In this rising tide of radicalism stood Félix-Gabriel Marchand, Mercier's successor and the Liberal leader in Quebec since 1892.

Soldier, farmer, capitalist, sportsman, poet, journalist and politician, Marchand was the Liberal Party's noble, steady, renaissance man. "He had an amusing and joyful wit, a moving spirit, a sincere and frank outlook; he had the goodness and the charity of a genuine Christian concern for others that was reflected in all his actions and in all his words," fondly remembered L.O. David. "There was nothing crude, trivial, mean, or shocking in him: he was, inside and out, a gentleman."[59] Marchand was born in 1832, the son of Gabriel Marchand and Mary McNider in St. Jean, a town on the south shore his father had helped found. Gabriel Marchand was a prosperous merchant who could afford schooling for his son in the Ste. Hyacinthe Seminary and, later, notarial studies.[60] After a long, romantic courtship, Felix-Gabriel Marchand married Hersélie Turgeon. Together, they had ten children.[61]

Marchand dabbled in many activities during his long career, but literature was his passion. He published often and his renown was so widespread by 1879 that the French Republic honoured him and his work by naming him Honourary Officer of Public Instruction. In 1891, Laval University bestowed upon him the title of Doctor of Letters as a reward for his literary accomplishments.[62] During his career as a journalist, Marchand never failed in serving his party. He founded Le Franco-canadien in St-Jean in 1860 and fought the idea of Confederation as its editor between 1867 and 1877. But Marchand was not a radical. He supported Mercier's coalition plans to remove the radical element from the Liberal party when it was in its nascent stages, he never antagonized the church, never invested his energies in seeking particularly progressive reforms, and only vaguely referred to Quebec's educational problems.

Marchand was first elected to the Legislative Assembly in 1867 to represent his native district of St. Jean and held that riding for 33 years. His quick mind, easy disposition, and virtuous sense of responsibility were immediately recognized and it was not surprising to see Henri Joly de Lotbinière name him to cabinet when the Liberal Party first held power in Quebec in 1878. Marchand was made Provincial Secretary and a few months later was given the post of Land Commissioner, a job he held for only seven months, as the government was quickly defeated when it finally faced the House.

Quickly proving his loyalty to the new party chief Mercier, he was called upon to assume the editorship of *Le Temps*, a Montreal daily conceived to oppose Beaugrand and *La Patrie's* early campaign against the Mercier leadership. When Mercier was swept to power in 1886, Marchand was named Speaker of the Assembly, and was chosen leader of the Parliamentary party after the crushing defeat of the Mercier troops in the 1892 election. His long experience in the legislative assembly, his almost divine gift for avoiding controversy, and the striking personality contrasts between him and his predecessor, made him a perfect choice as leader of a dispirited party. Nevertheless, the years in opposition were lonely for the discredited Liberals. Marchand was an admirable man, but not an effective leader of men. Still, he proved to be a steady hand and guided the Liberal caucus with some success. "He spoke effectively," recalled his son-in-law Raoul Dandurand, "but without warmth; eloquence was not his forte and he knew he did not have the magnetism that attracts and moves crowds—especially our crowds who are never insensitive to a well-crafted speech."[63]

While Marchand's task of endearing himself as leader was made easier by the fact that the parliamentary contingent was small, it was not easy to step into the legendary Mercier's shoes. The defeated premier would not disappear from the headlines. Ably defended by his former secretary F.L. Béique, Mercier was acquitted of the charges of corruption levelled against him in the fall of 1892, but his dream of a *Parti national* dynasty had been scuttled by his own negligence. His trial that fall and his strong, nationalist speeches in 1893 hardly allowed the modest Marchand a chance to make his own mark. Nonetheless, Marchand found strong support from a young generation of impatient Liberals which often flirted with radical ideas. Adélard Turgeon, F.G.M. Miville-Dechêne and Jules Tessier, in particular, attracted the attention of the parliamentary press corps with their eloquent speeches calling for change.

Indeed, Marchand's style of leadership allowed a propitious occasion for the radicals to show their mettle. Educational reform eventually made its way into the Liberal platform along with the traditional chorus for sound financial management. Most of the Liberal leader's efforts were spent trying to instill some peace in the party, even if that meant that he had to favour a few of the old radical demands. It was Marchand's task to hold together a fragmented, severely divided party in the face of Laurier's efforts to encourage a merger of Liberals and Conservatives within the confines of the Liberal Party organization. In a speech delivered in St-Jean during the federal election in June 1896, Marchand was even heard denouncing the conservative elements creeping into the party. "They are using subterfuges," he told a crowd of Liberals, "they seek to encourage our disputes and seek to disorient us—they want to divide us."[64] Marchand may have appeared weak in light of his uninspired opposition to the young turks, but Adolphe Chapleau, the Lieutenant Governor of the province was undoubtedly right when he observed that "it is in those individuals who appear indifferent that can be found the greatest resolves and endurance," when speaking privately about Marchand.[65] The Liberal leader in fact showed his true colours as well as his feelings towards the radical element of his party when tested by Godfroy Langlois's appointment to succeed Honoré Beaugrand as chief editor of La Patrie in the fall of 1895.

The Liberal press had been undergoing serious difficulties in the 1890s. The economic climate was tough on circulation figures, costs were up, advertising was down, and worse, La Presse proved an indefatigable competitor. Things had deteriorated to the point where Montreal's Liberal Party seemed unsure of its newspaper's own footing. Beaugrand's anticlericalism flared sporadically and unpredictably in some editorials and his fidelity to the Liberal leadership never seemed guaranteed. There was a high turnover rate in key personnel, clearly reflecting the difficulties of working with him. Beaugrand, moreover, was fighting chronic respiratory ailments that drained much of his energy. By 1895, *La Patrie*'s founder had resolved to distance himself from the daily grind of administration and began his search for a *dauphin*. Marc Sauvalle, the editor since 1892, did not fulfil Beaugrand's expectations, despite considerable party backing. Instead, paying no attention to the desires of the party leadership, Beaugrand sought Langlois at *Le Monde* and suddenly announced on October 25, 1895 that the job of general editor would be assumed by the 29 year-old. As such, he declared, *La Patrie* would continue to speak on behalf of the Liberal Patry. Langlois had eagerly accepted his old boss's offer and even ceased the publication of *La Liberté* so as to devote himself entirely to his new functions at *La Patrie*. *La Liberté* would appear for the last time in November 1895.

Marchand was furious at the Langlois nomination. "It appears to me that, considering the prejudice against the Liberal party in the catholic populace of this province, this article [announcing Langlois's appointment] can do a great deal of harm to Laurier in the task, already very difficult, that he is trying to accomplish," observed the Liberal leader. Marchand, moreover, was angered by Beaugrand's unilateral decision. "It is probable that our adversaries will depict all Liberals as responsible for *La Patrie*'s new attitude. I think it is urgent for the party to divest itself of this responsibility." "Is it not better to know immediately what the intentions of the new editor of *La Patrie* are," he impatiently asked Raoul Dandurand, "rather than wait for them to reveal themselves at an inopportune time?"[66]

Marchand's plea to his son-in-law for a disassociation of the Liberal Party from *La Patrie* quickly found an echo. Laurier, who also was concerned about the rising tide of radicalism in light of is preparations for the imminent election, was equally angered. "I do not recognize *La Patrie*'s self-given right to speak for the Liberal Party, and the views you state [in the article announcing Langlois's appointment] do not reflect the sentiments of this party," Laurier told Beaugrand. "Since I have been leader of this party, I have consistently worked to keep it within the broad directions of the English liberalism and it will not deviate from this road as long as I do remain in this position."[67]

If Beaugrand could not speak for the Liberal leadership, he could still do what he liked with his newspaper. The campaign Laurier and Marchand waged to distance the party from Langlois's radicalism was running into difficulties, especially in Montreal. Langlois would remain in his new position. Marc Sauvalle resigned as editor of *La Patrie* upon Langlois's arrival and established a daily called *La Bataille*, ostensibly to support the views of Laurier and Marchand and his first editorial openly reflected the conservative views of the Liberal leaders.[68]

Advanced Liberalism also found a fertile ground in the freemasonry of Quebec, one in which Langlois actively sought participation after becoming editor-in-chief of *La Patrie*. He joined the lodge of *Les Coeurs Unis* in Montreal on the eve of his 29th birthday in 1895. The freemasonry in Quebec was dominated by the Grand Lodge of Canada, and the Grand Lodge of Quebec, both of which were affiliated with the British masonry, a basically conservative movement. *Les Coeurs Unis* was a Montreal chapter of the Quebec organization.

Langlois's boss, Honoré Beaugrand, had deep roots with the Lodges. He had become involved with the Freemasons while he lived and worked in the United States, and had joined the King Philip lodge in Fall River in 1873, rising to the highest ranks within months. But with the 1890s, many French-speaking masons (the vast majority of them born between 1865 and 1870, which might suppose a generational reaction) had concluded that the Grand Lodge of Quebec was not fulfilling their understanding of what Freemasonry could contribute in Quebec. Language was an impediment to the spread of the Freemasonry, and it was concluded that the British practice of Freemasonry was incompatible with the "spirit of French masonry." The British lodge was probably still too respectful of the churches for anticlericals of the Langlois sort. On April

8, 1896, the young masons called a meeting of *Les Coeurs Unis* to discuss changes within the Grand Lodge of Quebec, and within four days it was decided to officially ask for an alliance with the French Masonry, the *Grand Orient de France* order. Godfroy Langlois joined the petitioning committee on that day, as did Léger Meunier. Langlois also sat on the committee given the task of determining what needed to be done to receive an official charter of the Paris order.

Things moved rapidly. Within days, an official request for a constitution was made, and Langlois proposed a name for the new lodge that was immediately accepted: it would be called *La Loge l'Emancipation*, and its motto would be *Reason, Labour, Liberty*. All that had to be done at that point was to await the decisions from Paris. On July 18, the official constitution was signed, and ten days later, the *Loge l'Emancipation* would be installed in the Old Fellow's Hall on Notre-Dame street, with nine members present. Among them were Achille Fortier, the composer and musician; Gaston Maillet, a dentist; Louis-Edouard Trudeau, an engineer; Félix Cornu, a doctor; Léger Meunier, a typographer; Alphonse Pelletier, a journalist; Ludger Larose, an artist; Lorenzo Prince, a journalist; and Godfroy Langlois. Dr. Cornu would head the local lodge; Godfroy Langlois, as the speaker of the lodge, would ensure that the rules and constitution of the lodge were respected.[69] Beaugrand joined *l'Emancipation* as an affiliate member in May 1897. Gonzalve Desaulniers would join in 1899.

The lodge never grew in membership beyond a mere handful of zealots, and never would constitute a broad audience for Langlois. While enthusiasm was strong for the lodge in its first year, members only met sporadically after 1899. Langlois nevertheless remained a staunch member of the Loge, rising to become its "venerable" president in 1901, succeeding Dr. Cornu. An inspection report submitted to the Grand Orient de France in early 1903 made particular mention of Langlois whose "energy and profound convictions" made him stand out.[70]

The party leadership's rapport with the reinvigorated radicals deteriorated further in the fall of 1896 when a letter written by Lieutenant-Governor Chapleau to Israël Tarte, Laurier's Minister of Public Works, was intercepted by Camille Piché, a Montreal lawyer and President of the *Club National*. Anticipating elections in Quebec, Chapleau told Tarte that thought had to be given to creating a political coalition of Liberals and Conservatives. According to Raoul Dandurand, the letter stated that Chapleau was willing to call upon Alphonse Nantel, a prominent Conservative, to form a government in which half the ministers, including Marchand, would be Liberal.[71] The radicals reacted vigorously and decisively, in a manner consistent with the practices of the Quebec intelligentsia: Eleven of them banded together to form a weekly, *Le Signal*. Among them were Paul Martineau, Philippe Demers (M.P. for St-Jean), Honoré Gervais, J.A. Drouin, David Lafortune, Camille Piché, Wilfrid Mercier, Gonzalve Desaulniers, Lomer Gouin and Godfroy Langlois. *Le Signal* proved to be a vehemently pro-radical, bitterly satirical weekly.[72] It was unequivocal in its defence of the "purity" and "incorruptibility" of Liberal principles. "All our collaborators are young enough to admire the legacies that have been given to us by the fathers of liberalism in this country," they proudly stated in their inaugural edition. "Confident in the integrity of our chiefs we will follow them into battle. But at the risk of delaying the victories, we will identify the weak flanks of the battalions."[73]

By "the weak flanks" of the battalions, the collaborators had two things in mind. First and foremost were the coalitionists of the Tarte-Chapleau school; the other weak area was the general political platform of the Liberal party. Lomer Gouin, significantly, was singled out as a leader of the mavericks. "In politics, Mr. Gouin is a Liberal, frankly and solidly Liberal. He is a partisan of reforms, he is a friend of progress," noted *Le Signal* in March 1897, as Gouin announced his candidacy for the upcoming provincial election.[74]

If the new radical-Liberal weekly freely advertised its admiration for Gouin, Godfroy Langlois's strong desire to press for educational reform was also noticeable. In the second edition, published November 21, 1896, *Le Signal* demanded a standardization of school books. As things existed, it was argued, parents were forced to pay prohibitively high prices for books of ephemeral use, something that harmed the quality of education throughout the province.[75] Typical of the Langlois style, the educational system of Quebec was singled out as a source of shame for the province. The critique was harsh and did not spare the church. "I am ashamed and I ask for pity from those compatriots who want us to drink from this chalice. It is enough," wrote "Dr.C". "I tell you that the punishment has been sufficient as it is and that there are no more obstacles for those who want to move ahead. It is in the Conseil de l'instruction publique that we find the sources of the humiliation that afflicts us, and it is to this body that we ask rehabilitation."[76] In February 1897, "Zéo" proposed that nothing short of free and mandatory school attendance would redress the inferior status of Quebec. "In order to overcome this damned ignorance the state must force apathetic, parsimonious, ignorant or needy fathers to let their children attend school: the state must decide which books should be used; the state must reexamine the manner in which it pays the teachers and judge them on their merits."[77]

Le Signal did not bear Langlois's imprint solely in its treatment of educational issues. "Coup de plume", Langlois's signature column, quickly pronounced itself in the finest of sarcasms on all issues. Indeed, Langlois seemed more comfortable as an occasional contributor to *Le Signal* than he did in the offices of *La Patrie*, although his presence in Beaugrand's editorial room was noticeable from the time he assumed his desk. The campaigns for educational reform he had instigated at *Le Clairon*, *l'Echo des Deux-Montagnes* and *La Liberté* were resumed. The negative reports of school inspectors, statistics and graphic depictions of a decaying church-run school system which were published in *La Patrie* clearly did not appease Marchand's anger. With the prospects of a provincial election, the old man despaired at *La Patrie*'s political attitudes. "We are, in reality, without an organ and without defense [...] against the French language press which has been making fire and brimstone against us for the last few months," Marchand again complained to Raoul Dandurand. "We win the debates in the legislature but our victories don't get a mention in the Montreal press and the public has no idea of what we are doing. The status of things is disastrous and if it continues there will be no point in us breaking our backs in the legislature as there will be little hope that our eloquence finds an echo outside."[78]

If Marchand felt he was having trouble with the troops in Montreal, fearing that *La Patrie* would do irreparable harm to the party with its unorthodox views, the situation in Quebec City was hardly better. Ernest Pacaud's *l'Electeur* had also succumbed to the radical verve and had begun to imitate *La Patrie*'s gesticulations. On December 22, 1896 *l'Electeur* was even placed on the Index by the Archbishop of Quebec City. "The bishops want war obviously," Laurier was heard to utter.[79] This incident only served to heighten Marchand's fear of an all-out war between a faction of his party and the church. "I hope that our friends in Montreal will understand, that in light of the upcoming battle, it will be necessary not to respond to this unprovoked aggression [...]," he told one of Montreal's chief political organizers, "the vote of June 23 [1896—the Laurier victory in Ottawa] must not be overturned."[80] Pacaud backed down, dissolved *l'Electeur* and founded *Le Soleil* instead. He promised to take the ruling to the Roman courts to appeal the Bishop's decision, but Beaugrand was infuriated: "All those men who refer to themselves as heralds of a new age appear on bended knee in front of the most arbitrary decisions, striking their chests with *mea culpas*."[81] "All you need is a pastoral letter to make the heads bow," lamented the radical, "and I look around in vain to see if there is still a Liberal worthy of the name who can protest this enslavement and this servility."[82]

Those words proved to be Beaugrand's swan song. Debilitated by his bronchitis, he finally opted to sell is newspaper to his childhood friend, Israël Tarte a month later. In his last article, published February 6, 1897 he told his readers he was leaving the reins of his cherished newspaper to a new generation, to "little Langlois—Godefroid [sic!] that I am happy will stay with the new editors of the newspaper."[83] Two days later, Langlois officially penned his first comment as chief editor for *La Patrie*. He was firm, but politely moderated his tone. "We will avoid those things which have tended to exacerbate the differences between our province's episcopate and the majority of parliamentarians—the majority of the electorate," he promised. Still, Langlois held firm to his ideal of a separation of church and state. The church, he argued, had to respect the public will in things temporal. "If this definition of the limits of the two powers [those of the church and those of the state] were accepted in good faith by all, the cause of our deplorable and ridiculous disputes would disappear." "We will be the defenders of political liberties," he warned, "we are taxpayers, free men, British citizens."[84] And Langlois did not miss the opportunity to press for educational reform: "Our people don't think that it is funny that the French province of Quebec is at the bottom of Confederation's list and often say that we should pay more attention to our own schools and less attention to the schools in Manitoba."[85]

Beaugrand's decision to force into the same political bed Langlois and Israël Tarte had many consequences. With his association at *Le Signal*, Langlois had repeatedly shown his hostility for the person who would now be his boss. In turn, the leadership of the party warmly supported Tarte and hardened its attitude towards Langlois even more as it prepared for eagerly awaited elections. The Conservative party, after all, was still a formidable opponent. In Montreal, it won the unambiguous support of *La Presse*.[86] Taxes had been raised under Conservative rule, admitted the Tory leaders, but only so as to allow the province to pay off the cost of Mercier's expensive policies. "I wish Mr. Tarte could see his way clear to come down and take charge of the provincial fight, as I must confess that I have great doubts about the outcome," lamented Robert Bickerdike, an important South Shore organizer in early March 1897.[87] If Mercier's political legacy was creating troubles for Marchand, Laurier was not helping his cause within his own party by responding affirmatively to Bickerdike's call for Tarte's political guidance.

Laurier did not hide his suspicion of radicals. In the formation of his cabinet, he had systematically avoided nominating controversial names. His selection of Quebec ministers included three English-speaking members and three French Canadians, including himself. What made Laurier's choices so controversial within the party was his disregard for the efforts of the radicals. Only Charles Geoffrion, who had laboured consistently, if quietly, for radical causes was nominated to a Minister-without-portfolio position. The rest of the Quebec ministerial contingent was anathema to radicalism. It included Henri Joly, the Premier of 1878, and few people had forgotten his denunciations of the radicals in the 1870s. Israël Tarte was an even more controversial choice. Tarte had never hidden his intentions to unite the moderate elements of the two established parties and was always considered an enemy by the radicals even though he joined the Liberal party in 1892. Insensitive to the radical protests, Laurier named Tarte to the politically-sensitive post of Minister of Public Works in June 1896. The Prime Minister's position *vis-à-vis* the radicals was made even worse by his two other choices of English Quebeckers: Charles Fitzpatrick and Robert Dobell, two Quebec City lawyers and former members of the Conservative party. Fitzpatrick was named Solicitor General and Dobell a Minister without portfolio. Sydney Fisher was also named as Minister of Agriculture.[88]

The Liberal press accepted Laurier's choices for cabinet as they were unveiled in July 1896, but the consensus was precarious and destined to hamstring Marchand's political march. François Miville-Dechêne, a prominent candidate in Quebec City, explained that patronage embarrassments triggered by Ottawa Liberals were discouraging good people from incurring the expenses to run for provincial office. "The unmovable senators who drove the party to ruin in 1878 will make us as unpopular as they made the Mackenzie government unpopular," complained Miville-Dechêne, "Already most of our best people refuse to serve."[89] Indeed, to manifest their alienation from the party executive in Ottawa, some openly supported candidates that were contesting the seats of incumbent Liberal deputies. Charles Langelier, another prominent Quebec City Liberal, pleaded with Laurier to straighten out the handling of patronage in the Quebec City area. The relative neglect suffered by the region since the advent of Laurier to power "created a dangerous malaise among us [...]. I tell you as a friend that the way patronage is run around here is doing us serious harm, you will see it later," he prophesied.[90] Clearly, the Liberal campaign in Quebec following the Laurier victory was not promising first because of obvious Tory strengths, but secondly because many self- described Liberal "fundamentalists" were fighting the Conservative infiltration of the party that Laurier, Tarte and even Marchand encouraged.

A first test was the candidacy of Joseph Shehyn in Quebec City. Mercier's former Minister of the Treasury, Shehyn was seeking a renomination. He seemed to be a most popular candidate and could conceivably unite the party behind him in the fight against the Conservatives. But he was challenged by a member of his own party by a certain Jean-Baptiste Thibaudeau, a former Conservative. Again, a frustrated Miville-Dechêne called upon Laurier to settle the issue. "Only you can put an end to this division by asking [Thibaudeau's organizer] Rochette to put aside his antipathies and his predilections and to support Mr. Shehyn. This should be done as quickly as possible, as the division worsens day by day."[91]

In Montreal, Henri-Benjamin Rainville sought the Liberal nomination for the St-Louis riding for the third time and his candidacy proved to be as contentious as Thibaudeau's in Quebec. He was nominated on February 17, 1897 but the debate triggered by his election left little doubt as to his unpopularity. The local riding association called for a new vote but Rainville was nevertheless re-nominated a week later. The Montreal *Witness* took a dim view of Rainville's candidacy, arguing that Liberal candidates should not be drawn from the ranks of the "clique" that ran city hall.[92] Efforts were made to present alderman Renaud to replace Rainville as Liberal candidate, but nothing came of it.

Miville-Dechêne's complaint to Laurier that Conservative infiltrations of the Liberal Party in Quebec City and Montreal were creating problems found an echo in the riding of Deux-Montagnes. Fortified by his rise to the chief-editor's chair at *La Patrie*, Langlois decided to submit his name for the Liberal candidacy in his family's riding. Supported by local Liberal celebrities, including Dr. Charles Marcil, a member of the Legislative Council and J.A.C. Ethier, the federal member of the region, Langlois was chosen by a nominating convention as the candidate to face the incumbent Conservative, J. Beauchamp. But Marchand decided to intervene. Deux-Montagnes had traditionally elected Conservative candidates, and the Sulpicians and the Trappists had intervened against the Liberals in the federal election of June 1896. Even though the priests had not succeeded in their campaign, the local strength of conservatism was a factor Marchand could not ignore.[93] Supported by other local Liberals who had complained of being ignored at the nominating convention, Marchand disallowed Langlois's candidacy and proposed instead Hector Champagne, a former member of the Conservative party. Negotiations took place among local party potentates and Langlois was finally forced to officially withdraw his candidacy. "The situation is really embarrassing," teased *La Presse*.[94]

His political career abruptly choked off, Langlois had no choice but to pursue his journalism and hope to find other tactics that would dam the osmosis of conservatism into Liberal ranks. But his sour experience at Deux-Montagnes was not the end of his troubles. Indeed, it took little time for Israël Tarte to challenge Langlois's inherited position in *La Patrie*'s newsroom. Two months after assuming the chief editor's post, Langlois was told to make room for a rising star in Liberal

ranks, one named Henri Bourassa. It was abundantly clear that
Bourassa and Langlois would not see eye to eye. The new
editorial director's politics could not be more dissimilar. "The
country is tired of these violent and acerbic fights," Bourassa
wrote in his inaugural editorial. In words that openly contra-
dicted the positions of *La Patrie* since Langlois had assumed *de
facto* command at the end of 1895, Bourassa continued:

> The confidence showed me by the leaders of the Liberal party
> by giving me the editorial control of their most credible
> organ in the Province of Quebec impresses me with obliga-
> tions I hope not to fail [...]. I feel no need to repeat it: In the
> field of religion, La Patrie is and will be frankly catholic, not
> catholic of this or that school, but catholic in a manner
> consistent with the heart and the spirit of the church, believ-
> ing in the dogma as it is taught by the church, obeying its
> discipline as it applies it. [...] I will defend the rights of the
> church when they are attacked. [...] I revere profoundly the
> sacerdotal character of the priest and the most august charac-
> ter of the Bishop. I see and respect in these men of God the
> authority of the church.[95]

Le Signal, *La Patrie's* impetuously radical younger brother,
did not take well to the news of Bourassa's assumption of
Langlois's editorial chair. "The entrance of Mr. Bourassa, the
M.P. for Labelle, will shortly bring about the disappearance of
Mr. Godfroid [sic] Langlois from that newspaper," wrote its
editorialist. "No one will deny that *La Patrie* was vigorously
and absolutely Liberal in the time Langlois, a professional
journalist, directed it, and we know a great number of people
who will regret this loss. There are still some of the old school,
you see, and there is a warm solidarity among those who are
not afraid to be a part of it. Let us hope that we are not about
to witness a decapitation or an immolation. Otherwise, we will
have our word to say," threatened *Le Signal*.[96]

Bourassa's fervent catholicism and his broadside against the
radicals created a fracas in *La Patrie's* newsroom that is not
difficult to imagine. Langlois was flanked by many of the more
anonymous radicals who worked at *La Patrie*, and it was

undoubtedly because of their support that he unequivocally prevailed. It was Bourassa, the Tarte choice, who decided to leave only a few days after assuming his post. "I had barely set foot inside," Bourassa confided to Laurier, "that I realized that someone had to leave. Having no personal interest in this enterprise, it was clear that if anyone had to leave, it was me. I had accepted the position with some repugnance, I leave it without remorse. On the contrary, the rather burlesque aspects of this adventure were rather entertaining."[97]

While *La Patrie* sorted out its personnel problems, the anxiously-awaited provincial election was called for May 11, 1897. It took little time for Edmund Flynn, the Conservative leader since 1896, to criss-cross the province in order to expound his programs. Marchand, much older and in less stable health, was more cautious in the length of his travels and on giving specifics to his promises: he concentrated his attacks on the past ministry and on the joyous prospects of having two Liberal French Canadians leading in Ottawa and in Quebec. It was, rightly complained *La Presse*, a rather dull campaign.[98] But interesting or not, the campaign tactics devised by Tarte and his lieutenant Raoul Dandurand dictated that Marchand concentrate his efforts in Montreal. One evening, thousands of people gathered at Sohmer Park, a popular east-end meeting place often used for outdoor circuses and vaudeville acts, to hear Marchand and his supporters speak out against the evils of Conservative tyranny. "Politics these days has so much charm that we noticed many representatives of the fair sex," sighed *La Presse*, confident that the population would heed its calls for a Conservative government.[99] Flynn's organizers were not to be outdone as they prepared a dramatic demonstration of support only two days later that attracted an estimated 25,000 people who marched in a spectacular torch-light parade from St-Lawrence Hall to Sohmer Park.[100]

In the end, when the polls closed in the evening of May 11, Tarte's strategy had borne fruit. With the normal 30.5% of eligible voters abstaining, Marchand's Liberals swept 52 of the 74 ridings and earned 54.5% of the popular vote. To the despair of *La Presse*, only one Conservative survived on the island of Montreal, and Flynn himself was barely reelected with a six vote majority. For many Liberals, this was the first victory since Joly's assumption to power. Nothing was due to Mercier, and the party, for the first time ever, had a solid mandate. At least eight of the Liberal members of the caucus were known to be in the radical camp: George Washington Stephens, Joseph Robidoux, William-Alexander Weir, F.X. Lemieux, Adélard Turgeon, François Miville-Dechêne, Tancrède de Grosbois and Lomer Gouin. *La Presse*, shaken by the results, complained that "the Conservative Party and Mr. Flynn have suffered a defeat they did not deserve" and carefully avoided congratulating the victorious Liberals.[101]

Secure in his victory, Marchand endeavoured to construct a cabinet that had to reflect the hybrid nature of the party without alienating any of its constituent parts. It promised not to be easy and Marchand even admitted publicly that he would be navigating treacherous water as he "awaited to launch his canoe": "I do not know what I will encounter," he told an audience at a post-victory banquet, "but no matter what the future brings, I will try to do one thing: to walk in the tracks of the one we all admire, the honourable Mr. Laurier."[102] Armed with the wisdom garnered during thirty years of political life, Marchand bravely set about his task.

Nobody could accuse Godfroy Langlois of not standing by his principles. Between 1892 and 1895, he had been publicly denounced by the church, by the leaders of the Canadian and Quebec Liberal parties and by his own boss Israël Tarte. His radicalism had been reproached and despite his provocations, he was still standing at the head of the largest French Liberal daily in the country. Evidently, he stood on the shoulders of many and with *Le Signal*, he had managed to connect with sympathizers to a new radicalism. Still, as Marchand tried his hand at building a cabinet, the young Langlois could do nothing but sit back... and wait.

Notes

1. *Le Glaneur*, 1890.

2. An account of Beaugrand's military exploits is in Pierre Bance, "Beaugrand et son temps" (Ph.D. thesis, University of Ottawa, 1964), pp. 14-16. Many aspects of Beaugrand's political career are nicely captured in the context of the smallpox epidemic of the mid-1880s. See Michael Bliss, *Plague: A History of Smallpox in Montreal,* (Toronto, 1991).

3. *Ibidem*, pp. 100-105.

4. *La Patrie*, 18 septembre 1879, cited in Bance, p. 249.

5. Nordmann, *La France radicale* (Paris, 1976), pp. 16-18.

6. Berthelot's biographer noted the *bons mots* and the good humour that animated the gatherings. See Henriette Lionais-Tassé, *La vie humouristique d'Hector Berthelot* (Montreal, 1934), p. 32.

7. Arthur Buies, *Reminiscences. Les jeunes barbares* (Quebec, 1892) p. 18.

8. See Victor Morin's account in his preface to Lionais-Tassé, op. cit.

9. On the important social, cultural and political roles of hotels and restaurants in Europe, see Jean d'Ormesson, *Grand Hotel: The Golden Age of Palace Hotels and Architectural and Social History* (London, 1984). No similar study of the social role of hotels has been attempted in Canada. For an entertaining American study, see Lewin Ehrenberg, *Steppin' Out: New York Nightlife and the Transformation of American Culture, 1890-1930* (Westport, 1981), chapter 2. Of interest is Francine Osborne, "Le Ritz-Carlton est le seul survivant de l'époque des grand hotels" *La Presse*, 18 juin 1984.

10. Arthur Buies, *Reminiscences*, p. 63.

11. See *Le Glaneur*, 1890.

12. Marcel Trudel, *L'Influence de Voltaire au Canada français, Vol. II* (Ottawa, 1945), p. 246.

13. See Jean Charbonneau, *Ecole Littéraire de Montréal* (Montreal, 1935).

14. Quoted in Rumilly, *Honoré Mercier et son temps, vol. II* (Montreal, 1935), p. 156.

15. PAC, H.J. Morgan Papers, Langlois to Morgan, n.d..

16. *La Patrie*, 13 octobre 1890.

17. *Ibidem*, editorial, 14 octobre 1890.

18. *Ibidem*, 21 octobre 1890.

19. For a dissident view, see Charles Langelier, *Souvenirs Politiques, Volume II* (Montreal, 1912), pp. 47-48.

20. See Pierre Bance, "Beaugrand et son temps" (Ph.D. thesis, University of Ottawa, 1962) pp. 130-132.

21. Trudel, op.cit., pp. 179-195. See also Jean de Bonville, "La Liberté de presse à la fin du XIXe siècle: Le cas de *Canada-Revue*," *RHAF*, mars 1978.

22. *l'Echo des Deux-Montagnes*, 14 juillet 1892.

23. *Ibidem*, 3 novembre 1892.

24. *Ibidem*, 27 novembre 1890

25. *Ibidem*, 11 août 1892.

26. *La Patrie*, 17 décembre 1892. As late as 1894, Langlois still declared himself an annexationist. See H.J. Morgan Papers, Langlois to Morgan, n.d.

27. *l'Echo des Deux-Montagnes*, 16 avril 1891.

28. *Ibidem*.

29. *Ibidem*, 14 juillet 1892.

30. *Ibidem*, 11 décembre 1890.

31. *Ibidem*, 27 novembre 1890.

32. Ibidem, 11 décembre 1890.

33. H.J. Morgan Papers, Langlois to Morgan, n.d. (probably 1894).

34. *l'Echo des Deux-Montagnes*, 27 novembre 1890.

35. It is difficult to agree with the contention that Langlois was a lifelong advocate of "British liberalism," even at this early stage of his career. See Ralph Heitzman for this view, "The Struggle for Life: The French Daily Press of Montreal and the Problem of Economic Growth in the Age of Laurier, 1896-1911" (Ph.D. Thesis, York University, 1977), pp. 288-89.

36. *La Liberté*, 9 mars 1893.

37. J.P.B. Casgrain, George Washington Stephens, *Les libéraux honnêtes répudient M. Mercier* (Montréal, 1892), p.9.

38. *Ibidem*. p.2.

39. *Ibidem*, p. 12.

40. Langelier, *Souvenirs politiques, Vol. II*, p. 205.

41. *L'Echo des Deux-Montagnes*, 17 novembre 1892.

42. *Ibidem*, editorial, 17 novembre 1892.

43. *La Presse*, 14 novembre 1892.

44. *La Liberté*, 1 décembre 1892. On Rodolphe Laflamme's assistance to Langlois in founding *La Liberté*, see the issue 14 décembre 1893.

45. On Langlois's promise, see *La Liberté*, 1 décembre 1892. On his declaration to Morgan see PAC, H..J. Morgan Papers, Langlois to Morgan, n.d. (late 1894?)

46. *Ibidem*, 16 mars 1893.

47. *Ibidem*, 2 mai 1895.

48. *Ibidem*, 27 décembre 1894.

49. *Ibidem*, 15 février 1894.

50. *Ibidem*, 31 janvier 1895.

51. *Ibidem*.

52. *Ibidem*, 9 mars 1893.

53. *Ibidem*, 23 mars 1893.

54. *Ibidem*, 18 octobre and 29 novembre 1894 are examples.

55. See Gérard Bouchard, "L'apogée et le déclin de l'ultramontanisme à travers le journal *Le Nouveau Monde, RS*, mai-décembre 1969.

56. L.O.David, *Le clergé canadien, sa mission, son oeuvre* (Montreal, 1896), p. 9. *Le Monde* is quoted on p. 109.

57. *Ibidem*, p. 117.

58. See Séraphin Marion, "Libéralisme canadien-français d'autrefois et d'aujourd'hui" in *CD*, 1962, p. 32. See also Marcel Trudel's discussion in *L'influence de Voltaire au Canada, Tome II* (Ottawa, 1945), p. 238-242.

59. L.O. David, *Souvenirs et biographies, 1870-1910* (Montreal, 1911), p. 135.

60. PAC, R. Dandurand-F.G. Marchand Papers, Joséphine Dandurand Diary, p.8.

61. The florid letters of the Marchand-Turgeon courtship have been preserved. See Archives du Québec à Québec (hereafter cited as ANQQ), F.G. Marchand Papers. For a more complete biography of Marchand, see Lionel Fortin, *Félix-Gabriel Marchand* (St-Jean, 1979).

62. A good cross-section of Marchand's work is found in *Mélanges politiques et littéraires* (St-Jean, 1899).

63. Marcel Hamelin (ed.), *Les mémoires du Sénateur Raoul Dandurand* (Ottawa, 1967), p. 12.

64. ANQQ, F.G. Marchand Papers, Speech, June 16, 1896.

65. Public Archives of Canada (hereafter cited as PAC), Joseph-Israël Tarte Papers, Chapleau to Tarte, May 17, 1897.

66. ANQQ, Marchand Papers, Marchand to Dandurand, 25 octobre 1895.

67. Letter quoted in *La Vérité*, 9 novembre 1895, cited in Marion, *op. cit.*, p. 28.

68. *La Bataille*, 14 décembre 1895.

69. See Roger Le Moine, *Deux Loges montréalaises du Grant Orient de France* (Ottawa, 1991) pp. 12-15. Le Moine conducted his research in Paris in the Archives of the Grand Orient de France.

70. *Ibidem*, the report in contained in Appendix III. See page 148.

71. *Les mémoires du Sénateur Raoul Dandurand*, p. 58.

72. *Ibidem*.

73. *Le Signal*, 14 novembre 1896.

74. *Ibidem*, 27 mars 1897; see also 15 mai 1897.

75. *Ibidem*, 21 novembre 1896.

76. *Ibidem*, 28 novembre 1896.

77. *Ibidem*, 13 février 1897.

78. ANQQ, Marchand Papers, Marchand to Dandurand, 13 décembre 1896.

79. As reported by *La Presse*, 7 janvier 1897.

80. ANQQ, Marchand Papers, Marchand to Dandurand, 28 décembre 1896.

81. *La Patrie*, 29 décembre 1896.

82. *Ibidem*.

83. *Ibidem*, 6 février 1897.

84. *La Patrie*, editorial, 8 février 1897.

85. *Ibidem*, 11 février 1897; see also 20 février 1897.

86. *La Presse*, editorial, 11 janvier 1897. On *La Presse*'s support for the Conservative party, See Pierre Godin, *L'information-Opium: Une histoire politique du journal La Presse* (Montreal, 1972). Less useful is Cyrille Felteau, *Histoire de La Presse, Tome 1, "Le livre du peuple", 1884-1916* (Montreal, 1983).

87. PAC, Laurier Papers, C747, R. Bickerdike to Laurier, March 1, 1897.

88. On the politics of constituting the first Laurier cabinet, see J.T. Saywell, "The Cabinet of 1896" in F.W. Gibson (ed.) *Cabinet Formation and Bicultural Relations* (Volume 6 of the Royal Commission on Bilingualism and Biculturalism: Ottawa, 1970).

89. PAC, Laurier Papers, C747, Miville-Dechêne to Laurier, 22 février 1897.

90. Laurier Papers, C747, Langelier to Laurier, 1 mars 1897.

91. Laurier Papers, C747, Miville-Dechêne to Laurier, 11 mars 1897.

92. *La Presse*, 15 février 1897.

93. Laurier Papers, C779, Tarte to Laurier, 6 octobre 1900.

94. *La Presse*, 15 février 1897.

95. *La Patrie*, editorial, 6 avril 1897.

96. *Le Signal*, editorial, 10 avril 1897.

97. Laurier Papers, C775, Bourassa Memorandum, "Encore aux lecteurs de *La Patrie*" n.d.

98. *La Presse*, editorial, 4 mai 1897.

99. *Ibidem*, 27 avril 1897.

100. *Ibidem*, 30 avril 1897.

101. *Ibidem*, editorial, 12 mai 1897.

102. *Ibidem*, 22 mai 1897.

CHAPTER III

MARCHAND
AND THE RADICALS

"There are still some of the old school,
you see, and there is a warm solidarity
that binds those who are not afraid
to be a part of it"

—*Le Signal , 1897*[1]

A S WITH ALL EXERCISES IN CABINET MAKING, Marchand's challenge in selecting his Ministers was to paper over the cleavages of geography, ethnicity, and ideology that characterized Quebec politics. One important party division, that which separated the "radicals" from the other Liberals, became a hot issue.[2] Indeed, even the newspapers of the day toyed with the notion that Marchand had to find an equilibrium between two ideological camps, the "Mercieristes" and the "Laurieristes", the former inexplicably being considered as more radical than the latter. Such labels were inadequate in that they were inconsistent (most Liberals had at one time been both Laurier and Mercier supporters, Marchand included), but they did convey the wisdom that two strong factions were waging a political war in the Liberal Party's bosom. "All we can say [...] is that the honourable Mr. Marchand has not been on a bed of roses since becoming Prime Minister", reported *La Presse* in late May 1897.[3]

Montreal radicals certainly were making life difficult for the new Premier with their incessant demands. Safely behind the editorial typewriter, Langlois saw the opportunity for the realization of the policy options he had advocated for close to seven years. "The Marchand government [...] can begin educational reform without fears," he editorialized following the Liberal victory. "What we want, what the province wants, is the uniformity of schoolbooks, a better and more practical education, competent teachers, better pay for teachers and that education be affordable for the poorest classes."[4] *Le Signal* echoed *La Patrie*'s demands. "The most serious [problem], at this hour," wrote "Paul" [probably Paul Martineau], "is a radical reform of our elementary school system."[5] "The remedy that is needed," the same "Paul" wrote a week later, "is mandatory attendance."[6]

Running parallel to policy demands were political ambitions. In a party so long deprived of patronage, Marchand was lucky he could count on Laurier to relieve some of the pressures. "Mr. Tarte told me yesterday that you were offering me your help to satisfy some of the ambitions that could make my work difficult," Marchand informed Laurier as he set out to form his cabinet.[7] His choices would not all be difficult, and guidelines did impose themselves. As *La Presse* noted, "public opinion would seem to dictate certain names that would be difficult to eliminate without causing some pain."[8] The protestant electorate had to be represented, and so did the Irish catholics. A balance had to be struck between the Quebec and Montreal representations, and some urban-rural equilibrium had to be achieved. In addition to the above criteria, Marchand also wanted men of quality. "I hope to be able to surround myself with colleagues of irreproachable characters who will be able to offer perfect guarantees," he told Laurier.[9]

Marchand did not go unassisted in his labours. Diplomatically, he sought the advice of party elders such as Henri Joly as well as those who had largely been responsible for his victory: Wilfrid Laurier and his Quebec organizers Israël Tarte and Raoul Dandurand. Joly offered advice that ignored too easily the realities that had brought Marchand to power. "In my view," Joly wrote, "it seems to me that you will never be as strong as you are today. This is the time for you to impose your views on your party — those who were elected explicitly to support you would offer no resistance today, in the immediate presence, so to say, of their electorates."[10]

Joly fully realized that Marchand was a moderate whose main intentions were to win over by his actions those whom the Liberal party had alienated during the Mercier years. Sober financial management was the key to the Liberal party's future according to Joly. But the former Premier was badly misreading the realities of Marchand's position *vis-à-vis* the radicals when he counselled that "as to the idea of launching the province in a new undertaking, however useful it may appear, don't think of it for the moment. Some people will complain, they will whine, but the majority is with you."[11] Joly's advice was thus of little help. Marchand's hands were not as free as Joly expected them to be. The debt incurred over five years of active support in opposition had to be repaid somehow and "radical" representation was necessary for the very survival of his ministry.

Israël Tarte rightly knew of these pressures, and strongly doubted whether Marchand could stand them. He privately suggested that Horace Archambault, a Montreal businessman of moderate predispositions, be asked to assume the Prime Ministership in the wake of the Liberal victory.[12] Lieutenant Governor Chapleau even contemplated the plan for an instant, but realized that Archambault could never win the support of a majority of Liberals and the idea quickly perished.[13] But Chapleau was fearful and still clung to the idea that the Liberal party could transform itself into a forum of moderate Liberals and moderate Conservative partisans. "The problem is in your hands," he wrote to Wilfrid Laurier. "I am counting on you in this task of pacification [...]."[14]

Chapleau reiterated his pleas to Tarte. "Do you want an unending war with no mercy against everything that is conservative in this province [...]?" he asked his old friend. "The feeling is unanimous: What is needed is an entirely new structure. Conservative ideas are not dead (since you are still alive); but the old machine hardly has any life in it anymore.

Moderation will be the salvation of this province and I have the hope that the church—the church that commands, not the church that lectures— will contribute in helping to bring about this moderation."[15] Clearly, Chapleau perceived the pressures exerting themselves on Marchand that Joly had not noticed.

Tarte did what he could. He pressed Marchand not to include George Washington Stephens in the cabinet. The latter had been a notorious "radical" all his life, had exercised the function of alderman in Montreal for 23 years and had been a Liberal member of the Legislative Assembly from 1880 until he was beaten in 1886. He had opposed Mercier's concept of a *Parti national*. "No one in Montreal is unaware of this fearless and irreproachable disciple of the old Liberal school," *La Presse* once remarked.[16] Stephens was a man destined for a cabinet position, having supported Marchand in the Legislative Assembly for five years. But Tarte had other priorities. "He is such a troublesome man that I would endlessly be suspicious of his presence in the government," he told Marchand.[17] Again, Tarte pressed to have Horace Archambault included in cabinet in place of Stephens. Even Laurier urged Marchand not to choose Stephens so that the latter could be free to take a Senatorial post "where his firm grasp of business affairs would be endlessly useful for us, and where, I think, he would find an atmosphere that would suit him better than the Legislative Assembly."[18]

There were other nominations to contemplate. Miville-Dechêne had to be a frontrunner. Similarly, Adélard Turgeon could not be ignored. His radical credentials,[19] like Miville-Dechêne, added to his popularity. Jules Tessier, a moderate, could not be ignored as cabinet material. Finally the old war horse Joseph Shehyn, a key organizer in Quebec City, a traditional representative of Irish interests and the most experienced man, having served as Treasurer for Mercier, had to be recognized. Marchand hesitated in choosing Shehyn over Dr. James John Guerin who fancied himself the representative of the Montreal Irish. Marchand decided to include both men in his cabinet. One to be left out in representing anglo-Irish interests was William Alexander Weir, the new MLA for Argenteuil county. Weir remained bitter at being passed over for a portfolio he thought he deserved[20] and would haunt Guerin in the caucus for many years.

Determining the representation of Quebec City and Montreal would be no less problematic. Both Tarte and Laurier were united in wanting to see Simon-Napoléon Parent in cabinet.[21] The member for St-Sauveur had distinguished himself as Mayor of Quebec City for five years. His administrative abilities also made him an excellent choice. But while he enjoyed the favour of potentates in Ottawa, Parent was far from popular on his own turf. "I will not hide the fact that there is a very strong movement against our friend Parent," Miville-Dechêne wrote to Marchand. "It should be easy to let him understand that he should complete his work at City Hall and that in a few months, he would find his place in cabinet."[22] What heightened Miville-Dechêne's hostility was the rumour that Turgeon would be forced to sacrifice his seat in cabinet in favour of Parent. Miville-Dechêne suspected Parent of being too close to the trusts — "it's one of the reasons for his weakness and that kills over here," wrote Miville-Dechêne.[23] In his eyes, Parent's prestige in Quebec City did not match Turgeon's and while the latter's loyalties were unquestioned, the same could not be said of Parent's. According to Miville-Dechêne, Parent was of those who were "incapable of defending themselves in the house, incapable of speaking on the hustings and who only benefit from overblown reputations. I would be very sorry if Mr. Marchand would choose as a colleague in Quebec men who [...] would be his secret enemies."[24]

It was even more evident that things were brewing in the provincial capital when it was rumoured that Joseph Robidoux would also be passed over. Robidoux, an assertive, articulate, radical-leaning law professor at McGill University, enjoyed quite a reputation among Montrealers. He had first been elected to the Legislative Assembly in 1884 and had served in the Mercier cabinet. "Robidoux was not an assiduous member of the 'council'," recalled the radical Arthur Buies, "but we would often find him in our closed meetings, where he liked to recall and recite the great authors of the day."[25] Indeed, Robidoux was of the sort that impressed people immediately.[26] He was a popular speaker, a sympathetic individual and a genuine leader who possessed strong "personal magnetism."[27] He was also ambitious, and his promises prompted his opponents to say that radical consequences would visit the province of Quebec if Liberals were carried to power because if elected, "Robidoux would become Prime Minister, and not Marchand."[28] Yet in spite of his popularity, Robidoux's access to cabinet was not assured. Also in the running for a position to represent French Montreal in cabinet was Henri-Benjamin Rainville, one of the most experienced public administrators in the Liberal caucus, having been alderman in Montreal since 1883 and an influential chairman of some of the City's most important Municipal Council Committees since 1886. Rainville, in his recurring fights with Beaugrand, had proven that he was not a friend of the radicals and *Le Signal* issued ominous political threats upon hearing the rumour that Robidoux would be passed over in favour of Rainville. "Villars" waxed menacing: "No ostracism, no cliques if party unity and order is desired in the ranks." He continued: "There are many liberals who are already in a bad mood and they do not want to see the party exploited for the benefit of a few castes and coteries. We are sincere and devoted partisans, we have made our share of sacrifices in the past struggle and this authorizes us to use the tone we are using today."[29]

Buoyed by *Le Signal*'s irreverence, Lomer Gouin, the newly elected member for St-Jacques, reaffirmed his links with radical liberalism. He and E.H. Bisson made representations to Marchand, apparently threatening him with embarrassing motions of non-confidence on the choice of Speaker if Robidoux was not elected to cabinet.[30] Laurier, on the other hand, was weary of Robidoux's radical influence and offered Marchand an eventual judicial seat for Robidoux in exchange for not admitting the popular law professor to the cabinet.[31] Understandably, the new Premier had a difficult task to perform as threats to the unity of the party were routinely broadcast by disgruntled factions. On May 24th, he finally introduced his cabinet, a formidable example in the art of compromise. "The work was painful," he confessed privately to Laurier a few days later. "You know all the difficulties a province such as ours holds when so many diverse interests and competing elements must be considered."[32]

To satisfy the party leaders in Ottawa, Marchand placed Horace Archambault and Simon-Napoléon Parent as Attorney General and Commissioner of Lands, Forests and Fisheries respectively. To placate the Irish of Montreal and Quebec he made both Joseph Shehyn and J.J. Guerin Ministers without Portfolio. To satisfy the protestants who had not only clamoured for many ministerial positions but had actually demanded, through the *Montreal Star*, that the finance portfolio be given "by natural right" to one of their representatives,[33] he made George Washington Stephens a Minister without Portfolio and H.T. Duffy Minister of Public Works. Marchand, in fact, kept the provincial treasury as his own responsibility and nominated fewer anglo-Quebeckers to his cabinet than any other previous Prime Minister.[34] Finally, Marchand gave in to radical demands by nominating four of the more tolerable radicals to the largest cabinet in the history of the province: Stephens, already mentioned; Turgeon; Miville-Dechêne and Robidoux. By keeping Tessier out of cabinet (and making him Speaker of the House), by ignoring totally the candidacy of the radical F.X. Lemieux, and by handing out only three of seven important portfolios to the radicals, Marchand did demonstrate that he still had the upper hand in directing party affairs, but that he was willing to accommodate them. Montreal, it must be noted, was favoured over all, receiving five of seven cabinet posts, with three of those going to the radicals.

The radicals had some good reasons to be happy. Montreal was largely represented in cabinet by people of their ilk. They had won their fight against Rainville's admission to cabinet, and Robidoux's nomination as Provincial Secretary sparked optimism. "Mr. Robidoux will almost be the Minister of Public Education," announced *Le Signal*. "The beautiful cause of education is in his competent hands, and we are happy that he has accepted the challenge."[35]

Observers of Quebec's Liberal party have often tried to depict the provincial organization as subservient to the aims of Laurier and the federal party, but in this case of the building of the Marchand cabinet, this was not true.[36] In the end, it must be said that Marchand acted on his own, and balanced the advice that came from Ottawa, against the demands and the threats formulated by the radical wing of the party. For sure, this was not a radical cabinet. Indeed, the presence of Archambault as Attorney General, of Parent as Minister responsible for Lands and Forests, of Duffy as Minister of Public Works and of Marchand himself holding the Province's purse strings would ensure a moderate tone in cabinet. *La Patrie*, perhaps reflecting the opinion held by Tarte, loudly applauded the formation of Marchand's new cabinet. "You have a great mandate," said *La Patrie*'s editorial, "You have our complete confidence. Whatever you will undertake will be well done."[37]

But not all political problems were resolved. While many did rejoice on May 24, many were bitterly disappointed to see the likes of Parent and Archambault take the places of deserving radicals, and Tarte's influence on the process was resented. Evidence of such animosity was quickly manifested as the Quebec City political rumour mill again ran at full tilt. On July 9th, *La Presse* reported that a conspiracy was being organized by the disgruntled in the party to redress the cabinet to a more "radical" posture.[38] Regardless of the validity of the *La Presse* story, the point was made, and Marchand stood warned of the troubles that would lie ahead if the situation was allowed to persist. Clearly, for the sur-

Name of small town in Ont mostly French

vival of his government, Marchand had to buy back the support of the radicals he had lost during his cabinet-making venture.

The radicals wasted no time in picking the next issue: The Lieutenant Governor Adolphe Chapleau. This onetime Premier of Quebec had been appointed to the post in 1892 by Canadian Prime Minister John Abbott, so as to guide the new Conservative regime in Quebec. Needless to say that to the radicals, he represented the most distasteful of remaining symbols of the long Conservative political hegemony in the province. Chapleau's term was to be renewed at the end of 1897 and the dilemma faced by Marchand in balancing moderate and radical interests was now faced by Wilfrid Laurier himself. Chapleau was a personal and political friend to the Prime Minister, and Laurier saw merits in trying to keep Chapleau in his position so as to facilitate the merger between moderate Conservatives and moderate Liberals both men looked forward to.[39] Unable to make a decision, Laurier, characteristically, stalled.

To the radicals who did not easily forget past precedents when Lieutenant Governors intruded in political affairs, Chapleau constituted a real threat to the Liberal administration. One member confirmed the antagonistic sentiments aroused by Chapleau. "There is in Quebec a great discontent about the Lieutenant-Governor, and that discontent increases with every day that passes," Laurier was told in early October 1897.[40] Pressures were mounting on both sides. Chapleau was writing that *La Presse* wanted to support the Liberals in Montreal, and that its editor, Arthur Dansereau, was ready to work for the party.[41] With the end of the summer of 1897 and early fall, the calls for replacing Chapleau grew louder. Chapleau could now read the writing on the wall. "I know Laurier is sincere on my account. But he is being overwhelmed and the partisans of the old *rouge* school are not giving up!" he told Dansereau.[42]

Laurier did begin to feel the heat. He hastily promised the job to François Langelier in the summer of 1897, but quickly

withdrew the offer.[43] Summer drifted into fall and no defini-
tive word had come from his office regarding the renewal of
Chapleau's mandate. "If Mr. Chapleau's mandate is renewed
after the expiry of his term in office," declared one letter,
"there will be an explosion of indignation as there has never
been in a political party and you will no longer be able to
count on the old partisans who have supported you for so
long.[44] Chapleau was equally unrelenting.[45] November was
drawing to a close and Laurier had still not made a decision.
More petitions followed. "The nomination of Mr. Chapleau
would be considered an act of treason against the Liberal
party, and this would be the beginning of the collapse of the
party and its ultimate ruin," declared one petition.[46] "Mr.
Chapleau's second term would be difficult for the province
to swallow," cautioned another.[47] Charles Langelier, whose
brother François had been promised the honour of being
named as Chapleau's successor, summarized dramatically the
general feeling among the radicals in the fall of 1897:

> If you give Chapleau a second term, or even prolong it for a
> few months, it will be a capital error, the great error of your
> life, it would be the dislocation of the Liberal party which is
> triumphant everywhere largely because of the great light you
> are shining on it. You will lose supporters you will never
> regain, you will compromise forever your future successes. I
> predict that there will be an outpouring of indignation you
> can hardly imagine now, but will inevitably take place. That
> you do not nominate my brother is immaterial. That you
> would leave Chapleau, that would be too humiliating, too
> much. Those who make you believe that these sentiments are
> not felt generally are either misinformed, are deliberately
> misguiding you or are plainly blinding themselves.[48]

Faced with such militancy, Laurier yielded and forced
Chapleau to retire. The radicals, who had staked party unity
of the issue, had won the fight. On December 30, 1897,
Chapleau held a dinner for all the members of the Legislative
Assembly and officially announced his retirement.[49] To the
radicals, the first link of the Chapleau-Tarte-Dansereau axis

of Conservative infiltration had been broken. Chapleau's successor, nonetheless, would be a disappointment. They still hoped to have one of them nominated to the Lieutenant Governorship but Laurier decided against it. A week after Chapleau retired, it was announced that Louis-Amable Jetté, a moderate Liberal since the late 1860s would be the new representative of Queen Victoria in Quebec. "Mr. Jetté is a striking example of what can be accomplished with work, moderation, sound principles and good behaviour," L.O. David said of his old friend. "He has made his way quietly, without impatience and without noise, without upsetting the natural flow of things."[50]

To Marchand, an ally of Jetté's since the 1870s, the choice seemed judicious enough, but something had to be done to appease Langelier who since December had scurried about the province denouncing Chapleau and those who supported him. He promised Laurier that Jetté would be highly respected by the cabinet,[51] but demanded at the same time that the provincial government's expenses incurred in the upkeep of the residence of the Queen's representative be drastically cut.[52] Perhaps this was his way of showing to the radicals (never big monarchists) that he, at least, had heard their views.

Marchand was quickly learning the art of appeasing radicals with astutely chosen symbolic gestures. Still, the threats of impending factional feuding in the wake of the announcement of his cabinet had an impact on him. To buy peace, Marchand consulted Robidoux and it was decided that the only measure that could assuage the disgruntled was a bill reforming the educational system. Robidoux took his cue from the party newspapers and *La Patrie* and *Le Signal* both clamoured for reform: "This is the hour of progress, the wind is blowing in the directions of reform: Let us be of our time and raise our sails to these strong winds," admonished *Le Signal*'s "patriote" while advocating educational reform.[53]

Langlois wanted to go further to inspire the radicals. Immediately following the Marchand victory, he lectured on the French Republic of 1848 and published his discourse that fall. *La République de 1848* reflected Langlois's burning desire for reform. "It is a page of the democracy's beautiful pageant that I invite you to read and meditate," this unabashed admirer of republicanism told his readers.[54] "Believe me," he wrote, "I profoundly admire the revolution of 1848 because it was the affirmation of popular sovereignty, because the people removed, almost without bloodshed, those who were selling it out, because the sons of 1789 reconquered their freedom to give to the nation a government of the people for the people."[55]

Langlois's glowing description of the republic of 1848 did not merely coincide with the radical press's attempts to convince Marchand of the merits of introducing reformist legislation. "1848" was chosen because it could be interpreted as the seed of modern reformist liberalism, just as Marchand's advent to power was perceived as the opportunity to establish new norms in the role of the state in Quebec. According to Langlois, France had shed its chains in 1848 and had taught other nations to attack absolutism and seek emancipation. Out of the republic came suffrage extensions, reductions in work hours and reforms in public education.[56] "The seed of liberalism and of progress that was sown by the men of 1848 has grown in a rich soil," argued Langlois.[57] Indeed, the French Third Republic was seen as a continuation of the abruptly aborted reforms of 1848. Just as France had recovered from its ignominious defeat in 1870, Langlois hoped to see Quebec follow the same route. "Here, in the province of Quebec," he told his readers, "we have followed with immense pride the monumental task of reestablishing our old mother country which we still love and we applaud, with heart and soul, the result of 25 years of the republican regime."[58] It was Langlois's hope that the use of historical examples such as these could legitimize whatever radical reforms the Marchand government would initiate.

Langlois's opuscule was received favourably in many circles, but some reviewers did perceive the amateur historian's

ulterior motives. "Mr. Langlois applauds without any mis-
givings the progressive works of the second and third republics of France: we would note nonetheless that his study is
incomplete and without purpose [...]," argued the Conservative *La Minerve*. "We are not ready to accept the judgements
made by Mr. Langlois on the men and their acts during these
three revolutions, or rather, the three republics. We believe
them to be on the contrary to be inspired by ideas that are
evidently not at all similar to ours."[59] Ottawa's *Le Canada*
also perceived Langlois's bias. "[The text] is far too imbued
with radicalism in its republican principles to judge this
period of France's history with the perfect impartiality that
we are to expect from a historian."[60]

Marchand, never a vigorous proponent of educational
reform, decided to seek educational reform along the lines
prescribed by the radical faction during that summer of
discontent over Chapleau. His actions paid eloquent testimony to the clout the small clique now possessed. The
Premier's thoughts on the matter were a mystery. David
described him as "honest, moral, religious, humbly practising
what he firmly believed, as frankly liberal as he was catholic,"[61] and there is no doubt that Marchand considered his
past as a good catholic to be a guarantee against any church
opposition.[62] As Langlois was making speeches around the
province, the Premier decided to act. He announced at the
end of July that Robidoux would be placed in charge of
reforming the educational system of the province. Marchand
then enlisted Paul de Cazes, an author as well as the general
secretary of the *Conseil de l'instruction publique*, to help the
reform. In August, he named Paul Martineau, a radical
lawyer, alderman and frequent contributor to *Le Signal* to
the Montreal School Board (or Commission). The choice of
Martineau was obviously repugnant to the conservative
members of the commission. Twice, immediately following
the Martineau nomination, the members of the board deliberately failed to reach a quorum.[63] Marchand, for his part,
retreated with Robidoux and Archambault at Paul de Cazes's

summer home on the Ile d'Orleans in late August to nail down an education policy.[64]

To secure some support from the church that summer, Robidoux sought out Mgr Merry del Val, the Papal delegate to Canada to discuss the general orientation of the Marchand government's intentions. In what detail Robidoux disclosed his plans to the prelate was unclear, but he did secure the Papal representative's support. Perhaps because he had witnessed very radical educational policies in Europe, Merry del Val had no reservations in giving his general approval of the Marchand initiatives.[65] Marchand worked on his own to seek allies in the church, and knowing full well that the impetuous Paul Bruchési, the new Archbishop of Montreal and the *de facto* leader of the church in Quebec, would be overtly opposed to the measures proposed, addressed himself to another papal legate, the Cardinal Rampolla. "Today," Marchand concluded in his letter to Rampolla, "the issues of education are on the agenda and everyone in the province recognizes that certain reforms have become necessary. We hold dearly to the realization of these reforms that are demanded by public opinion, and we do not want to hurt some of the members of our episcopate. As I am sure you know, there already exists some suspicion of our motives."[66]

The issue would lay dormant, save for the rhetoric in the Liberal and radical press until the government revealed its intentions in its first Throne Speech. The bombshell of November 23, 1897 stunned the Archbishop of Montreal. Bruchési immediately cabled both the Premier and the Lieutenant-Governor, urging them to retract the government's plans to introduce reformist legislation in the field of public education.[67]

Marchand's decision not to reveal his plans to the Episcopate before the bill was presented to the Assembly was indeed surprising. Did he fear the reprisals of the radicals should Bruchési or any other notable church leader in the province publicly condemn the initiatives even before they were introduced? Marchand's cool secrecy regarding this sensitive matter was perhaps revealing of how tenuous his grip on the party leadership really was. Unable or unwilling to reach Bruchési and explain the pressures to which he was subjected, Marchand proceeded. Dandurand oddly added another dimension to the problem. As he put it, "Mr. Marchand could not risk the retraction of this bill without risking a serious conflict of races and beliefs in the province."[68]

Desperately, Bruchési insisted that Marchand not present his reform bill to the Legislative Assembly. "I see in these plans the threat of discord among our population, the cause of unfortunate discussions that will work against our race, the cause of divisions among catholics and, perhaps, the cause of a conflict between the episcopate and the government," menaced Bruchési in a letter that arrived a few days after the throne speech.[69] Even while invoking the Pope's views on the subject of public instruction,[70] Bruchési obviously suspected the pressures under which Marchand was working. "I trust you will raise this matter with your cabinet," the Archbishop noted while encouraging Marchand to drop the matter.[71] Marchand responded to the letter almost twenty days later and revealed that his hands were tied. "The movement was considerable and could not be stopped without danger. I thought it possible, in guiding this movement instead of trying to stop it, to satisfy public opinion while maintaining it within the bounds of orthodoxy and respect for religious authority."[72] The proposed law, argued Marchand, was not as radical as some expected for it left the church to oversee religious instruction and maintain the religious character of the schools. Courteous as ever, Marchand again explained that he could not remove the bill from the Assembly's agenda "without compromising my reputation as a public figure and without raising in the province a dangerous and deep agitation I could not take responsibility for."[73]

Chapleau, fighting for his own survival, bore witness to many of Marchand's political constraints. "He could not withhold the announcement of his government's intentions in the Throne Speech without serious inconveniences, and even the rupture of the cabinet, considering the mix of elements with which it is composed," Chapleau told Bruchési.[74] Marchand's position was thus clear, and the clout of the radicals in the party and in the cabinet could be appreciated by all observers. To abandon the projected law would have forced Marchand to lose face, forced him perhaps to retire, and thus leave the party open for the radicals to command. "The shelving of our school bill," Marchand told Chapleau, "would bring about the resignation of many members of the cabinet and could cause such grave consequences I could not be responsible for."[75]

The effect of the proposed reform was to reduce the influence of the church and increase the responsibilities of the state. The essential point of the law was that it replaced the Superintendent of Public Instruction, the non-political chief executive of the educational hierarchy, with a Minister of Education. The Catholic Council of Public Instruction was to be reduced to the capacity of an advisory body to the minister responsible. "It was [...] the way to contain within just limits the popular movement that has erupted recently regarding our elementary schools, while maintaining the authority of the Conseil de l'Instruction Publique," argued Robidoux.[76] In effect, the Liberal proposal established a *de facto* Minister of Education, but ensured that the educational bureaucracy would not be part of the state. All the same, the arm's length relationship between the two bodies would be ended.

The bill was tabled by Robidoux on Wednesday December 22, 1897. "We want more children to know how to read, we want our youth to be better educated," Robidoux told the Legislative Assembly in his introductory speech, "but we are of those who believe that God must be present everywhere in education, and that before we can begin to develop intelligences and physical strengths, we must inculcate our children with a love of truth, we must strengthen their resolve and teach them to raise their eyes to the heavens before asking them to gaze down to their books."[77]

The fierce opposition of Edmund Flynn's Conservatives was not diminished by Robidoux's eloquence. Branding the bill as saturated with perfidy and filled with carefully masked radical tendencies, Flynn categorically opposed the intentions of the bill as well as its measures. Indeed, to all Conservatives, the bill represented but a first step toward obligatory, free, and secular schools. For this reason, a law that would establish a Minister of Education had to be opposed. Even Israël Tarte urged the Premier to drop the matter. "Those unhealthy elements that hanged Mercier and dishonoured our party for so long must be resisted," he urgently wrote to Marchand the day after the bill was presented.[78]

Without denying that the Robidoux bill constituted but one first step, Marchand repeated the refrain made familiar by the radicals:

> May it be well understood, once and for all, that religious instruction will be respected and maintained in our schools. But alongside this instruction, there must be the education in secular things: It is this part of the system, in my view, that is defective and which requires a serious reform, so that our youth can acquire all the competence required to place it at the same level as its counterparts in our sister provinces, and thus place it in a position to struggle for life.[79]

The bill passed its second reading on January 5, 1898 and was finally passed, after a few days of review in Committee, by the Legislative Assembly. It was then sent for approval to the Legislative Council, Quebec's upper house, where the radical cause of educational reform took a turn for the worse.

If Bruchési had been unable to move Marchand and the radical members of the Liberal cabinet, he had allies among the number of Conservatives who held the majority in the Legislative Council. The upper house consisted of ten Liberals and thirteen Conservatives in 1898, including three former Premiers: Boucherville, Ouimet and J.J. Ross.[80] These men, two of whom had played leading roles in the Ministry of Education's abolition in 1875, led the charge in the Legislative Council with the help of Thomas Chapais. Their main argument was that the proposed law would place public instruction in the arena of partisan politics, of electoral fluctuations and of the abuses of patronage. Chapais chided the cabinet for giving in to radical pressures. "There are some who want to drive us to state socialism in the field of education," he told the Council, "and others who do not have the courage to resist that current."[81] The vote in the Legislative Council divided itself along party lines, with the majority of Conservatives winning the battle, 13 votes to 9.

In the face of defeat, many of the Liberals swore to reintroduce the bill at another session, appended to a bill abolishing the Upper House entirely. But at this point, Israël Tarte and other moderates of the party redoubled their efforts to convince Marchand not to renew his attempt at school reform. Since Bruchési's nomination as Archbishop in early 1897, Laurier and Tarte had cautiously approached the church in the hopes of striking a new peace with the episcopacy, but feared that their efforts would be undermined by provincial initiatives. Marchand's acquiescence to the will of the radicals had dramatically slowed the process of the desired rapprochement. "Mgr Bruchési wants to be a Cardinal," Tarte cautioned Laurier a few months after the education bill was defeated, "and he expects that you would support his candidacy in Rome. I think it is the best policy for us to follow. It is important, however, not to let it show in Quebec City [...]. If we can capture the religious influence of this metropolis [Montreal], our policy will have borne great fruit."[82]

Tarte's role in convincing Marchand to drop the education bill was critically important. "Mgr Bruchési begs that in the interest of the peace we have concluded with him that we do our best so that the Marchand government not introduce its plans to create a Ministry of Public Education in the next session," he told Laurier in late 1898. "I must admit that I share in part the Archbishop's opinion [...]. After all, what is the point of opposing the opinions — the prejudices maybe, if you like — of the Episcopate, now that it begins to look at us in a kinder light than in the past? You have no idea of the progress we have made among the clergy."[83]

The radicals, for their part, were not willing to concede defeat. Tancrède de Grosbois, the Liberal Member for Shefford, threatened in February 1898 to present a private member's bill that imposed a fine to parents who neglected to send their children to school.[84] Godfroy Langlois was equally distressed at the outcome of the educational reform bill, but remained optimistic, hoping to go to war against the Legislative Council. "The Marchand government will not allow itself to be stopped in its progressive march," he declared, "Born of the ranks of the people, responsive to the best interests of the people, it will accomplish its mission with intelligence, devotion and firmness. It matters not how the Legislative Council will attempt to block its way."[85]

Langlois's optimism notwithstanding, Marchand's government became rather timid following the education bill debacle. The actions of the Legislative Council over the issue had made the point that it could even refuse the government the funds necessary to continue its rule. A representative illustration of the lengths Marchand went to in order not to alienate the slim Conservative majority in the Legislative Council was his policy on the federal senate issue. Senate reform had always been favoured by the radicals, particularly because the upper chamber was controlled by those who had reaped the benefits of almost thirty years of uninterrupted patronage. In Quebec, Godfroy Langlois had been a major proponent of the abolition of the Senate, on the grounds that its existence posed a threat to the legitimacy of the democratically-elected House of Commons. His publication *Sus au Sénat* was reproduced in full or in part in all the Liberal newspapers of the day. Frustrated by his own experience with the Senate, Laurier decided to act in 1898. Unsure as to how the Senate could be abolished in light of the absence of an amending formula in the *British North America* Act, Laurier asked the provincial administrations to pass motions in their legislations proposing the abolition of the Senate.

At the end of June of that year, Laurier contacted Marchand to enlist his support. Marchand was non-committal. "The proposition you offer in your letter," responded Marchand, "raises so many important objections that, notwithstanding my personal wish to be of help to you, I am compelled to ask you not to insist for an immediate answer."[86] Laurier nevertheless pressed on with his demand, hoping that Quebec would make the first pronouncement on the matter and give an example to the other Liberal provinces in the Dominion. Pressured, Marchand submitted Laurier's proposal to cabinet, and collected the answers he predicted. "Aside from Turgeon and Robidoux, who said nothing, the other members raised objection after objection. They are of the view that the initiative should be taken by another province."[87]

Marchand, who had decided to resume work on a new educational bill, explained this situation frankly to Laurier a few days later. A motion could not be passed in the Legislative Assembly condemning the Senate because "it would be dangerous for the Liberal party in our province and because it would provoke the rejection of our education bill and our money bills in the Legislative Council."[88] Marchand offered, all the same, to ask the provincial legislature to second a motion passed in the House of Commons. Laurier would again appeal to members of Marchand's cabinet, but ended soon thereafter his attempts to abolish the Canadian Senate.[89]

The anger of radicals in the aftermath of the defeat of the educational reform bill focused more and more on the subject of Israël Tarte, a close associate of Premier Marchand. He had never been welcomed by the radicals of the Liberal party and was not immune to their tantrums after Marchand was elected to power. "They are asking Laurier for your head," Arthur Dansereau had told Tarte a week before the Marchand victory.[90] "It is a war to the death," Chapleau had warned him in the wake of the Liberal triumph, "with pick-axes or with knives in the back—they will make use of whatever is handy—[...] the government of Quebec is now part of the movement."[91] In what Tarte's biographer euphemistically called a "difficult partnership,"[92] Tarte immediately felt the cold blade of resentment as the radicals maneuvered to deprive his *La Patrie* of governmental advertising.[93] In those days, the Provincial Secretary was responsible for the distribution of advertising patronage, and in the Marchand cabinet, that post was held by none other than Joseph Robidoux. Barely a week after the government was sworn in, Robidoux awarded to *Le Signal,* the radical, anti-Tarte publication the contract to print government announcements in Montreal, thus favouring it over *La Patrie.* Tarte's response, in a letter to Raoul Dandurand, was bitter. "In light of the strange attitude of *Le Signal* towards me, it is very humiliating [...] to see oneself forgotten," he confided to the Premier's son-in-law and confidant. "I want to get to the bottom of this. Robidoux was unhappy with me and I want to know how he has acted in this affair."[94]

Concern about Tarte rose from other quarters. Ernest Pacaud, the editor of *Le Soleil* in Quebec City spoke against Tarte.[95] But the most vocal was Charles Langelier, who was bolstered by the support of Philippe-Auguste Choquette, a Quebec City lawyer and former MLA for the riding of Montmagny. Another to speak out was Calixte Lebeuf, who attacked Tarte for hampering the provincial party's autonomy and for sabotaging *La Patrie.* "*La Patrie,*" he declared, "has become the exclusive organ of Mr. Tarte alone since he has purchased it. It has not been the organ of the government of Quebec, nor of the friends who are in power in Quebec."[96]

Much of the opposition to Tarte, as it reached a crescendo in 1898, emanated from the "clubs" that formed the propaganda structure of the Liberal Party in Quebec. The nature of such organizations, while crucial to the continued militancy of the Liberal loyalists, has not been understood as an autonomous part of the party structure by historians. There existed a great variety of clubs. Many were named to support the people who founded them, such as the *Club Laurier*, the *Club Robidoux*, the *Club Préfontaine* and even the *Club Tarte*, so as to keep fresh the loyalty of party workers. Others became the organizations of special interests groups. The oldest, for instance, was the *Club Letellier* in Montreal, which was founded in 1879 to support a famous politician but that increasingly distinguished itself as a defender of the interests of the working class and as an important source of radical opinion. The *Club Geoffrion* also harboured many radicals, almost all of whom were workers.[97] The *Club National* and the *Club de Réforme* seemed to be the domain of the more bourgeois radicals. The *Club libéral des entrepreneurs*, on the other hand, was noted for its moderation. During the cabal against Tarte, all the clubs were inextricably involved in the fight. The *Club Geoffrion* initiated the fight when it invited Calixte Lebeuf to speak against Tarte, and the latter was warmly applauded. But the *Club Laurier* executive denounced the *Letellier* and *Geoffrion* clubs for their criticisms of Tarte, though it was not clear if they spoke for the rank and file.

It took little time for the normally uncontroversial presidencies of these clubs to become hot political items. Even at this level, the opposition to moderates of the Chapleau and Tarte ilk invading the Liberal Party took root in fertile soil. In January 1898, one of Tarte's sons, Louis-Joseph, was dismissed from the vice-presidency of the *Club Letellier* by a vote of members. A few months later, in April 1898, the members of the Club deposed their president Oscar Beauchamp for not having taken part in denouncing Tarte. He was succeeded by the anti-Tartiste J.O. Lambert.[98] The following August, a movement to depose Lambert was launched, only to be crushed a few weeks later when Lambert was reelected in a general vote.[99]

The autumn of 1898 was marked by a sharp rise in club activism, largely as a result of the brewing discontent with

Tarte. Laurier, unable to attend all meetings, feared the negative impact of such dissent on party discipline. In vain, he sent letters to club presidents to steady their support, but the tide of protest quickly proved unmanageable. Even Raoul Dandurand, still unsure of the nature of his own radicalism, was repudiated for trying to pacify the discontented. At a sitting of the *Club National* before Christmas 1898, he protested the actions of "the young 'clubbists' who spend their time screaming after Mr. Laurier's colleagues and who risk creating discomfort in our ranks in doing so."[100] Desperate, Dandurand consulted Tarte in order to find a new solution: "Is not time for Mr. Laurier to intervene?" he asked. "I have noticed that it is those frustrated job seekers, in Quebec City as much as in Ottawa, that become anti-Tarte. They don't dare speak out against Marchand or Laurier."[101]

Laurier saw this as more than a dispute over patronage, and although there was no doubt that patronage issues did play a role in shaping this crisis, it was not the root cause. He chose to defend his friend Tarte in an open letter to Dandurand. By stating that some of the most illustrious politicians (citing his hero Gladstone particularly), had changed their political allegiances, Laurier exhorted all members of the party to keep their organization open to the best minds, regardless of their political pasts.[102] Ignoring Laurier's gauche dismissal of the rebels as students "who should return to their studies and to discussions of the issues our country must face in the future", the executive of the Club Letellier held its ground. "What we reproach of Mr. Tarte is not to have changed, but to have stayed the same. We want to fight not only the degenerated Conservatives, as does Mr. Tarte, but Conservatism in all its essence, even that of Macdonald and Cartier."[103] J.O. Maillé, representing the radical ranks of the *Club Geoffrion*, replied to Laurier's criticisms publicly: "This club protests and believes that before trying to find Tories in our ranks, Sir Wilfrid should begin to find those disguised Tories in his cabinet, and in the cabinet in Quebec City."[104]

As *La Presse* astutely remarked in December 1898, there
seemed to be three parties in Quebec. The Conservatives, the
"light red" and the "bright red".[105] The problem lay in
identifying who belonged to which group. One event did
shed light on the state of the Liberal Party's factions. Indeed,
the difficult year of 1898 would end much as it had begun,
with Charles Langelier denouncing his party. On two previous occasions, during the 1892 election and in an 1897
by-election, Langelier had sought the Liberal candidacy but
had found the opposition of the moderate Liberals like Israël
Tarte and Henri-Benjamin Rainville overwhelming.[106] Undaunted, Langelier promised to exact his revenge.[107] Now in
Lévis, supported by the tacit silence of Pacaud's *Le Soleil* and
by the Conservative *L'Événement*, which was only pleased
to abet discord in the Liberal party, Langelier sought his
revenge, as he said, against Tarte.[108] In December 1898, he
decided to return to active political life by running in a
provincial by-election in Lévis on the promise that he would
act as a counter-weight to the "traitors" in the Marchand
cabinet. Langelier, strategically, never mentioned any names
and most of the campaign press coverage was invested in
attempts to outguess him.

Indeed, Langelier's campaign gave voice to a vigorous
movement of radicals in Quebec City. As in Montreal, a
political club acted as crucible for the movement. J.A. Lane,
"a man of the working class,"[109] an outspoken opponent of
Liberal conservatism, and President of the proletariat-domi-
nated *Club Mercier*, summarized the views of the discontented, and called for a ringing endorsement of the Langelier
candidacy. "I belong to the old school of Liberals: that of the
bright reds," he told a meeting of the *Club Mercier* on
December 2, 1898. "I will never be a *bleu*, nor a light red—I
am a bright red. [...] What have the Laurier and Marchand
governments done for the old fighters?"[110]

Marchand was paralysed. "Mr. Langelier is feared among
the cabinet members, that is obvious", laughed *L'Événement*.
"They are not oblivious to the fact that if Mr. Langelier

entered the Legislative Assembly, it would not be long before many deputies would gather around him, thus forming an important faction that could constitute a serious danger for the government."[111] Equally fearful of being overturned by the Legislative Council, Langelier's threat of dividing the ranks of the Legislative Assembly made it impossible even for those radicals who wanted to stay in power to sit idly. While the *Club Laurier* in Montreal pronounced itself in favour of Langelier,[112] Raoul Dandurand and Miville-Dechêne spoke out against Langelier. "The friends of yesterday speak to each other without listening. One supports Langelier and the other for Marchand, without being able to explain their motives," noted *La Presse*.[113]

Langelier won the Liberal nomination, and went on to defeat his Conservative opponent, in what *La Presse* (suddenly made aware of the issues) called a frank denunciation of Tarte and of his lieutenants Marchand, Miville-Dechêne and Dandurand. "The events of yesterday," it noted, "have delivered a fatal blow to the regime of compromises and as such will shine in the political annals of this province."[114] Elated by his success, Langelier immediately sent thanks to Laurier for not denouncing him. "What an election campaign I did!" he exclaimed. "Do we not have here the teachings of the old Liberal Party in whose school I was taught?"[115]

Despite the agitation following the Legislative Council's rejection of the educational reform bill, and the addition of the impetuous Langelier to their ranks, the radicals seemingly rallied behind their moderate leader to preserve the Liberal administration. Marchand had earned their trust by nominating a few of their members to cabinet and by at least attempting to instigate educational reforms. In 1898, the government did involve itself in educational affairs by publishing and distributing, free of charge, to all first grade students, a reader. Albeit a small measure, the initiative was pregnant with significance. The radicals had clamoured for free, standardized textbooks, and Marchand's bill guaranteed state sponsorship. A bill to abolish the upper house was also introduced in good time, but was predictably defeated. To further please the radicals, Marchand pressed for Lomer Gouin to be admitted to the Conseil de l'Instruction Publique and immediately promised to invest $35,000 more a year on Quebec's educational system (an increase of over 8%), despite his austerity measures. Provincial government contributions in education actually rose by $55,000 during the first year of Liberal administration, a 15% increase. Total moneys directed into education also rose during Marchand's stay in power. $3,031,211 had been invested in education by the Flynn administration in 1896-1897. That figure had risen to $3,452,754 in Marchand's last budget year, 1900-1901.[116] In light of the French Third Republic's experience of educational reform, there was little in the 13.2% increase in educational spending Marchand allowed to quench the radicals' thirst for change, but most were convinced that little could be done for the time. Public education on the issues of public schools and upper houses, many concluded, had to be intensified so as to force politicians into action.

Radical Liberals reacted differently. Langlois's *La Patrie*, which continued to be filled with Tarte-inspired optimism, took the defeats of the administration in stride, and continued to press for educational reform: "Time works wonders, the obstacles will disappear and our program will be fulfilled."[117] The *Club Geoffrion*, however, was typical of the impatient and denounced Marchand's compromise measures in the field of education as a "farce".[118]

After the heated flurry of programmes and dreams of 1897-98, the administration quietly set about its task of sound fiscal management and took little interest in anything else. By playing with numbers, by assuring that the provincial governments got its share of revenue from the federal authorities,[119] Marchand succeeded in restoring a balanced budget. Indeed, so uneventful were provincial politics after 1898 that the newspapers paid but a minimum of attention to Quebec City. To a world concerned with the outbreak of the Boer War, the Boxer rebellion in China, the Spanish-

WOULD THAT HE WERE WITH US NOW!!

American war, to say nothing of the spectacular murder trials in Rawdon and St-Canut, the parliamentary workings of an old man and his becalmed party constituted little of journalistic interest.

Marchand could take some pride in the way he had handled, and in many ways hampered, the flexing muscles of radicalism. The radicals manifested their frustrations in 1897-98 on many issues. Indeed, so effective were their campaigns that Marchand was forced to implement policies for which he was not personally predisposed. Their attacks also made political casualties of some of his closest political friends. Chapleau proved impotent in the face of their multi-pronged onslaughts. Israël Tarte, whose influence seemed to pervade the party in 1897, continued to be the object of radicalism's scorn, but unlike Chapleau or Arthur Dansereau, proved capable of weathering the storm by securing some allies within the radical ranks. Marchand was able to survive by maintaining a careful balancing act. He knew that the traditional *rouge* confusions over the necessary means to accomplish desired ends had not altogether disappeared, and he took advantage of those weaknesses. He may have been criticized for giving the radicals a platform, but he was also aware of the consequences of not allowing them to speak. The Montreal *Witness,* for example, chided Marchand for not being sufficiently aggressive with the radicals. "He did not ride roughshod either over his opponents or over his followers," its editorialist wrote. "He was aware of wrong things on the part of the latter that he did not succeed in preventing."[120] Marchand, much to the credit of his political survival, chose not to brutalize the radical faction. It had demonstrated its unity, managed to impose its presence in cabinet and did affect policy initiatives to an unprecedented extent. He did his best to govern in a difficult internal political environment, and succeeded.

The radicals certainly did not disappear. Langelier wrote to Tarte following his victory and evoked the familiar fable of the hog and the hare. A wild sow, he recounted, one day presented herself at the rabbit's doorstep and asked for his hospitality. An obliging fellow, the hare accepted, only to find a few days later that the sow had given birth and that there was no more room for him in his own house. Unable to move the intruder, the rabbit had to abandon his abode. "The Liberal Party is determined not to play the role of the hare," Langelier told Tarte.[121] Langlois, for his part, continued to work at *La Patrie*, working to make sure that the hare had all the weapons necessary to repel the sow. Radical *rougisme* was undergoing a rigorous revision in *La Patrie*'s editorial rooms, a reorientation orchestrated by Langlois that, ironically, did not always displease Tarte.

Notes

1. *Le Signal*, 10 avril 1897.
2. See Jean Hamelin and Louise Beaudoin, "Les cabinets provinciaux, 1867-1967", *RS*, septembre-décembre 1967. See also Bernard Chevrier, "Le ministère de Félix-Gabriel Marchand" *RHAF*, juin 1968.
3. *La Presse*, 25 mai 1897.
4. *La Patrie*, editorial, 15 mai 1897.
5. *Le Signal*, 15 mai 1897.
6. *Ibidem*, 22 mai 1897.
7. ANQQ, Marchand Papers, Marchand to Laurier, 14 mai 1897.
8. *La Presse*, 18 mai 1897.
9. PAC, Henri Joly-de-Lotbinière Papers, M 794, Marchand to Joly, 14 mai 1897.
10. ANQQ, Marchand Papers, Joly to Marchand, 16 mai 1897.
11. *Ibidem.*
12. See allusion to Tarte's plan in PAC, Joseph-Israël Tarte Papers, Chapleau to Tarte, 17 mai 1897.
13. *Ibidem.*
14. Laurier Papers, Chapleau to Laurier, 15 mai 1897.
15. Tarte Papers, Chapleau to Tarte, 17 mai 1897.
16. *La Presse*, 29 mai 1897.
17. ANQQ, Marchand Papers, Tarte to Marchand, 12 mai 1897.
18. *Ibidem*, Laurier to Marchand, 24 mai 1897.

19. Marcel Trudel identified Turgeon as a "Voltairian", no doubt because of his early writings in *l'Action Libérale*, a Quebec City publication of the early 1890s.

20. *La Presse*, 22 décembre 1897.

21. ANQQ, Marchand Papers, Tarte to Marchand, 12 mai 1897.

22. *Ibidem*, Miville-Dechêne to Marchand, 19 mai 1897.

23. *Ibidem*.

24. *Ibidem*, Miville-Dechêne to Marchand, 21 mai 1897.

25. Arthur Buies, *Reminiscences* (Quebec, 1892), p. 30.

26. *Ibidem*, p. 31.

27. Charles Langelier, *Souvenirs politiques, Volume II* (Montreal, 1912), p. 38.

28. *La Presse*, 25 mai 1897.

29. *Le Signal*, 15 mai 1897.

30. As reported in *La Presse*, 26 mai 1897.

31. ANQQ, Marchand Papers, Laurier to Marchand, 24 mai 1897.

32. Laurier Papers, C750, Marchand to Laurier, 28 mai 1897.

33. *La Presse* denounced the *Montreal Star*'s position as "injurious to all the other races and religions that make up our population" in its editorial of 14 mai 1897.

34. See Robert Boily, "Les hommes politiques du Québec" *RHAF (Numéro spécial en honneur du centenaire canadien)* 1967, p. 605.

35. *Le Signal*, 29 mai 1897.

36. *La Presse*, 25 mai 1897. The day after the cabinet was unveiled, *La Presse* stated that "it is generally recognized that the plans for the new ministry were drafted in Ottawa." Hamelin and Beaudoin, *op.cit.*, also uphold the theory that Laurier was fully implicated, but offer no evidence.

37. *La Patrie*, editorial, 24 mai 1897.

38. *La Presse*, 9 juillet 1897.

39. Chapleau's ambitions are well desribed in John Saywell and Blair Neatby, "Chapleau and the Conservative Party in Quebec" *CHR*, 1, March 1956. See also Tarte Papers, Chapleau to Tarte, 18 mai 1897; Chapleau to Tarte, 31 mai 1897.

40. Laurier Papers, C757, Pelletier to Laurier, 4 octobre 1897. See also C744, Chapleau to Laurier, 16 novembre 1896; C748, Chapleau to Laurier, 2 avril 1897.

41. *Le Signal*, 27 février 1897.

42. Tarte Papers, Chapleau to Dansereau, 27 juin 1897.

43. The letter offering the position is reproduced in full in P.A. Choquette, *Un demi-siècle de vie politique* (Montreal, 1936), p. 125. The rumour is confirmed by Tarte in PAC, J.S. Willison Papers, Tarte to Willison, 16

December 1897. See also Laurier Papers, C751, Langelier to Laurier, 28 octobre 1897.

44. Laurier Papers, C750, petition, 4 octobre 1897.

45. *Ibidem*, C752, Chapleau to Laurier, 15 novembre 1897.

46. *Ibidem*, C751, petition, 5 octobre 1897.

47. *Ibidem*, C751, Chouinard to Laurier, 6 octobre 1897.

48. *Ibidem*, C. Langelier to Laurier, 18 octobre 1897.

49. *La Presse*, 3 janvier 1898.

50. L.O. David, *Souvenirs et biographies, 1870-1910* (Montreal, 1911), p. 91.

51. Laurier Papers, C753, Marchand to Laurier, 7 janvier 1898.

52. ANQQ, Marchand Papers, Marchand to Laurier, 9 février 1898.

53. *Le Signal*, 4 septembre 1897.

54. Godfroy Langlois, *La république de 1848* (Montreal, 1897), p. 1.

55. *Ibidem*, p. 14.

56. *Ibidem*, p. 52.

57. *Ibidem*, p. 62.

58. *Ibidem*, p. 63.

59. Godfroy Langlois Papers, File O, clipping of *La Minerve*, n.d.

60. *Ibidem*, *Le Canada*, n.d.

61. L.O. David, *Souvenirs et biographies, 1870-1910* (Montreal, 1911), p. 136

62. PAC, Raoul Dandurand-F.-G. Marchand Papers, Joséphine Dandurand diary, p. 95.

63. *Le Signal*, 14 août 1897.

64. Dandurand-Marchand Papers, Joséphine Dandurand Diary, p. 95.

65. ANQQ, Marchand Papers, Marchand to Rampolla, 19 novembre 1897. On the politics between the Holy See and Canada see Roberto Perrin, *Rome in Canada: The Vatican and Canadian Affairs in the late Victorian Age* (Toronto, 1990).

66. *Ibidem*.

67. ANQQ, Paul Bruchési to Marchand, telegram, 22 novembre 1897.

68. Dandurand-Marchand Papers, Dandurand to Mgr Merry del Val, n.d. (1906?) Much of the correspondence on this issue has been reproduced in *Les mémoires du Sénateur Raoul Dandurand*.

69. ANQQ, Paul Bruchési to Marchand, 22 novembre 1897.

70. *Ibidem*.

71. *Ibidem*.

72. Archives de la Chancellerie de l'Archevêché de Montréal (hereafter cited as ACAM), Paul Bruchési Papers, Political Correspondance file, Marchand to Bruchési, 11 décembre 1897.

73. *Ibidem.*

74. ANQQ, Marchand Papers, Chapleau to Bruchési, 8 janvier 1898.

75. *Ibidem*, Marchand to Chapleau, 7 décembre 1897.

76. ACAM, Bruchési Papers, Marchand to Bruchési, 8 janvier 1898.

77. Full text is reproduced in *La Presse*, 22 décembre 1897.

78. ANQQ, Marchand Papers, Tarte to Marchand, 23 décembre 1897.

79. *Ibidem*, "Discours de l'hon. F.G. Marchand sur la loi de l'instruction publique," 28 décembre 1897, p.2.

80. See Edmond Orban, *Le conseil législatif de Québec, 1867-1967* (Montreal, 1967),, pp. 260-267. See also Louis-Philippe Audet, "La querelle de l'instruction obligatoire" *CD*, 1959; Victrice Lessard, "L'Instruction obligatoire dans la province de Québec de 1875 à 1943" (Ph.D. thesis, University of Ottawa, 1962)

81. Thomas Chapais, *Discours sur la loi de l'instruction publique, 10 janvier 1898* (Quebec, 1898), p.3.

82. Laurier Papers, C758, Tarte to Laurier, 21 juillet 1898.

83. *Ibidem*, C 761, Tarte to Laurier, 3 décembre 1898.

84. Lessard thesis, *op.cit.*, p. 25.

85. *La Patrie*, editorial, 12 janvier 1898.

86. Laurier Papers, C758, Marchand to Laurier, 28 juin 1898. See also Laurier Papers, C763, Laurier to Marchand, 8 février 1899. Marchand's speech on the Legislative Council is reproduced in full in *La Presse*, 20 mars 1900. On the eventual dissolution of the Council in 1968, see Edmond Orban, "La fin du bicaméralisme au Québec" *CJPS*, 2, 1969.

87. *Ibidem*, C 763, Tarte to Laurier, 21 février 1899; see also Dandurand-Marchand Papers, Tarte to Dandurand, 6 mars 1899.

88. Laurier Papers, C 763, Marchand to Laurier, 1 mars 1899.

89. *Ibidem*, Laurier to Parent, 3 mars 1899.

90. Tarte Papers, Dansereau to Tarte, 19 mai 1897.

91. *Ibidem*, Chapleau to Tarte,.16 juillet 1897.

92. Laurier L. Lapierre, "Politics, Race and Religion in French-Canada: Joseph-Israël Tarte" (Ph.D. Thesis, University of Toronto, 1962), p. 344.

93. On Tarte's patronage expectations, see Dandurand-Marchand Papers, Tarte to Dandurand, 23 mai 1897.

94. *Ibidem*, Tarte to Dandurand, 30 mai 1897.

95. Laurier Papers, C752, Pacaud to Laurier, 6 décembre 1897. J.S. Willison, editor at *The Globe* in Toronto also covered the Langelier affair in some detail and attracted Tarte's fury. See PAC, J.S. Willison Papers, Tarte to Willison, 16 December 1897.

96. On Chapleau's warning, see Tarte Papers, Chapleau to Tarte, 16 juillet 1897. See also *La Presse*, 2 avril 1898; Tarte Papers, A. Germain to Tarte, 20 avril 1898.

97. Tarte Papers, A. Germain to Tarte, 20 avril 1898.

98. *La Presse*, 14 avril 1898.

99. *Ibidem*, 5 octobre 1898; 6 octobre 1898.

100. Laurier Papers, C761, Dandurand to Tarte, 22 décembre 1898.

101. *Ibidem*.

102. Dandurand-Marchand Papers, Laurier to Dandurand, 26 décembre 1898.

103. *La Presse*, 14 janvier 1899.

104. *Ibidem*, 11 janvier 1899.

105. *Ibidem*, 5 décembre 1898.

106. See Rainville's comments, *La Presse*, 16 décembre 1897.

107. Laurier Papers, C752, Langelier to Laurier, 26 décembre 1897.

108. *Ibidem*, C745, Langelier to Tarte, n.d.

109. *Ibidem*, C773, Langelier to Laurier, 8 février 1900.

110. *La Presse*, 3 décembre 1898.

111. As cited in *La Presse*, 5 décembre 1898.

112. *Ibidem*, 9 décembre 1898.

113. *Ibidem*, 5 décembre 1898.

114. *Ibidem*, editorial, 20 décembre 1898.

115. Laurier Papers, C761, Langelier to Laurier, 27 décembre 1898.

116. Province de Québec, *Annuaire statistique du Québec, 1916* (Quebec, 1916), pp. 227-228.

117. *La Patrie*, editorial, 11 mai 1898.

118. *La Presse*, 1 mars 1899.

119. Laurier Papers, C757, Marchand to Laurier, 11 juin 1898.

120. *The Witness*, editorial, 26 September 1900. In a similar vein, see *The Gazette*'s editorial for the same day.

121. Laurier Papers, C745, C. Langelier to Tarte, n.d.

CHAPTER IV

THE RISE OF LIBERAL PROGRESSIVISM IN MONTREAL

"Iron discipline, that is to say the blind approval of the worse dirt to protect a party, no longer exists, at least not with the Liberals any way. Sound public opinion no longer tolerates such discipline which was invented to obliterate independence, liberty, energy and virility."

—*Le Signal, 1897*[1]

A VERY INTERESTING MEETING of the fledgling *Club ouvrier independant* was held in late October 1898. Its members had gathered in a hall at the corner of Parthenais and Ste-Catherine streets in east-end Montreal not to discuss the presence of Israël Tarte in the Liberal party, but to discuss the latest propositions for reforms to the City of Montreal's Charter. A few aldermen had been invited to speak on the latest suggestions, and while some declined the request, a few did address the issue, but only in a typically vague, evasive manner. Dissatisfied with the responses, J.A. Rodier, a worker at *La Presse*, then took the stand. He declared that the projected charter was an abomination in that it addressed none of the issues raised by the workers of Montreal. He argued against the undemocratic financial qualifications still required to run for aldermanic seats or for the mayoralty and eventually summarized his short speech with a denunciation of "capital's" corruption of city politics.

Responding to Rodier's speech a few moments later, J.G. de la Durantaye, a journalist from *La Patrie*, countered the arguments against capitalism. He told the assembly that there was no doubt that efforts had to be made to improve the city's Charter and the conditions of the working class but that it was not necessary to overturn the established order to reach that goal. He declared that industrial relations was too serious a matter to be judged not "from an exclusively personal point of view, but from the point of view of the general interest and of the harmony that must exist between all the classes of our society."[2]

That small altercation revealed many things about politics in Montreal at the closing of the nineteenth century. It was significant that the issue of the legitimacy of capitalism was raised in discussing not the lofty topics of tariffs or excise taxes, but in examining civic politics. The radical Liberals, in meetings like that of the *Club ouvrier independant*, discovered that there was a growing discontent among segments of the population that it really had never addressed before. It recognized that Liberalism was no longer responsive, and fearing the formation of a third party, sought to demonstrate to people like Rodier that the ideal of a humane capitalism held real meaning among some Liberals. It was in the crucible of metamorphosing Montreal that radical Liberalism shed its mid-nineteenth century colours, broadened its network of adherents, and devoted itself to the concerns of the urban masses. The first phase of this transformation consisted in revising the party image at the local level — the level that arguably affects the day-to-day lives of most people and that consequently played the greatest role in legitimizing the capitalist system.

As a seasoned observer and participant in radical politics, J.G. de la Durantaye probably was dismayed to see himself outflanked on the left by Rodier. As an associate of Godfroy Langlois since their earliest days at *Le Clairon*, he epitomized *La Patrie*'s evolving approach to politics in Montreal and its drive to redefine liberalism at the turn of the century. As editor of *La Patrie*, Langlois grew increasingly sensitive to the transformations that industrial capitalism had wrought to Montreal. "He observed with particular interest the conduct and the efforts of the public leaders as they grappled with the issues of the day," remembered a *La Patrie* colleague: "His constant preoccupation compelled him to study the emerging problems that modern times were bearing and to measure the impact of the solutions required. Everywhere he saw necessary reforms that had to be undertaken."[3] Langlois, like others such as Lebeuf, Beaugrand, Langelier had challenged Liberalism to address the new problems since the early 1890s, but the disconcerting answers yielded by conventional wisdom about the nature of politics in general, and of Liberal policies and practices in particular, spurred him to break party discipline and establish in *La Patrie* the basic parameters of what can be best described as an incipient Liberal progressivism.

Indeed, it was ironic that Godfroy Langlois managed to cultivate a working relationship with the arch-enemy of the radicals while working at *La Patrie*, especially since Tarte had attempted to replace him with Henri Bourassa less than a month after assuming control of Beaugrand's newspaper. It was not easy. "It was probable that our friend Langlois was uncomfortable with us, hampered as the head of a staff that was receiving its instructions and its directions from higher offices and which with every day dedicated *La Patrie* to the appeasement of discussion, to encouraging the union of moderate elements and to the reconciliation of political factions that had been fighting for some time," remembered Charles Robillard, a reporter at the time, "this policy did not conform to this impetuous temperament."[4] Tarte's duties in Ottawa undoubtedly made things slightly easier for Langlois as the Minister of Public works left the mundane operations of the daily to his sons. The result was an enduring display of editorial tensions.

To Langlois's dismay, *La Patrie* could never again be a genuine publication of "combat" it sometimes had been under Beaugrand's leadership. The Tartes were eager to enlarge their share of Montreal's newspaper market and had little patience for their editor's endless harangues. Their publication's pious tone would oftentimes be interrupted with explicit and graphic descriptions of violent crimes and gory hangings. Indeed, Langlois's presence at the editorial desk was sometimes merely indicated by the daily's attention to international news, labour affairs and reports on educational matter. "Coups de Plume", which of course followed its author wherever he went, was the only resort for Langlois's frisky, sarcastic pen.

Still, if the mercurial journalist was forced to curb his zealous demands for reform, his superiors were not always successful in muzzling him. Archbishop Bruchési paid particular attention to newspapers. He was acutely aware of the sensationalist tendencies of Montreal's competing dailies and relentlessly attempted to persuade the editors to curb the editorial excesses. Repeatedly he decried the emerging "yellow" journalism. "I am ready to protect the [youth] and however painful may be the task, I will not fail," he once told the Tarte brothers. "Journalism in Montreal has taken a character that can only be deplored. Yet, I thought I could count on the solemn promises that I am sure you have not forgotten."[5]

La Patrie, despite the Archbishop's pleas, remained a sensationalist rag under the direction of the Tartes. Eugène Tarte, the elder of the brothers, was not overly concerned with ideological and political issues. As Henri Bourassa later recalled, he was nothing but "a vulgar shopkeeper who has no conscience of his journalistic responsibilities. For him journalism is a 'business' much like the manufacturing of boots or the building of a railway."[6] Often, the competition with *La Presse* forced *La Patrie* to compromise the pledges made to Bruchési on numerous occasions. On February 14, 1899, for instance, *La Patrie* withheld its publication of a story in Quebec City, but *La Presse* did not. Angered by the Archbishop's double standard, Eugène Tarte raged: "I certainly do not see why we should let our newspaper suffer," he told Bruchési. "The people are thirsty for this type of thing, and I am convinced that in Quebec City they will say that our newspaper is ill-informed, that we cannot afford the means by which to report the news and this will hurt us: *La Presse*'s agent in Quebec will profit from this, I am convinced, and will use the arguments that I have just used."[7]

If the Tartes had difficulty in pleasing the Montreal Archbishop over routine coverage of crime stories, their task was made all the more arduous when Langlois got his way. With every critical article published on education, the overly sensitive Bruchési considered that the church's moral authority was placed on trial, and did not fail in protesting the publication of such pieces. Following one letter, Tarte's response to the Archbishop spoke volumes of Langlois's place in the newsroom and in the party. "I had given strict orders to my editors not to discuss any religious question, or of education without consulting me," he assured the Archbishop.

> You have no idea of the struggle I have to wage every day against a number of people, thankfully they are not numerous, who believe that because our newspaper La Patrie is the organ of the Liberal party, that we are radicals and that we must demolish everything.[...] I have had to keep in my offices, for political reasons, some editors that I would like to see a hundred miles from here; you are not without knowing, Monsignor, that in life, one has to pull many strings and although I have done by best to muzzle my editors, disagreeable things happen now and then.[8]

Tarte's pleas for moderation in Langlois' comments were in vain. The sad dimensions of the school question in Quebec were easy targets for the sensationalist *La Patrie* as horrible stories of exploited young women hired to teach and maintain a school house for a salary of less than $100 a year were recounted.

If the rapport between the Tartes and Langlois was often tense, the relationship between Laurier and Langlois was always cordial, founded on a mutual respect. Laurier was never slighted in *La Patrie*, which consistently hailed him as the "true representative of the aspirations of Canadians, of French Canadians particularly."[9] The many letters exchanged between Laurier and Langlois revolved around a great many common concerns. Langlois sporadically offered policy counsel to Laurier, but seldom met with any success. (As early as 1897, Langlois had privately pressed Laurier to establish a law against usury.)[10]

Langlois avidly supported Laurier generally, but his vigour was weakened by the issue of the Boer War. Like many in Quebec's francophone intelligentsia, Langlois objected to the Canadian role in South Africa being proposed by the English language press.[11] "Canada does not have, and cannot have the ambition to play a role in European diplomacy," *La Patrie* editorialized in early November 1899. "We are ready to defend the soil we inhabit and the British flag that protects it, but it is entirely different for us to go beyond our role and to throw ourselves in the whirlwinds and the wars Europe is always threatened with."[12] *La Patrie* responded critically to the pro-intervention "imperialists", choosing to examine the deep implications of the conflict on Canadian policy. "The programme of these brave people," Langlois wrote of the imperialists in an article that recalled the tones he had used when commenting on the Manitoba schools question, "is no more, no less the enslavement of the French Canadians, their political annihilation by any means— even by the force of arms, if they were capable."[13] Reflecting on the dark shadows cast on English-French relations in Quebec in the wake of a pro-imperialist McGill student riot in March 1900, Langlois sounded pessimistic. "It is being asked if we are going to civil war," he wrote. "It cannot be imagined that the French Canadians will tolerate outrages of this sort [...]. It is out of the question to believe that confederation can function if such doctrines are not immediately repudiated by the sound-thinking partisans of both political parties."[14]

It was on the relatively neutral grounds of international affairs that Tarte was able to defuse some of the radical anger directed towards him. He did not support a Canadian presence in the Boer War.[15] In this respect, he spoke for many of the "radicals" and the Boer question might have saved his political life among Liberals for a time. Tarte would be grudgingly acknowledged as one of the Liberal party chiefs, even if not all gladly accepted to see him at Laurier's side. One "vieux rouge" was still unhappy. "You must rid yourself of Tarte!" Louis Fréchette urged Laurier in 1900. "That man is making you lose everything you gain with your personal popularity [...] Tarte is corrupt, he is a liar, he is a traitor, a man who enriches himself on the public purse, [...] an individual one would think is being paid by your opponents to sap your popularity and drive the party to ruin."[16]

If Langlois and Tarte agreed on the threat imperialism posed to the survival of Confederation, they also agreed that there certainly was something wrong with the Liberal party at the local level. Durantaye, Langlois and the people who assembled around his editorial desk, argued that the Party was obviously not reacting to the demands of mass politics. Though a Liberal, it was Langlois's old boss Raymond Préfontaine who was now the mayor of Montreal. With him at the helm, Liberals were faced with the scenario that their party would lose the working class's general support, and the main reason seemed to be because the party was increasingly seen as the party of special interests.

The people at *La Patrie* did not discover that "capital" was corrupting politics in the late 1890s when Raymond Préfontaine was first elected Mayor. The echo of Calixte Lebeuf's famous *cri de coeur* in 1889 was still ringing in their ears, and they did not forget that the maverick had denounced Préfontaine in particular.[17] Langlois, for his part, had often written about the corrupting influence of industrial magnates in setting tariff rates. What made the issue of corruption so urgent in 1898 was the mounting challenge of the left. So as to prevent further erosion of Liberal support and reaffirm the virtues of the capitalist system, some Liberals proposed a two-pronged resolve: First to clean the party so as to give it more democratic credibility and second, to make better use of the levers of government power so as to address the grievances of an increasingly disaffected segment of the population. The second resolve opened doors to many suggestions. In the process, the generation of radical Liberals that emerged in the wake of Mercier's defeat was reinvigorated with a new mission at a time when the once promising efforts at the provincial level seemed stalled by the party leadership. It merged with other reform Liberals who had not been active at the provincial level and together they gave life to a new philosophy of interventionist government and democratic party politics. The realization that the survival of Liberals depended on their treatment of civic affairs, and not only national and provincial issues, was a critical phase in the rise of Liberal progressivism. The new creed was born out of a fear of the left, as radical Liberalism sought to redefine itself.

During his short stay at *Le Monde*, Langlois had established and promoted a regular column whose expressed purpose was to talk about and to the working class. Urbain Lafontaine's "Causerie Ouvrière" was a comprehensive feature of the daily that actually sought to "explain" the working class to the governing classes, but more importantly, to itself. It constituted a dialogue between the classes that Langlois was eager to pursue at *La Patrie*. "Chez les ouvriers" and later "Le monde ouvrier" illustrated this desire to address the labouring classes in Liberal terms. Langlois considered the working man's support to be of critical importance to the Liberal party, even though the vast majority of labourers could not exercise the franchise. Regardless, *La Patrie* took it upon itself to argue on behalf of the working classes in its various crusades. Langlois, for instance, linked the cause of improving education with the fate of the working class. "What we want," he said often, "is education to be accessible to the poor classes."[18] But Langlois's concern for the disaffection of the working man went far beyond the bounds of educational issues. He reproached the government in the spring of 1897, when the Flynn Conservatives imposed a ten dollar deposit on plaintiffs who demanded court action to rectify disputes. An additional ten dollars per day was also imposed if the matter could not be settled by the court on the first day. Clearly, such a "user fee" made justice available only to those who could afford it. "With such a system," argued Langlois, "only the rich can plead and seek justice before the tribunals."[19]

Langlois extended his support for the working class to the labour unions. He applauded the triumphs of the unions "to protect their membership from capital, when the latter is unjust and tyrannic,"[20] but made his position clear: He supported trade unions as long as they kept within the confines of an apolitical agenda. As his colleague Durantaye had done at the meeting of the *Club ouvrier independant,* Langlois endlessly attempted to convince his working class readership that most capitalists were well intentioned, and that there was little to be gained in listening to people like Rodier. The prospect of a Labour Party in Montreal simply unnerved *La Patrie*'s editor. "Workers beware!" he said in 1899, "do not compromise your sacred cause by removing it from other issues, by isolating it, by drowning it in a greater whole."[21]

Langlois's motivations in constructing the grammar of a new liberal ideology were political as much as they were ideological. Eager to demonstrate that labour had its place in the Liberal party, Langlois admonished Laurier to address the concerns of the working class. On one occasion, fearing a haemorrhage of support flowing from the Liberals to the Labourites as two of *La Presse*'s employees (Rodier included) founded a Labour Party in Montreal, Langlois pressed Laurier to rebuke publicly "that handful who profit of *La Presse*'s publicity to make war on the government, to give themselves a mission and an authority that they do not have and will never have."[22] Parallel to his exhortations to the Prime Minister, Langlois urged labour not to forget Liberal-

ism. "The workers have more to gain in allying themselves
to the government," Langlois wrote in March 1900, "to bring
interest to their situation, men of heart and of good conscience, eminent citizens like Mr. Laurier, than to place
themselves in the hands of simple typos from *La Presse*."[23]
Langlois's distrust of activist Labour was reflected when he
even criticized Eugene Debs's Social Democratic Party for
trying to alienate the working class from the whole of
society.[24]

Langlois's concern about the working class political opinion prompted *La Patrie* into adopting increasingly progressive postures. The increasingly obvious high concentrations
of economic power worried Langlois more and more. This
question, he thought, provided an issue in which the Liberal
Party could prove its mettle before the eyes of the working
class. "Liberals have understood that the principal cause of
wrong has been the organization of these manufacturing
leagues," he wrote in 1897, "of these combines that dissipate
competition between producers, and they have committed
themselves [...] to kill these leagues and to readjust the tariff
on more equitable bases so as to relieve the shoulders of the
worker, but without harming the manufacturer."[25]

Langlois's campaign against the trusts gave the Liberal
Party something of an anti-business profile few in the party
could agree with. Laurier, in particular, refused Langlois's
invitations to address the working classes, and did not take
particularly well to Langlois's seemingly anti-business crusades. In 1899, for example, an important Montreal financial
institution, the Banque Ville-Marie, had jeopardized its de-
positors' holdings through a series of obviously bad investments. Langlois published numerous critical articles
regarding the bank's business practices and was reproached
by Laurier himself. The editor defended his position by
pointing out that he had the support of the Banque Jacques-
Cartier and the National Bank in his criticisms of the Ville-
Marie interest as well as the support of a great number of
businessmen and "hundreds" of "good" Liberals. "You will

admit, Sir Wilfrid, that in the interest of our newspaper we could not simply watch *La Presse* and *The Herald* battle it out while keeping our arms crossed," thundered Langlois. "We have taken a vigorous attitude that has won us thousands of adhesions and which has certainly not harmed the government, since it furnished it with an opportunity to define its position on a defective law. For indeed, in the first days, people were saying: Why is the government not intervening?"[26] In his desire to see the Liberal Party move to the left, Langlois pressed the government into interventionist policies. Not surprisingly, he looked abroad for examples of state intervention to give credibility to his views and never failed to highlight French examples. He roamed the planet for other examples. In January 1902, to cite but one example, he lauded the New Zealand government's strict new "socialist" regulations regarding working conditions, hoping that the experience of that nation would set an example for all.[27]

La Patrie's incipient Liberal progressivism was perhaps amorphous, but when juxtaposed with Langlois's call for educational reform, the editorial mindset of the daily reveals a greater clarity. Strikingly, the philosophy did not end at the tip of the editorialist's pen: there was also a philosophy of praxis here and *La Patrie* did not shirk the responsibility of applying its somewhat vague philosophy of liberalism to the hard realities of Montreal's political arena. If it was still difficult to tell what exactly it and its adherents stood for, it was far easier to distinguish what Liberal progressivism stood against. It was during the municipal elections of 1898 — events that paralleled the rejection of Marchand's educational reform bill and the campaign against Adolphe Chapleau — that divisions among Liberals first seriously began to show how deep the chasm separated the "moderate Liberals" and the born-again radical Liberals really was.

There was no formal political "organization" of Liberals in Montreal. Because power emanated from political clubs, editorial rooms and from public offices, the control of the party was never clear. Indeed, power within the Liberal party in Montreal was often hotly contested between the elected members and the extraparliamentary apparatus. Senators, MPs, MLAs, aldermen, Mayors, Club presidents and even newspaper editors all vied for preeminence in what all considered to be the most important nexus of power in the province. Liberal power in Montreal was, for the last decade of the nineteenth century, held mainly by Raymond Préfontaine. An experienced lawyer and politician, "the key to our organization in Montreal," as privately acknowledged by Israël Tarte,[28] Préfontaine considered himself a *rouge*. He had distinguished himself in the annexation procedures of Hochelaga to Montreal in 1883 and thereafter represented the region in Montreal's Municipal Council. Préfontaine soon was named chairman of the Council's Roads Committee and was literally controlling the local Liberal machine through this office at the turn of the century.

Préfontaine had no difficulty in reconciling his self-imposed *rouge* label with his notorious actions in favour of the interests of the big gas, tramway and electricity companies. If anything, his use of the label highlighted its corruptibility, something radicals had realized as early as 1889 when Calixte Lebeuf had denounced him along with Honoré Mercier. Those allegations had made no dint in Préfontaine's political armour, as he was enormously popular with east-end Montrealers. His position as the "boss" of the Liberal party in Montreal was still unassailed in late 1897, when Israël Tarte, eager to make himself more popular with the new generation of radical *rouges*, sponsored an attack on Préfontaine as the latter announced that he was seeking the mayoralty in the February 1898 election.

Why would Tarte involve himself in this struggle? He shared with Préfontaine an unquestionably similar outlook. But as Henri Bourassa remarked years later, it was not out of character for Tarte to attack erstwhile friends. "He was unquestionably catholic and patriotic, but that did not deter his resolve in matters that were contrary to his convictions," Bourassa observed, "he had something of the Corsican in him."[29] There is another explanation, however, and it lies in Tarte's visceral hatred of corruption. He had left the Conservative party over corruption scandals, and would do his best to ensure that the Liberal party remained unsullied. Concerned by the federal electoral campaign in 1896, Tarte did not mince his words when reporting on the Montreal situation with Laurier. "As far as the organisation of the party is concerned, we are wasting very precious time right now," he told Laurier. "Our people have so many things to do for themselves in the [Montreal] Municipal Council that the Party issues forcibly become secondary. [...] I have told you before and I repeat it again, municipal affairs have completely rotted the party here and I would want to see the municipal council in hell."[30] Langlois also knew Préfontaine well. Dejected by his law school experience, Langlois had secured a clerkship in Préfontaine's prestigious law office in 1888. He was obviously not comfortable in the surroundings of Préfontaine's firm and opted to join the radical Rodolphe Laflamme's office a few months later.

La Patrie's crusade against Raymond Préfontaine's bid for the mayoralty, therefore, suited the political demands of many people. January 1898 was, for Israël Tarte, a difficult time[31] but to prove his loyalty to the renewed radical ideals, he found a perfect target in identifying with Langlois's fight with Préfontaine. Langlois, in turn, was more than eager to put into practice his ideas on the needs to reaffirm the legitimacy of the state. Together, they went after Préfontaine's political skin and that of his two closest lieutenants, Henri-Benjamin Rainville and Cléophas Beausoleil.

Like Préfontaine, Rainville and Beausoleil were old names in the Liberal organization. Rainville was born in the village of Ste-Angèle-de-Monnoir in 1852. He studied at the Collège de Ste-Hyacinthe and in the Collège de Ste-Angèle-de-Monnoir. Like Laurier, he studied law with the radical Joseph Doutre and attended McGill before he was admitted to the bar in 1874. In addition to his studies, he was a regular at the sessions of the Institut canadien during the 1870s and once suggested that the American system be emulated in educational matters and that Quebec should make schools free and controlled by secular authorities.[32]

Rainville was first elected as alderman in Montreal in 1882 and quickly shed his reputation as a radical. In 1886 he began a nine-year term as Chairman of the Municipal Council's Lighting Committee and felt so strong in his position that he challenged Honoré Beaugrand's progressive mayoralty in 1887. Beaugrand easily defeated him in this battle, the first of many between the two men. In 1890, Rainville was Mercier's candidate for the St-Louis riding in Montreal and was challenged by Beaugrand for the Liberal nomination. Rainville won the nomination, and narrowly defeated Beaugrand who decided to stand against him as an independant Liberal. Two years later, circumstances were repeated as Beaugrand again challenged the incumbent. Both this time were defeated by the Conservative candidate. Through all this, Rainville retained his important position in City Council. In 1896, he had been made Chairman of the Finance Committee.

The second most important of Préfontaine's allies was Cléophas Beausoleil. "That damned man" (Tarte's words[33]) had always sided with the more moderate Liberals, consistently hoping to thwart the radical initiatives. He had been an alderman since the early 1880s, he was a close ally of Rainville, and was equally seen as destructive to the Liberal cause by La Patrie's editors and directors.

La Patrie, ably assisted in this campaign by the Liberal Montreal Herald and its fiery editor J.C. Walsh, chided the Préfontaine clique for not producing a programme. "The boss's way is nearly always the taxpayer's wrong way," lamented the Herald.[34] Despite the Liberal newspaper's demands, Préfontaine had little reason to formulate an electoral platform. No one contested his election, and it was soon obvious that he would be acclaimed Mayor of Montreal. Rainville had already been acclaimed alderman. Clearly only a small circle of Liberals perceived the corruption of the Préfontaine team. Indeed, there seemed to reign a certain consensus outside radical circles regarding its candidates. Even Hormisdas Laporte, identified by historians of this period as a "reformist", signed Préfontaine's nomination card.

If Préfontaine's candidacy seemed to raise little opposition from Montreal's body politic, some members of his electoral "machine" were not as fortunate. Ten people were elected by acclamation, leaving only fifteen wards to be contested. Of these, six became battlegrounds for Liberals. M.B. Connaughton was challenged by Daniel Gallery in Ste-Anne ward. Joseph Gauthier contested R. Dufresne's seat in Hochelaga (Préfontaine's stronghold) and Clément Robillard opposed Joseph Brunet, a notorious Préfontaine crony.[35] The most obvious Liberal squabble was Honoré Mercier's (son of the former prime minister) challenge to Cléophas Beausoleil. La Patrie, happily abetting the fight against Beausoleil, openly supported those individuals who contested the Préfontaine Liberals. It supported Henry Ekers and Jimmy Cochrane in St-Laurent ward. It even endorsed Frank Sullivan's bid against "reformer" Herbert Ames in St-Antoine. Ames had no political relation to Préfontaine, but his brand of "reform", and his ties to the Conservative Party made him a reformer of little relevance, obviously, in La Patrie's editorial rooms.[36]

Cléophas Beausoleil reacted bitterly to the radical challenge to his incumbency. "This provocation will bear fruit," Beausoleil complained to Laurier. "The Minister of Public Works really wants a division in the Liberal party that supports you and that trusts you. I am compelled to add that La Patrie's attitude will lead to this: the defeat of its candidate and the humiliation of that small circle that agitates to the indifference and the hostility of the population."[37] Equally angered by the doubts cast publicly upon his honesty by all members of his own party, Préfontaine also addressed himself to Laurier and cabled the Prime Minister with the following message: "Most respectfully but urgently appeal to you to put an immediate stop to the attempt of the two

Liberal organs *Herald* and *La Patrie* to ride me out of the party—or I must defend myself."[38] Even Adolphe Chapleau, the now deposed Lieutenant Governor, grew frightened by the spectacle of moderate Liberals like Tarte and Préfontaine squabbling. Desperately, he urged Tarte to restrain his editor. "Is there no way for you to respect Préfontaine?" he asked. "It is no longer a matter of wrecking everything; things have to be put together again."[39]

Despite the anger engendered in part by *La Patrie*, electoral results were not all that favourable to the radical cause. Préfontaine, as expected, was elected by acclamation, as was most of his "machine". Consolation could be found in the fact that anti-Préfontaine Liberals such as Paul Martineau, George Sadler, I.H. Stearns, Henry Ekers, Richard Turner, Daniel Gallery and George Washington Stephens had been elected. It was a modest triumph, but a victory encouraging enough to sustain further efforts. "*La Patrie* will monitor more closely than ever before the evolution of municipal affairs," promised Langlois upon hearing of Préfontaine's acclamation. "What matters above all," he concluded, "is to restore the public's confidence in our municipal institutions."[40]

Préfontaine, Rainville and Beausoleil emerged unscathed from the campaign, but some damage was done. Negative sentiment against Beausoleil had reached Premier Marchand's office when Laurier urged the Quebec Premier to give Beausoleil the posts of License Commissioner and Sessions Judge so as to get him out of active politics. Aware that awarding patronage to Beausoleil would not curry favour among the radicals who endlessly haunted him, Marchand declined. "For right or wrong," he told Laurier, "there exists in Montreal a broad distrust of the way this man would carry out his functions."[41] Marchand instead chose Philippe-Auguste Choquette, an unrepentant radical who had denounced Mercier and helped Langelier in the scathing 1898 Levis provincial by-election. Clearly, Liberal progressivism, though still in its formative stages, was being heard.

Langlois learned many lessons from his experience of the 1898 municipal election. For one thing, his thoughts on the necessity of redefining radicalism into a Liberal progressivism had to be spread. He chose the best propaganda unit: the club. Soon after the election, Langlois was made director of the Montreal Citizens' Association and in the fall of 1898 he played a key role in the founding of The Reform Club, and was named its secretary.[42] In December 1898 Langlois was also elected President of the *Association de la presse de la province de Québec*, placing him as leading spokesman for Quebec's Press industry and providing him with a convenient platform (and the ubiquitous, sumptuous banquets) from which he could voice his views.[43]

Municipal affairs continued to offer a laboratory for his thinking. Préfontaine's two years as mayor did little to assuage *La Patrie* and the Liberal progressives. Tarte continued to perceive Préfontaine as a liability to the party in Montreal, and did not fail to inform Laurier regarding partisan discontent. Reporting on some bribe the Mayor of Montreal had received (a bribe that included money from Georges Parent, the cabinet minister's son), Tarte noted that "our friend has again made the type of gesture with which he has become familiar at City Hall. It is out of the question for me, or rather for the government, to sanction such speculation. You have seen that Préfontaine had been abandoned by our best partisans...."[44] Beausoleil's reputation had not improved either. Sensing the damage this unpopular man could cause to the party, Laurier was finally convinced by Tarte of the necessity of removing him from municipal politics. Beausoleil was thus named by the Federal government as Postmaster in Montreal a few months before the 1900 municipal elections.[45]

The city elections of 1900 showed clearly the divisions of the Liberal Party in Montreal between the emerging Liberal progressive faction and the rest of the party. Seven of the twenty aldermen elected by acclamation were Liberal progressives: Gallery, Sadler, Ekers, Clearihue, Robillard,

Turner, Bumbray and Martineau. The 1900 elections also saw the launch of a new reformist group led by Herbert Ames and vaguely identified as "La Réforme". Indeed, the first salvo against the Préfontaine machine was thrown by Raoul Dandurand, now a Senator. Saying that he represented "La Réforme", Dandurand challenged pro-Préfontaine Olivier Faucher for the Liberal nomination in the St-Antoine Sud division. Dandurand was defeated at the nominating convention (much to the delight of the pro-Préfontaine *La Presse*),[46] by the local appeal of his opponent. "The Hon. Dandurand now ousted from the municipal arena, the Ames organization now has a broken back," editorialized *La Presse*. In fact, *La Presse*'s comment only bore witness to the importance of the Liberal party in the Ames organization.[47]

Dandurand's brief, ill-fated campaign was *"La Réforme's"* only real action. It was Calixte Lebeuf, the notorious radical who had prophesied Mercier's downfall and the corrupting influences of Préfontaine and Beausoleil in 1889, who set the tone of the election when he contested Henri-Benjamin Rainville's nomination in the Quartier-Centre district. "For a long time, and especially for the last two years, municipal affairs have been poorly conducted at City Hall," Lebeuf argued in *La Patrie*. "If they [the electors] want a change, if they want to break the chain that is stifling the city, they should vote against Rainville who is the linchpin that moves that chain."[48] *La Patrie*'s editors launched their own attacks. "Alderman Rainville represents a regime whose actions we have condemned," argued its editorialist. "Mr. Rainville is, above all, the excellent friend of the monopolies."[49] On the other hand, *La Presse*, as ever a supporter of conservative Liberals and Tories, noted that Lebeuf's candidacy was literally a joke and that Rainville deserved the people's support.[50]

The 1900 election proved another small success for Liberal progressivism. Lebeuf defeated Rainville and with Beausoleil out of the race even before it was started, two of the pillars of the corrupt Liberal "machine" had been removed. In addition to the eight Liberal progressives elected by acclamation, were added the fiery Lebeuf, Senator H.J. Cloran, a founding member of the Montreal Trades and Labour Council and L. Arsène Lavallée. Last but not least was Lomer Gouin, who was elected in the Quartier Est division.

The collapse of the Préfontaine machine was not simply the result of "disclosures of City Council's irregularities nor because of the city's financial problems during the late 1890s," not was it the result of a non-partisan "reformist" campaign directed against him.[51] Préfontaine lost support because members of the Liberal party, his own party, had rebelled against his corruption. George Washington Stephens and Honoré Beaugrand had fought the Préfontaine clique without success throughout the mismanaged 1890s, but what made the difference was the rallying vision of an urban, progressive Liberalism at a time when the bourgeoisie faced an increasingly alienated working class.

With the 1900 municipal election, the position of the progressively-minded Liberals was enhanced. It was significant that the most vital forces in challenging the Préfontaine machine had emerged from Liberal ranks. Consistently, the spearhead of reform had been *La Patrie*. Why? As Durantaye realized at the meeting of the *Club ouvrier indépendant*, the party had a major image problem to contain and something had to be done to rethink the ideological components of liberalism.

It was in the hothouse of municipal politics that radical liberalism was redefined. Of course, much was inherited from the varied *rouge* movements of the nineteenth century, but that ideological bag of loosely defined principles, values and symbols was transformed to fit a new era, in ways that made it often unrecognizable to those who had studied the politics of the Union period and the early years of Confederation. Anticlericalism survived the death of the *Institut canadien* and continued to thrive in the twentieth century as did the glorification of the ideals of liberty, equality and fraternity. It was particularly as they sought to respond to new socio-economic pressures, that many of the radicals matured into a body of opinion I call Liberal-progressivism. Broadening the narrow ideological parameters set by their nineteenth-century forefathers, the new Liberal radicals addressed issues born of the experience of industrialization and urbanization. As they formulated their grievances, they proved to be as resolutely hostile to political bosses as some of their ancestors had been hostile to the church. Their aim was to make the ideology of liberalism a living one, one that responded in a practical way to the changes besetting their world, one that would ensure the survival of the bourgeois-capitalist system and preserve basic principles of individual liberty and free-market economies. For the Liberal-progressives, this meant challenging the assumptions of a liberalism dedicated to economic "liberty" and forcing on this system of beliefs an appreciation of how liberalism had to respond when the very economic freedoms it was conferring to the few were curtailing the freedoms of the majority.

This urban progressivism in Quebec was expressed by French-speaking reformers. Inspired by modern American studies of "progressivism", studies of the movement of reform perceived progressivism in Quebec as a West-end, largely anglophone, business elite that wanted to see an end to the abuses of patronage wrought by the populist East-end politicians.[52] Adapting to the Montreal situation historian Richard Hofstadter's point that non-Anglo-Saxons were often hostile to the idea of reform,[53] historians tacitly came to the conclusion that French-Canadians generally sided with the unscrupulous "bosses" while the anglophone *grande bourgeoisie* clamored for reform and searched for a business-like order.[54]

The evidence demonstrates indeed that, much as in the United States, or Europe for that matter, most progressives in Quebec were urban-based and that many of them were closely tied to business interests.[55] There is a doubt, however, that they were recruited among those classes Hofstadter referred to as "victims of an upheaval in status".[56] Liberal progressives were acutely aware of the necessity of building bridges to the working class, and were far more concerned about achieving social harmony among the classes to worry seriously about a decline in their own status. Indeed, all the accepted definitions of American progressivism have proven too narrow or too broad to be of relevance in understanding Quebec's experience. Many, if not most, of the reformers were French-Canadian, thereby further negating the validity of the ancient ethnic model of progressivism. Similarly, countless people who shared the exact same qualifications as the progressives fought reform every inch of the way. Socio-economic categorizations, therefore, explain little.[57] There is little doubt, that as with their American and European cousins, Liberal progressives were liberal thinkers.[58]

A new inspiration nourished the politics of Montreal's radicals at the turn of the century. While many people spoke the great phrases of reform, few deigned to leap into the political fray. The desire to seek an engagement distinguished the Liberal progressives from those salon reformers. Indeed, the vital part of the reform movement grew out of the conviction that various interests were corrupting Liberal politics in Montreal and in Quebec City. The only solution, it was concluded, was to clean-up the party, but not to eradicate it. As events unfolded, it was evident that the campaign to remove the "corrupt" on the local scene fol-lowed the exact same battle lines as the struggle between the "radical" and the "conservative" factions of the Liberal party. In sum, to best understand the politics of progressivism in Quebec, a political classification must be made. Interestingly, the most dynamic "progressives" shared one thing in com-mon: They were foot soldiers in the Liberal army, disgrun-tled with the conservative inclinations of their leaders.

Langlois epitomized the trend. His sharpened editorials in the Liberal Party's main organ, and his relentless urging that the party's credibility be bolstered so as not to alienate the working class, convinced a number of Liberals that it was no longer in the interest of the party to keep Préfontaine and his lieutenants as chiefs. The discovery that corrupt Liberals were seriously harming the party fuelled the attacks on Préfontaine and his clique.

Langlois participated in the battle, but would not celebrate the results of the elections with his colleagues at *La Patrie*. On January 24, 1900 he married Marie-Louise Hirbour, the 17 year-old daughter of Stanislas-Emmanuel Hirbour. Hirbour, who had completed his notarial clerkship with the future Premier Marchand in 1866, had moved to Butte City, Montana where he made a fortune in copper mining. He returned to Canada with his family in 1898, and died soon thereafter. One of Butte City's most remarkable pioneers left an estate valued at over $500,000.[59] The ceremony uniting Godfroy Langlois to his young bride took place on January 28, 1900 at St-Louis-de-France church before Father Gustave Bourassa (Henri's older brother). Godfroy and Louise then left Montreal for a two- week honeymoon in New York City and Washington D.C.[60] Langlois's marriage in the catholic church certainly colours the principles he personally harboured as a freemason. While his enemies believed he was an atheist, his religious convictions did not prevent him from marrying the catholic Louise. Such was the double life lived by these Freemasons. Gonsalve Desaulniers, a political and personal friend, lived a similar experience as a freemason who married in the catholic church and who insisted on having his children baptized. Desaulniers would often insist that he was not a freemason. Langlois never denied it.

By the time Langlois had returned to Montreal and had moved with his wife to their new lodgings on Ste-Famille street, eight of the nine Préfontaine incumbents who had been challenged were defeated (two- thirds of the aldermanic seats were won by acclamation). *La Patrie* even boasted that almost all the candidates it had supported had emerged victorious. "We asked for these new men because municipal reform is needed. Our voice was heard."[61]

Of course, the fight against Préfontaine had not proven to be a total success. The leader of the clique retained his post. Préfontaine's candidacy had gone practically unchallenged by the weak, rival "reform" candidate, W. Doran. Préfontaine's emaciated clique continued to govern (or not govern) in Montreal, and the eleven Liberal progressives were politically unable to redirect municipal policy in a truly reformist fashion. Still, Langlois and the people around him could be satisfied with their efforts at the dawn of a new century. The newly-fanged "Liberal progressives" had proven their might in the 1900 municipal election, their first real victory since the defeat of the educational reform bill in early January 1898.

Notes

1. *Le Signal*, 31 juillet 1897.
2. *La Patrie*, 26 octobre 1898.
3. *La Patrie*, 10 janvier 1943, in Langlois Papers, Scrapbook A.
4. *Ibidem*.
5. Archives de la chancellerie de l'archeveché de Montréal, Paul Bruchési Papers (RLBr), Newspaper Correspondence file, Bruchési to "Au directeur de *La Patrie*, 22 février 1903.
6. Henri Bourassa Papers, Private Collection, Bourassa to L. Hacault, 2 mars 1910.
7. Paul Bruchési Papers (RLBr), E. Tarte to Bruchési, 15 février 1899.
8. *Ibidem*, I. Tarte to Bruchési, 31 mai 1898.
9. *La Patrie*, 30 août 1897.
10. Laurier Papers, C750, Langlois to Laurier, 15 juillet 1897.
11. On the pressures being exerted on Laurier by elements of the English-language press, see Carman Miller, *Painting the Map Red: Canada in the Boer War* (Montreal, 1993).
12. *La Patrie*, editorial, 6 novembre 1899.
13. *Ibidem*, 13 novembre 1899.
14. *Ibidem*, 3 mars 1899.
15. PAC, J.S. Willison Papers, Tarte to Willison, October 20 1899; November 22, 1900; November 28, 1900.
16. Laurier Papers, C777, Fréchette to Laurier, 15 juin 1900.
17. See Chapter II.
18. *La Patrie*, 15 mai1897.
19. *Ibidem*, 1 avril 1897.
20. *Ibidem*, 6 septembre 1898.
21. *Ibidem*, 22 mars 1899.

22. PAC, Laurier Papers, C 774, Langlois to Laurier, 24 mars 1900.

23. *La Patrie*, 18 mars 1900.

24. *Ibidem*, 16 août 1897.

25. *Ibidem*, 29 novembre 1897.

26. Laurier Papers, C 768, Langlois to Laurier, 2 août 1899.

27. *La Patrie*, 18 janvier 1902.

28. Laurier Papers, C 739, Tarte to Laurier, 1 mars 1895.

29. Henri Bourassa Papers, Private Collection, Bourassa to L. Hacault, 2 mars 1910.

30. Laurier Papers, C 739, Tarte to Laurier, 7 novembre 1894.

31. See chapter III.

32. N.S. Robertson, "The Institut Canadien: An Essay in Cultural History" (M.A. Thesis, University of Western Ontario, 1965), p. 37.

33. Laurier Papers, C 761, Tarte to Laurier, 30 novembre 1898.

34. *The Montreal Herald*, Front page editorial, 15 January 1898.

35. *The Gazette*, editorial, 29 janvier 1898.

36. *La Patrie*, editorial, 29 janvier 1898.

37. Laurier Papers, C 753, Beausoleil to Laurier, 11 janvier 1898.

38. Laurier Papers, C 753, telegram, Préfontaine to Laurier, 16 janvier 1898; See also Préfontaine to Laurier, 7 janvier 1898.

39. Tarte Papers, Chapleau to Tarte, n.d. (context indicates sometime in January 1898).

40. *La Patrie*, editorial, 20 janvier 1898.

41. Laurier Papers, C761, Marchand to Laurier, 28 décembre 1898.

42. It is interesting to note that it was Langlois who introduced the Club to the Prime Minister, asking him to be the honorary president. See Laurier Papers, C 761, Langlois to Laurier, 29 décembre 1898.

43. *La Patrie*, 3 décembre 1898.

44. Laurier Papers, C761, Tarte to Laurier, 30 novembre 1898.

45. *Ibidem*, C769, David to Laurier, 13 octobre 1899.

46. Though *La Presse* always professed to being neutral, it certainly was not. Not only did it advocate social conservatism, it also pursued political Conservatism. On its conservative social outlook, see Ralph Heintzman, "The Struggle for Life: The French Daily Press of Montreal and the Problem of Economic Growth in the Age of Laurier, 1896-1911" (Ph.D. thesis, York University, 1977), pp. 12, 16-26. On *La Presse*'s support of the Conservative party, see Pierre Godin, *l'Information-Opium: Une histoire politique du journal La Presse* (Montreal, 1973).

47. *La Presse*, editorial, 18 janvier 1900.

48. *La Patrie*, 22 janvier 1900.

49. *Ibidem*, editorial, 23 janvier 1900.

50. *La Presse*, editorial, 24 janvier 1900.

51. Michel Gauvin, "The Reformer and the Machine: Montreal Civic Politics from Raymond Préfontaine to Médéric Martin" *JCS*, 13, 2, Summer 1978, p. 17.

52. For this view, see Michel Gauvin, "The Municipal Reform Movement in Montreal, 1886-1914" (M.A. thesis, University of Ottawa, 1972); Francine Nagant, "Politique municipale à Montréal, 1910-1914: l'échec des réformistes et le triomphe de Médéric Martin" (M.A. thesis, Université de Montréal, 1982).

53. Richard Hofstadter, *The Age of Reform* (New York, 1955), pp. 181-186. See also S.P. Hays, "Politics of Reform in Municipal Government in the Progressive Era" *PNQ*, October 1974. Both emphasized the point that reform came from the "governing classes". It should be mentioned that others have brought to light the reformist impulses of the working and immigrant classes. On this see J.J. Huthmacher, *Senator Robert F. Wagner and the Rise of Urban Liberalism* (New York, 1968) and John D. Buenker, *Urban Liberalism and Progressive Reform* (New York, 1973).

54. P.A. Linteau, "Quelques réflexions autour de la bourgeoisie Québecoise, 1850-1914" *RHAF*, 30, 1, juin 1976. For the argument that Progressivism in America was essentially conservative and business-oriented, see Robert Wiebe, *The Search for Order* (New York, 1967); Gabriel Kolko, *The Triumph of Conservatism* (New York, 1963) and J. Weinstein, *The Corporate Ideal in the Liberal State, 1900-1918* (Boston, 1968). On Canada's conservative experience of progressivism, see J.C. Weaver, "'Tomorrow's Metropolis' Revisited: A critical Assessment of Urban Reform in Canada, 1890-1920" in Alan Artibise (ed.), *The Canadian City* (Toronto, 1977). See also D. Russell, "H.B. Ames and Municipal Reform" (M.A. thesis, McGill University, 1971).

55. Liberalism as a philosophy among Quebeckers has a long tradition. It has been examined by Paul-André Linteau, René Durocher and Jean-Claude Robert, who considered it to be the "triumphant" ideology at the turn of the century. See *Histoire du Quebec Contemporain: de la confédération à la crise (1867-1929)*, (Montreal, 1979), pp. 603-608. Liberalism as an expression of French Canadian businessmen in Montreal is examined in Fernande Roy, *Progrès, harmonie, liberté: Le libéralisme des milieux d'affaires francophones à Montréal au tournant du siècle* (Montréal, 1988). Based on a reading of weekly business publications, Roy describes liberalism around three themes. She concludes that ultimately the liberalism adhered to in the business publications was of a conservative nature. Regrettably, her study does not include the political activities of businessmen, which were tremendously self-contradictory, and which would add many vital dimensions to an understanding of the "liberalism" they espoused.

56. Hofstadter, *Age of Reform*, p. 135. On the middle class profile of progressivism in America, see George Mowry, "The Californian Progressive and his Rationale: A study in Middle-Class Politics" *MVHR*, September 1943. See also Wiebe, Kolko and Weinstein, *op. cit.*

57. The best criticism of the works on progressivism, particularly in their use of socio-economic categorizations, is still Peter G. Filene, "An Obituary for the Progressive Movement" in *AQ*, XII, Spring 1970.

58. The literature on the liberal nature of progressive movements in America at the turn of the century is rich, even if there is little agreement on the exact definitions of a liberalism. See J.D Buenker, *Urban Liberalism and Progressive Reform* (New York, 1973), David Mark Chalmers, *The Social and Political Ideas of the Muckrackers* (New York, 1964), Louis Filler, *Crusaders for American Liberalism* (Yellow Springs, 1939), Charles Forcey, *Crossroads of Liberalism* (New York, 1961), Louis Hartz, *The Liberal tradition in America* (New York, 1955), R. Hofstadter, *The Age of Reform* (New York, 1955), J.J. Huthmaker, *Senator Robert F. Wagner and the Rise of Urban Liberalism* (New York, 1968), David W. Levy, *Herbert Croly of the New Republic* (Princeton, 1985), C.C. Regier, *The Era of the Muckracker* (Gloucester, Mass, 1932), David Seideman, *The New Republic: A Voice of Modern Liberalism* (Westport, 1986), J. Weinstein, *The Corporate Ideal in the Liberal State, 1900-1918* (Boston, 1968), Arthur and Lila Weinberg, *The Muckrackers* (New York, 1961), S.P. Hays "The Politics of Reform in Municipal Government in the Progressive Era" *PNQ*, October 1964.

59. Langlois Papers, Scrapbook A, p. 14.

60. On the Langlois-Hirbour wedding, see Langlois Papers, File E.

61. *La Patrie*, editorial, 2 février 1900.

CHAPTER V

THE MARCHAND SUCCESSION

WHEN FÉLIX-GABRIEL MARCHAND rose to give his budget speech in the winter of 1900, newspapers reported that he was visibly very ill. His daughter, Josephine Dandurand, manifested a general concern: "You are tired, sick, harassed, disgusted and how do you hope to help yourself?" she scolded her father, "with a stronger dose of disgust. It cannot go on like this—you absolutely need to renew yourself morally and physically." In vain, she pleaded with her father to join the Dandurand family for a holiday in France. "With new strengths, you can be sure that courage will return. [...] At your age, one cannot abuse of one's strengths," she urged him.[1]

Marchand was suffering from the advanced stages of arterial sclerosis. Unable to travel to Europe, very fatigued, he spent the summer of 1900 with a daughter in Quebec City. He would never recover. By the end of August, the oldest Premier in Quebec history was dying. Charles Langelier, Liberal MLA for Lévis, already worried about the succession, coldly suggested to Laurier that some thought had to be given to the future of the Liberal Party in Quebec. "That is pretty well it for Mr. Marchand. He will be dead before a month, probably before. It's only a matter of days," he advised Laurier. Langelier suggested that Lieutenant-Governor Jetté would make a good Premier.[2] Feigning disinterest, Laurier dismissed Jetté as a possible candidate for the moment, and rejected Langelier's implication that Laurier was the one to make the choice. "Mr. Marchand's colleagues will make the final choice," Laurier responded.[3] The Prime Minister of Canada had his own problems to worry about. As Laurier campaigned for the re-election of his government in Ontario on the evening of September 25, Marchand breathed his last with his family around him.

Laurier hurried to Quebec City to attend the Marchand funeral a few days later. Rumours abounded regarding the new leadership, and a number of Liberals wanted to be heard on the succession. Joseph Robidoux, the charismatic minister who had gallantly defended the educational bill and opposed the influence of Israël Tarte, was especially favoured by the radicals. Langlois and others organized a round robin of signatures in support of Robidoux and sent it to Laurier.[4] Senator Alphonse Pelletier was also considered to be in the running,[5] but the links of the government leader in the Senate with the Quebec City caucus were really too meagre for his name to be seriously considered. A third candidate, Israël Tarte's first choice in 1897, was Horace Archambault. The experience garnered over his ten years as Legislative Councillor made him a credible candidate, but his close links with the Préfontaine clique all but wrecked his chances.[6]

Laurier, who had promised a month earlier to leave the question of the Liberal party leadership to the Parliamentary caucus, wasted no time in imposing his preference. He ignored the important petition in favour of Robidoux and declared that Simon-Napoléon Parent, the ever efficient Minister of Crown Lands, would succeed Marchand. This was not the first time that Laurier had moved to keep Robidoux out of power. It will be remembered that he urged Marchand not to include him in the provincial cabinet in 1897.[7] Five days after Marchand's death, Parent was sworn in as Premier of the Province. Miville-Dechêne and Turgeon immediately declared themselves unwilling to serve under Parent.[8] The charismatic Robidoux was crushed by the announcement, resigned his cabinet seat, and was never heard from again.

The radical faction was despondent in the face of this display of command politics. As Charles Langelier put it, "Mr. Robidoux [...] had more party experience than Mr. Parent and on numerous counts, had superior qualities that were suited to the post of Prime Minister."[9] Even *La Presse* was surprised by Laurier's choice. "In terms of conventional wisdom, the hon. Mr. Robidoux was designated as the successor to Mr. Marchand. He had the seniority, a striking social and intellectual superiority, the almost unanimous support of his colleagues in the house [...] How is it that at the last moment [...] it would be Mr. Parent [...] who would be chosen?"[10] *La Patrie*, stunned, tellingly restricted itself to politely describing Parent as a man with a clear mind.[11] *L'Événement*, a Conservative daily, perhaps had the best description of Parent's political life until he was, literally, made Premier. "Mr. Parent," its editor wrote, "is one of those lucky men who arrive at high places with the most surprising ease. He does not possess the great qualities a party should wish to see in its leader. He does not have Mercier's talent, or Marchand's prestige. He does not exude any of the magnetism that made his predecessors popular. But, for right or wrong, he has carved himself a reputation as an administrator. Time will tell [...]."[12] Ernest Pacaud, a close personal friend of Parent and the editor of *Le Soleil*, the Liberal organ in Quebec City, seemed alone in accepting Laurier's choice. "No man is more similar to Mr. Marchand in his qualifications to become Prime Minister than Mr. Parent," he argued.[13] Seldom in Quebec history had such a political kiss of death been administered.

Simon-Napoléon Parent was born in 1855 in the small village of Beauport, the son of a merchant. He completed legal studies at Laval and in 1877 had married Marie-Louise Gendron, the daughter of a Beauport timber inspector. His rise in the ranks of the Liberal party had been steady, but unspectacular. He had won a seat as alderman in Quebec City's municipal council in 1890. That same year he was elected in the riding of St-Sauveur to the Legislative Assembly. He was 35 years old, and had caught the eye of Wilfrid Laurier and Israël Tarte. Four years later, as the provincial capital suffered difficult times, he was named Mayor by the city councillors. In 1897, Marchand was looking for a good business-minded man to oversee the thorny problems of the crown lands, and despite the objections of the *rouges* in the party who screamed that Parent was dangerously tied to the local trusts, named Parent to cabinet to oversee Crown Lands. The new recruit did not disappoint, and was recognized by the federal Liberals as an individual worthy of encouragement.

A quiet, unassuming man, content to mind his own business, Parent seemed aloof and wholly oblivious to his fellow politicians. He had none of Marchand's political authority, indeed, Parent's looks militated against authoritative postures. His long sideburns and mustache could not conceal his thin lips and delicate features. It looked as though his sideburns were shaved so as to run parallel to the curve of his nose. A thin man with a tendency to paunch, Parent's tie hung uncomfortably round his neck. In the company of the exuberance that made so many of his political contemporaries famous, Parent looked decidedly ill-at-ease. In Max Weber's terms, Parent was probably the least "charismatic" man in government, which only served to undermine his personal authority in the eyes of those in the party who wanted Liberalism to be bold and challenging in Quebec. In an age where political reputations were made of fiery stump performances, Parent, indeed, was cruelly ill-equipped.

Parent could live with the criticisms; he was a surprisingly independent politician. He was successful in business, and made his political contacts in this *milieu*. He was a man of private pleasures, given occasionally to revelling in the small luxuries of hotel life. His passion was bridge. Games often began on the train from Montreal and would not end until the small hours of the following morning in the Château Frontenac. But even his skilled game of cards could not repair his debilitated political persona. "Constantly preoccupied with administrative problems and solutions, your father was not very communicative," wrote one observer of the new Premier to Paul Parent in 1935.[14] Parent always left of task of presenting and defending bills to others, choosing to avoid confrontation. "Parent had none of the necessary qualities to be the leader of a government," argued the fiery Philippe-Auguste Choquette. "He always had [...] a sore throat that prevented him from partaking in the debates."[15]

Perhaps Parent's most unforgiving flaw was his reluctance to tailor his style. His forte was administration, he was satisfied with that, and he lacked any ambition to improve on his political image. He seldom ventured out of Quebec City (except for the occasional game of cards, it appears), never uttered a view of Liberal goals or philosophy, and never reached out to the hearts of the partisans in the manner of Laurier, a Mercier, or even a Marchand who was a terrible speaker, but who exuded an unquestionable sincerity. There was none of that critically important "emotional bond" between leader and follower that allows for success.[16] For the Liberals, Parent seemed satisfied to be the invisible leader of the party in Quebec.

Parent made some adjustment to Marchand's cabinet when he assumed the leadership of the government, but most ministers kept their posts. Turgeon and Miville-Dechêne, who had threatened to resign upon hearing of Parent's nomination to the Premiership, reconsidered their views and decided to stay on. Three positions were thus open: Marchand's, Robidoux's, and Shehyn's, who had left for the Senate a few months earlier and who had not been replaced by Marchand. Miville-Dechêne was moved to Agriculture while H.T. Duffy, Marchand's Minister of Public Works, was promoted to the post of Treasurer. To replace Duffy, Parent tendered an olive branch to the radicals by naming Lomer Gouin at Public Works. This surprised all but Langlois, who accorded more attention to Gouin than to the new Premier in his coverage of the new cabinet in *La Patrie*. Anglophone newspapers were far less positive, although they were pleased to have an anglophone as responsible for the Treasury. "Mr. Gouin's ability as a legislator has never been marked," noted *The Gazette*. "His record otherwise is against him. He is a poor substitute for Mr. Marchand. The choice of a non-entity was less menacing. His entry in the administration will hurt where he is best known. His advancement will create a conviction that the wrong element is paramount in the councils of the government's party."[17] *The Gazette* was keenly aware of the political significance of Gouin's entry in cabinet, something Parent was careful to counterbalance. He named Henri-Benjamin Rainville as speaker of the House—a favourable signal to Montreal's business community. Parent kept for himself the position of Minister of Lands, Forests and Fisheries, another favourable sign to the business community.

Armed with a new cabinet, Parent surprised everybody when he asked that the Provincial Legislature be dissolved on the day following Laurier's triumphant reelection on November 15, 1900. As he told the Lieutenant-Governor, his nomination to the Premiership of the province "while not meeting with any disapproval, as far as I know anyway, did surprise the expectations of a certain segment of the population." [18] Clearly, Parent felt the urgent need to show that he could win. Only with a new mandate could he be able to exercise his authority with any freedom and with the respect of his opponents in the party. Although the government still had two years left in its own term, Quebec was immediately plunged into a three-week electoral campaign.

Parent's platform was strikingly unoriginal, limiting himself to saying that Marchand's work would be continued. Pressing for clearer policy directions, L.O. David spoke for many when he said that "the new government will have to do more for colonization."[19] Colonization was uppermost in the minds of many, and Parent did address the issue.[20] The cause of educational reform had been pushed to the top of Liberal priorities and here again Parent promised to continue Marchand's course. Above all, Parent made it clear that he was devoted to the concerns of the province's business community. He said he called an election soon after Laurier so as to avoid the "depressions" in the business world during electoral times. By calling an election immediately, he argued, an unnecessary economic "downswing" would be avoided. The best option, therefore, was to take advantage of the depression already cause by the national election![21]

The rushed electoral campaign was not much of a contest. Thirty people, all Liberals, were immediately declared elected by acclamation. Five of the forty-four remaining ridings were undecided not because of inter-party challenges, but because the conflict between radical and conservative elements within the Liberal party moved from the local to the provincial level. In Chambly, the radical M. Perrault challenged former Conservative Antoine Rocheleau, who this time ran as a Parent Liberal. In Chateauguay, F.X. Dupuis's reelection was challenged by Narcisse Laberge, another local radical. Similar situations existed in the Verchères and Iberville ridings. For Parent, however, the most important challenge was taking place in the Quebec-Est riding. H. Thauvette, Parent's candidate, was challenged by J.A. Lane. Lane was an impenitent radical and had been a vicious critic of Parent as Mayor of Quebec City. Extremely popular with segments of the working class, his candidacy posed a serious threat to Parent.

The Liberals scored a record-breaking triumph on December 7, 1900. If elections by acclamations are ignored, the Liberals had garnered 56% of the popular vote, while the Conservatives culled 43.8%. Yet these figures hardly tell the real story because 36 Liberals won their elections by acclamation. One evaluation of the popular vote, taking into account elections by acclamations, put the percentage of Liberal votes at 84.9% of the total. The Conservatives were trounced. They won seven seats in comparison to the 67 seats won by the Liberals, a reduction of 17 people on their side of the Speaker's chair.[22]

The radical challengers to the Parent Liberal nominees fared less well in this lightning-speed election. Lane would be the only new radical addition in the house, something which could not compensate for the serious loss of Robidoux, who had announced that he was quitting politics when Parent asked the Lieutenant-Governor to dissolve the Assembly.

There were now nine progressive Liberals in the Legislative Assembly: Stephens, Weir, Gouin, Turgeon, Grosbois, Miville-Dechêne, Langelier, Cochrane and Lane.

Parent's government had reason to feel at ease. The opposition was small, Liberalism had a strong mandate, although it remained very unclear as to what its priorities should be. Parent, characteristically, said little. Some tendencies were decipherable, but one theme stood out: The Quebec government would remain fiscally and administratively conservative.

Parent never envisioned the expansion of state services the Liberal progressives demanded in the field of education, and this was quickly made noticeable as the new parliament began. "Public education is probably the first and most important basis we must consolidate," he did say in his response to the criticisms of the throne speech. "We have before us the example of neighbours, richer than we are, it is true, who make enormous sacrifices and who spare nothing for their elementary schools," he noted. "The government is convinced, of this people can be sure, of the primordial importance of such policies. It is willing, as the government which preceded it, to do the impossible in improving our educational system. [...] The truth is that we will proceed in an orderly, methodical and sure way, but that we will move ahead."[23]

Parent was challenged by members of his own party to make a progressive step forward in education soon after he uttered those words. Tancrède de Grosbois, the member for Shefford, proposed a bill in mid-March 1901 that would have forced the parents of children aged 8 to 13 years to send their children to school at least for 16 weeks per year. The measure was remarkably lax. Loopholes were provided so a child could be excused from attending classes for reasons of distance, handicaps, or proof that he or she was receiving good instruction at home. Grosbois's bill was supported by William Alexander Weir, H.T. Duffy and others, but created divisions even among the ranks of those who prided themselves in their progressive views of government policy. Adélard Turgeon, for instance, spoke out against the measure, arguing that the measures proposed by Grosbois would infringe on the individual's freedom of choice. He also said that it would threaten the clergy's authority. "In the interest of our nationality," he said, "the legislature should do nothing that could separate the people and the clergy."[24] Turgeon, seconded by Lomer Gouin, proposed, all the same, that the matter be referred for later discussion and Grosbois's bill was defeated by a vote of 55 to 7. Support for the measure came, in part, from surprising sources, from individuals were had not associated themselves in the past with educational matters. The seven in support of it were Ernest Roy, Charles Langelier, Côme- Séraphin Cherrier, W.A. Weir, James Cochrane, J.B. Prévost, and Grosbois himself. The radicals were not silenced. A few days later, J. Allard, the member for Yamaska, proposed that school taxes be abolished. The net effect of that law, Turgeon argued again in defence of the government, "would be free schools, and the government would not stand for it."[25] Turgeon, who for a decade had associated himself with progressive policies, seemed to have renounced them completely.

That wasn't good enough for Godfroy Langlois. In March 1901, as Grosbois's bill was being debated, he published in *La Patrie* numerous school inspection reports that displayed the lamentable state of Quebec's education and the high rate of absenteeism among the enroled students. He argued in favour of raising teachers' salaries and improving the physical condition of schoolhouses and reducing the cost of books. He published Mme Dandurand's impassioned speech urging the government to raise the salary of the 1469 teachers who earned less than one hundred dollars.[26] "We have an exercise in persuasion to undertake," he editorialized. "It is more than time to open one's eyes and to act."[27]

Grosbois's bill rode the cresting wave of Langlois's harsh criticism of Quebec's educational system. Though his cherished project of a secular Ministry of Education had been scuttled in 1898, Langlois never failed to hail the Robidoux bill as the solution to Quebec's problems. "It is the school system that has made of the American Republic a robust, progressive, energetic, practical, free, so proudly American, people," he declared in January 1901.[28] The need to prepare the next generation for a continental "struggle for life" necessitated that the system be imbued with a greater sense of realism, and Langlois, in his own incisive way, revealed his own recipe for a sound curriculum: "We should not lose sight of the fact that three quarters of the college-level students who return to the world in the liberal professions or in commerce need a general education, a practical education; they must be taught mathematics and English, they must be taught to master their French. Finally, the system should encourage them to cultivate a certain virility, a strength of character, a strong will, sound, great ambitions that do not require a life in a monastery or the devotion of the religious."[29]

Annoyed by Langlois's innuendos regarding the church's responsibility for denying not only humane working conditions for the province's teachers, but also for stalling French Canada's evolution, Archbishop Bruchési resumed his complaints to Tarte in the wake of the Grosbois affair. Tarte's response again shed some light on why Langlois could not simply be dismissed. "I have myself reprimanded my son on the exaggerations of *La Patrie* in the field of public education," he reassured the Archbishop. "Unfortunately, I do not have the time to control the newspaper. [...] I thank your Lordship for entrusting me with your views on this state of things which would not exist if a more experienced hand wielded the pen at *La Patrie*. Your Lordship should only know how difficult it is to find men capable of running a newspaper."[30] Clearly, Montreal was not devoid of talented journalists capable of heading *La Patrie*'s editorial department. Tarte refused Bruchési's request of firing Langlois because it was politically impossible to do so. As a colleague of Langlois at *La Patrie* remembered the crusades for educa-

...chool picture, on the wooden sidewalks of Collège Ste-Thérèse (1880). Godfroy ...anglois (not quite in focus) appears in the front row, second from left.

...he Langlois cottage, near Comeau, Quebec, *circa* 1904. In front, the young Roger(l.) ...d Roland(r.) Maillot, future founders and owners of the populaire *Petit Journal*.

Portrait of the young intellectual as a radical, *circa* 1885. An elbow on the table, a book in hand, and a piercing stare straight into the camera's lens were all the accessories needed.

Godfroy Langlois and his political (possibly Freemason) friends, after a day's boating in the Thousand Islands. Seated, unsmiling: Charles A. Geoffrion, Minister without Portfolio in Wilfrid Laurier's cabinet. He was flanked on one side by Senator Joseph-Philippe Casgrain and by Norman W. Trenholme, who was about to be named judge in Montreal. On the other side was J.A.C. Madore, the M.P. for Hochelaga, and J.A. Drouin, the Vice-President of the Club National. Léger Meunier, typographer, sat in the grass. Standing in the middle was Godfroy Langlois, the editor-in-chief of the Liberal Party's French daily in Montreal, *La Patrie*. The others remain unidentified except for their last names: "Senecal", "Talibert" and "Archer".

From the Canada Newspaper Cartoonists Assocation. Captioned 'Montrealers a
we see'em, Godfroy Langlois was simply identifed as 'M.L.A., St. Louis Division
Montreal, and Managing Director, *Le Canada*'.

Caricature of Langlois leaving the purity of his newspaper (and the country) to represent Quebec in Europe, with the Devil following in his footsteps. Circa 1912.

Reims, 1918. Godfroy Langlois (second row, far right) was accompanied by the Mayor of Montreal-North, Albert Brosseau. Their role was to supervise the voting by Canadian soldiers, who exercised their rights 'even in the trenches'.

Cannes, February 1922. Langlois and his daughter Marcelle take the brisk winter Riviera sea air on *La Croisette.*

The last happy days, relaxing in Petit-Colombes, near Paris, circa 1923...

...and the dignified old war-horse, alone and
in exile, at Le Perreux, near Paris, circa 1925.

tional reform, "we were often told to mind our own business at *'La Patrie'*, that issues in public schooling were best left to the relevant authorities, etc., etc. We were dangerous beings destined for eternal flames. People really went to extremes in those days."[31] If the fate of the Grosbois bill had frustrated *La Patrie*'s dreams of improving the lot of teachers in Quebec, the issue of the Carnegie grants in the fall of 1902 only redoubled Langlois's resolve.

Three Canadian cities had accepted the American industrialist's challenge to match his offer of money so as to finance the establishment of municipal libraries: Vancouver, Winnipeg and Halifax. Langlois and *La Patrie* urged Montreal's aldermen to meet the necessary conditions required to receive the $150,000 Carnegie offered. "Montreal owes it to its dignity to have a civic library," Langlois argued repeatedly.[32] Indeed, Montreal soon remained the only important city in North America not to have a municipal library. The church opposed the project for fear that it could not control the quality of the books on its shelves. In vain, Langlois proposed a compromise solution in which a commission composed of clergy and laity would be established in order to manage the Carnegie-funded municipal library,[33] but Bruchési remained firmly opposed to the idea and the project was scuttled.

Langlois's stature as a leading spokesman of the progressive faction of the Liberal party was becoming clear at this time. His personality attracted many people, not the least among his co-workers. "As a colleague," fondly remembered Charles Robillard, "Godfroy Langlois had endearing personal qualities. Of a great simplicity, warm, affable and obliging, a friend of the good clean joke, he knew how to bring a gaiety to everyday conversation. He certainly was not lacking in finesse, or in humour. His open and frank laughter put everyone at ease. His inquisitive eyes sparkled vividly behind those spectacles that were always ready to fall from their frail perch. [...] The intransigeance of his principles was forgotten when in close company, and people only saw before them the most humble and charming of men."[34]

Langlois took advantage of his senior position at *La Patrie* to invest Liberal progressivism with better defined aspirations of state intervention in educational and economic matters. In gestures that recalled Hector Berthelot's fun Sunday night "ten-o'clock gins," Langlois often allowed his home to become a forum for progressive discussions. Anticipating the birth of a daughter in the fall of 1900, he and his wife had moved to more spacious lodgings on Laval street a few doors down from the house where Emile Nelligan wrote some of the best poetry in the French language. The luxurious new house, bordering the trendy St-Louis square, proved inspiring for the new breed of "radicals". Langlois hosted the meetings in his study, a marvellous room lined with rows of books, stacks of newspapers, curios and paintings. "The conversation was quickly animated," recalled Charles Robillard, one of the regulars in attendance. "All the questions of the hour were dissected religiously, and in the middle of the commentaries and the jeers one could see a parade of the personalities of the day who made things happen."[35] The failure of the campaign to match the funds of the Carnegie Foundation convinced Langlois that *ad hoc* bull sessions with his journalists would not sufficiently broaden the political appeal of educational reform. "In this task of intellectual, social and economic renewal, he would have wanted to enlist all men of enlightenment and good will," noted Robillard.[36]

Langlois set himself to work, remembering the examples French politics could offer him. In November 1901, Langlois articulated the need for an organized group to advance ideas regarding education reform.[37] It took a year before the fruits of these reflections flashed on the political stage. On the heels of the rejection of the Carnegie Foundation's offer, the *Ligue de l'Enseignement* was officially founded in Montreal on October 9, 1902. Not surprisingly, in light of Langlois's participation, its name deliberately evoked the ghost of the French *Ligue* of the same name, an association founded by Jean Macé in 1866 and the first home to a great many, if not most, Third Republic radicals. In Montreal, the organization was stacked with members of the Liberal progressive wing of the Liberal party.

Its first president was Olivier Faucher; Godfroy Langlois was named vice-president and secretary. Estimates of its membership indicate that it reached its peak only a few months after it was created, in January 1903, when 400 people declared themselves members, but the only published list enumerated slightly less than two hundred names. As it was inaugurated, a manifesto affirming the rights to education was published, again reflecting Langlois's views.[38]

Indeed, if the French *Ligue de l'Enseignement* acted as an umbrella for secular, republican, radical and simply charitable groups,[39] the ligue Langlois was associated with was demonstrably far more moderate than he would have liked. Its membership was almost totally Liberal, but the moderate wing of the party was as strongly represented as the radical camp, at least on paper. The Board of Directors reflected this tendency. Two known Liberal progressives, Godfroy Langlois and Dr. L. Laberge, were Vice-Presidents; and Paul Martineau and Achille Bergevin, two outspoken progressives who had played key roles in the founding of *Le Signal* with Langlois, were present among the eight directors on the board. If anything, the membership of the *Ligue de l'Enseignement* demonstrated a reaffirmation of Liberal progressivism and Langlois's willingness to tone down his rhetoric in order to attract more people into considering the virtues of educational reform.

Langlois made good use of his personal contacts with recruiting members for the Ligue. (Newsmen—and women—were allowed to become members without paying the required $1.00 annual membership fee.) His father, Joseph Langlois, and his brother-in-law J.E. Valois both figured on the list. Old friends like Ephrem Taillefer and E.H. Tellier (who had launched *Le Clairon* with Langlois in 1889) and J.D. Leduc (who had launched *L'Echo des Deux-Montagnes* and *La Liberté* with Langlois in the 1890s) could be counted among the members as was Philippe-Auguste Choquette,

A.P. Pigeon, the publisher of the hilarious *Canard*, and Camille Piché (who had also worked to launch *Le Signal*). Senators Béique, Shehyn, Forget, Dandurand and Joseph-Philippe Casgrain were prominently cited as members as were numerous M.P.s and M.L.A.s, including Philippe Demers, active in founding *Le Signal*, and Louis-Philippe Brodeur, the Speaker of the House of Commons in Ottawa. Noted local Montreal progressive Liberals like Gilbert Marsolais, James Cochrane, L.A. Lapointe and Clément Robillard, two of the recently elected Liberal progressive aldermen, were part of the census.

Langlois also made use of his Freemason brothers. Ludger Larose, Adelstan de Martigny, Joseph Fortier and Gaston Maillet, founding members of the *Loge l'Emancipation* with Langlois in 1896 were present. Gonzalve Desaulniers, who had joined the lodge in 1899, also became a member of the *Ligue*. What was most remarkable about the composition of the Ligue's list of adherents, however, was the fact that many of Liberal progressivism's political enemies were present. Adélard Turgeon who 18 months earlier twice denounced state involvement in education was prominently named as were Henri-Benjamin Rainville and Horace Archambault! Names of known "radicals" were listed alongside people like F.O. Dugas, M.P. for Montcalm and F.X. Dupuis a freemason and the M.L.A. for Chateauguay; two men who like Turgeon opposed state involvement in education.[40]

To solidify further moderate support for his ideas Langlois even invited Laurier to join the new group. "I know that the question of the schools in Quebec interests you highly, because you understand the prestige and the greatness our race could achieve with better schools and curricula that are more practical and better organized," Langlois told Laurier. "[...] We would love to have your adherence, we wish to see you among our membership."[41] Laurier declined the offer.

Langlois submitted a program for the approval of the new society on November 21, 1902. It was a remarkably toned-down enumeration of the goals and principles Langlois had defended since the beginnings of his career. The goal was to give each individual equal opportunity to reach his personal potential. "It is the state's responsibility to ensure that no one, not even the poorest, be forgotten at the banquet that is intellectual life, for elementary education has become a right that nobody should be deprived of." Careful to emphasize that it did not "want to destroy or to break, on the contrary, it wants to improve, perfect, complete," the *Ligue* pronounced itself in favour of improving the salaries and qualifications of school teachers, of increased subsidies from the provincial government, of enforcing current education legislation, of building clean, "sanitary" schools and of a centralization of the school system's administration.[42] What was striking was the obvious absence of school book uniformity, of mandatory attendance, of secular education and of free education.

Notwithstanding the moderation of the principles espoused by the *Ligue*, it was not clear in what measure there ever existed a consensus among its members. Certainly, all pronounced themselves in favour of educational improvements, but many of these same people also publicly opposed the massive imposition of the role of the state in the affairs of public instruction. Most, however, were probably content to continue to perceive formal education as a privilege, rather than "a right no one should be deprived of" as the *Ligue*'s manifesto stated.[43] Langlois's creative effort in lobbying for support was bound to fail. Perhaps the lack of consensus is best reflected in the fact that less than half of the alleged "members" actually paid their dues.[44]

Though it was never formally condemned by the church, the *Ligue* did not live long. It was strongly denounced by publications professing to speak for the church,[45] and was roundly denounced as a Masonic conspiracy in 1904,[46] but the *Ligue* really collapsed under its own heavy weight of inconsistencies. From the beginning, the *Ligue de l'Enseignement* had trouble generating its own steam because it could not convince moderate Liberals of the necessity of acting in lieu of mere philosophizing. The association had practically evaporated by late 1903, when it celebrated its first birthday. By 1904, it had, for all intents and purposes, been abandoned. It is difficult to perceive the disintegration of the *Ligue* as the fruit of the dissatisfaction of the "moderates" in the organization, in light of its very moderate ambitions. One wonders if it was not stillborn,[47] the victim of a bad mix of incompatible aspirations.

The Liberal progressives who had remained guardedly content with Marchand's initiatives in the field of education were quickly disillusioned with Parent's promises to continue on the same course of reform. While provincial government expenditures in the field of education dropped only slightly during the first year, the impact of Parent's policies was made clearer in the following three years. It was decided that the already impoverished parishes would have to contribute a greater share of their tax revenues to education. In 1903-1904, provincial government expenditures in education dropped 3.2% from $484,964 to $464,280. The 1904-1905 fiscal year saw that figure raised to $480,760, a 2.4% increase. Yet the provincial government was spending less money in education in 1905 than in the 1901-1902 fiscal exercise, which was Parent's first budget-year. Total moneys directed to education from local taxes and from the provincial treasury grew very slowly under Parent. $3,453,754 had been directed into education from all sources in the last year of the Marchand administration. In a booming economy, Parent only allowed a 2.1% increase in 1901-1902, a considerable 5.6% increase in 1902-1903, a 2.7% increase in 1903-1904 and a 7.0% increase in 1904-1905.[48]

Despite favourable economic conditions, the development of an educational vision stagnated under the Parent administration, and the Liberal progressives responded by establishing the *Ligue de l'Enseignement*. That attempt to convince the moderate element of the Liberal party of the necessity of educational improvement failed miserably. Langlois and the Liberal progressives rapidly lost a forum but the setback did not dull their resolve to battle for reforms. They were looking forward to taking their battles elsewhere by 1903 anyway. The Liberal progressives had reacted to the Liberal Premier's refusal to pursue reforms and the obstinacy of the church leaders, but had failed to rally enough members of the party to form a strong reform constituency. Again inspired by the example of the Third French Republic, the progressives of the Liberal party had attempted without success to press their party into more reformist positions, although they had succeeded in affirming their intention to pursue the issue. This further episode of disagreement between moderates and progressives, in the end, only served to envenom relations between the factions of the Liberal party and embitter Liberal progressives attitudes to Simon-Napoléon Parent's leadership.

Notes

1. ANQQ, Marchand Papers, Joséphine Dandurand to Marchand, 28 mai 1900.
2. Laurier Papers, C778, Langelier to Laurier, 31 août 1900.
3. *Ibidem*, Laurier to Langelier, 4 septembre 1900.
4. *Ibidem*, C810, Langlois to Laurier, 30 mars 1904.
5. *La Presse*, 27 septembre 1900.
6. *Ibidem*, 1 octobre 1900.
7. See chapter III.
8. Choquette, *op.cit.*, pp. 162-163.
9. Charles Langelier, *Souvenirs politiques, Vol. II* (Montreal, 1912), p.40.
10. *La Presse*, editorial, 1 octobre 1900.
11. *La Patrie*, 1 octobre 1900.
12. *L'Evénement*, 1 octobre 1900.
13. *Le Soleil*, 1 octobre 1900.
14. ANQQ, Parent Papers, Henri Kieffer to P. Parent, 28 décembre 1934.
15. Philippe-Auguste Choquette, *Un demi-siècle de vie politique* (Montreal, 1934), p. 163.
16. See K.J. Patnam, "Charisma and Political Leadership" in *PS*, vol XII, 3, 1964, p. 345. On the problems of placing too much importance on

the vague concept of charisma to the detriment of understanding the hard realities that often account for political alliances, see Carl J. Friedrich, "Political Leadership and the problem of Charismatic Power", *JP*, February 1961; Léon Dion, "The Concept of Political Leadership: An analysis," *CJPS*, vol. 1, No. 1, 1968. For a broader definition of charisma see Edward Shils, "Charisma, Order and Status" *ASR*, April 1965.

17. *The Gazette*, editorial, October 1, 1900.

18. Parent Papers, Parent to Jetté, 13 novembre 1900.

19. Laurier Papers, C781, David to Laurier, 23 novembre 1900.

20. There has been some debate as to what importance colonization actually occupied in the political sphere. Michel Brunet accused Quebec's politicians of spending too much time on the matter to the detriment of the hard realities of promoting industrialization. Scholars have since disputed his claims. On the importance of colonization, see Brunet's "Les trois dominantes de la pensée canadienne-française: agriculturalisme, anti-étatisme, et messianisme", in *La présence anglaise et les canadiens* (Montreal, 1958). A.I. Silver saw "colonisation" as an expression of the French-Canadian sense of mission. See his "Some Quebec attitudes in an Age of Imperialism and Ideological Conflict" *CHR*, 4, December 1976. One historian of this period has observed that colonization was not a great concern. See Ralph Heintzman, "The Struggle for Life: The French Daily Press of Montreal and the Problem of Economic Growth in the Age of Laurier, 1896-1911" (Ph.D. thesis, York University, 1977). A discussion of Parent's practices regarding colonization is in Patrice Dutil, "The Politics of Progressivism in Quebec: Godfroy Langlois and the Liberal Party, 1889-1914" (Ph.D. thesis, York University, 1987), p. 259-264.

21. Parent Papers, Parent to Jetté, 13 novembre 1900.

22. Jean Hamelin, Jacques Letarte et Marcel Hamelin, "Les élections provinciales dans le Québec" *CGQ*, 7, octobre 1959-mars 1959, figure X.

23. Parent Papers, Response to the Throne Speech debates, 1901.

24. *L'Enseignement Primaire*, Avril 1901, p. 486. Cited in Victrice Lessard, "L'instruction obligatoire dans la province de Québec de 1875 à 1943" (Ph.D. thesis, University of Ottawa, 1962), p. 36.

25. *La Patrie*, 9 mars 1901.

26. see *La Patrie*, 16 mars 1901.

27. *Ibidem*, editorial, 19 mars 1901.

28. *Ibidem*, editorial, 3 janvier 1901.

29. *Ibidem*, 25 juin 1898.

30. ACAM, Newspapers Correspondence File, I. Tarte to Bruchési, 26 avril 1901.

31. *La Patrie*, 10 janvier 1943. This document was found in the Godfroy Langlois Papers, Scrapbook A.

32. *La Patrie*, 16 octobre 1902.

33. *La Patrie*, 16 mars 1902.

34. *La Patrie*, 10 janvier 1943.

35. *Ibidem.*

36. *Ibidem.*

37. See *La Patrie*, 20 novembre 1901.

38. It is reprinted in Daniel Latouche and Diane Poliquin Bourassa (eds.), *Le Manuel de la Parole: Manifestes québécois. Tome 2, 1900 à 1959* (Montreal, 1975), pp. 31-42.

39. Catherine Auspitz, *The Radical Bourgeoisie* (New York, 1982).

40. The list is published in a pamphlet published by the Ligue, *La question de l'instruction publique dans la province de Québec* (Montreal, 1903).

41. Laurier Papers, C796, Langlois to Laurier, 26 novembre 1902.

42. Ligue de l'Enseignement, *La question de l'instruction publique dans la province de Quebec* (Montreal, 1903), p. ii.

43. A discussion of the Ligue's program can also be found in Ruby Heap, "La Ligue de l'enseignement, 1902-1904: Héritage du passé et nouveaux défis" *RHAF*, décembre 1982.

44. See Jean-Claude Charbonneau, "The Lay School Movement in Quebec since 1840" (M.A. Thesis, McGill University, 1971), pp. 96-132.

45. For example, see Pierre Savard, *Jules-Paul Tardivel, La France et les Etats-Unis* (Quebec, 1967), pp. 430-432.

46. See Henri Bernard, *La Ligue d'enseignement: histoire d'une conspiration maçonnique à Montréal* (Montreal, 1904). It is worth noting that the masons took great pride in Langlois's work. In June 1903, the Loge L'Emancipation officially requested that the Grand Orient de France put forward Langlois's name for the Légion d'honneur as a reward for those efforts. See Roger Le Moine, *Deux Loges montréalaises du Grant Orient de France* (Ottawa, 1991) p.44.

47. For a different interpretation of the failure of the Ligue, see Ruby Heap, *op.cit.* As it is fairly evident that many people who allegedly belonged to the Ligue were in fact hostile to state-imposed reform, it is difficult to agree with her thesis that the Ligue was scuttled by the moderates who distrusted the radical proposals. The Ligue collapsed not because the moderates left it, but because the radicals quickly realized that such an association was doomed to failure in its attempt to convince moderate opinions of the need for a more ambitious educational strategy.

48. Province de Québec, *Annuaire statistique du Québec, 1916* (Quebec, 1916), pp. 227-228.

CHAPTER VI

FIGHTING THE EVIL TRUSTS

"Must we be bled dry?"
—Godfroy Langlois, 1904[1]

THE SHORT CAREER OF THE *Ligue de l'Enseignement* in Quebec was only a symptom of the dissatisfaction of Liberal progressives with the Parent regime. That discontent flared again over Parent's arbitrary treatment of forestry and hydro-electricity issues. "It saddens us, we the old Liberals, to see the work of over 25 years destroyed by the vanity and the autocracy of that small-footed potentate," the irrepressible Alfred Lane wrote to Sir Wilfrid. "For me and your friends, that Parent remains Prime Minister for a time or that he leaves does not matter to us personally. But while he refuses to govern, it is the Liberal party that suffers. He [Parent] could not care less if the Liberals stayed in power or lost it, as long as his private business goes well and continues to stuff his purse. We live in Quebec under a regime or terror; it is the politics of 'believe or die' that dominate."[2]

It was not the threat to the "colons" represented by Parent's forestry policies, however, that preoccupied the Liberal progressives. It was hydro-electricity. This was a new issue, and it would become as important in defining Liberal progressivism as had educational reform and the nature of Préfontaine's leadership. At stake, to those who sympathized with Liberal progressivism, was the reputation of Liberalism at a time when both the municipal and provincial governments were obviously protecting certain companies. The issue caused a regrouping of Liberal progressives. Louis Hartz explained it best when he wrote that in the mind of the radical liberal, "if the trust were at the heart of all evil, then Locke could be kept intact by smashing it."[3] Godfroy Langlois distinguished himself in being among the first to diagnose the evil of the trusts in Montreal, but more importantly, in fighting it.

Montrealers, like all their urban counterparts, were concerned with the costs and conditions required to allow private public utilities to operate. In Ontario, municipalities quickly noticed the advantages of securing a publicly-owned utility that could supply light, heat and power to businesses and homes at the cheapest rates. Their campaign, most notably that of Adam Beck, to take over the electrical companies, gradually won support among the business community and the citizenry.

In Montreal, and in Quebec generally, many politicians and journalists also called for public ownership of utilities but their campaigns fell on deaf ears. Geography, in part, served to undermine their cause: Quebec possessed many cataracts that could be harnessed for power supply. But there was also a greater number of companies in the utilities business. A final factor played a key role in Quebec's case: the lack of understanding between the provincial and municipal governments over utility policy.[4] One such case of misunderstanding and business influence at the provincial level revealed the lines of struggle between the progressive and the conservative factions of the Liberal party in Quebec. It festered over many years on the issue of the powers and prerogatives of the Montreal Light, Heat, and Power Company.

The issue arose when the Parent government, in its very first session, moved to incorporate a new electricity company that had been formed by Herbert Holt and Rodolphe Forget. It proposed to give a provincial charter to the Montreal Light, Heat and Power Company, an amalgamation of the Montreal Gas Company, managed by Herbert Holt; the Royal Electric Company; the Montreal and St-Lawrence Light and Power Company and the Imperial Electric Company. What made this charter so important, in addition to the sheer size of the operations it would be creating, was its clause 10 which stated that the company could expand and install its works without the preliminary consent of the municipality:

> The company will, in the City of Montreal or in any other location situated in the province of Quebec, within a radius of one hundred miles from the said City, have access and establish under and on the streets and public roads, all the lines, channels, conduits and other installations that will be necessary for its business, all its works being completed as fast as possible and under the direction of the municipality in which the works are situated.[5]

While the Montreal Light, Heat, and Power Company was not yet big enough to be regarded as a monopoly at the time of its incorporation, the municipal government reacted promptly upon learning of the controversial stipulation. On March 11, a week before it was introduced to the Assembly, the Municipal council elected to send a protest delegation to Quebec City. Herbert Ames proposed that Hormisdas Laporte, Paul Martineau, Calixte Lebeuf, Arthur Gagnon and Frank Hart (all but Laporte having distinguished themselves in fighting for educational reform or against the Préfontaine clique), be sent to make representation to the provincial government. Following much discussion over the efficiency of sending such a large delegation, and of the cost of sending them to Quebec City, it was moved that the delegation be limited to Hormisdas Laporte and Paul Martineau.[6] The debate over the size of the delegation was but an example of the tragic divisions among the "reformers" in City Council as Liberal progressives argued in favour of a big demonstration while other were more concerned about the cost of such a foray. The two-man delegation was eventually sanctioned by a vote of 14 to 5, but in the end, many informal representations were made to Quebec City, including that of Lebeuf.

Godfroy Langlois immediately echoed the concern in *La Patrie*. "Where are we heading," he asked. "What wrongheadedness is pushing our legislators to give to [...] the promoters of this exaggerated bill [...] powers so broad, so arbitrary? [...] It is a nonsensical, intolerable bill that we denounce today." "Protest immediately and vigorously," he excitedly urged Montreal's politicians.[7] Deaf to the demands of Montreal's Liberals, F.X. Dupuis, M.L.A. for Châteauguay, presented the private bill incorporating the Montreal Light, Heat, and Power Company on March 15. Reaction in Parliament was swift. The first phase of formal Liberal opposition took place in the Private Bills Committee. J.J. Guerin proposed an amendment that would prohibit the Montreal Light, Heat and Power Company from working without municipal approval. The motion was rejected.[8]

W.A. Weir and Lomer Gouin instantly pronounced themselves against the bill. "A door is being opened wide for a new monopoly whose goal it is to swallow all the small companies. [...] Before four or five years, the population will complain about this monopoly and about those who will have given it life," declared Gouin. Weir then proposed an amendment to the contentious clause 10 stating "as long as the consent of each municipality involved has been previously received."[9] Such an amendment would have hamstrung the consortium as it gave the municipalities some sort of bargaining power. Without it, municipal authorities were exposed to virtual extortion. By granting these exclusive privileges to one company, the provincial legislature was giving the Montreal Light, Heat and Power Company the right to install its equipment before all others, thus filling the streets with wire and equipment, placing itself in a position to safely offer lower rates to its customers temporarily as it had a *de facto* monopoly of street space. Newcomers would be discouraged by the prospects of having to abide by city regulations in the face of such competition, and would likely be faced with selling out to the trust. Free of competition, the Montreal Light, Heat, and Power Company would consequently raise its rates. The amendment to paragraph 10 was rejected by a margin of seven votes in the Legislative Assembly. Gouin, recognizing the futility of opposing such display in favour of the Holt-Forget trust, did not vote. Adélard Turgeon, on the other hand, was conspicuous in his rejection of the amendment.

Remarkably, the bill still did not get much publicity in the press, and encountered little challenge in public. It was sent to the Legislative Council where it ran into unexpected opposition. J.C. McCorkill, a Liberal, proposed after the second reading of the bill on March 22, that the words "with the consent of the municipalities" be amended to clause 10. The motion was rejected by a vote of 13 to 10 and among those who opposed the amendment was Horace Archambault (Tarte's protégé), Speaker of the Legislative Council and a representative of the Montreal region.

McCorkill was tenacious. Again, he moved that the words, "that the streets where the company will build its tunnels etc. will be indicated by the municipal authorities," be added to the clause.[10] Despite his efforts to safeguard the City's rights, McCorkill's amendment was promptly rejected and the bill was sent for Royal Assent. The Montreal Liberal progressives continued their pressures on Parent by taking their fight to the Lieutenant-Governor on March 25 and submitting to him the following resolution:

> That the Council of the City of Montreal, in special meeting assembled, hereby protest most emphatically against the treatment accorded to Montreal and its environments in the passage by the legislature of Quebec of a bill to permit the Montreal Light, Heat, and Power Co. to operate in, under, and over the streets of this city without the previously obtained consent of the municipal authorities having jurisdiction and this Council hereby petitions his honour the Lieutenant-Governor of the Province of Quebec praying him to withhold his assent from the said bill.[11]

The resolution was approved and cabled to Quebec, in vain.[12] Lieutenant-Governor Jetté was convinced, however, that the bill had such support in cabinet that not signing it would bring about a major crisis. "Our friends in the Ministry stood by the bill and apparently the Governor, rather than bringing about a Cabinet crisis, has signed the bill," reported Charles Porteous, a member of the Montreal Light, Heat, and Power Company Board of Directors.[13] On April 5, 1901, the Board of Directors for the new company was organized in Rodolphe Forget's office. Herbert Holt was made president with a salary of $25,000. James Ross was made first Vice-President and Rodolphe Forget second Vice-President. Other board members included L.J. Forget, Robert Mackay, Montagu Allan, Charles Porteous, F.C. Henshaw and, last but not least, Henri-Benjamin Rainville.[14] With capital amounting to 17 million dollars, the Montreal Light, Heat, and Power Company was one of the largest corporations in Canada.

The incorporation of the Montreal Light, Heat, and Power Company had an immediate impact on the political structure of Montreal's City Council. Mayoral and ward elections being held every two years, the Council had to submit itself to electoral judgment in February 1902, less than a year after the Montreal Light, Heat and Power Company was granted its charter. The target, this time, was to be Préfontaine who had survived the onslaught of 1900, and who had done nothing to represent the city's interests in the Montreal Light, Heat and Power affair.

The progressives of the Liberal party were fast off the mark in seeking a contender for Préfontaine's position this time. Shedding their respect for the custom of alternating French and English-speaking mayors, three senators prepared themselves to run for the top job: J.P. Casgrain, F.L. Béique and Raoul Dandurand. "I think you can present yourself as able to take the fight to Préfontaine, if he decides to run again, and I am not sure of that," Israël Tarte confided to Dandurand. "You will have the support of the English, and I am convinced that you will break his back in the French neighbourhoods. I will fight him tenaciously in *La Patrie*. If the Liberal party does not have enough honest people to fight honestly, my personal opinion, offered without prejudice, is that men like Préfontaine do more harm than good for a party."[15]

The Liberal progressives finally settled for two nominees from their ranks: Dr. Ernest Lachapelle, the President of the Provincial Board of Health and James Cochrane, who was both an MLA and an alderman. Lachapelle was pressed into running by Senator Casgrain and by Godfroy Langlois who supported him avidly in *La Patrie* and presented himself against Préfontaine on frankly progressive platforms. He had witnessed first-hand the deterioration of Montreal's sanitary conditions and had often pledged himself in favour of many of Langlois's proposals. Lachapelle would join Langlois later that year as a member of the *Ligue de l'Enseignement*.

Lachapelle's candidacy was a direct French-Canadian challenge to Préfontaine. Even Langlois acknowledged in *La Patrie* that should Préfontaine retire from municipal politics, Lachapelle would withdraw.[16] Cochrane's effort, on the other hand, was predicated on the widespread assumption that Préfontaine would retire from city politics and that events would follow tradition's dictates so that an anglophone would succeed a francophone in the Mayor's office.

The barrage against Préfontaine in *La Patrie* was merciless. Sensing that he could no longer be supported by an adequate number of Liberals in Montreal, Préfontaine finally announced that he would withdraw from the race and threw his support to Richard Wilson-Smith, who had been Mayor from 1896 to 1898. Lachapelle abandoned the contest upon hearing the news, and Dandurand and the other French-speaking hopefuls also agreed to withdraw. Liberal progressive support was thus given to James "Jimmy" Cochrane.

Cochrane, like Lachapelle, had close ties with the Liberal progressives. In the Legislative Assembly, where he represented a Montreal riding, and on the local Montreal political scene, where he was an alderman, he always lent a good helping hand in various crusades. He had supported Grosbois's educational reform bill and would also become a member of the *Ligue de l'Enseignement*. Fluently bilingual, Cochrane spoke the language of the working classes. Even so, Cochrane's personal character threatened a schism in Liberal ranks, something the old radical L.O. David feared greatly. Now Clerk of the City Council in Montreal, David urged Laurier to intervene and convince Cochrane not to run against Préfontaine or his designated heir. "I fear that Cochrane's candidacy will foil the plans of those who believed it wise to elect an amiable Englishman and not a Cochrane. Both the friends of Préfontaine and of Lachapelle are wondering what they should do if Cochrane does not retire his candidacy [...]."[17]

Laurier refused to intervene, and even told David that he liked the idea of Cochrane running, even though his candidacy did not hold out any hope. Préfontaine and Cochrane should both retire from city politics, Laurier said, leaving Wilson-Smith to be elected by acclamation.[18] But if Laurier was willing to support Cochrane in his own silent way, Godfroy Langlois and W.A. Weir were among his most vocal supporters. So strong indeed was Cochrane's position that Préfontaine arrogantly decided to return to the contest at the end of January 1902, a week before the polls were to open. Préfontaine's candidacy was disallowed on a technicality. Judge François Langelier's decision (the same radical Langelier who had been promised Chapleau's position by Laurier in 1897) thus improved Cochrane's standing against the popular Préfontaine. To promote his candidacy, a great demonstration was organized on the day following Préfontaine's disqualification at Sohmer Park, even though it was one of the coldest days of the year. *La Presse* reported that over 600 people attended the speeches made by a host of noted progressive Liberals. Among them were Senators Joseph-Philippe Casgrain and H.J. Cloran, J.A.C. Madore, J.A. Drouin, Camille Piché, Gonzalve Desaulniers, G.W. Stephens and Godfroy Langlois. One wonders how they managed to be heard over the extraordinary brouhaha reportedly created by the marching band hired for the occasion.[19]

Cochrane won a close race, and the reformists at City Hall saw their ranks swell. Not only was this a victory for those who had opposed Préfontaine for so long, it was also the beginning of the steady downfall of the conservative Liberals in Montreal. The Liberal progressive victory was so impressive that it prompted Senator H.J. Cloran to declare that Cochrane's triumph represented far more than the mere outcome of an election. It was, he said, "the victory of the people against capital."[20]

If the Mayoral race created a stir, the aldermanic contests were far less agitated. Thirteen aldermen were elected by acclamation, and of them only three belonged to the Préfontaine machine. Nine Liberal progressives were acclaimed: Martineau, Lapointe, Ekers, Carter, Sadler, Robertson, Stearns, Clearihue, and Robillard. The remaining seventeen contests reflected many of the same electoral tendencies. The seven Préfontaine candidates who faced reelection were defeated. On the Liberal progressive side, Lebeuf was reelected, as was John Bumbray, Richard Turner, Daniel Gallery and two newcomers: J.C. Walsh, editor of the Montreal *Herald* and S.D. Vallières. Liberal progressives fared well in the elections, but still did not muster enough power to take a majority of the seats in City Council. Those without identifiable party allegiances would hold the balance of power.

The relationship of newspapers to the political parties at the turn of the century continued to be as important as before. Considering the inundation of new political ideas, moreover, to secure and maintain a voice in the daily literature was indispensable.[21] To the Liberals in Quebec, newspapers were a constant headache in that they were as unpredictable as they were expensive. In every region of Canada, Laurier was at pains to ensure the loyalties of the editors who professed to be at his service. Simon-Napoléon Parent, for his part, had reason to be complacent. As far as the press was concerned, he really had nothing to fear.

Anglophone Liberal newspapers in the province supported him consistently, and French journals rarely even mentioned his name. *Le Soleil*, directed by Ernest Pacaud, was wholeheartedly devoted to the Premier, and whatever Godfroy Langlois might feel, Tarte evidently permitted little to be said against the Premier in *La Patrie*.

The press world in Quebec was dramatically altered in October 1902, however, when Israël Tarte, Laurier's staunch defender and friend, announced that, as he no longer shared Laurier's views on trade policy, he would resign from the Liberal party. Tarte's departure would leave a vacuum in the Liberal party's Montreal organization. Laurier was losing his most visible moderate representative, a gifted political organizer, and, just as importantly, was losing the continuous support of *La Patrie*. The reaction among the party faithful was predictably mixed. Moderates viewed the loss as serious for party organization,[22] others, such as George Washington Stephens, illustrated the attitude of many progressives. "I am delighted that you have got rid of Tarte," he told Laurier. "It will prove a blessing to the government. We have all been disgusted with his overbearing vanity—He is a good type of the modern politician who forgets that he is in office for the good of his country."[23]

Tarte's departure triggered a three-month struggle for influence between the progressive faction and the conservative faction of the party. Laurier needed a replacement for Tarte in cabinet, and suggestions came fast and furious. The Prime Minister was leading in two directions. Senator F.L. Béique, a patron of the Liberal progressives was a possibility.[24] But Laurier also wanted to see his good friend, the discredited Raymond Préfontaine, in cabinet.

Laurier's first move was a surprise. To replace Tarte, James Sutherland was promoted from Minister without Portfolio to Minister of Public Works. Langlois was unhappy. "The moral effect of the loss of the Public Works portfolio would be great," he told the Prime Minister.[25] A cabinet post was still open for a Quebec representative, nonetheless. Laurier wavered. Béique or Préfontaine? The mere rumour of a Préfontaine appointment roused vehement antagonism among the Liberal progressives who desperately wanted to be represented in the national cabinet. "Then Préfontaine is going to be in cabinet?" asked a crusty old partisan. "Canada does not want men like him in cabinet. His reputation has been made right here in Montreal in every shape. The papers cannot consistently support him. We had enough of Tarte, now let us have men of untarnished reputation."[26] So eager was Dandurand to see Préfontaine out of Ottawa, that he even suggested to Laurier that he be appointed as a replacement for Lieutenant-Governor Jetté.[27]

Remarks made by members of the progressive faction seemed to hit their mark and Préfontaine felt that he had to defend his political record in light of the harsh criticism levelled against him. "I hear, to my great surprise [...] that some people [...] have [...] deliberately poisoned your thoughts and those of certain of your colleagues on my account," Préfontaine told Laurier. "I am even more surprised to learn at the same time that these people have had a great effect on you with regards to me, and that would explain the flagrant injustices I have had to suffer politically since the arrival of our friends in power [since the municipal election of 1902]."[28]

Suggestions continued to flood into Laurier's office. Lomer Gouin was touted as a likely candidate to replace Tarte,[29] but Laurier finally opted for his friend Préfontaine. Laurier was betting on the residual popularity Préfontaine still enjoyed among the masses of Montreal, but the act constituted a deep disappointment for the Liberal progressives who hoped to see Préfontaine out of politics forever. Their foe won a by-election in December 1902 and joined the Laurier cabinet soon thereafter as Minister without Portfolio. The radicals, for the moment, had been foiled.

In January 1903, the expected finally happened: Israël Tarte broke the ties between *La Patrie* and the Liberal party, pledging that his newspaper would be a forum of *independent* thought.[30] Laurier had long anticipated the loss of the daily and had struck a party committee soon after Tarte's firing from cabinet to look into the question of launching a new newspaper. Senator Béique soon offered enough capital to start the venture, and the preparations for a new publication were initiated at the end of January of 1903.

If Béique had majority ownership in the new venture, Laurier reserved for himself the task of appointing the editor.[31] Three names deserved serious consideration, according to Laurier. Jules Helbronner, an editor at *La Presse*; Marc Sauvalle, the ever loyal assistant-editor also at *La Presse*; and Godfroy Langlois, who was still toiling under the Tartes. Langlois was Béique's favourite, and Laurier seemed to agree with his choice. That was not to say that all Liberals were in agreement, far from it. Arthur Dansereau, chief editor at *La Presse* who had suffered the sting of Langlois's pen since 1896, wanted to see his colleague Helbronner at the helm of the new Liberal newspaper. Langlois, in his opinion, was "a burned out little mind incapable of maintaining popular views."[32] Ernest Pacaud, the owner-editor of *Le Soleil* in Quebec City, was as bitter as Dansereau on Béique's suggestion. "Would it really be Godfroy Langlois as director of the new paper? If yes, this would be a really bad start. *Le Soleil* would not get along with such a comrade-in-arms. We do not share the same ideas and I could do nothing except continue to combat his eccentricities," he told Laurier.[33]

Laurier's choice was made sometime late in January 1903. Helbronner had no intention of leaving *La Presse*, and Sauvalle was not considered to have the business acumen necessary to start mass-circulation daily paper. Laurier settled on Béique's protégé Langlois "because he certainly has the qualities of a businessman and that would be a great advantage for the newspaper's success." Still, the Prime Minister remained concerned by his choice: "I worry about his character," he confided to Béique, "[...] you will have to hold his reins, otherwise he will buck."[34]

Laurier had seen the political wisdom of appointing Langlois director-editor of the new Liberal organ. The Prime Minister cited Langlois's excellent business sense, but his choice was made for political reasons. Indeed, for the same reasons he had denounced Langlois when Beaugrand had named him editor of *La Patrie* in 1895, Laurier nominated him director of the new Liberal paper. Langlois had been criticized in 1895 for being a radical and thus unrepresentative of the Liberal point of view, and now was being embraced as the new editor because he was a leading member of an increasingly muscular faction of the party, the Liberal progressives. It had taken a while, but Langlois had gained enormous political clout in Montreal in the intervening years. Laurier's appointment of Préfontaine to the cabinet had to be counterbalanced by the choice of a Liberal progressive, and no better opportunity presented itself than the nomination of a Liberal progressive at the helm of the French voice of Liberalism in Montreal. Only then could the progressive faction be placated.

Laurier met with Langlois at the end of January 1903 to discuss the tone and orientation of the new publication. Armed with a personal guarantee that the newspaper would remain loyal to the Liberal party in all circumstances, Laurier gave his new director the green light to commence preparations on what would be a morning publication called *Le Canada*, and Langlois quickly set out to do his job. Within three weeks, he had gathered over $10,000 in advertisement contracts and already perceived a brilliant future for the Liberal venture. "I am convinced now more than ever," he told Laurier, "that *Le Canada* will become popular and will accomplish magnificent business."[35] Despite his enthusiastic predictions, however, Langlois had to face serious financial problems. The $25,000 Senator Béique invested to start up the newspaper could not cover all the expenses. *Le Canada*'s purchase of the *Toronto News*'s press had quickly emptied its purse and Langlois felt justified to complain to Laurier. "If the public knew that we had founded a newspaper with such a small sum, we would be laughed at," lamented Langlois.[36]

Even as the new morning paper hit the streets for the first time on April 4, 1903, the organization was not complete. The presses purchased in Toronto had yet to arrive and permanent lodgings for the paper had not been found. It was only in late May, almost two months after the paper first appeared, that the journal was published on its own press in its own building. *Le Canada* was located at 73 rue St-Jacques, in the heart of Montreal's journalistic and business world.

The newspaper circulation figures prospered, despite its financial handicaps. In early May, Langlois could report that over $35,000 in advertising contracts had been secured and that about 10,000 copies were being published each day. "We are therefore the most widely circulated morning newspaper in Montreal and in the province of Quebec," Laurier was told. "I would dare to believe that you will not regret having given me the direction of *Le Canada*."[37] But the need for working capital got worse as *Le Canada*'s sales rose by an average of a 1000 copies every week and advertisement contracts reached $45,000 by July 1903. "It is time, high time, that you do something for *Le Canada*," Langlois again complained to Laurier:

> It appears to me, dear M. Laurier, that it should be easy enough to find funds for *Le Canada*. Mr. Tarte knew where to find them whenever he needed them for *La Patrie*.
> The government is the one most directly affected by the development, the success and the prosperity of our newspaper. The government cannot, consequently, cross its arms and leave us in a jam[...].
> I know of some of our friends who, in gratitude for a Senate position, would give $20,000 or $25,000 to the newspaper.[38]

Unable to count on donations from potential senators, Langlois had to turn to other methods to balance his books. To bring down the cost of production, he cut the salaries of his employees in early November only to find that the old

Toronto News press could no longer manage the great increases in the newspaper's circulation. Langlois celebrated *Le Canada*'s first birthday by announcing to Laurier that he only had enough money in his till to pay off the fixed costs of the paper's production.[39]

In spite of the financial difficulties, *Le Canada* made an immediate impact on the political life in Montreal. First, there was a settling of accounts. Liberal progressivism gladly divorced itself from Israël Tarte as Langlois, no doubt venting the frustrations he had lived with for six years, mercilessly insulted his old boss in the pages of *Le Canada* during the summer of 1903. Tarte instigated legal proceedings against his former employee for libel in October. Langlois appeared at the Court house accompanied by Lomer Gouin, who had been retained as legal counsel, and the case was heard by none other than judge Philippe-Auguste Choquette, the same man who had cooperated so closely with Charles Langelier in the bitter anti-Tarte Lévis by-election of 1898. Ambushed, Tarte quietly dropped his case.

Feeling free as he had been when directing *L'Echo des Deux-Montagnes* and *La Liberté*, Langlois undertook to purify his vision of Liberal progressivism in the context of the Montreal, Light, Heat and Power Company's economic and political clout. In April 1903, as *Le Canada* went to press for the first time, the directors of the Montreal Light, Heat, and Power Company asked the Lighting Committee of Montreal's City Council to reimburse the $778 it had deducted from the company's invoice because of defective service.[40] Until that time, the Montreal Light, Heat, and Power Company had not received much attention. The reasons for this were simple. The company still faced competition from the Lachine Rapids Hydraulic and Land Company, which enjoyed the support of many industrial and financial interests in Montreal and which itself had purchased three small steam stations which would allow it to compete with the Montreal Light, Heat and Power Company in the city.[41] But the competition was short lived, as the Montreal Light, Heat, and Power Company bought out its competitor in 1903. With that purchase, people finally realized that the Montreal Light Heat and Power company was now in complete control of the Montreal market.[42]

These new revelations fuelled the Liberal progressive campaign during the municipal elections of 1904. The Liberal progressives were challenged as never before by the conservative faction of the Liberal party who saw it in its interests to protect the concerns of the Montreal Light, Heat, and Power Company. This was made obvious in the municipal elections of 1904 when the legitimacy of this company's privileges became an issue.

James Cochrane had disappointed many with his lacklustre performance as mayor. Sensing the opportunity of running against a weak incumbent, Ucal-Henri Dandurand (no relation to Raoul Dandurand) declared that he would run against Cochrane. Dandurand, an obscure quantity most political observers had never even heard of, was a long-time protégé of Raymond Préfontaine, and a member of the Liberal party. Dandurand's candidacy was viewed dimly by many in the Liberal party. "Either Dandurand will be elected by inexcusable means and with people of dubious reputations, making his election one in which no one will be able to take pride, or he will be crushed, which will help neither the government, nor Préfontaine," commented L.O. David. "Why is it that Préfontaine is always on the suspicious side that never says anything good. I would understand voting for Cochrane, but for Dandurand, it is simply ridiculous and even dangerous for the party."[43]

Undaunted, Dandurand ran on the promise that he would secure cheap rates for electricity in Montreal. His candidacy, however, raised even more doubts when it attracted the public support not only of Préfontaine, but also Henri-Benjamin Rainville, who was a director of the Montreal Light, Heat, and Power Company. Even *La Presse*, now increasingly aware of the threat posed by the hydroelectric monopoly, began to reconsider the political support it had traditionally given to various individuals. "No good reason can be put forward to defend Mr. U. Dandurand's candidacy," declared *La Presse*, "at a time when many names can be invoked to fight him and to convince the electors of the dangers to the city his election would bring about."[44]

Dandurand was quickly branded as the protector of Herbert Holt's Montreal Light, Heat, and Power Company. To fight him, Hormisdas Laporte, a long-standing reformer of no obvious political affiliation, soon also declared his candidacy for mayor. He naturally was seen as the anti-trust candidate. The hapless Cochrane stood in the middle, unable to define where he stood on the issue. Concluded *La Presse*: "the character of the opposition and of this struggle is now in clear focus: It is either the triumph or the defeat of the monopolies."[45]

In light of the dramatic struggle for the mayoralty, the aldermanic contests were far less exciting, as 20 of the 36 aldermen were acclaimed two weeks before polling day. Langlois and *Le Canada* had reason to adopt a rather aloof attitude. Fifteen Liberal progressive incumbents had been returned without even having to face opponents. Gaspard Desserres, a Liberal newcomer who had distinguished himself with bitter criticisms of the Montreal Light, Heat and Power Company was also elected by acclamation. The Liberal progressives had finally won the race before it even started. Only S.D. Vallières, Henry Ekers and Paul Martineau were challenged.

Conspicuous during these elections was Henri-Benjamin Rainville, the Speaker of the Legislative Assembly who had so eloquently defended the incorporation of the Montreal Light, Heat, and Power Company in 1901 and who had been rewarded with a position on its board of directors. In this election, Rainville ran in Duvernay ward, and Calixte Lebeuf, the legendary radical who had defeated him in the 1900 race, inexplicably broke with his past and ran with Rainville's support in Quartier Centre ward. It seemed as though the Holt-Forget trust was ready to defend its ground. Seven politicians could now be easily detected as protectors of the trusts: Lebeuf, who finally revealed that he would act as the

Montreal Light, Heat and Power's attorney, Giroux, Rainville, Larivière, Ouimet, Lespérance and Chaussé. The trust had candidates willing to defend its interests at a time when it was most needed. Indeed, Montreal was to renegotiate its gas contract during the 1904-1906 tenure, as well as debate the contentious issue of burying electrical hardware, a costly and monopoly-threatening proposition to the Montreal Light, Heat and Power Company.

The party, as L.O. David feared, was again divided. From the middle of January 1904 until the election in February, the "trustards" were denounced in speeches, editorials, and telling cartoons. In the end, the association with the Montreal Light, Heat and Power Company proved politically lethal. Hormisdas Laporte was triumphantly elected Mayor, defeating Dandurand by a record margin. Lebeuf was not reelected and Rainville was trounced, although two of the trusts' defenders, Larivière and Chaussé, were reelected. The turncoat Lebeuf was humiliated and was denied the reimbursement of his candidacy's deposit. The only Liberal progressive casualty in the election was the veteran Paul Martineau, who lost by an handful of votes. In all, nineteen Liberal progressives would sit on City Council. Fifteen of them had won by acclamation, and four more were elected in regular contests: Gallery, Ekers, Vallières and J. St-Denis, the Liberal who defeated Calixte Lebeuf.

The Montreal Light, Heat, and Power had become a political issue capable of destroying those who did not handle it carefully. Liberal progressivism in Montreal had found an issue that would legitimate its rebirth after three difficult and often unbearable years under Simon-Napoléon Parent. The discovery that some business interests were corrupting Liberal politics fuelled Liberal progressivism.[46] "Must we be bled dry?" cried out a Langlois editorial in February 1904. The Montreal Light, Heat, and Power had again asked for a 20% increase in its lighting rates in order to pay off its acquisition of the Lachine Water and Land Company.[47] Indeed, the Liberal progressive faction had found an issue likely to

strengthen its coalition. Though they still did not enjoy a
majority of the seats in Municipal Council, they had finally
defeated the Préfontaine machine Goliath and served warning to the protectors of the trusts that Liberalism would not
be its shield. Langlois could speak of a "liberal renaissance"
in February 1904 with a rare confidence.[48]

Notes

1. *Le Canada*, editorial, 22 février 1904.
2. Laurier Papers, "de St-Roch" to Laurier, 27 février 1902. For Parent's
   early comments on Lane, See Laurier Papers, C781, Parent to Laurier,
   23 novembre 1900.
3. Louis Hartz, *The Liberal Tradition in America* (New York, 1964). p. 232.
4. On this point, see C. Armstrong and H.V. Nelles, "Contrasting Development of the Hydro-Electric Industry in the Montreal and Toronto
   Regions, 1900-1930", *JCS*, Spring 1983, p.7.
5. *La Presse*, 16 mars 1901.
6. McGill Special Collections, H.B. Ames Papers, "City Council Diary,
   Sept.1, 1900-Sept. 1. 1901" pp. 125-126.
7. *La Patrie*, editorial, 14 mars 1901.
8. PAC, W.D. Lighthall Papers, Vol. 2. Lighthall to William Minto, March
   15, 1901.
9. *La Presse*, 16 mars 1901.
10. *JCLPQ*, Vol. XXXV (Quebec, 1901), pp. 96-98.
11. H.B. Ames Papers, Diary, op.cit., p. 135.
12. It is interesting to note that the City of Westmount also registered
    similar complaints. See Lighthall Papers, Vol.2. "Petition to his honour
    the Lieutenant Governor in Council," March 25, 1900.
13. Cited in C. Armstrong and H.V. Nelles, *Monopoly's Moment* (Philadel-
    phia, 1986), p. 143.
14. *La Presse*, 6 avril 1901.
15. PAC, Dandurand-Marchand Papers, Tarte to Dandurand, 24 octobre
    1901.
16. *La Patrie*, editorial, 20 janvier 1902.
17. PAC, Laurier Papers, C790, David to Laurier, 22 janvier 1902.
18. *Ibidem*, Laurier to David, 25 janvier 1902.
19. *La Presse*, 31 janvier 1902.
20. *Ibidem*, 3 février 1902.
21. Paul Rutherford, *The Making of the Canadian Media* (Toronto, 1978),
    pp. 65-72.

22. Laurier Papers, C795, Monet to Laurier, 31 octobre 1902.

23. *Ibidem*, Stephens to Laurier, October 22, 1902.

24. *Ibidem*, Dansereau to Laurier, 21 octobre 1902.

25. *Ibidem*, C796, Langlois to Laurier, 5 novembre 1902.

26. *Ibidem*, "An Old Liberal" to Laurier, November 5, 1902.

27. *Ibidem*, Dandurand to Laurier, 31 octobre 1902.

28. *Ibidem*, C795, Préfontaine to Laurier, 22 octobre 1902.

29. See, for example, Laurier Papers, C 790, Anonymous to Laurier, n.d. (#61175-61182).

30. *La Patrie*, 4 janvier 1903; Dandurand-Marchand Papers, Tarte to Dandurand, 5 janvier 1903.

31. On Laurier and political patronage see Gordon T. Steward, "Political Patronage under Macdonald and Laurier, 1878-1911" *ARCS*, Spring 1980. See also Paul Stevens, "Wilfrid Laurier: Politician" in Marcel Hamelin (ed.) *Les idées politiques des premiers ministres du Canada* (Ottawa, 1969); Gordon T. Stewart, *The Origins of Canadian Politics* (Vancouver, 1986) and Geoffrey Simpson, *Spoils of Power: The Politics of Patronage* (Toronto, 1988).

32. Laurier Papers, C792, Dansereau to Laurier, 20 octobre 1902.

33. *Ibidem*, C797, Pacaud to Laurier, 28 janvier 1903.

34. *Ibidem*, Laurier to Béique, 27 janvier 1903.

35. *Ibidem*, C789, Langlois to Laurier, 23 février 1903.

36. *Ibidem*, C802, Langlois to Laurier, 3 juillet 1903.

37. *Ibidem*, C800, Langlois to Laurier, 12 mai 1903. Many feared that *Le Canada* would not surpass *La Patrie*. See Laurier Papers, C801, Fréchette to Laurier, 8 juin 1903; Laurier to Fréchette, 9 juin 1903.

38. *Ibidem*, C803, Langlois to Laurier, 3 juillet 1903.

39. *Ibidem*, C810, Langlois to Laurier, 12 avril 1904.

40. *La Presse*, editorial, 25 avril 1903.

41. John Dales, *Hydroelectricity and Industrial Development in Quebec, 1898-1940* (Toronto, 1957), p. 104.

42. *Ibidem*, p. 105.

43. Laurier Papers, C817, David to Laurier, 16 janvier 1904.

44. *La Presse*, editorial, 21 janvier 1904.

45. *Ibidem*.

46. On this point, see R.L. McCormick, "The Discovery that Business Corrupts Politics: A reappraisal of the origins of progressivism", *AHR*, April 1981.

47. *Le Canada*, editorial, 22 février 1904.

48. *Ibidem*, editorial, 6 février 1904.

CHAPTER VII

THE TRIUMPH

SIMON-NAPOLÉON PARENT'S second anniversary in power, in November 1902, was a happy occasion. Even Charles Langelier could report at the beginning of 1903 that "the affairs of the party are going very well here. Never have our friends in the Assembly been so united. Caucus has been most agreeable. No complaints against the Ministers."[1] *La Presse*, a consistent and hearty supporter of Parent, was under the same impression. "All the members are in perfect agreement on all points with the Parent cabinet," it observed.[2]

If things seemed to run smoothly within the parliamentary caucus, the same could not be said about the extra-parliamentary party where the apparent consensus was rapidly decaying. Montreal's municipal politics had shown since 1900 that Parent's allies were not well received in some circles. Even in Quebec City, his supposed fortress, Parent enjoyed far from unanimous support. In March of 1903, the exuberant Alfred Lane embarrassed the Premier in the Legislative Assembly to the point where Parent complained to his friend in the federal cabinet, Charles Fitzpatrick. "He took me apart on the issue of amending the charter of Quebec City," Parent lamented, "he said in front of the entire assembly that he did not recognize me as the leader and that he had the full confidence of Sir Wilfrid. His speech, in sum, was that of a complete political adversary."[3] Some of Lane's speeches evidently hit their targets, but pressures were being exerted from all sides. Indeed, by the winter of 1904, sensing his declining popularity, but citing health reasons, Parent let it be known that he was preparing to step down. Apparently, the post of chairman of the commission responsible for the construction of the proposed National Transcontinental Railway from Moncton to Winnipeg had been proposed to him. The rumour circulated that he would be replaced either by Horace Archambault of Adélard Turgeon, two men who had, among other things, repeatedly defended the Montreal Light, Heat, and Power Company's interests.[4]

Prompted by such annoying prospects, Godfroy Langlois revealed his thoughts on the leadership of the Quebec party to Laurier. "I believe it to be my duty as a good Liberal to tell you again that the rise to power of either Mr. Archambault or Mr. Turgeon would be absolutely contrary to the accepted interests of our party in the province of Quebec," he told the Prime Minister of Canada in a sensitive and passionate letter worth quoting at length.

> If you want the province of Quebec to be governed by the Forgets [refering to Rodolphe Forget, a founder and Vice-President of the Montreal Light, Heat, and Power], then this arrangement would be suitable. You remember, no doubt, I remember and everybody remembers the role played by Mr. Archambault, by Mr. Turgeon, by Mr. Rainville in that scandalous session when the Montreal Light Heat and Power made it rain or shine at will in the provincial parliament. [...] At this point, the Liberals of the province of Quebec wish and desire to see Mr. Parent retire, because he has driven your party to insignificance and unpopularity in the last three years. They ask for a Prime Minister who will not be compromised, a man with sufficient probity and energy to give our party the prestige and the popularity it has lost.
>
> You will not find, I am sure, serious and sincere Liberals in the entire city of Montreal who would not tell you that the advent to power of either Mr. Archambault or Mr. Turgeon would be filled with peril for the Liberal cause.
>
> In either case, dear Mr. Laurier, if a change in Prime Ministers must throw us, bound hand and foot, in the offices of the Forgets, I would much rather stay under the Parent regime. [...]
>
> But I wish to repeat that to stay longer under the Parent regime is, for the Liberal party, to walk to an inevitable disaster.[5]

If some of Montreal's Liberal progressives were still hesitant to condemn the Premier during the municipal elections of 1904, Parent's actions in the spring of that year only reaffirmed the perception of many regarding his corruption. In May, the Legislative Council adopted a resolution that aimed at restricting any future power company from penetrating an area without the consent of the local authorities. In other words, the conditions that allowed the Montreal Light, Heat, and Power Company to expand and exercise its virtual monopoly in Montreal would not be extended to its competitors. The Holt-Forget trust, however, would be allowed to retain the prerogatives it had received earlier.

Langlois's *Le Canada* saw in this new rule that the Montreal Light, Heat, and Power Company would be protected by blatant double standards. "Why does the upper house now want to close the door to competitors? At the risk of dishonouring itself forever, it cannot become the champion of private corporations and serve the interest of a trust." The Legislative Council was preventing fair competition in Montreal, according to Langlois. "We estimate," he continued, "that it [the Montreal Light, Heat, and Power Company] treats the public in a provocative fashion by increasing, as it has, its electricity rates and its prices for gas to onerous levels. It will have more respect for the poor taxpayer when it feels the heat of competition."[6]

The matter came to the political forefront when the Legislative Council decided to exercise its new authority as the Shawinigan Electric Company, the Terrebonne Electric, and the Laval Electric (all relatively small companies), applied for their charters. In all three cases, the provision given to the Montreal Light, Heat and Power was denied them. The Canadian Light and Power Company's bid for a charter was also affected. For Langlois the outrageous move was a deliberate attempt to curtail the powers of the potentially strong competitor in Montreal.

In the Liberal party, anger focused on Horace Archambault, who had again protected the interest of the trust. In vain, Archambault defended his position to Wilfrid Laurier. "I have in no way influenced the opinion of any member of the Legislative Assembly or in the Legislative Council on those bills," he pleaded: "Two or three of our friends came to see me about them, and I told them that these were private members bills and that they were free to vote on these measures according to their own views."[7] Lomer Gouin again denounced the bills proposed by his colleagues. In a splendid speech, he excoriated the house for its disregard of the rights of Montreal's citizenry, and moved that the bill incorporating the Montreal Light, Heat, and Power Company also be amended so as to ensure that municipalities be consulted before it expanded. His motion was rejected.[8] *La Presse* had incisive words regarding the majority who had rejected Gouin's amendments: "This majority is not political, it is exclusively financial and for private interests. It is composed of Liberals and of Conservatives united by maneuvers that have been evident since the beginning of this session," wrote *La Presse's* editor. In conclusion, the latter astutely predicted that "the last word in this painful affair has not been said and the trust could well learn that some victories come at a dear cost."[9] Indeed, the parliamentary session of the "electricity trust"[10] would haunt Parent for the next months.

Protest also came from Quebec City. Echoing Alfred Lane, recriminations now came from Philippe-Auguste Choquette. Intransigent, infuriated, Choquette had spent four years as a judge in Montreal and was impatient to return to active politics. He considered himself a *vieux rouge*, and consistently lived up to his profession of faith. A member of the Quebec legislature in the late 1880s, he had virulently opposed tying Liberal fortunes to Mercier's *Parti national*, had supported Charles Langelier in the politically bloody anti-Tarte Lévis 1898 by-election, causing Laurier to angrily dismiss him as a mere "kicker".[11] He had retired from active politics when Marchand named him to the bench in 1899 over Cléophas Beausoleil. Choquette has lived the transition from radical *rougisme* to Liberal progressivism at the turn of the century. He had joined Langlois's *Ligue de l'Enseignement*, but could not actively participate in electoral contests in light of the necessary impartiality a position on the bench required. Like most radicals, Choquette had hoped to see Joseph Robidoux lead the Liberals after Marchand's death and had never warmed to the idea of Parent leading the party. "I have always opposed Parent, I always will," he admitted to a reporter. "I was a judge when they made the mistake of choosing him as leader, as Prime Minister of the French province of Quebec. What could I do? Shrug and keep quiet. If only I could have spoken!"[12]

But Choquette could no longer repress his political ambitions. He had trouble hiding the fact that he wanted to be mayor of Quebec City, a post still held by his hated nemesis, Simon-Napoléon Parent. In 1903, he had been frustrated in his attempt to buy out Ernest Pacaud's *Le Soleil*, which was staunchly in support of Parent. Parent had complained of Choquette's intentions, insisting that the latter had published vicious articles against the government in a Quebec-area newspaper in part owned by Choquette, *Le Courrier de Montmagny*.[13] Laurier agreed that Choquette should not be allowed to have access to *Le Soleil*. He told Parent that it was difficult to muzzle the impetuous Choquette and counselled patience, while scolding Choquette:[14] "Is it not a publicly known fact that Parent is the constant object of your attacks?" Laurier wrote to the dissident, "and that every time you find yourself with a circle of friends, poor old Parent is pitilessly torn to shreds."[15]

Choquette decided to rebuild his base of support in the old capital, and it was Laurier, ironically, who offered him the opportunity. Notwithstanding diverging views on Parent, Laurier wanted Choquette to use his considerable prestige to organize the Liberal forces in the Quebec City area for an election he was planning for the fall of 1904. Choquette accepted Laurier's offer of returning to politics on the condition that a Senate seat would be his, or at least the Speakership in the Commons.[16] Laurier flatly refused to consider Choquette's bid for Speaker, but did intimate that a Senate seat would be forthcoming if things worked out in Quebec City.[17] By the summer of 1904, Choquette had decided to leave his post as judge and to seek the post of chief Liberal organizer in the Quebec City district.[18]

Within weeks, the two Quebec City power companies announced that they had jointly agreed to raise their rates by 25%. The issue of electricity rate increases gave Choquette an ideal atmosphere in which to re-enter politics.[19] The issue provided him with a platform on which to criticize Parent as both mayor and Premier. Choquette successfully completed the job Laurier had assigned him for the November 1904 election and was duly compensated with the Senate seat he so desired. The unexpected provincial election, however, created a rift between Choquette and the Quebec City party establishment.

Traditional explanations have suggested that Parent called a snap election in November 1904 to ride the coattails of the Laurier victory and take advantage of a discouraged and distraught Conservative Party, as he had done in 1900. This reason can only explain part of the decision. Parent surprised everybody with his announcement, including all of his cabinet ministers. He had long claimed that he would resign after the federal elections, and indeed, many people counted on his resignation.[20] But Parent knew that the progressives in his party were finding new steam with Godfroy Langlois heading *Le Canada*, Lomer Gouin pestering the government in the Legislative Assembly over hydro-electric policy and now "Senator" Choquette firmly at the helm of the Liberal organization in Quebec City. Parent had to reaffirm his authority and needed the right occasion. The Laurier victory in November 1904 provided a perfect opportunity to catch the Liberal progressives off-guard and to save his own political skin. He could count on their loyalty to the party and to Laurier, and certainly did not expect them to challenge the incumbents. Lomer Gouin, already the most talked-about successor to the Premiership, had just lost his wife and could be expected to be incapacitated by grief for a time.

With these calculations in mind, Parent called the election on November 6, with the nomination deadline set on the 18th and the election itself on the 25th. There would not be enough time to organize support, generate propaganda and win nominating conventions in such a short time. The radicals would only embarrass the party, he undoubtedly thought, and Laurier surely would not let them. Parent's announcement of the election reflected well these factors. "During the last session, and since," he said, "the press and others have raised accusations against certain members of the Assembly and against the entire magistrature of Quebec. The good name and the honour of the province demands that these detractors of our provincial assembly be in a position to prove their accusations and to identify to the electors those among their representatives who have been guilty of the alleged acts of corruption that are allowed to weigh against the entire legislature. If these accusations are well founded, the elections will provide opportunities for the accusers to make their cases and to have the guilty judged by the people, who is in such matters the sovereign arbiter. The members of the government and the members of the legislature who support the government are ready to face their detractors face to face, in front of the free and independent voters of the province, to show the malice and the falseness of the accusations levelled against them by their adversaries."[21]

Confident though he seemed to appear, for *La Presse*[22] and Tarte's *La Patrie*[23] were to support him in Montreal, Parent could not count on the active backing of Laurier who, exhausted from his own campaign, was leaving for a desperately needed rest in Colorado. Nor could he count on support from the emerging progressive wing of his party. Indeed, it took much less time for the Liberal progressives to organize than Parent anticipated. Almost six years of struggle against the Préfontaine clique had brought together many people who were naturally inclined to fight Parent.

Le Canada did its partisan duty by pledging its support to Parent in its November 7 editorial, but that same night, Godfroy Langlois immediately set out to mobilize his supporters. The Liberals of his riding were meeting to choose their candidate that evening. Judging this to be a routine matter, the Chairman offered the Liberal nomination to the incumbent, Henri-Benjamin Rainville, the Speaker of the Legislative Assembly and the *bête noire* of all progressive Liberals. As a cable sent by Parent was read confirming the Premier's personal endorsement of his candidacy, Rainville had a right to think he had clinched the designation as the Liberal candidate. It was then that Godfroy Langlois demanded the right to speak. Standing before the howling crowd he interrupted the proceedings and defiantly proposed that the nomination be put to a vote. The Chairman refused to agree to Langlois's request, but he was shouted down. Only a dozen people out of approximately sixty were favourable to the incumbent, according to press reports. It was immediately clear that the Rainville nomination was not popular, and the meeting soon turned into a frenzied debate. Numerous people argued in favour of Langlois's motion and demanded that the nomination be put to a vote. Albert Saint-Martin, the fiery labour leader, eloquently defended Langlois's audacity. Langlois also received support from his aldermen friends, including Louis A. Lapointe and Louis Payette who spoke loudly in his favour. By 11:00 p.m., the meeting had reached an unresolvable impasse, and it was agreed that another nominating convention be held the following day.

Concerned with this unexpected challenge, Parent appealed to the federal Liberals to placate Langlois. "I have learned that Mr. Godfroy Langlois, editor at *Le Canada*, intends to present himself in opposition to the hon. H.B. Rainville," Parent informed Senator Béique, Langlois's boss. "In the spirit [...] of avoiding a division between the Liberals of that district," he concluded in his letter, "I pray of you and of your friends to use your influence so that Mr. Langlois does not persist in his demands that could only create embarrassment for the government."[24] Béique, a long-time supporter and sponsor of Liberal progressivism in Montreal, refused to intervene, although he was sensitive to the divisive impact Langlois's challenge to Rainville could present. "I appreciate the necessity of avoiding division among the Liberals, but the best way to accomplish this is not to go against public opinion, especially here," he told Parent, adding that "there were in the legislature that was just dissolved, Liberal and Conservative elements that were harming the well understood interests of your government as well as those of the public, and it is urgent to make them disappear."[25]

Parent finally realized that he was in trouble in Montreal. F.X. Dupuis, the member for Châteauguay and a loyal Parent supporter, observed that "the war against the trust [...] has been openly declared [...] by many, but it is but a pretext for most of them, for those who have been shooting you in the back for four years. Your friends here [...] should have known this and advised you in light of this."[26] Dupuis's letter bore witness to Parent's bad interpretations of Montreal's political history since 1898. Worse still, according to Dupuis, the only people supporting Rainville were the members of the Conservative party and a few select Liberals such as the detested Archambault and Préfontaine!"[27]

Parent's stubborn support for Rainville and others who had supported the Montreal Light, Heat, and Power Company angered many other Liberals. Lomer Gouin marched into the Premier's office and tendered his resignation from cabinet, on the grounds that cabinet solidarity had been breached by the Premier as he had not consulted any of his colleagues in deciding which candidates should enjoy cabinet support. Parent refused his resignation, and significantly, Gouin did not persist. He knew his base of support had not yet proven itself, and that he needed more support in the caucus for a resignation to have the *fracas* he wanted.

As Montreal Liberals anxiously waited to see the outcome of the scheduled party convention in the St-Louis riding, it was obvious that Rainville was not a popular man. Close to six hundred people gathered in the Salle St-Joseph on November 8. Ucal Dandurand, the defeated mayoralty candidate earlier in the year, nominated Rainville, and thirteen men raised their hands in his favour. The crowd instantly hollered its support for Langlois, a quick count was taken, and the short, rotund journalist was hoisted to the platform and offered the nomination.

Langlois proudly accepted the honour, and took his seat on the platform to listen to some of his supporters regaling themselves with what had just taken place. Senator Raoul Dandurand raged: "Well then, gentlemen," he intoned, "will the representative of the Montreal Light, Heat and Power Company have the audacity to present himself before you and say 'I have mocked you, I have fooled you, now re-elect me!' I do not think, gentlemen, that Mr. Rainville will dare act in this fashion. He will not want to oppose this nomination, he will not do it."[28] Others rose to speak in favour of Langlois, including labour leaders such as Senator H.J. Cloran, one of the founders of the Montreal chapter of the Trades and Labour Congress.

Langlois eventually stood before his electors and spoke eloquently, choosing to direct his pitch to those who had come to overthrow Rainville. "I present myself the champion of people's rights against the 'trusts' who have crushed and intimidated us," he said. "The trusts will not prevent me from speaking and to attempt to make my views known [...]. I will bring my attention to bear on the all-important issues of colonisation and of public education. We must tool the new generation for the struggle for life and it is to this great question that I will be devoted."[29]

Dandurand and Langlois were wrong to assume that Rainville would accept defeat and fade away. Instead, the incumbent declared that he would run for reelection on an "Independent Liberal" ticket, ranting publicly that a Legislative Council seat would be his if he was defeated. Parent evidently supported Rainville's resolve to ignore the nominating convention's decision, as he said nothing to counter that boast. It was then that some of Quebec's most powerful Senators protested to the party's chief arbiter, Wilfrid Laurier: "If you think like me that the nomination of Rainville to the Council would be a misfortune, you would be right to talk about it with Parent," thundered Dandurand. "What we all think here about Rainville we also think about Archambault who is also in the trust."[30] Senator Béique added another voice to the dissenting chorus. "The issue in the St-Louis division, presents itself, it seems to me, in a similarly unpredictable manner in other ridings, especially where the provincial cabinet members are seen," he told Laurier. "We will only avoid division in our ranks, the division the Conservatives are counting on, as long as we have a Government in Quebec City in which we can have total trust. [...] There must be in our party the elements of progress, of honesty and of vigilance that the circumstances require: some new men of value [...].[31]

Similarly, Dandurand summarized the situation to Parent himself in an unequivocal manner: "Rainville will be crushed in St-Louis because he coldly sold out his electors and the city of Montreal to the Montreal Light and Heat that has done its best to intimidate us since it has become the master of the area," he argued. "Don't believe that we are oblivious to the influences that have borne on the two levels of the legislature in the constitution and the protection of this trust. We even know who has an interest in Forget and in the Light and Heat."[32] Continuing, Dandurand spared no words in attacking Parent over the possible nomination of Rainville to the Legislative Council:

> [...] the Legislative Council that must be composed of independent and steady men has not responded to our expectations because of the fact that certain Councillors had an interest in the Light and Heat. Now, I hear that Mr. Rainville is bragging that he can be named to the Legislative Council within 24 hours of his defeat or of his withdrawal.

It is against this public calamity that I come to protest in the name of the city of Montreal. If we have not been able to receive justice from the Council over the last few years, what will the next twenty years be like if you install there the direct representative of the trust?

It is in the name of common sense and of elementary justice that I urge you to beware.[33]

Defending the moderates of the Liberal party was Israël Tarte, who focused his ferocious attacks on his former editor. Questioning Langlois's credibility and exhuming the latter's mysterious links with the *Loge l'Emancipation*, Tarte conjured up scenarios of a province governed by Langlois and godless hooligans if Rainville was defeated.[34] Raymond Préfontaine, for once united with Tarte, confided to Laurier that he expected to see Rainville win his battle against Langlois. "Being in full sympathy with Rainville who has always been, for over thirty years, one of my loyal friends [...] I have all reasons to believe that Rainville will be elected," he told Laurier.[35]

Langlois was not alone in challenging Parent's cabinet. J.C. Walsh, the mercurial editor of the Liberal Montreal *Herald* went after John James Guerin, a lacklustre Minister without Portfolio. Walsh's candidacy, also opposed by Parent,[36] was orchestrated by alderman Daniel Gallery, a pillar of the Liberal progressive movement since its inception in the late 1890s.[37] Things went scarcely better for Parent in Quebec City. Senator Philippe-Auguste Choquette was complaining publicly that the articles he was submitting to *Le Soleil* were being censored by Parent's loyal friend, Ernest Pacaud. Laurier was livid at Choquette's taunts. "I have always believed and I believe still in Parent's honesty. I have always deplored and I deplore still the attacks which he has had to suffer," Laurier tenaciously held.[38] Choquette had agreed to work as an organizer in the provincial election, but quickly came to the conclusion that Parent was double-crossing members of the party in the Charlevoix riding.[39] Parent was apparently supporting a P. Dauteil, a former Conservative and a friend of Rodolphe Forget of the Montreal Light, Heat, and Power Company, who was challenging the local nominating convention's choice, an act which infuriated Choquette. The Liberals of the riding had elected Dr. Synotte, a radical whose campaign had been organized by Choquette. He hurried to Parent's residence upon hearing of the declaration to get an explanation. "Instead of speaking as a gentleman, [Parent] spoke like a spoiled-brat," Choquette later recalled.[40] "If you are not happy, go to hell!" Parent told him, "I have already got the majority elected!"[41]

"It is you who will soon go to hell!" responded the Senator as he stormed out of the house.[42] Choquette promptly set out to support the local radicals in the Quebec-Est and Quebec-Ouest ridings. On the day of the election, Choquette publicly branded Parent as a "miserable traitor" for supporting Dauteil against Synotte. Immediately, the capital city was afire while Parent mounted a campaign to discredit Choquette. Choquette held an open-air meeting on St-Valier street the following day but was subjected to a hostile demonstration of opposition when he spoke. Dodging stones and facing relentless heckling, Choquette and his supporters sought refuge in a nearby tavern on rue des Fosses where he resumed his criticism of Parent: "There are members who have thought like me for a long time on the subject of the Prime Minister and the only thing that stopped them in this moment of battle was party solidarity. Before long we will be rid of this autocrat and parvenu [...]. Enough of this reign of terror [...]. Mr. Parent is incapable of anything, and he has but one talent, that of organizing hoodlums to break the heads of those who don't think like him."[43]

Choquette repeated his threat to launch a newspaper that would compete with Le Soleil's hegemony over Liberal debates in the capital city, but before any of his supporters could speak, the power supply to the tavern was cut, throwing the assembly into frightening darkness. Things got worse as the bullies that had pelted Choquette earlier on the street were forcing their way into the confused meeting.[44] Panic erupted, and the assembly broke up instantly, with Choquette literally running for his life.[45]

The election was marked with Liberal strife. With 35 Liberals elected by acclamation following the announcement of a partial boycott of the election by the Conservatives, Liberals fought other Liberals in seventeen ridings. The Conservative Party contested fifteen ridings. Four constituencies became battleground between Liberals and local Labour parties, and in this great tide of reform only one seat was sought in the name of the "Ligue nationaliste".

Parent and the Liberal party won a resounding victory, exactly as Parent had predicted. In the end, 38 Liberals won by acclamation, and 30 more were elected at the polls. The Liberals improved on their 1900 standing by winning 68 seats (one more than in 1900), and by maintaining roughly 87% of the popular vote, if elections-by-acclamations are taken into considerations. The Conservative Party held onto most of its seats, losing only one.[46] Parent's inner circle fared less well, however. Langlois defeated Rainville by 225 votes and Walsh beat J.J. Guerin with a 397 vote plurality. Choquette's influence was felt in Quebec City as incumbent Liberals in the Quebec-Est and Quebec-Ouest ridings were defeated by radicals of Choquette's ilk, and as Dr. Synotte was elected in Charlevoix. Clearly, Choquette had some success.

What had also been wrecked was party discipline, and Parent had to glue together the pieces of his fractured cabinet with a fortified progressive wing shadowing him. "There are strong spirits who want to change everything," observed S. Chérrier, the member for Laprairie.[47] But Laurier was as optimistic as ever. "There were a few setbacks as it is inevitable in these contests, but even those setbacks do not appear to offer serious dangers," confidently remarked the vacationing Prime Minister.[48]

On November 28, three days after the most crushing electoral victory ever recorded in Quebec history, Lomer Gouin arranged to meet Choquette in Quebec City. Adélard Turgeon joined them. It was decided that the campaign of public criticism against Parent that had been instigated by Godfroy Langlois should be continued. Two days later, when both Gouin and Turgeon threatened to resign if Rainville was named a Legislative Councillor, Choquette called on the newly elected members of the Liberal party not to commit themselves to supporting the Premier. "Let me tell you that I ask you to do this in the interest of the party; and that when you will know all the reasons that have led me to make this request, you will be satisfied," Senator Choquette explained in a letter addressed to each new Liberal parliamentarian, hoping no doubt that there would be a solidification of progressive opinion within the party.[49]

F.X. Dupuis, the member for Châteauguay, and Parliamentary Godfather to the Montreal Light, Heat and Power Company, responded publicly to Choquette's request. "From which authority do you personally attempt to decapitate the Liberal government of the province of Quebec? And you hold this conduct while our leader Sir Wilfrid Laurier is absent," Dupuis chided Choquette.[50] Privately, the Parent loyalist then asked Choquette to deliver his proof of Parent's dishonesty. "Not only do I invite you to give me these details, but I challenge you to do so. If there are things in my political life that prevents me from walking with pride, I want to know, and, if you are a gentleman, as I believe you are, you will speak frankly."[51] Choquette released Dupuis's letter to the press and their subsequent exchange also found its way into the pages of the dailies, with Dupuis staunchly defending his leader. The final publication of the letters was made on December 24th, with Choquette summarily ending the battle. "You are the only one to write as you do," he told Dupuis in an open letter. "Stay in your ridiculous interpretations."[52]

Political discussions that Christmas turned to the unity of the Liberal party and the future of its leader in Quebec. The task of mending the wounds and seeking compromise was proving insurmountable and Laurier decided to cut short his Colorado holiday in order to settle the Quebec question. "I hope the trip did some good to the boss," mused Charles

Langelier. "It is time he returned, because there is a lot of squabbling in the party. It is a good thing we are strong. He should do well to come to Quebec City to consult the friends, because there is a considerable movement against Parent."[53] Laurier not only had to confront the cold of Quebec City in winter, but the cold war that had paralysed his party in his own backyard.

Laurier followed Langelier's suggestion. Almost as soon as he arrived in Canada, he made arrangements to meet Gouin and Langlois at the Windsor Hotel in Montreal to investigate the situation.[54] Laurier then travelled to Quebec City where he dined with Choquette and various members of the Legislature. A few of the known "Parentistes" who had been invited, such as Cyrille Delage and Georges Tanguay, were apparently ordered by Parent not to attend the diner, and did not appear. Laurier was furious at Parent's disrespect of the reconciliation process. Hoping to end the tensions, Lieutenant-Governor Jetté then invited Wilfrid Laurier and Parent to dine at Spencerwood, but again Parent called off his engagement at 7:30 p.m., saying that he was "indisposed".[55] Laurier, twice snubbed by his own protégé, promptly returned to Ottawa.

Parent's credibility, never strong but badly undermined by years of neglect, was rapidly eroding. After the election, Senator J.H. Legris, who had presided over a Royal Commission called a year earlier to examine the management of Quebec's Crown Lands and who had found nothing substantial to criticize, suddenly changed his mind and lambasted the Parent administration's of lands, accusing it of corruption. Choquette, vigilant as ever, added oil to the fire by publicly supporting Legris's conclusions. In a desperate attempt to keep the issue out of the public eye, Parent instigated libel suits against the two Senators.

Until January 1905, the only public indication of a party revolt was the Choquette-Dupuis exchange of insults in December. Few words were said to the anxious press, and the Liberal journals were mute. *La Presse* decided to encourage the Liberal struggle. "The public has the right to know which of the members of the legislature support the Hon. Parent; which of the members who want to depose him and which of the members have no opinions," demanded the daily, which sent a similar letter to all MLAs.[56] Seven Liberals answered *La Presse*'s poll. The first, not surprisingly, was F.X. Dupuis.[57] Four other backbenchers voiced their support for Parent, and two declared themselves undecided. Indeed, it remained as difficult as ever to discover who in the parliamentary caucus supported Parent and who did not. Parent did seem to enjoy the dedicated support of many of his anglophone partisans. "Those revolting hotheads in Quebec must be brought to their senses," wrote Tom Trenholme, an eastern county organizer. "If Parent is defeated it will be the beginning of trouble in this province—the English speaking businessmen have every confidence in Parent [...] the trouble is that Parent is too good an administrator for the young ambitious fellows. We want no repetitions of some of the past," he wrote to Laurier, "the serious people are satisfied as things are, let us have no change if possible."[58]

It seemed as though Laurier was content to leave Parent to his misery. "You do not seem to understand the gravity of the situation," he was told, "or you are being misled by the political appearances of our province."[59] Under pressure to act, Laurier resumed his efforts to reconcile the diverging factions of his party in Quebec. The Prime Minister saw Choquette again in Ottawa on January 14th, and managed to convince him to formulate an agreement. Plans were made for Choquette to meet Parent at Senator Pelletier's home in Quebec City. "I hope that you will meet him and that you will leave things as they are until that meeting," Laurier urged Parent.[60] Unimpressed, Parent again refused to meet Choquette in neutral territory. On the night of January 30, he sent his closest aide Alexandre Taschereau to Choquette's residence in order to arrange a meeting between the two adversaries at Taschereau's home. This time, it was Choquette who refused, allegedly for fear of blackmail.[61]

While this was going on, Parent attempted to restore his personal credibility on his own. He chose to initiate a *rapprochement* in late January with Dominique Monet, the newly elected member for Napierville and a close friend of Henri Bourassa. He asked Monet to join the cabinet as Minister without Portfolio, and Monet intimated that while he was interested, he would have to defer his decision. Parent had selected Monet as a suitable candidate because the latter was known to have some personal friendships with progressive Liberals, with conservative Liberals and with the nationalists. The Premier's initiative was not unanimously popular. Raymond Préfontaine shared his worries with the Premier, as did other deputies who considered themselves more deserving.[62] The choice of Monet was tactical: It was a last-ditch attempt to secure the support of a majority in the Legislative Assembly. By choosing Monet, he undoubtedly thought, his willingness to accommodate his detractors would be demonstrated. Monet sought the advice of Langlois, who urged him not to accept the offer, as did the impulsive Olivar Asselin. Henri Bourassa, Monet's mentor, was indifferent, while Israël Tarte urged him to join.[63] Monet finally accepted Parent's invitation and arrived in Quebec City on the night of February 1st. He met Parent at the Château Frontenac and dined with him as they discussed the future of the Quebec cabinet. It was decided that Monet would be sworn in as fast as possible. The deed was done the next morning.

After his swearing in, Monet met Parent and Archambault in the Premier's office. Monet's introduction to the cabinet was discussed for about half-an-hour before the scheduled luncheon cabinet meeting. As they entered the cabinet room, Gouin resolved to act. As he wrote later, "the determining fact took place on February 2nd [...] I have nothing to say against Mr. Monet—I have against Mr. Parent who did not tell me one word of Mr. Monet's entrance—Proof that I was no longer useful [...] I judged that in the interest of the province I had to give my resignation."[64]

That night, Gouin, fortified by the newly elected supporters, forged alliances. A natural ally in cabinet was W.A. Weir. Born in 1858, Weir had attended McGill and taught at McGill's teachers' college before pursuing studies in law. He was admitted to the bar in 1881 and had been elected to the provincial parliament in 1897. In 1903, under pressure to replace George Washington Stephens who had retired in 1901, Parent had made him a Minister without Portfolio. Weir had exemplified Liberal progressivism in his fights for the Grosbois bill, against the Préfontaine machine and against the Montreal Light, Heat, and Power Company. Gouin was approached by Adélard Turgeon also. The latter was of a considerably different political breed: a dashing athlete[65] who had repeatedly spoken against educational reform and who had never said a word against the Montreal Light, Heat, and Power Company. Turgeon's views had become remarkably conservative on most socio-economic matters, and certainly no longer resembled the young-turk radical who had mercilessly pestered the Boucherville and Flynn administrations in the early 1890s. Langlois undoubtedly argued against involving Turgeon as he had in 1904, but Gouin felt a need to compromise in order to attract even broader opposition to Parent. Turgeon remained one of the most experienced cabinet ministers in Quebec and a senior party man capable of giving respectability to the dissenting movement. Besides, Turgeon hated Parent with a passion, always had, and always would.

The trio submitted a collective letter of resignation from cabinet on February 5, 1905. They stated as the main reason for their action Parent's lack of trust in his cabinet. The unilateral dissolution of the Assembly in November, the support given to individuals of dubious reputations without cabinet approval, and finally the secret swearing in of a new minister were cited by the three resigning ministers as proof of a lack of trust. "The malaise felt by the public and of which you are solely responsible convinces us that you do not possess the confidence of the electors of this province," they concluded.[66]

Parent, who only two months earlier had headed the greatest electoral victory in Quebec history, was now in deep trouble. "The cabinet is in complete crisis, discord reigns among us," it was reported to Laurier.[67] Archambault and McCorkill, Parent's Minister of Finance since 1902, departed for Ottawa immediately to explain the situation to Laurier and left the political rumour mill running at capacity. Rainville was widely expected to be named to cabinet as a member of the Legislative Council to fill the void left by the three resigned Montreal-area ministers. Parent was also rumoured to be extremely ill, and Archambault was expected to fill the Premier's shoes while Parent took a vacation in Florida. Nothing was said officially to confirm any of those rumours. Parent could hardly leave to escape a crisis that had been brewing in his party since he had assumed high office.

Choquette was happy with the turn of events. "Now that Mr. Parent is half-broken as Prime Minister, we will take the war to him on the municipal grounds, we will destroy his false reputation as an administrator, the questions of lighting, of tramways and of ferrying will be debated. Our program will include the election of the mayor by the people, as it is done elsewhere," he asserted to a reporter, following the resignation of the three ministers.[68] Again, as he had done in November, Choquette elaborated plans to launch *Le Libéral*, a newspaper that would compete with Pacaud's *Le Soleil*.

The accusations of the three departing Ministers did not seem to shake the Premier from his torpor. "Parent is wrong to hang on to power," observed the old radical L.O. David. "You cannot make the people believe that one can put aside values such as honour and dignity to conquer and keep power, and that one can indifferently absorb the grossest of accusations without responding, without appearing to even understand their importance and their reach! Besides, what is the point of so many plots when in the end, one still has to leave?" he asked Laurier.[69]

Despite the many rumours that a new cabinet was to be reconstructed rapidly, Parent found the task difficult. With the inflow of Liberal progressives into the party as a result of the November 1904 election, Parent knew that his new executive had to meet expectations or be defeated in the Legislature by his own party. His best talents, moreover, were quickly pledging their allegiance to the revolt. Unable to forge an alliance of his own, Parent asked the Lieutenant-Governor to delay the opening of the new Parliament. In the Château Frontenac, meanwhile, a caucus of over fifty Liberal Party members was organized by Gouin's allies on the night of February 8. It was in the elegant lobbies and hallways of this grand hotel that the Liberal progressives played a critically important role. Gouin's challenge to Parent's authority did not automatically receive the approval of what essentially was still a very conservative caucus. One can safely speculate that it was on that evening of political arm-twisting, cajoling and persuading that the legitimacy of the Gouin challenge was established. The three former cabinet ministers spoke to the crowd gathered, as did Godfroy Langlois. Also speaking were Camille Piché, the federal member of the Parliament for the Montreal riding of Ste- Marie; and Achille Bergevin, a journalist who had succeeded Tancrède de Grosbois as deputy in the Legislative Assembly for the riding of Shefford. Both men had long been members of the Liberal party, and had repeatedly proven their loyalty to progressive Liberalism. Piché, always active at the Club level, had helped found *Le Signal* in the mid-1890s with Godfroy Langlois, and had taken an active party in the fight against the Préfontaine clique. Bergevin had often spoken in favour of radical educational reform. Both men had been leading members of the *Ligue de l'Enseignement* and Bergevin had been a member, like Langlois, of its board of directors. A motion of support for the three dissenters was passed with the support of 43 Liberal members of the Legislative Assembly.[70]

Parent's supporters held a similar caucus in the same hotel, but only 38 people showed up at room 119 to listen to Monet,

Archambault and McCorkill give speeches.[71] It was now clear that Parent no longer commanded the backing of a majority of Liberal MLAs, but not being pressed to constitutionally to call the Assembly into session, the argument was that he would hold on to power for eleven more months! Laurier again took it upon himself to convince Parent to resign, hoping to arrange it so that neither he nor his protégé would lose face.

On Sunday February 12, Turgeon and Gouin as well as Parent and Archambault met with Laurier and Raoul Dandurand in Ottawa. Gouin and Turgeon lunched with Laurier and took the 6:00 p.m. train back to Montreal, while Parent finally met with Laurier later that evening. Despite Laurier's renewed attempts to seek reconciliation, Parent staunchly refused to bargain. Three days later, defiant as ever, Parent finally accepted the resignations of his ministers.[72] Parent would thus govern the province with a depleted cabinet of yes-men: Archambault, McCorkill, Monet and Robitaille. A week later, Parent announced that the Legislative session would open on March 2, 1905. Clearly, something had broken since his meeting with Laurier. "Our party is going through a crisis right now whose consequences could be disastrous for the future," the beleaguered Premier confided to Senator Pelletier. "I want to avoid a disaster at all cost [...]. My health is weakened and, no matter what happens now, I cannot stay much longer at the head of the government of Quebec."[73] Parent told Pelletier that he would try to save face by announcing at the opening of the session that a committee would be established to investigate the charges laid against him by Senators Legris and Choquette. Confident of an exoneration, he told Pelletier he would then resign.

Two days after he wrote that letter, Parent finally unveiled his cabinet. The only addition was Némèse Garneau, a lacklustre backbencher. On March 2, as scheduled, the provincial parliament met for the first time since the election. Parent suggested that the dissident MLA Auguste Tellier (who had supported Gouin in the Château Frontenac caucus) be approved as Speaker by the Legislators. A brief throne speech was read, and Parent then rose to address the Assembly. The atmosphere was tense as he denounced those who had accused him of corruption. He proposed that an all-party committee be established to investigate the charges made against him, and sat down.

For the two ensuing weeks the committee headed by Liberal A. Girard made the headlines. On the fifteenth of March, a report was tabled in which Girard admitted that there was little evidence upon which to accuse the Premier. Confident that his honour had been salvaged, Parent lunched at Spencerwood, the Lieutenant-Governor's residence for the last time, and then silently submitted his resignation to his host. Laurier was the first to congratulate his dejected protégé: "I congratulate you on having emerged victorious from all these challenges and to have won, on all counts, the honours of the war."[74]

Parent's honour might have been saved in the eyes of some by the Girard Committee, but Parent was as detested as ever by the progressive faction of the Liberal party. Parent would leave public life four months after recording the greatest electoral victory in the history of the province in as silent a way as he had entered it: unnoticed. The progressives who had worked to unseat him and who had fought his attitudes and policies were the victors. Some could not resist putting in a last few punches. "It is your turn now to recognize that past services count for little in politics. They mattered not in your view on certain occasions (this is the normal effect among those who are intoxicated by power) you are now served in the same manners you served others [...] odd thing, don't you think?" the old radical Louis Fréchette sarcastically told Parent. "Last fall, you were threatening me with destitution for having served dirty intrigues, you were far from suspecting that of the two of us I was not the one to have to pack his bags."[75]

Fréchette was not alone in kicking up his heels to celebrate. Liberals told the reporter of the Montreal *Daily Wit-*

ness that were "elated over what they termed the happy deliverance at last of the province and the party from the tyrannical rule of an autocrat and a boss, who neither by education nor instinct was fitted to lead them, and whose tenure of power had only been maintained by intrigue and a system of espionage and slavery that was altogether foreign to Liberal principles and disastrous to the reputation of Liberalism."[76]

Parent's lonely and quiet departure left the party in a vacuum. It was on March 22, a day after Parent quit, that Gouin was called upon to form the government. He enjoyed the support of the Liberal progressives, but not all Liberals. That night, an anxious Dominique Monet sat at the desk of his Château Frontenac room and left his impressions to Sir Wilfrid Laurier. Monet predicted misfortune for those who might replace him in cabinet. "The history that is recorded, that which goes beyond the lies and the intrigues of politics," Monet observed, "will sully the reputations of those who will have picked up portfolios in the baggage of the Liberal army that was derailed by the treachery of those who should have led it."[77] As Monet perceived it, the hour of revenge had struck, but the party's destiny would not be decided exclusively by the confident new Premier. Debts had to be repaid. Monet identified Adélard Turgeon, obviously, as one of the ministers who had resigned with Gouin in February, as eager to collect his due. Similarly, Monet considered the Langelier brothers, Charles and François, as powerful forces who had long opposed conservative politics in the Liberal party. All had political axes to grind and Monet knew that Gouin could not afford to ignore them or their wishes.

As important as the Langeliers and the Turgeons were, however, Monet only mentioned them as an afterthought. "The party," he told Sir Wilfrid, "is in the hands of Camille Piché, Godfroy Langlois and Achille Bergevin." Such a remark said much about the ascendancy of progressivism in the Liberal party at the time. Monet's mention of Langlois, whom Laurier had tried to distance from the party ten years earlier, must have made the Prime Minister frown.

In its own way, Monet's letter said much of what has become known at the Gouin "coup" of 1905, but the power struggle which had toppled Simon-Napoléon Parent had remained mysterious.

Godfroy Langlois's role was pivotal. It was he who personally triggered the crisis by challenging Rainville during the election, harnessed that current of discontent within the party and managed to convince radicals that they had to react to emerging issues. Gouin did not single-handedly wrest power from Parent. As Monet rightly observed, the party was largely in the hands of Montreal's Liberal progressives, men like Langlois, J.C. Walsh, Camille Piché, W.A. Weir, Philippe-Auguste Choquette and Achille Bergevin. Turgeon, who because he had been a member of the revolt and because of his seniority, was touted in the press as Parent's logical successor, had to be passed over. Lieutenant-Governor Jetté undoubtedly knew that Turgeon would never succeed in controlling the radicals.

Le Canada seemed content. "With Gouin and Turgeon as leaders, the Liberal party will walk proudly on the road to progress; our programme will take off, our work will expand; our party will affirm itself," wrote Langlois, confident that Liberal progressivism had finally taken hold of the party.[78]

The resignation of Parent in March 1905 was the climax of an opposition campaign that was given spark in March 1901 when the Montreal Light, Heat, and Power Company was given a charter and when the Grosbois educational reform bill was defeated. Those incidents reaffirmed the divisions within the Liberal party, but they also provided issues to unite those elements of the party who considered themselves reformists. It was their resolve that led the fight to rid the party in Montreal of its corrupt "bosses", to compel Marchand to propose education reform, that prompted the Grosbois educational reform bill and the *Ligue de l'Enseignement* and to fight over the incorporation of the Montreal

Light, Heat, and Power Company. Unlike Marchand, Parent had repeatedly failed to realize the potency of radicalism within the ranks of his own party. Parent cared little for the jostle of party politics and paid little attention to the demands of members. To his credit, Lomer Gouin had recognized the vitality of the Liberal progressive movement and had consistently supported it since 1896 when he helped launch *Le Signal*. He took full advantage of its vitality and of its talent. Langlois, who had done more than any other single individual to transform radical *rougisme* into Liberal progressivism, was only too happy to see his old friend finally take the reigns of power.

Notes

1. Laurier Papers, C798, C. Langelier to Laurier, 16 janvier 1903.
2. *La Presse*, 20 février 1902.
3. *Ibidem*, C799, Parent to C.Fitzpatrick, 31 mars 1903.
4. *La Presse*, editorial, 31 mars 1904.
5. Laurier Papers, C810, Langlois to Laurier, 31 mars 1904.
6. *Le Canada*, editorial, 21 mai 1904.
7. Laurier Papers, C813, Archambault to Laurier, 17 juin 1904.
8. *La Presse*, editorial, 30 mai 1904.
9. *Ibidem*, editorial, 3 juin 1904.
10. Session nicknamed as such by *La Presse*, editorial, 1 juin 1904.
11. Laurier Papers, C788, Laurier to Choquette, 24 octobre 1901.
12. *Ibidem*, 24 novembre 1904.
13. Laurier Papers, C805, Parent to Laurier, 21 octobre 1903.
14. *Ibidem*, Laurier to Parent, 26 octobre 1903.
15. PAC, Philippe-Auguste Choquette Papers, Laurier to Choquette, 26 novembre 1903.
16. Laurier Papers, C817, Laurier to Choquette, 26 novembre 1903.
17. *Ibidem*, Laurier to Choquette, 25 janvier 1904; see also C819, Quebec Superior Court Transcript, 2 février [1905], (#94507).
18. *La Presse*, 22 septembre 1904.
19. *Ibidem*, editorial, 29 août 1904.
20. Laurier Papers, C819, Quebec Superior Court Transcript, 2 février [1905], (#94508).

21. ANQQ, Parent Papers, "Aux électeurs de la province de Quebec" 8 novembre 1904.

22. Laurier Papers, C807, Dansereau to Laurier, n.d. [November 1904].

23. *La Patrie*, editorial, 5 novembre 1904.

24. Laurier Papers, C 817, Parent to Béique, 8 novembre 1904.

25. *Ibidem*, Béique to Parent, 9 novembre 1904.

26. Parent Papers, F.X. Dupuis to Parent, 9 novembre 1904.

27. *Ibidem*; Dupuis's observations are corroborated by La Patrie, 17 novembre 1904.

28. *Le Canada*, 9 novembre 1904.

29. *Ibidem*.

30. Laurier Papers, C817, Dandurand to Laurier, 9 novembre 1904.

31. *Ibidem*, Béique to Laurier, 10 novembre 1904.

32. *Ibidem*, Dandurand to Parent, 9 novembre 1904.

33. *Ibidem*.

34. Best example is *La Patrie*, editorial, 25 novembre 1904.

35. Laurier Papers, C817, Préfontaine to Laurier, 21 novembre 1904.

36. *Ibidem*, C832, McCorkill to Laurier, 10 mars 1906.

37. *Ibidem*, C817, Guerin to Laurier, 17 novembre 1904.

38. Choquette Papers, Laurier to Choquette, 1 novembre 1904. See also Laurier Papers, C 818, Laurier to Choquette, 2 janvier 1905.

39. Laurier Papers, C819, Quebec Superior Court Transcript, 2 février [1905], (#94508).

40. *Ibidem*.

41. P.A. Choquette, *Un demi-siècle de vie politique* (Montréal, 1936), p. 167.

42. *Ibidem*.

43. *La Presse*, 25 novembre 1904.

44. *Ibidem*.

45. Parent Papers, H.T. Simard to G. Tanguay, 27 novembre 1904.

46. Jean Hamelin, Jacques Letarte, et Marcel Hamelin, "Les élections dans la province de Québec," *CGQ*, 7, septembre 1959-mars 1960, figure XI.

47. Parent Papers, Cherrier to Parent, 27 décembre 1904.

48. *Ibidem*, Laurier to Parent, 5 décembre 1904.

49. There is a copy of this letter in the Parent Papers, but it is reproduced in full in *La Presse*, 5 décembre 1904.

50. Parent Papers, Dupuis to Choquette, 6 décembre 1904.

51. *Ibidem*.

52. *La Presse*, 24 décembre 1904.

53. Laurier Papers, C818, C. Langelier to R. Boudreau, 22 décembre 1904.

54. *La Presse*, 27 décembre 1904; Laurier Papers, C818, Laurier to Langlois, 24 décembre 1904.

55. PAC, Lomer Gouin Papers, Vol. 12., rough draft of sequence of events, n.d.

56. *La Presse*, 12 janvier 1905.

57. *Ibidem*, 13 janvier 1905.

58. Laurier Papers, C819, T.Trenholme to Laurier, n.d.; see also C805, Trenholme to Laurier, November 15, 1903. Trenholme's remarks exemplify a good deal of English Quebec's opinions. Support was so strong for Parent among some of them that the St-Antoine division of the Montreal Reform Club, a chapter dominated by anglophone membership, sent the party leader a motion of support even after he had resigned as Premier. See Parent Papers, petition, April 1, 1905.

59. Laurier Papers, C817, Anonymous to Laurier, 13 janvier 1905.

60. Parent Papers, Laurier to Parent, 14 janvier 1905.

61. Laurier Papers, C818, Choquette to R. Boudreau, 30 janvier 1905.

62. Parent Papers, Prévost to Parent, n.d., Préfontaine to Parent, 9 janvier 1905.

63. *Ibidem*, Monet to Parent, 19 janvier 1905. On Langlois's remarks, see Robert Rumilly, *Histoire de la Province de Quebec, Vol XI, S.-N. Parent* (Montreal, 1930), p. 202.

64. Gouin Papers, Vol. 12, rough draft of sequence of events, n.d.

65. *La Presse*, 19 mai 1905.

66. Gouin Papers, Vol. 12, rough draft of sequence of events, n.d.

67. Laurier Papers, C818, Anonymous to Laurier, n.d..

68. *La Presse*, 3 février 1905.

69. Laurier Papers, C819, David to Laurier, 4 février 1905.

70. Gouin Papers, Vol. 12, Procès verbal , Château Frontenac, 8 février 1905.

71. *Le Canada*, 9 février 1905.

72. Gouin Papers, Vol. 12, Parent to Weir, Gouin and Turgeon, 15 février 1905.

73. Parent Papers, Parent to Pelletier, 22 février 1905.

74. Laurier Papers, C821, Laurier to Parent, 22 mars 1905.

75. PAC, Louis-Honoré Fréchette Papers, C13988, Fréchette to Parent, 21 mars 1905.

76. *The Witness*, editorial, 22 mars 1905.

77. Laurier Papers, C821, Monet to Laurier, 22 mars 1905.

78. *Le Canada*, 22 mars 1905.

CHAPTER VIII

THE CITY REFORMER

*"In truth, we longer know to which side to
turn to get an explanation
of what is going on in City Hall."*

—*Godfroy Langlois, 1907.*[1]

OR THE LIBERAL PROGRESSIVES, the Gouin "coup"
held the promise that there would be change in the way
municipal politics were carried out and in the manner
policy would be formulated. The triumph over the protectors of the Montreal Light, Heat, and Power Company in
the 1904 municipal race and Parent's loss as credibility as
leader of Liberals and as Premier of the Province, was bound,
they hoped, to allow Liberal progressives the freedom to flex
their muscles.

Simon-Napoléon Parent left the provincial political scene
in the spring of 1905, but remained Mayor of Quebec City
and continued to spawn controversy in the region as his war
with the Liberal progressives continued unabated in the
capital. Parent's resignation from the Assembly left a seat
vacant and the resulting by-election in the riding of St-Sauveur was to be held in October 1905. The contest pitted J.A.
Rochette, a Parent protégé, against Dr. Charles Côté, who
was running on a Liberal-Labour ticket, but was really being
fought between Choquette and Parent. Côté won a landslide
victory on October 14, 1905,[2] thereby confirming the further decline of Parent. Some Liberals, nevertheless, held a
final banquet in honour of their deposed Premier. Laurier
and other federal Liberals such as Charles Fitzpatrick and
Rodolphe Lemieux were present, but provincial notables
were conspicuous in their absence. Gouin boycotted the
dinner, and no recognizable Liberal progressive faces were

among the crowd: the party was still decidedly split in Quebec City and the fight between Choquette and the former Premier was not over.[3] "I can assure you that the masses are with that valiant fighter Choquette," Turgeon told Laurier.[4]

Parent lost the taste for battle once and for all after the St-Sauveur by-election. He held his position of Mayor only tenuously. Since 1904, Choquette had threatened Parent's position in City Hall and chances were now rather slim of him collecting a sufficient number of votes among city councillors to be reelected as Mayor. Choquette's threats, once easily discounted by Parent, had to be taken seriously. Parent announced in January 1906 that he would not seek reelection as mayor, and resigned in favour of Georges Tanguay. Parent's resignation was accepted unanimously by City Council, without discussion, as it was widely expected that Louis-Alexandre Taschereau would replace Parent after the next municipal election, since Tanguay was only a temporary solution.

Upon hearing Parent's announcement, Choquette immediately announced his candidacy. Laurier, who had pleaded with Choquette not to continue the fight against Parent in City Hall, immediately urged him to withdraw his name lest it "damage the party's honour" further in the provincial capital. Choquette and others responded angrily. "We do not see where the party's honour is jeopardized, because in this race, it is a question of saving our municipal politics from the [...] party [...] that would continue the nefarious works of the bad Parent administration," Laurier was told. "You knew that the majority of municipal electors are favourable to the candidacy of the honourable Choquette against Mr. Taschereau and that in obliging Choquette to withdraw you are favouring Mr. Taschereau who is the heir to the bad Parent regime, to your detriment."[5]

Choquette saw things in light of the fight that had split the party the winter before. "I do not hide the fact that, if the fight continues, it will be disagreeable and disastrous from the point of view of the party," Choquette told Laurier. The Senator then offered a compromise. He would withdraw his candidacy only if Taschereau did the same, and even offered to support a mutually-acceptable third candidate.[6] Laurier went to work on that offer and managed to convince Taschereau to withdraw in favour of Georges Garneau. He succeeded, and cabled Choquette to urge him to do the same.[7] Choquette finally agreed to the compromise.[8] If Laurier met with some success in calming the tempestuous relations within his party in Quebec City, the *Parentistes* continued to feel discrimination in the doling out of patronage, and as late as 1907, Taschereau would complain that he and all of Parent's friends were routinely being humiliated.[9] Still, nothing further emerged in Quebec City to cause Laurier or Gouin any more headaches.

The same could not be said about the situation in Montreal. Whereas the fight between progressive Liberals and their conservative counterparts was kept alive in Quebec City by easily identifiable leaders, Liberal progressive leadership in Montreal was faced with critically important decisions. None of the issues was as important as the hydroelectric question, the same knotty political problem that has spurred Liberal progressivism in the first years of the twentieth century.

In many ways, a small revolution in utilities policy took place in mid-March 1905 when Lomer Gouin, fairly secure in thinking he would soon become premier, introduced to the Legislative Assembly an amendment to the Canadian Light and Power Company's charter, granting it the same privileges allowed to the Montreal Light, Heat, and Power Company in 1901 — the same prerogatives that had been denied to this company in 1904. The amendment to the Canadian Light and Power's charter granted the same development rights to this company as those accorded to the Montreal Light, Heat, and Power Company, with the *proviso* that the Canadian Light and Power could not charge more than the minimum rated imposed by the Holt-Forget company. The motion created a stir within the coalition that had been struck by Langlois's electoral bid in November 1904. People like Senators Dandurand and Béique feared that the Assembly was committing the same mistakes made in 1901, endangering yet again Montreal's autonomy. Gouin firmly disagreed. "Your principles are commendable, but the situation is exceptional," Gouin told Raoul Dandurand. "This monopoly was created by the legislature; the duty of the legislature is to kill it. I see no other way to crush it than to create competition. It is undoubtedly wrong to impose on the municipality's autonomy; but in this case, it is a wrong to create a greater good. For to refuse competition is to protect the trust."[10]

By the time Gouin assumed the Premiership, it looked as if the Montreal Light, Heat and Power Company's days as an omnipotent trust were over. Two months later, however, the City of Montreal voted to extend to the Montreal Light Heat and Power a 15 year gas contract on the condition that its price be reduced by 5 cents a year until 1910. The vote provoked by alderman Louis Payette's "deal" divided the Liberal progressive contingent in City Council. Twenty aldermen voted in favour of the deal, fourteen voted against. Among those who voted for the Montreal Light, Heat and Power Company were Louis Payette, L.A. Lapointe, Arsène Lavallée, Clément Robillard and J. St-Denis: men who had fought together to defeat those who had supported the electricity trust. The politicians who voted against the contract (all Liberals in good standing) formed the core of Liberal progressivism over the next five years: Aldermen Vallières, Robertson, Levy, Clearihue, Turner, Sadler, Ekers, Gallery, Bumbray, Walsh, Nelson, Stearns and Desseres.[11]

Louis Payette, who had supported Godfroy Langlois time and again, soon emerged to dominate local Liberalism in Montreal, much as Raymond Préfontaine had done a few years before. Born in 1854 in Montreal, Payette had become a successful contractor whose works included the Gare Viger and the Church of St-Louis-de-France in Montreal as well as

Quebec City's prestigious Château Frontenac hotel. A member of the Liberal party since the late 1880s, the handsome and energetic Payette had always confounded his critics by supporting the progressive side of Liberalism at times and the conservative side at others. In the winter of 1904 he had won St-Louis ward with the support of Henri-Benjamin Rainville but had proven to be a key mover against Rainville when Langlois challenged the Parent protégé in the provincial election of that year. With his actions in 1906, Payette had put the doubts to rest: he was now a protector of the trusts.

Perhaps more surprising, in light of this apparent slipping in reformist zeal, was the Liberal progressive reaffirmation of the need to municipalize the system. If Payette was now moving out of the fold, Calixte Lebeuf, who had been one of the original leaders of the Liberal progressive movement but who had chosen to support the Holt-Forget trust in the 1904 election, was returning. He declared in the wake of the Payette deal that "the cost of living is too high for the price of gas not to come down. The actual reduction is far too little. I was against municipalisation, but in the face of what is happening today, I am wondering if it would not be better for the city to produce its own gas itself. If I had been elected to City Council, I would not have voted with the twenty who adopted the resolution."[12] W.D. Lighthall, the fiercely independent Liberal Mayor of Westmount, similarly argued that "the natural and reasonable system would appear to be control of its franchises by the municipality, and fair and generous bargains made with capital to operate those franchises, so that the municipality might not be carrying out businesses out of its line, but at the same time would have a proper check on the companies doing such business."[13]

Langlois was predictably outraged. He wanted to see the Montreal Light, Heat, and Power Company expropriated. "The idea that public services should be under the absolute control of the public and free of all other foreign influences is not owned by any one person or any one party," he raged. "It is such a simple idea that it comes to mind of all the people."[14] Langlois's campaigns against the Holt-Forget trust did not abate after the many triumphs of 1904 and he soon came to the conclusion that the only solution to the problem of the high cost of energy in Montreal was the purchase of the Montreal Light, Heat, and Power assets. He wanted public ownership of the utilities but Langlois knew that his hopes would be more realistic if he simply called for stricter regulation so as to allow more companies to compete on an equal footing with the Holt-Forget trust.[15]

Provincial Liberals seemed interested in the matter, even if many local Montreal aldermen were not. Early in the winter of 1906, an innovative response to the situation was presented to the Legislative Assembly. The bill proposed by the Gouin government provided Montreal the right to expropriate the Montreal Light, Heat, and Power Company's street hardware as well as the right to construct and manage underground wire conduits. Led by Mayor Hormisdas Laporte, Montreal's City Council reacted quickly to the new initiative by passing by-law 343, which forced hydroelectric companies to bury their wires. The law was a significant step in trying to control the utilities and certainly reflected Liberal progressive thinking. The idea was to remove from companies like the Montreal Light, Heat, and Power the opportunity to monopolize street space with lamp posts, wires and various other paraphernalia. While few cables could be safely strung up, there existed little danger of burying a multitude of cables underground. It followed, therefore, that companies would be able to challenge the Montreal Light, Heat, and Power in areas it could not dream of approaching. This act was not immediately implemented, however, as Montreal was not voted the funds necessary to carry out the plan.

The disillusionment of the Liberal progressives was almost palpable during the 1906 municipal election as apathy reigned in this contest. 22 of the 40 aldermen were reelected two weeks before the election through acclamations, and seven of them belonged to Liberal progressive ranks. Two of the fourteen Liberals who had voted against extending the Montreal Light, Heat and Power Company decided to retire: Aldermen Vallières and Robertson announced that they would not contest the next election. Disillusioned by the impotence of the mayoralty in the face of strong opposition, Mayor Hormisdas Laporte similarly declared that he would not continue the fight and seek reelection.[16]

To follow tradition, an anglophone candidate had to be selected to succeed Laporte, and two men intimated a willingness to present themselves for the job. Henry Ekers, a Liberal party member and an alderman who had repeatedly voted against the Montreal Light, Heat, and Power Company, said he would run. Senator H.J. Cloran also wanted to run. He had been an active Liberal progressive, and an influential member of the labour movement. To Langlois, who feared a split in the progressive vote, such candidacies posed a dilemma. Cloran had always been most supportive of his work. When he declared his candidacy in early December 1905 at the *Club Papineau,* Cloran even reiterated his support for Langlois's crusades for educational development.[17] It was thus not surprising to see Langlois support his colleague for a time in *Le Canada.*

But Ekers was more popular, and Cloran knew it. He pulled out of the race after a few weeks, so as to ensure that the progressive vote would find cohesion in this otherwise lacklustre campaign. Facing Ekers would be W. Doran, the same man who had unsuccessfully contested Préfontaine's reelection in 1900. The gas purchase issue seemed forgotten. Even *La Presse*, which also supported Ekers, reflected on this curious race. "The great battle was supposed to be fought on the gas issue and especially on the votes given last May," its editorialist noted. "Yet, to everyone's surprise, our colleagues have until today remained completely mute on this issue [...]."[18]

Liberal progressives were mute after Cloran's withdrawal from the race. Some of them, including J.B. Bumbray and George Sadler, chose to support Ekers's candidacy. But Ekers also won the support of his friends of old like L.A. Lapointe, Louis Payette and Arsène Lavallée, three former progressive Liberals who had pressed for the acceptance of the gas deal with the Montreal Light, Heat, and Power Company. There was little to say, as it was evident that the popular and experienced Ekers would win the election handily. Remaining Liberal progressives were resigned to the fact that successive mayors had repeatedly proven their impotence in the face of the influence of the trusts on City Council, and were too demoralized to campaign effectively. Laporte's tenure, in sum, had been a total failure.

Langlois, who was being criticized severely on other issues, chose to keep a lower profile in this campaign. In his own ward, Dr. J.F. Gadbois presented himself as the official candidate of the "Citizen's League" and was supported publicly by George Washington Stephens. Like Langlois had done in the provincial election of 1904, Gadbois campaigned in St-Louis on a reformist platform, arguing in favour of the City's autonomy, for improved sanitary conditions, better water, more efficient streetcar service, and against the Montreal Light, Heat, and Power Company. Gadbois did not live in the St-Louis ward, but won a handsome victory, nonetheless, because of the very progressive nature of his platform and because his opponent, Placide Daoust, had served the Préfontaine clique for years. This constituency, increasingly populated by Jewish immigrants, consistently supported progressive candidates.

Gadbois's success notwithstanding, the electoral results must have been a disappointment for Langlois. While Ekers did win the mayoralty by over 3000 votes, it was evident that even the reformists lost much support in this uninspired campaign. Pillars of the Liberal progressives movement such as Daniel Gallery, Gaspard Desserres, George Sadler, J.B. Clearihue, J. Bumbray and R. Turner were elected. The big disappointment was J.C. Walsh's unexplainable defeat. While comforts could be taken in the fact that Ucal Dandurand had again lost his bid to be elected alderman, the news

225

that Napoléon Giroux and Médéric Martin were elected
could not have been well received. Giroux was notorious for
his unabashed support of the Montreal Light, Heat, and
Power Company and had defeated a very weak incumbent.
Martin also came with a dubious reputation. Worse still,
three of the turncoats who had voted for the Payette proposal—Lapointe, Robillard and Lavallée were elected by
acclamation. There only remained a handful of Liberal progressives in Municipal Council after 1906. Any hope that this
reformist movement could have affected local policies was
shattered by a failure to agree on a common platform.

There was still some debate on the question of electricity
in Montreal with Ekers's inauguration, created in part by the
composition of the important City Council committees,
which reflected the victory of conservative Liberalism in the
February 1906 election. Louis Payette, who had orchestrated
the 1905 bill to extend the Montreal Light, Heat and Power
Company's contract, became Chairman of the Finance Committee. His supporter H.Y. Yates was made Chairman of the
critically important Fire and Lighting Committee. A few
months later, in May 1906, a sub-committee was established
to negotiate a deal with the Montreal Light, Heat, and Power
Company composed of Aldermen Payette, Labrecque and
Mercier.

While negotiations with the Montreal Light, Heat, and
Power Company proceeded in the midst of Liberal progressivism's disillusionment, some of the Gouin administration's
initiatives did allow for a ray of hope. In early February 1906,
Adélard Turgeon proposed a bill that would prohibit any
power company from establishing itself on Jacques-Cartier
Lake in the Laurentians. Such restrictions were welcomed,
and at least some of the backbenchers were of the opinion
that the state should nationalize the production and distribution of hydroelectricity. On February 15, Maurice Perrault,
Liberal member for Chambly, gave a long speech in the
Assembly in favour of the nationalization of public utilities.[19] It was in the context of the backdoor negotiations with

the Montreal Light, Heat and Power Company and some of the thought being expressed in the provincial legislature that Langlois pursued his campaign against the trust. In November 1906, *Le Canada* had launched an investigation to compare the cost of electricity and gas in Montreal with those of other cities in Canada and in the United States. Langlois's conclusions were clear. Montrealers were being gravely exploited. It was even disclosed that the Montreal Light, Heat, and Power Company charged 33 percent less in Westmount (where it still faced competition), than in the rest of the Montreal areas. The solution was to municipalize, but city fathers proved unwilling, despite their platforms, to do anything about it.[20]

In 1907, the negotiations subcommittee of the Fire and Lighting Committee released its proposal. In an acrimonious debate, Payette proposed that City Council allow the Montreal Light, Heat, and Power Company an extra five years on its 15 year contract with the City. Payette's actions, now supported by *La Presse*, roused anger from many corners. Dr. Gadbois, L.A. Lapointe (who had supported Payette in 1905) and George Sadler led the fight against him, accusing Payette of selling out the city and of acting in bad faith by scarcely showing up for debates.[21] The Payette motion was narrowly passed after seven hours of intense debate, by a 21 to 19 margin and the debate left a bitter aftertaste in the mouths of many Liberals. "For the future, I think we will have to take the battle to Ottawa and Quebec City," a dispirited Dr. Gadbois told a reporter. "It is up to our members of Parliament to do the rest. We have done all we could."[22] The City's contradictory demands both for extra powers to counter the pressures of utility monopolies and extra privileges for the Montreal Light, Heat, and Power Company undoubtedly bewildered the Quebec Legislative Assembly.

Godfroy Langlois, who again raged against the second Payette proposal in *Le Canada*,[23] responded to Gadbois's demand for provincial action and led a delegation of reformist Montreal aldermen to the Premier's office. They exhorted Gouin to act against the Payette deal that pronounced themselves quite satisfied with their meeting. Langlois promised an even greater demonstration of opposition to the Payette proposal.[24] Ten days later, a chartered Canadian Pacific coach pulled into Quebec City carrying 150 irate Montrealers who wanted to make the trip to protest the Payette proposal. Among them were the 19 aldermen who had voted against the deal. It was again Langlois who introduced the delegation to cabinet, and Gonzalve Desaulniers, the radical poet and associate of Langlois during the 1890s, resurfaced to speak on behalf of the protesters.[25]

Langlois's efforts were not in vain. Evidently, if the Montreal Light, Heat and Power Company had numerous friends in Montreal's City Council, it had fewer allies in the Legislative Assembly. The annual subsidy to the City of Montreal was ratified that year in a way that allowed the city to tax at will the use of its street underground, thereby opening access to funds that could be applied to the burial of cables and wire. Moreover, the Province legislated that the Montreal Light, Heat, and Power Company bury its cables in city conduits. The Gouin administration went further. It placed a ten-year ceiling on any hydroelectricity contracts negotiated between the city and the power companies, and imposed that a referendum be held to ratify any longer-term agreements. In March 1907, the Legislative Assembly arranged to permit the City of Montreal to borrow up to $5 million to finance the burying of cables, and voted a motion accepting the principle that the City of Montreal acquire the materials necessary to establish its own gas company and power plant once its contract with the Holt-Forget company had expired.[26] Unfortunately, the Legislative Council, still dominated by Conservatives, rejected the last clause.

Langlois could rejoice in a partial victory nonetheless. It was clear that Liberal progressivism had found, for the moment, a new generation of leaders. L.A. Lapointe and Arsène Lavallée, (who both had supported the first Payette deal) had both distinguished themselves in speaking out in defence of the rights of the city. Together, they had managed to attract the support of six non-Liberals and divide in almost equal halves the Municipal Council. The Montreal Light, Heat, and Power Company thus suffered serious setbacks in 1907, but it still would control the electricity costs in Montreal. It had lost a battle, but the war raged on.

Surprisingly, the controversy over the rights of the Montreal Light, Heat, and Power Company and the Payette initiative did not have dramatic political reverberations. Indeed, Louis Payette's political fortunes thrived on the notoriety he acquired in 1907 to the point where he confidently announced his candidacy for Mayor in November 1907 when Ekers, exhausted, declared that he would not seek reelection. Payette was immediately supported by a who's who of conservative Liberals: James McShane, the old Liberal, supported Payette as did John James Guerin, who had been ambushed and defeated by J.C. Walsh in the provincial election of 1904. Ekers immediately lent his support as did aldermen N. Giroux and Médéric Martin. All in all, fifteen aldermen supported Payette, ten of whom had voted in favour of his controversial motion the previous year. The only Liberal progressive to support him was, surprisingly, Clearihue.[27]

For a long time, it seemed as though Payette would be elected by acclamation. Disgusted with the behaviour of his party in municipal affairs, Langlois initially said little in *Le Canada* about the municipal race, except to warn his readers of the unpredictable nature of city politicians. "Declarations on the attitude they expect to adopt on the issues of gas and electricity should be demanded of all the candidates in the next municipal election," he editorialized. "Let us demand written declarations especially."[28] Liberal progressivism seemed in disarray as its unofficial leader stubbornly refused to throw their hats in the mayoral race. Most Liberal party members seemed resigned to support the Payette candidacy, *faute de mieux*.

It was then that Philippe Roy, Liberal MLA for St-Jean and a former speaker of the Legislative Assembly, indicated a willingness to oppose Payette. He was supported by Maurice Perrault, MLA for Chambly, who again spoke in the assembly in favour of municipalizing utilities. But there were problems with Roy's candidacy. He did not live in Montreal, for one thing, and was almost unknown to Montreal Liberals. More embarrassingly, he had followed Parent's lead in 1901 when the Montreal Light, Heat, and Power Company had been given its charter.[29] Finally, party potentates were not favourable to his candidacy. Laurier indicated privately that "if I was a voter in the city of Montreal, I would certainly vote for Payette who has more experience in City Council than any other competitors. As to our friend Roy, he is certainly too late and would only confuse the rank and file."[30] L.O. David concurred. He told Roy that in the interest of the party, he had better not present himself. "Payette has his faults," David conceded, "but he is frankly Liberal and he has many friends."[31]

As in 1906, Langlois was in a difficult position. He had no sympathy for Payette, no matter what the party establishment had to say in his favour. Roy, on the other hand, had grown to be a friend, as both men developed a close rapport in the Legislative Assembly. Roy often supported Langlois's controversial motions in Quebec and also owned a substantial number of shares in *Le Canada*.[32] Roy, moreover, regretted sincerely his 1901 posture. With little time remaining in the campaign, he mounted an impressively progressive platform, promising to put the trust in its place and to abolish property qualifications for aldermen and mayoralty candidates, and was successful in finding support at the eleventh hour. While *La Presse* continued to support Payette, at least 400 Liberals opted to oppose him and chose to encourage Roy when he finally announced his candidacy and officially unveiled his platform on January 21, 1908 at a meeting in Montreal's Monument National. J.C. Walsh supported Roy as did Senator Béique. Senator Cloran spoke in favour of Roy at the meeting as did Dr. Gadbois and labour spokesman Gustave Francq.[33] *Le Canada*, ignoring the will of Laurier and David, declared itself in favour of Roy. "Today as yesterday, we cannot approve of the men who formed the bloc [of 21] to favour an odious monopoly," its editorialist wrote. "It is not without some regret, however, that we must intervene today because Mr. Payette was always a friend of the Liberal cause and, if he has erred on the question of lighting and followed the wrong path in a few other circumstances, we know that he has often served the city well with his extensive business experience and his vigorous and informed point of view."[34]

Finally, the 1908 Municipal race was focused on the issue of utility regulation, and Payette felt pressed to explain himself before the electorate. "I declare that I am absolutely independent of all trusts," he told an audience in St-Henri late in the race. "We had to deal with the issue in order to resolve it. [...] We had to deal with the Company. We were not free, since the company has a provincial charter. We could not stop it from selling its gas and its electricity. In return, the company asked us for the impossible, for such things as a fifty year contract. We refused, but we still had to deal with the company. We gave our conditions. [...]. Don't you think that if we had sold out, we would have given more in exchange for favourable rates?"[35]

Le Canada's support notwithstanding, Roy's last minute campaign did not attract enough support. While Payette's mainstay of support rested with the "21" who had voted in favour of his hydro proposal, only two of the "19" who had opposed Payette's bill actually rallied publicly to Roy. When the votes were tabulated, Payette had scored an overwhelming victory, beating his adversary by almost 3000 votes. The City Council stayed largely unchanged as 25 (out of 40) aldermen were elected by acclamation. The only defeated incumbent was Houle, a Payette supporter. Solace could also be found in the fact that Henri-Benjamin Rainville (who had tried to be elected in Quartier-Centre) was again defeated.

Though it ended in total failure, the Roy candidacy seemed to have relaunched the Liberal progressive movement's assault on the Montreal Light, Heat, and Power Company.

The renewed vigour became apparent a few months later, when the Canadian Light and Power Company secured an agreement to sign a electricity purchase contract with the City of Montreal.[36] Negotiations were held up as the city insisted that the deal had to conform to the ten- year limit imposed by the provincial government. The company argued that this was an insufficient guarantee. The Canadian Light and Heat Company was offering to charge less than the Holt-Forget Company, but argued that it could not even break even on its investment within the prescribed ten years. Three years alone, it submitted, would be needed for construction and market build-up alone. City Council, for its part, offered no other incentives.[37] In the meantime, the Montreal Light, Heat and Power Company's electricity contract with the City (not to be confused with the gas contracts) was to expire by the end of 1908, and City authorities were reluctant to accommodate the trust. The Holt- Forget Company offered to renew its street-lighting contract for $75 a year per arc-lamp. The City rejected the offer and pronounced itself willing to offer $60 a year per arc-lamp. The Montreal Light, Heat, and Power Company threatened to shut off all lamps on January 1, 1909 if no contract was signed or if an arbitrator was not named; it also threatened to raise the fees to upwards of $200 per arc-lamp/year starting on April 1, 1909. "I challenge the company to shut off its lamps on January 1st," declared alderman L.A. Lapointe. "It knows too well that the entire city would rise up against it. She will continue to give us light and will charge us the going commercial rate [...]. The Company asks that the dispute be submitted to arbitration. We refuse because we know all too well that we would lose, and that the arbiters would be like puppets in the hands of the company."[38]

Urged by Dr. Gadbois,[39] Mayor Payette effected a surprising reversal on this issue. "For me, there is only one way out," thundered the angry Mayor at the suggestion that the dispute be settled through arbitration:

> No one can say that the city cannot provide its own light at a better price that the company can with its steam power and the hydraulic works of its aqueduct. Is money needed? I commit myself to find some whenever the city will need it. Some say the city has no right to produce its own electricity. Do they believe that the province would refuse us the permission if we asked for it? Let us plan a strategy and build our own plant. It can take a year or two, but no matter. In the meantime we will pay the company what it wants. The other companies who have made us offers such as the Saguenay, will sell us what they can and the Montreal Light, Heat, and Power will sell us the balance at its own price. The day we have our own electricity plant, we will get rid of it. And if after that we secure the right to provide electricity to consumers, it will be the death of the company.[40]

Langlois must have choked in reading Payette's declaration, but the latter's defiance suddenly put winds in the Liberal progressive sails. Only two years earlier, it was Payette who had led the march against Liberal progressivism with his blatant protection of the Holt-Forget trust. Yet by 1909, Payette had again transformed city politics and recovered the trust of many disaffected Liberal progressives.

Payette's return to the progressive fold naturally sharpened the conflict between conservative Liberals and the rump of Liberal progressives. In February 1909, when it came time to ratify routinely the composition of Council committees, a group led by aldermen Giroux and Mercier (both Liberals) contested the composition of most of the Committees. They had allies. On February 8, Giroux proposed that new committees be established and, to everybody's surprise, his motion was carried by a one-vote margin. Giroux had long wanted the patronage-rich Roads Committee Chairmanship for himself, and had tried in vain to secure it after the 1908 election. A year later, he was successful. With the "Giroux Committees" some of the biggest Liberal progressives were swept away from their already precarious positions. Larivière lost the Chairmanship of the Roads Committee to Giroux and found himself in limbo. Lavallée and Sadler were also unceremoniously dumped. Only Levy retained the Chair of the relatively unimportant Public Sidewalks Committee. While Lapointe was allowed to keep the Chair of the Finance Committee, he would preside over a board of certified Giroux supporters. New names thus emerged to prominence: Levesque, Dagenais, Lesperance and, last but not least, Médéric Martin.[41]

As the forces of reactionary Liberalism wreaked havoc on City Council Committees, the conflict between the Montreal Light, Heat and Power Company and the embattled City Council reached an impasse. Payette was now a lame-duck mayor, and it was unclear who was governing the city. In Quebec's Legislative Assembly, Liberal progressives took initiatives to clean up the Montreal mess. At the first session following the Giroux "coup", Godfroy Langlois presented a bill aiming at incorporating another potential competitor to the Montreal Light, Heat, and Power Company, the "Merchant's Light, Heat, and Power Company." This firm wanted to produce and transmit electricity in the neighbourhood bounded by Craig, Ontario, Bleury and Parent streets. Apparently, 500 merchants had already pledged their patronage, and the company had capital amounting to $1.5 million. The bill was accepted, given a second reading on March 23, 1909 and eventually was passed.

Langlois seemed adamant in making sure the company he was supporting would compete with the Holt-Forget trust. On March 25, he proposed an amendment to the Merchant Light, Heat, and Power Company's charter stating that the company would not have to seek the approval of the municipal government anywhere on the island of Montreal, Beauharnois or Châteauguay to install its hardware. Surprisingly, and despite the protests of some in Montreal City Council who argued that this again constituted a threat to the city's autonomy, the amendment was approved by a vote of 39 to 10.

Langlois was not acting simply on behalf of a company. He succeeded in pressuring the Legislative Assembly to accept a further amendment to the Merchant's charter that would prevent it from ever fusing with either the Montreal Light, Heat and Power Company or with the Canadian Light and Power. Afraid of a potential future temptation to consolidate and forge a monopoly, Langlois demonstrated the progressive faith that competition was the only solution that offered itself to Montrealers in light of the government's refusal to finance a complete takeover. With the establishment of a Public Utilities Commission which was forged a few weeks later by the Legislative Assembly, progressive Liberals in the Assembly expected fair competition and fair prices in Montreal for the benefit of industry and of consumers.

Less than a week after proposing those amendments, Godfroy Langlois introduced a further measure in the Legislative Assembly that aimed at correcting the abuses of a confused, corrupt and aimless Montreal City Council. Seconded by J.C. Walsh, he proposed to the legislature that a "Board of Control" be added to Montreal's administrative structure. Such a reform was not unique in its kind. Many cities in North America had found such offices necessary to review City Council decisions, and Langlois struck a nerve with his bill. "There is one project to which the French Canadian population could never oppose too much," wrote *La Presse*'s editorialist, once again siding against Langlois: "it is the Board of Control proposal [...] of which Mr. Langlois has made himself the sponsor in the legislature."[42] *La Presse*, like many conservative politicians, feared that the Board of Control would allow a minority to dictate to the majority. As various camps formed themselves, Langlois proposed in Quebec City that a referendum be held on the question in Montreal.[43]

Langlois's proposal found great support. Gouin ordered that a Royal Commission be formed to examine Montreal's administration. Judge L.J. Cannon, from Trois-Rivières, was asked to head the inquiry, and quickly set himself about the task of hearing testimony. "Everything is in disarray," the Commission was told in September by none other than Mayor Louis Payette. "Disunion reigns; there is no trust anywhere and no reforms are made."[44] Payette charged that the factionalization of Montreal City Council, with the race for patronage it engendered, cost the city budget at least 20 percent more than what should be reasonably spent. Like his old friend Langlois, Montreal's Mayor suggested that a Board of Control be established and even went further than Langlois in suggesting that the ward system be abolished entirely.[45] Giroux, speaking on behalf of conservative Liberalism, opposed vehemently any plans for a Board of Control.

Cannon submitted his damning report to Cabinet in December 1909. He accused outright nine aldermen of corruption and his conclusions regarding the politics of City Council were, to say the least, unflattering. The majority of aldermen, Cannon charged, ran the city so as to favour their families and friends, much to the detriment of Montreal as a whole. He argued that since 1902 Montreal's administration was "saturated with corruption," the result of political patronage. "City Council consists today of groups and coteries that struggle with each other to the point where they lose sight of the higher interests of the community," Cannon concluded.[46]

As Cannon supported the proposal that a Board of Control be established, another of Langlois's initiatives was rewarded with support. A referendum on the idea of a Board of Control was held, and it proved again that Langlois, and *Le Canada*, which avidly argued the case for it in its pages, could read and respond to the will of the electorate. Montreal's electors, indeed, voted their approval of a reduction in the number of aldermen and to establish a Board of Control.

On December 21, 1909, another referendum on the munici-
palization of electricity was held. 1909. *Le Canada* demanded
that the electorate support it, and it did.[47] Less than 10% of
the eligible voters made their voices heard, but again, it was
a sign that the political winds were changing in Montreal.
"We will now be able to make an experiment of municipalisation," exclaimed alderman Roy, one of the prime movers
of the plebiscite. Langlois could not have hoped for more.

Still, the years following the great Liberal progressive
electoral gains of 1904 and 1905 were a great disappointment.
Chances for innovation were lost, hopes were dashed, things
remained almost untouched. The City Council had bloated
to forty members, an enormous number of people with
insatiable appetites for political patronage. Liberal progressives were sadly disoriented. As the Roy campaign in the
winter of 1908 had amply demonstrated, leadership was
sorely lacking. Hormisdas Laporte, a man of great courage
and vision, lost the taste for battle quickly, so did his supposedly progressive Liberal successor Henry Ekers. Worse, they
were not replaced. Few people stood up against the two
Payette bills, except in Quebec City, and here Godfroy
Langlois and those who supported him distinguished themselves.

The net result was an ideological derailment, and Liberals
such as aldermen Napoléon Giroux and Médéric Martin
enjoying *de facto* power. The ideas for urban reform were
there, heatedly advocated in *Le Canada*, ardently argued in
the Assembly, and momentarily (if clumsily) brought to the
electorate by the Roy candidacy, but Langlois's call for
measures to remedy Montreal's alarmingly high infant mor-
tality rate, pathetic public sanitation standards and dirty
water were ignored. Effective competitors to the Montreal
Light, Heat, and Power Company were spawned, regulations
controlling the utilities were decreed and administrative
reforms were imposed from Quebec City, but the political
will to follow through on all those initiatives was lacking in
Montreal. Liberal progressives who had won the hearts and

votes of Montreal's electorate in 1904 lost almost all their support from Montreal's largely apathetic electorate. Even though Payette returned to the Liberal progressive fold in early 1909 and denounced the Montreal Light, Heat, and Power Company, the upshot was a divided and ineffective Liberal progressive contingent in Municipal Council.

As Langlois, *Le Canada* and a few aldermen diligently kept the ideals of progressivism alive in the Liberal party, many former allies defected, for a variety of reasons, to the side that was protecting the trusts. Some of the people who had supported Langlois in the earlier years wandered away from, or simply abandoned, the ideology that had brought them to so close to power. Many of them changed sides outright and joined the ranks of the conservative Liberals who had supported Préfontaine and Parent in an earlier time. Liberal progressivism's loss of cohesion highlighted its weak leadership at the local area—a political sphere that had been so critical in giving the ideology its issues, its shape and its tone.

It was a difficult time for the Liberal progressives at *Le Canada* who stubbornly clung to ideals, and Langlois's remark in early 1907 about not knowing where to turn for explanations was very revealing. Langlois and the staff of *Le Canada* watched Montreal city politics and the Liberals who dominated it with exasperation and disbelief. Langlois did what he could as a member of the Legislature. He led the delegations from Montreal to protest the Payette deals before the provincial cabinet, he sponsored the bill to grant a charter to the Merchant's Light and Heat Company and fought gallantly to graft a Board of Control onto Montreal's political structure.

Still, it was clear that many of Langlois's erstwhile allies, men who fought the Préfontaine and Parent machines alongside him, no longer subscribed to the views that filled the pages of *Le Canada*. Strong disagreements over the nature of urban reform isolated the journal's uncompromising vision of Liberal progressivism, and Langlois had supported Roy's candidacy in 1908 when it was clear that the party establishment in Ottawa was favourable to Payette. "Langlois helps himself to *Le Canada* when it comes to municipal affairs to make himself some friends," complained the always reformist Senator Béique to Laurier in early 1909.[48] Clearly, upper-echelon Liberals were increasingly uncomfortable with Langlois's actions in the municipal political arena.

Notes

1. *Le Canada*, editorial, 16 janvier 1907.
2. *La Presse*, 16 octobre 1905.
3. *Ibidem*, 20 octobre 1905.
4. Laurier Papers, C829, Turgeon to Laurier, 18 novembre 1905.
5. *Ibidem*, C827, Anonymous to Laurier, 12 janvier 1906.
6. *Ibidem*, C826, Choquette to Laurier, 20 janvier 1906.
7. *Ibidem*, C827, Telegram, Laurier to Choquette, 9 février 1906.
8. *Ibidem*, Telegram, Choquette to Laurier, 10 février 1906.
9. *Ibidem*, C843, Taschereau to Laurier, 10 février 1907.
10. PAC, Dandurand-Marchand Papers, Vol.1, Gouin to Dandurand, 10 mars 1905.
11. *La Presse*, 9 mai 1905.
12. *Ibidem*, 10 mai 1905.
13. PAC, W.D. Lighthall Papers, Vol. 1. Memorandum, 5 April 1905.
14. *Le Canada*, editorial, 20 octobre 1905.
15. *Ibidem*, 20 mai 1904.
16. *La Presse*, 8 janvier 1906.
17. *Ibidem*, 9 décembre 1905.
18. *Ibidem*, editorial, 20 janvier 1906.
19. *La Presse*, 16 février 1906.
20. *Le Canada*, 13 novembre 1905.
21. *Ibidem*, 8 janvier 1907.
22. *Ibidem*, 5 février 1907.
23. *Le Canada*, editorial, 8 janvier 1907.
24. *La Presse*, 15 février 1907.
25. *Ibidem*, 27 février 1907.
26. *Ibidem*, 28 février 1907.
27. Clearihue further demonstrated his estrangement from the Liberal progressives by running against Dr. John Finnie in the provincial elections held in June 1908.

28. *Le Canada*, 8 janvier 1908.

29. *La Presse*, editorial, 25 janvier 1908.

30. Laurier Papers, C857, Laurier to David, 11 janvier 1908.

31. *Ibidem*, David to Laurier, 10 janvier 1908.

32. *La Presse*, 4 février 1908.

33. *Ibidem*, 22 janvier 1908.

34. *Le Canada*, editorial, 29 janvier 1901.

35. *Ibidem*, 25 janvier 1908.

36. *Ibidem*, 7 juillet 1908.

37. *Ibidem*, 13 octobre 1908.

38. *Ibidem*, 9 décembre 1908.

39. *Ibidem*.

40. *Ibidem*, 11 décembre 1908.

41. *Ibidem*, 9 février 1909.

42. *Ibidem*, front page editorial, 12 avril 1909.

43. *Ibidem*, 22 avril 1909.

44. *Ibidem*, 2 septembre 1909.

45. *Ibidem*.

46. *Ibidem*, 13 décembre 1909.

47. *Le Canada*, editorial, 11 décembre 1909.

48. Laurier Papers, C872, Béique to Laurier, 2 février 1909.

CHAPTER IX

THE RADICALISATION OF GODFROY LANGLOIS

*"Can you tell me why you call yourselves
French Canadians? You, French?
But why? [...] You have no painters, you
have no serious writers, you have no
sculptors, you have no poets... Fréchette
maybe and another young one ...
But Christ, you have no men,
you have no men. It is up to you
journalists and to the students to prepare
the future and shape the taste and habits of
a country. But the students! You come to
teach them and they insult their professors
[...] Ah! But what do you understand as
progress? You have progressed backwards
for the past twenty-five years."*

—*Sarah Bernhardt, 1905*[1]

*... I felt I had to go to France so as to
replenish my old French faith, for none, I
think, has been more French than me.*

—*Godfroy Langlois, 1909*[2]

IT WAS EARLY IN THE EVENING of November 21, 1905.
Le Canada's reporters were still streaming into the offices,
sitting down to file their stories for the next day's edition,
still bantering about the student demonstration they had
witnessed the day before in front of the building. There had

been delays in the composition and Godfroy Langlois had decided to postpone his return home.

Momentarily distracted, Langlois leaned to his window and noticed policemen hurriedly approaching *Le Canada* from all directions. Another demonstration? Evidently, the police authorities had been alerted that Laval students had once again marched off the campus, in formation, carrying red flags and singing funeral hymns. The police immediately surrounded Langlois's downtown office. He waited, the police waited, but no students arrived.

The police had been foiled. Indeed, the students were marching, but had instead turned north on St. Denis street and were headed for St-Louis Square, the quaint park on which Langlois's domicile faced. Langlois and the detachment, upon hearing the new developments, headed in the same direction. As he approached Laval street, a sudden fright shook him. Something was really happening on the square. He drew closer to the manifestation and quickly realized that people were indeed demonstrating in front of his home. He saw flames, and fearing for his wife and child, raced home to see the red flags set ablaze and himself being burnt in effigy by approximately 300 students. While Langlois's driver guarded the front door, armed with a 12-gauge rifle, more police were called in, including mounted officers, and the demonstration was brutally scattered. Approximately 30 people were injured, and one student was arrested.[3] A year almost to the day since his rousing victory over the defenders of the "trusts", the deputy for St. Louis was being denounced by students. "Poor Langlois," wrote Armand Dugas, a spokesman for the young demonstrators, "one would think that everyone has agreed to declare war on him."[4]

Impelled by his successes as a journalist and as a politician, Langlois had given a new direction to *Le Canada* since Liberal progressivism's victory over Parent. As he sought to explain his increasingly radical philosophy of nationalism, politics, economics, society and the reasons for why he thought French Canada was not progressing as others, Langlois alienated many people, including some of his erstwhile supporters. Indeed, as Langlois attempted to move Liberals in the direction of the French Radical left, his position in the Liberal progressive movement as well as in the party was being questioned. Sarah Bernhardt's scathing remarks about French Canada's manhood and its students that November found an echo in *Le Canada* and Langlois's anti-nationalist excesses ruffled more than a few party feathers. Archbishop Bruchési raged against the excesses of French theatre in a letter read in all Montreal churches: "We defy the most brilliant orators and the most celebrated actresses to come here to our city and ridicule our history or insult the honour of the Canadian name, for we know that they would receive hisses rather than applause."[5] *Le Canada*, and Langlois, who had published the names of society leaders who were seen attending her performances, were caught in the Bernhardt affair, which earned him as much student protest as Bernhardt herself during her notorious trip. "Langlois's presence [...] costs us the adhesions among the clergy and among a good number of Conservatives every day," affirmed L.O. Dugas, father of the student spokesman and himself the member of Parliament for Montcalm. He told Laurier that "another consequence, by no means the least important, is the apathy of youth [...]. The students of Montreal are irritated by *Le Canada* and if this continues at all, the Liberal party risks alienating Liberal youth."[6] The Prime Minister agreed, and told Dugas that "a radical change" was in order.[7]

In fact, there was little Laurier could do about Langlois in late 1905, even if he was increasingly uncomfortable with some of the editorial and managerial decisions made at *Le Canada*. The beginnings of the daily had been financially troubled, and problems continued to plague its editors. In desperate need to illustrate his chronic shortage of cash to party magnates, Langlois dismissed Charles Marcil, his Parliament Hill correspondent in Ottawa in February 1905.[8] Such a tactic, Langlois argued, would allow him to save money for a down payment on a new printing press. By early

1905, the newspaper's subscriptions had climbed to 21,000 issues a day and 18,000 each Saturday and the old press simply could not manage.[9] Laurier was infuriated when learning that the Liberal organ in Montreal would no longer have a parliamentary correspondent in Ottawa. "Do you not think that what you call a savings could not not at all be a savings, on the contrary, but a bad tactic? Can a newspaper increase its circulation if it does not have all the available news, if it is not as interesting if not more interesting than its competitors?"[10] Insulted by Laurier's gratuitous accusations, Langlois (who wanted to rely on party insiders to report "the news") wrote a thunderous reply. "The businessmen who direct our managing board believe that the time has come to make ends meet in the administration of our newspaper and they have resolved to reduce certain expenditures, including the Ottawa correspondent," Laurier was told. "Our till is in such as state that we must at all cost adopt a more economical, if not parsimonious, approach."[11]

If some aspects of Le Canada's administration annoyed Laurier, Langlois's ideological experiments also began to alienate Liberals of all hues. His incessant calls for a purification of the party in Montreal, Quebec city and Ottawa; for a greater role of the state; and his vitriolic denunciations of nationalism cost him much support among those who had supported him at the turn of the century. It made his position as the Liberal party's chief scribe vulnerable to an attack from an exasperated party establishment. "The beaten path was repugnant for him," remembered Charles Robillard, a coworker. "He adventured himself in new directions, audacious directions, risking the frightening of important groups of the party he wanted to serve. His independence of character, his inflexible will to remove the obstacles and to see his ideas triumph, and his clear vision of the goals that had to be reached disconcerted even the most hardy reformers of his entourage."[12] The radicalization of his views and the consequent isolation he suffered as many of Montreal's Liberal progressives waxed increasingly moderate, served to weaken the overall thrust of Liberal progressivism. Langlois's experience in the years following the Gouin "coup" highlighted the bifurcation of Liberal progressivism.

By 1906, the affairs of *Le Canada* seemed to stabilize. Langlois had managed to overcome the company's precarious financial situation, and because of the continuously growing readership of the morning daily, could look forward to better times. While he never shirked his administrative responsibilities, his first interest always remained writing, and as such managed to make an imprint on the newspaper's content. Langlois turned away from the yellow journalism he had tolerated at *La Patrie*. *Le Canada* was sober in its look and feel, and more likely to reprint a good speech than report the intimate details of a murderer's lifestyle.

That was not to say that Langlois did not indulge in muckraking of his own. His professionalism and intellectual vigor attracted top-notch journalists. Marc Sauvalle, who had been passed over in favour of Langlois for the director's position at *Le Canada*, left *La Presse* late in 1903 and found his way to Langlois's journal, as did a number of emerging politicians. Olivar Asselin, the fiery leftist nationalist, worked for Langlois until the end of 1904. Jules Fournier, another impetuous character, was hired from *La Presse* in mid-1904 and promoted to the post of political editor for a short time in 1906. It is interesting to note Langlois's occasional collaboration with some members of the *Ligue nationaliste*. Fournier, indeed, contributed to *Le Nationaliste* while editing *Le Canada*. Yet Langlois never adhered to this emerging nationalist thinking. His relationship with Henri Bourassa's apostles throws as much light on the variety of opinions which warred within *nationaliste* thinking as it did on his own understanding of nationalism and its application in French Canada.

While Laurier was in power, many French Canadian thinkers were reevaluating Quebec's role in Confederation. The Riel rebellions and the school crises had forced many, Langlois included, to conclude that the *status quo* no longer fit the realities of French North America. The notion of survival was on everyone's lips and many blueprints for Quebec's future were produced. Some, like Edmond de Nevers, were pessimistic about French Canada's chances for survival. For many conservative thinkers, the key to survival lay in a redefined nationalism, one that borrowed much from Catholic doctrine but affirmed the distinctiveness of Quebec's society and of its mission to ensure the survival of the French language on North American soil. To that end, Henri Bourassa and a sizeable portion of the *Ligue nationaliste* believed that French Canada's survival depended on a shielding from the effects of urbanization and industrialization. To survive in the face of inexorable socio-economic changes, French Canada had to securely anchor its modernization in its traditional attitudes, mores and customs.[13]

What differentiated Langlois's evolving nationalistic ethos from that of Bourassa was the nature and function of nationalism. Bourassa saw it as a means to an end: to preserve French Canada as Catholic and French. Langlois saw in nationalism little that could be of use, except perhaps as a unifying force that could bring together the reformists (a case in point was in his campaign to create a distinct Masonic lodge for francophones in Quebec in the mid-1890s). Worse still, Langlois feared the nationalists themselves, perceiving them as reactionaries who fought reform. Bourassa, for his part, feared the impact of Langlois's influence, especially on the students. "I noticed that young people were moving away more and more from sound religious and national ideals," he told Jules-Paul Tardivel in April 1904, in a letter explaining the ideological underpinnings of the *Ligue nationaliste*. "The ideas of the defunct *Canada-Revue* of *Débats* and the more veiled, and perhaps more dangerous ideas of Langlois at *La Patrie*, then of *Le Canada*, of Beauchesne at the *Journal*, were winning over new adherents. A group of young people, not very religious, but sincerely nationalistic, wanted to affirm themselves. I could not have succeeded in having them make an essentially catholic newspaper, but I found a derivative in prodding them in the nationalistic movement. I convinced them to accept the idea that to be anti-catholic was to be anti-patriotic and that to preserve the French Canadian nationality, it was necessary to maintain the influence of the catholic clergy."[14]

Obviously, Langlois never supported Bourassa's catholic, conservative ideology nor the nationalistic movement it spawned. Like Herbert Croly, and a few other notable American progressives, he had hoped that nationalism could fuel reform,[15] but unlike the French, German and the old *rouges* of the nineteenth century, Langlois was slowly turning away from nationalism altogether.[16] On those rare occasions when Langlois pretended to "speak for the nation", he did it while scolding his fellow citizens for not progressing fast enough, never to congratulate them. Although there is no doubt that Langlois believed in a national "good", he did not believe in a need for a national "ideal". He preferred to speak for the individual. If many of them were French Canadian, so be it. But Langlois often spoke with equal passion about the considerable Jewish element in his riding as well as about English Canadians. To him, a Liberal progressive was by definition a patriot, for he aimed at improving the whole of society by allowing the individual a chance to struggle for life with the right tools. His liberalism only reinforced his desire to see Canada strengthened by its cultural duality. "In the game of public interests, commercial and industrial, let us not be simply provincialists," he argued. "Let us work to make of our nine provinces a great nation, united, strong, proud, based on the most profound tolerance and the most complete freedom."[17]

Evidently, Langlois did not lose hope in Confederation, but was acutely conscious of a "slipping", a "*reculade*" in Quebec's industrial and commercial life when compared to the rest of Canada. "We should be of our time and of our era," he wrote in 1904. "We must at all cost give a stronger, more practical, more modern education to our youth [...]. Let us compete with our anglophone friends and fellow citizens on the basis of strength, energy, of thrusts towards the intellectual advancement of our masses, towards the moral and material development of the country and let us organize together the march of Canada to the future."[18] As he continued his travels both in English Canada and in the United States, his admiration for the two societies only grew. He marveled at the "extraordinary intensity" of industrial life in Butte City, Montana in 1902.[19] Increasingly, he openly compared Quebec's industrial and educational performance with that of the rest of North America. Langlois's observations made him pessimistic about Quebec's future and he criticized those in the province — nationalists — who argued that the province was more virtuous. Langlois, unlike a great many nationalists, no longer saw English Canada as a cultural menace, but as a society that had much to teach Quebec.[20] Le Canada's unflattering comparisons of Quebec with Ontario added bitterness to the debate about reform. In a heated discussion in the Legislative Assembly on educational issues, Langlois was castigated by the Liberal member from Chicoutimi, Dr. Jobin, for asserting that Ontario did more for education than did Quebec. Coldly referring to the facts as he understood them, Langlois rejected Jobin's reproach. The figures, he argued, spoke of a need for a Ministry of Education, and there was nothing treasonous in demanding action.[21]

Langlois's reaction against the nationalists could thus be explained as an attempt to instill some order in Quebec's social, economic and intellectual agenda. More than the notion of nationalism, Langlois distrusted the nationalists. "St-Jean-Baptisme" as Langlois derogatively styled the new conservative nationalism, was to the editors of Le Canada an outright falsification of the realities of Quebec's state and a distraction from the solving of the problem's most pressing problems. "Mr. Bourassa refers to himself as a Liberal on every issue, but he is masking the 'castor' and 'tory' characteristics that are revealed by his actions," wrote Langlois in 1907.[22] Langlois's sense of patriotism rejected complacency and idle glorifications. "The Canadian fatherland must occupy our hearts and our soul," he told a journalists' banquet in 1903. "It must be loved by means other than the ephemeral and artificial 'St-Jean Baptisme' thrusts that feed the illusion that we are the greatest and freest people on earth. That optimism and that excess of vanity have until now only hampered our course towards the future. We are not the greatest people, believe me, our schools are too modest and inadequate, our public school system is too neglected, our evaluation has been too timid and our attitudes are still too unsure."[23]

Phrases such as these raised the ire of many students and more than a few politicians. It was simply a part of Langlois's sorting out of Quebec's ideological baggage. Room had to be made for his ethos of Liberal progressivism, even if that necessitated throwing some aspects of the political culture overboard and quoting with such love people like Sarah Bernhardt, who since her first trip to Canada in 1880 had been an inspiration to the radicals in Quebec.[24] Langlois's rejection of Bourassa's conservatism and his need to reconcile national destiny with improved individual liberties prompted him to codify his ideas along the evolving features of French Radicalism.

Langlois's fascination with France did not wane as he grew older. His sentiment for the Third Republic, as it suffered highs and lows, only grew fonder. If he sought inspiration in the writings of the older radicals in the late nineteenth century, he wholeheartedly espoused what the radicals now pointed to as a unifying ideology: *solidarisme*.

Solidarisme, the brainchild of Léon Bourgeois (1851-1925), was an early doctrine of welfare-state liberalism. Bourgeois had been a politician for almost twenty years when he formulated the foundations of his philosophy in the mid-1890s. He was one of the founders of the *Parti radical* in 1901, a party that openly stated that Bourgeois's notions formed the crux of its beliefs. Bourgeois's innovative ideas were not lost on French Canadian radicals, although it took time for them to digest them. *Le Signal*, the radical journal of Montreal Liberals in the late 1890s openly expressed the admiration of the new generation of radical rouges for Bourgeois as early as August 1897.[25] Feeling unfettered by the party line, Langlois began to apply Bourgeoisian concepts in his daily observations at *Le Canada*.

Bourgeois's mission, like Langlois's, was eminently political. He wanted to reconcile radical impulses of individualism with the modern realities brought about by an often reckless capitalism. Man is not born free, Bourgeois concluded. From the time he is born he incurs debts: to his family, to his society, to his country. Those debts, he argued, were amassed in a series of unwritten contracts, and had to be honoured as much as the individual could afford.[26] The French radicals, according to Bourgeois, had to respond to this political reality.

It was in the twentieth century that Bourgeois's ideas attracted attention to the point where it bound together fiercely independent radicals into a party. In 1901, on the occasion of the birth of the new *Parti radical*, Bourgeois clearly distilled for the first time the creed of *solidarisme*, which is worth quoting at length: POLAND 1990

> The goal is to organize society politically and socially according to rules of reason, that is to say according to the total development of the human person in every human being, according to the total realization of justice in all the relations between human beings. *Faith in reason.*
>
> The method proceeds from the conception that all associations tend to develop towards a higher state by the coordinated evolution of all of its singular elements. *Faith in progress.*
>
> The Radical Party expects the progressive improvement of society to be the product of a moral and intellectual evolution of each of the members of society. Education is thus recognized as important, the essential motor of progress, which will make revolutions unnecessary. *Faith in schools.*
>
> The morality of enlarging solidarity to a political principle must, in social policy, make way to a network of insurances:

The nation will only enjoy peace when it will have created a complete package of insurance that will protect every individual from the risks of sickness, of unemployment, of disability, of old age. *Faith in national solidarity.*[27]

VERY ANTI MIKE HARRIS

While its agenda never stopped evolving, *solidarisme*'s orientation remained clear. In the words of historian J.E.S. Hayward, *solidarisme* was "opposed alike to liberal economism, marxist collectivism, catholic corporatism and anarchist syndicalism, though having something common with them all."[28] Bourgeois was certainly always careful to avoid socialism: There was no desire to confiscate property or profits. "*Solidarisme* required men to cooperate not in production or in the division of wealth, but in insuring themselves against the risks of life," observed British historian Theodore Zeldin: "Equal wages were neither possible nor desirable, but a minimum wage was necessary. In the name of justice and illness, accident or unemployment insurance were a social duty. Taxation should exist not for the purpose of levelling incomes but to support common services, though each should contribute in proportion to his income. Education should be free. The important thing was that the only limit to a man's ascent should be his natural abilities."[29]

Part of Langlois's attraction to the French Radical notion of *solidarisme* may be explained by the overriding concern French radicalism devoted to education. This impulse fit neatly into Langlois's own agenda for Quebec. Bourgeois, for one, had been active in pressure groups that had advocated educational reform since his earlier days in politics. From 1895 to 1898 he had succeeded Jean Macé as the President of the French *Ligue de l'Enseignement*, and his influence in that organization was pervasive. In 1900, the *Ligue* congress voted in favour of Bourgeois's goal of *solidarisme*.[30]

If *solidarisme* appealed to reformers of education, education was in turn a cornerstone of solidarisme's model of a perfect society. In order for the individual to repay his debt to society as completely as possible, he had to be as productive as possible. An efficient, educated individual was an asset to the state and to society not only because he was more likely to support the system, but because he would reduce the weight on the state's shoulders in the long run. In order for the educational system to perform efficiently, however, reforms had to be enacted. From 1881, elementary schools in France was free to all children. In June 1882, the government decreed that parents were obliged to educate their children of both sexes until the age of 13. Still, more than a quarter of France's schoolchildren were still in the hands of the church-run private schools and most radicals found these figures unacceptable.[31]

With the René Waldeck-Rousseau and Emile Combes ministries at the turn of the century, the radicals made concrete their ideals in a secular society. In 1901, certain catholic orders were dissolved under the stress of strict regulations. Clerical education was suppressed, as a virtual revolution was imposed on the French religious establishment. Diplomatic relations between France and the Vatican were cut off. As Langlois barely muffled his applause in his articles on the French political scene, the church in Quebec grew restless.

Langlois's keen interest in the working class also made him all the more susceptible to absorbing Bourgeois's philosophy of the state and formulation of liberalism. As "coups de plume" was transplanted to Le Canada after Langlois's departure from Tarte's La Patrie, so was "Chez les ouvriers." The journalist's initiatives in pushing the Liberal party to the left had motivations that resembled those of Bourgeois's solidarisme. Langlois aimed to show his working-class readership that the Liberal party was ready and willing to acknowledge and act on its demands. More than the majority of his colleagues, moreover, Langlois was conscious of the fact that the Liberal party had to perform in order to be accepted. This meant that action was needed at a time when workers' parties of all kinds were sprouting in Montreal. In 1906, he urged Laurier again to address the workers on Labour Day so as to "return the faltering opinions to the Liberal party."[32]

252

It was through Langlois's dialogue with the working class that the principles of Liberal progressivism assumed clearer outlines. Following Bourgeois's lead, his progressive creed called for a greater, though limited, state involvement in the economy in order to safeguard the rights of the individual as well as the legitimacy of the capitalist system. Like the French radicals, and to some extent the Asquith Liberals from 1908 to 1914, Langlois welcomed enthusiastically a rethinking of the state's role in society. He often wrote glowingly about French socialism, and Jean Jaurès, the leader of the socialist movement in France, piqued Langlois's curiosity. *Le Canada*'s editor never shied from publishing "for documentary purposes" Jaurès's socialist speeches. Despite his admiration for the French socialist leader, however, Langlois refused to stretch the bounds of his understanding of Liberal progressivism to include Jaurèsian visions.[33] Indeed, when Keir Hardie, the popular British socialist, visited Canada, Langlois manifested his apprehensions regarding socialism. "Mr. Hardie's socialism expresses an ideal that is obviously not bereft of nobility and that reveals a sense of humanity that we are pleased to recognize," said Langlois. "But that socialism has strong collectivist tendencies—and here, already, we begin to move away from him."[34]

Socialism was no solution for the working man, argued Langlois. "We are all workers or children of workers," this merchant's son reasoned. "Canada is the land of workers *par excellence*. We are all, from the smallest to the oldest, the authors of our fortunes and of our destinies. Here there are no privileged classes, no feudal fortunes, no omnipotent magnates: the rule of work is a common obligation."[35] Langlois's exaggerations in describing Quebec's society were not gratuitously or condescendingly offered. He was not deaf to the particular demands of the working class and used them to justify his own agenda. "We are not of those who believe our present society to be perfect and who consider it a crime to attempt to improve it," he assured his readers.[36] Like Bourgeois, Langlois was concerned that the capitalist state

was no longer fulfilling its task of legitimizing the existence
of the capitalist system. The educational system worked at
odds with the requirements of modern life. The state's function was confused and ill-designed in light of modern oppres-
sions and attacks on liberty of choice. He undoubtedly shared
the French radical's fear of a reaction of the working class.
"Today you see on the other side of the Atlantic that dark
cloud of trusts who diminish the light of human liberties and
that already throws shadows on the shores of the old world.
If you leave the worker to be weak, alone, without support
and without social aid, in that cold that is more intensely felt
with each day that passes, do you know where he will go?
He will revolt, he will turn to violence, to chimera," Bourgeois told the first congress of the *Parti radical* in 1901.[37]

To protect the individual, Bourgeois saw the state take on
the role of limiting the strength of the "trusts". As much as
Langlois, he feared a calcification of freedoms wrought by
great industrial and financial empires. "The general interest
of the country, the liberty and the fate of all, must be
preserved from their growing domination," Bourgeois said
in 1901, "either through legislation that could put an end to
speculating or by legislative measures that could create
within the state certain monopolies and public services as
they are needed and which affect national defence as well
agricultural and industrial production."[38] Active state involvement in certain areas was a fundamental premise of
solidarisme thinking. "The state is a human creation," Bourgeois affirmed. "It can only intervene to reestablish equality
between all the parties to a contract. What is now required
of democracy is an accurate estimate of the contributions and
levies of everyone. The state is nothing more than the under-
writer to those contracts. It will therefore have to give to
those who are creditors, and ensure that debtors pay."[39]
Solidarisme refused to make the state superior to the individual. The role of the state had to be appreciated, but it could
not be deified. Contrary to socialism, in the words of Jean-
Thomas Nordmann, an observer of the French radical tradi-

tion, *solidarisme* translated public rights as an expression of individual rights. This vision fit perfectly with Langlois's thinking on the ideological directions of the Liberal party. Upon reviewing a *Parti radical* pamphlet in a 1907 editorial, Langlois could hardly contain his enthusiasm for the radical conception of the role of the state. Albert de Chabanne's *Le libéralisme devant la raison* argued that the state had a moral role to perform in order to grant the individual his freedom. "It is of the 'liberalism' examined in this book that we speak and not of English liberalism, the conservative liberalism, the old liberalism," exclaimed *Le Canada.*[40]

The challenge in avoiding the alienation of the working class in this era of growing industrial power, according to Bourgeois, lay in having the state minimize the amount of "debt" a person could accumulate. The answer was a sharing of the risks of modern life. To borrow historian Theodore Zeldin's phrase, "Bourgeois saw society as a giant mutual insurance company."[41] Premiums, of course, had to be paid, and Bourgeois considered than an enlightened taxation system would improve the state with sufficient resources to protect individuals from running great risks in the course of their daily lives. Godfroy Langlois applied Bourgeois's ideas instinctively, and was outspoken in his demands that the Province of Quebec levy higher direct taxes on its rich citizens so as to alleviate the misery of society's poor. "Liberals, and Conservatives, are wrong to instill in people a fear of direct taxation," Langlois argued in the Legislative Assembly in February 1906. "If a government presented itself before the people and proposed that what we could call a national contribution for the maintenance of our roads and our public schools, this proposal would not be refused."[42]

Langlois ensured that *Le Canada* remained an active participant against the trusts and those politicians who supported it. The call for state-sponsored competition against the Montreal Light, Heat, and Power Company was not a knee-jerk reaction to all problems of monopoly capitalism. Considering the sour experience of railway building in Quebec, for instance, *Le Canada* had balked at the idea that railways should be nationalized in 1903.[43] Nevertheless, more and more industries were increasingly considered suitable for massive state involvement. "Our entire industrial and commercial system is permeated by them," Langlois declared of the trusts two months after his election to the Legislative Assembly. "There is not one area of human activity that is exempt. Must there be an insurgency against all those combines that are nothing but associations put together to more or less force the public to pay a certain price for the merchandise and the services of their members? A social revolution might as well be undertaken."[44] Unfortunately, Langlois only expanded cryptically on the concept of the "social revolution" he advocated. He never really argued for a "social revolution" as much as an intellectual one, especially among politicians, in order to avoid a veritable "social revolution".

Langlois's advocacy of state insurance concepts was typically Bourgeoisian. In the fall of 1907 the government of New York disclosed its findings of price fixing in the insurance industry. Langlois faithfully published numerous accounts of poor investments of premiums, of exploitation of the clientele, and of exorbitant salaries paid to company executives.[45] He pressed the Quebec government to establish a parliamentary commission to study the possibilities of state insurance.[46] State-sponsored life insurance in the province of Quebec, according to Langlois, could offer an honest administration, hardy initiative, and above all, an understanding of the population it serviced. "With this assurance," he wrote as early as 1905, "no fear of failure, no extravagant administration costs, premiums reduced to their lowest values, compatibility with the interests of all the population. This is the quintessence of mutuality, with the most absolute security."[47] A few months later, Langlois demanded that higher taxes be levied on insurance companies in Quebec. He observed that only three of the 35 insurance companies who did business in Quebec were owned by Quebeckers. Fourteen of them were from Ontario, 16 were American, 7 had headquarters in Great Britain and one was from Manitoba. "Those companies have taken from the people of our province about $5.5 million dollars," Langlois told the Legislative Assembly. "Of that number, only $575,000 went to the companies of our province. It is therefore fair that these foreign companies pay an income tax here that is at least as considerable as what they pay in their own country."[48]

The best example of *Le Canada*'s philosophy of the state can be culled from its reactions to the old age pension debate in 1908. Langlois advocated measures that would have helped the elderly who were no longer capable of working. He disagreed with federal M.P. Ralph Smith's proposal that these pensions be made universal, however. Langlois was unfavourable to the notion that all could benefit equally from the measure. His idea was that, barring the establishment of an income tax that would recover some of the moneys needlessly handed out, an affordable insurance, and better payouts, should only be available to those in need.[49] In the debate on old-age pensions, Langlois again manifested his intellectual debt to the French radicals. He made no attempt to hide that debt as he was warmly applauded after his annual toast to the Third Republic during the Bastille Day banquet in Montreal in 1907. "We have common origins," he told the President of the Canadian chapter of the Alliance française. "French Canadians love France as much as you do and what we love of France is its democracy, its love of liberty. We have borne witness with pride to its recovery during the last thirty years." Taking advantage of the occasion to swipe at those "nationalistes" who denounced the Third Republic's excesses, he said: "There are some who believe that there are movements of revolt in France, but those of us who understand the French pay no attention for we love that nation whose brain is in activity rather than those whose brains are anemic."[50] The conservative daily *La Vérité* reacted violently to a similar speech made by Langlois a year later. "You insist a great deal, Mr. Langlois, on the state of *liberty* in France today; is it ignorance or meanness?" went the editorial. "The *liberty* only exists there for those who do wrong, the Free-masons have a freedom of action, the Jews too; the catholics, do they have it? What do you mean, Mr. the director of *Le Canada*, by the fecundity of the works of *modern* France? Is it the *Ligue de l'Enseignement* and other organizations who work to dechristianize the church's eldest daughter? [...] It is worth noting, in France mainly, that Mr. Langlois is only expressing his personal views and those of a handful of *francissons* who have nothing in common with French Cana-dians."[51]

La Vérité's stinging remark about Langlois's ideas having little in common with French Canadians was finding an echo in many reaches of the Liberal party in Quebec. Where Langlois had been recognized as a true spokesman of the progressive Liberals in the past, many now found his remarks to be a threat to the party. Among those who deserted him were many Liberal progressives who had supported him with *Le Signal*, and in his crusades against the corruption of the Raymond Préfontaine clique and against those who pro-tected the Montreal Light, Heat, and Power Company. Lan-glois was becoming too radical, and was pushing Liberal progressivism too far in the direction of French radicalism. This was not to say that Liberal progressivism was defeated— far from it— as people continued to believe in the desirability of educational reform, the need for government involvement in pensions, and in the virtues of controlling utilities. Rather, a gulf was being created between him and some of his former followers as disagreements erupted over the means and the tone of the rhetoric required to meet the desired ends.

The student riot led by Armand Dugas in 1905 was a symptom of Liberal disagreement. Many opposed Langlois's anti-nationalism and critical comments regarding Quebec's increasingly evident "retard." It was their way of punishing him for parroting the searing remarks made by Sarah Bern-hardt in November 1905. There was much truth to what he uttered at the 1909 Bastille Day banquet in Montreal: he had

demonstrated more than anyone in Quebec that he was a
follower of what one historian called the Third Republic's
"official ideology" of *solidarisme*.[52]

Notes

1. Cited in Georgette Weiler, *Sarah Bernhardt et le Canada* (Quebec, 1973), pp.37-38.
2. See *La Presse*, 15 juillet 1909.
3. The best account of the event is in *La Presse*, 22 novembre 1905.
4. Langlois Papers, Scrapbook A, p.22, unidentified newspaper clipping, n.d.
5. The 1905 Bernhardt affair is well described in Ramon Hathorn, "Sarah Bernhardt and the Bishops of Montreal and Quebec" Canadian Catholic History Association *Historical Studies*, Vol. 53, (1986), pp. 97-120. Bernhart was invested with a strong symbolic value by the radicals ever since her first trip to Quebec in 1880. On the importance of symbolism in history and historiography, see Robert Darnton, "The symbolic element in History", *JMH*, Vol 58, No. 1, March 1986. On the *rouge* politics surrounding the first Bernhardt visit, see Dutil thesis, *op.cit.*, pp. 1-5. See also Ramon Hathorn, "Sarah Bernhardt et l'accueil montréalais" *RHLQCF*, Vol. 5, 1983.
6. Laurier Papers, C829, F.O. Dugas to Laurier, 26 novembre 1905.
7. *Ibidem*, Laurier to Dugas, 28 novembre 1905.
8. *Ibidem*, Langlois to Laurier, 2 février 1905.
9. *Ibidem*, Langlois to Laurier, 10 janvier 1905.
10. *Ibidem*, Laurier to Langlois, 3 février 1905.
11. *Ibidem*, Langlois to Laurier, 7 février 1905.
12. *La Patrie*, 10 janvier 1943.
13. Although scholars have lavished attention on Bourassa, much of his thinking remains shrouded in mystery. Some have argued that Bourassa was progressive in many of his observations, while others have depicted him as essentially conservative. The most succinct descriptions of Bourassa as "progressive" are in Michael Oliver, "The Social and Political Ideas of French Canadian Nationalists, 1920-1945" (Ph.D. Thesis, McGill University, 1956) and Joseph Levitt, *Henri Bourassa and the Golden Calf* (Ottawa, 1972). Among those who have highlighted Bourassa's conservatism, see Susan Mann Trofimenkoff, "Henri Bourassa and the Woman Question" *JCS*, 10, 1975, and C. Michael MacMillan, "The Character of Henri Bourassa's Political Philosophy" *ARCS*, Spring 1982. The most recent discussion of the works on Bourassa is Joseph Levitt, "Images of Bourassa", *JCS*, 13, 1978. One of the best works to describe the mindset of Bourassa and his followers is

Arthur Silver, *The French Canadian Idea of Confederation, 1864-1900* (Toronto, 1982).

14. Henri Bourassa Papers, Private Collection, Bourassa to Tardivel, 20 avril 1904.

15. On Herbert Croly's nationalism, see David W. Levy, *Herbert Croly of the New Republic* (Princeton, 1985) and Charles Forcey, *The Crossroad of Liberalism* (New York, 1961).

16. Nationalism was a by-product of liberalism in the nineteenth century. On the importance of nationalism in German liberalism, see James Sheehan, *German Liberalism in the nineteenth Century* (Chicago, 1978). An interesting study of twentieth century liberal nationalism in Germany is Moshe Zimmermann, "A Road not Taken—Friedrich Naumann's Attempt at a Modern German Nationalism" in *JCH*, 17, 1982. Nationalism in France was also best defined by the radicals, until the neo-conservatives challenged them with a new Catholic, xenophobic creed. See Sanford Elwitt, *The Making of the Third Republic* (Baton Rouge, 1975) and R.D. Anderson, *France, 1870-1914: Politics and Society* (London, 1977). The rise of the "new right," while ignored in Canada, has been examined in some detail by European historians. Briefly, for France, see Robert Soucy, *Fascism in France: The Case of Maurice Barrès* (New York, 1972); Eugen Weber, *Action Française: Royalism and Reaction in Twentieth Century France* (New York, 1962); William D. Irvine, *The Boulanger Affair Reconsidered* (London, 1989) and Julien Benda, *La trahison des clercs* (Paris, 1927). The issue of the "new right" in Germany is treated in Geoff Ealey, *Reshaping the German Right* (New York, 1980). On Italy, see Alexander de Grand, *The Italian Nationalist Association* (New York, 1978) and A. James Gregor, *Young Mussolini and the Intellectual Origins of Fascism* (New York, 1979). On the importance of nationalism in nineteenth century Canadian liberalism, see Jean-Paul Bernard, *Les Rouges* (Montreal, 1971).

17. *Le Canada* , 10 septembre 1906.

18. *Ibidem*, 4 septembre 1904.

19. Laurier Papers, C 796, Langlois to Boudreau, 27 octobre 1902.

20. *Le Canada*, 31 août 1906.

21. *La Presse*, 2 mars 1906.

22. *Le Canada*, 30 juillet 1907; see also 30 novembre 1906.

23. *Le Canada*, 9 décembre 1903.

24. On the significance of Bernhardt's first visit to the *rouges*, see Patrice Dutil, "The Politics of of Liberal progessivism in Quebec: Godfroy Langlois and the Liberal Party, 1889-1914" (Ph.D. thesis, York University, 1987), pp. 1-5.

25. See *Le Signal*, 7 août 1897.

26. On the origins of *solidarisme*, see J.E.S. Hayward, "Solidarism: The Social History of an Idea in Nineteenth Century France" *IRSH*, 9, 1959.

27. See Bourgeois's preface to Ferdinand Buisson, *Le radicalisme* (Paris, 1901), cited in George Lefranc, *Les gauches en France* (Paris, 1973), p. 159.

28. J.E.S. Hayward, "The Official Social Philosophy of the Third Republic: Léon Bourgeois and Solidarism" *IRSH*, 6, 1961, p. 21.

29. Theodore Zeldin, *France 1848-1945* (London, 1973), p. 658.

30. Cited in J.E.S. Hayward, "Educational Pressure Groups and the Indoctrination of the Radical Ideology of Solidarism, 1895-1914" *IRSH*, Vol. VIII, part 1, 1963.

31. Maurice Larkin, *Church and state after the Dreyfus Affair* (New York, 1974), p. 2.

32. Laurier Papers, C 836, Langlois to Laurier, 4 juillet 1906.

33. See *Le Canada*, 18 mars 1904; 8 juillet 1905; 29 juillet 1905 for examples.

34. *Le Canada*, 30 juillet 1907.

35. *Le Canada*, 3 septembre 1905.

36. *Le Canada*, 5 septembre 1905.

37. Jean-Thomas Nordmann, *La France radicale* (Paris, 1976), p. 85.

38. _____, *Histoire des Radicaux* (Paris, 1970), p. 125.

39. *Ibidem*, p. 134.

40. *Le Canada*, editorial, 17 août 1907.

41. Zeldin, *op.cit.*, p. 658.

42. *La Presse*, 9 février 1906.

43. *Le Canada*, 28 mai 1903.

44. *Ibidem*, 19 janvier 1905.

45. *Ibidem*, 9 october 1907.

46. *La Presse*, 24 mars 1908.

47. *Le Canada*, 19 octobre 1905.

48. *La Presse*, 9 février 1906.

49. *Ibidem*, 5 février 1908.

50. *La Presse*, 15 juillet 1907.

51. *La Vérité*, 18 juillet 1908.

52. J.E.S. Hayward, "The Official Social Philosophy of the Third Republic: Léon Bourgeois and Solidarism" *IRSH*, 6, 1961.

CHAPTER X

THE DOWNFALL OF GODFROY LANGLOIS

WHEN THE LEGISLATIVE ASSEMBLY RESUMED its work after the "Gouin Coup", it seemed as though the problems of the past were forgotten. Senator Philippe-Auguste Choquette was optimistic: "Local politics are going very well," he informed Sir Wilfrid in May 1905. "Every one seems happy and already notices a great difference in what is being accomplished in Parliament, as well as in the conduct of the Assembly and in the committees, etc." "The party," he valiantly concluded, "will be stronger from the point of view of morale than it has been since 1897."[1]

Choquette, who had finally bought control of *Le Soleil* in April 1905, was not alone in relishing the fruits of Liberal progressive triumphs. Godfroy Langlois, sitting in the Legislative Assembly for the first time, was equally hopeful that the party "morale" would reflect Liberal progressive instincts, even if the location of his desk relative to the members of the cabinet was perhaps revealing of the way he was already being perceived by the party leadership. Because the Liberal victory had been so overwhelming, members of the governing party had to sit alongside the opposition. Seated almost directly opposite Gouin was Langlois—an arrangement that illustrated well the relationship the two men would share for the next ten years, especially over the critical issue of educational reform.

Gouin fulfilled the hopes of the Liberal progressives on the issues of controlling the hydroelectric industry. They heartily sponsored Gouin's attempts to foster competition against the Montreal Light, Heat, and Power Company and certainly were favourable to the Premier following the establishment of a Board of Control in Montreal and the provincial Public Utilities Commission. Educational reform, however, proved to be a fault line where Liberal progressives would divide. A measure of the importance of educational reform in Godfroy Langlois's mind can be gauged from his performance in the Legislative Assembly. In the nine years he sat in the Legislative Assembly, there were a total of 195 recorded votes. Godfroy Langlois voted in favour of his government 104 times, was absent on 83 occasions, but voted against the Premier on only eight occasions, all of them dealing with the educational motions he or some of his allies would propose. Langlois, demonstrably content with most aspects of Gouin's administration, voted with the government 92.9% of the time. Restrained by the realities of factionalism in the party, Gouin chose to accommodate the views of conservative Liberals in the sensitive area of educational policy and was forced to withdraw his usual support for Langlois when it came to discuss these matters. The latter was isolated by progressive Liberals like Gouin who shared the same ideals, but— and this is a significant condition—who adopted wider time frames to see the full implementation of reforms.

Hot on the heels of the "coup", Gouin spoke out more clearly than at any other time of his life to explain where he stood. As it was the legal tradition, the new cabinet faced the electorate to reaffirm its legitimacy. All were acclaimed except the Premier himself who was challenged by the leader of the *Parti ouvrier*. Evidently, Gouin had already begun the process of welding together the broken pieces of his party so as to ensure that the Liberal coalition would not come apart under his leadership as it had under his predecessor Simon-Napoléon Parent. Among the first five names signing the Premier's nomination form were dedicated Parent supporters such as Préfontaine, Rainville, and Archambault! Albert Saint-Martin, who had spoken in favour of Langlois during the 1904 election, contested Gouin's election.

Saint-Martin had always been an adamant supporter of left-leaning Liberal clubs, and often admitted being an admirer of Félix-Gabriel Marchand's educational policies. He quit the party in the winter of 1905 as soon as he heard "that the workers wanted to organize a workers' party."[2] Indeed, Saint-Martin seemed to speak as the disgruntled Liberal progressive he had once been. Chiding Gouin for not fulfilling promises made to the Liberals, he asked: "You promised the nomination of a Minister of Public Schools, your party having even designated the individual who would occupy that position [Langlois?]. Why have you not even tried to make that nomination?"[3] Forced to speak out, Gouin initially pretended to adopt a distinctly neutral position, even if he did address the issue of education. "If there are needs, ideas and demands that the government must satisfy," Gouin said, "those are the needs that are felt in the school, it is those ideas that are oriented towards education, it is those demands that are formulated to improve the lot of teachers." Then, striking a decidedly Liberal progressive chord, he said to a crowd of partisans gathered in the Ecole Montcalm that "education is, in fact, the most important of political, economic and social issues facing men, because it contains the solution to all the others."[4] But Gouin was careful not to alienate the more conservative Liberals who had signed his nomination card. "We are not doctrinaire," he told the same crowd, "we recognize that policy is not a matter of opinion, of prejudice or of passions. Well understood, it is a science; it should even take its place among the sciences that are said to be experimental."[5] Gouin, who sometimes dared to experiment, won his election handily. Saint-Martin, gathering less than ten percent of the total vote, lost his deposit.

For his part, Langlois (who found himself without a cabinet post) wasted no time in trying to steer the cabinet's agenda from his seat opposite the Premier when Parliament resumed late in April 1905. Relentlessly, the new member for St-Louis prodded the government into releasing figures on all sorts of matters. The power of Quebec City never intimidated Langlois. For the $800 he was paid annually for his legislative duties, he was asked to be in the capital for an average of five to six weeks a year, generally in February or March. Members were routinely entertained at Spencerwood, the Lieutenant-Governor's mansion, or in the Speaker's quarters. Some days the Assembly sat for only a half-hour, while at other times debate lasted into the small hours of the night. Most MLAs did not sit on Mondays or Fridays, allowing many of them the opportunity to return to their ridings, and in the case of Langlois, to attend to the business of running a daily newspaper. So comfortable was Langlois with political life that he literally dominated the 1905 and 1906 sessions with his incessant queries, jibes and numerous motions. His first bill, perhaps more closely related to advertising revenue than with the issues with which he was most closely associated with, aimed at allowing dentists to advertise their services in newspapers.[6]

The newly elected Liberal progressives did not wait long to be heard on the subject of school reform and church authority after the Gouin "coup". On May 11, 1905, Langlois rose for his first major speech to the Assembly and proposed a three-pronged package of educational reform. He was harshly critical of the administration of public education in the province and openly accused the system's superintendent of doctoring field reports so as to avoid embarrassment.[7] He demanded that more teachers' colleges be established and asked that the central examiner's office—the institution that granted teaching licenses—be abolished. Because of the shortages of staff it was obvious that the office was granting certificates to people ill-suited to teaching. Finally, he urged the government to consider reducing the number of school boards so as to permit a greater centralization and a more standardized and equitable educational policy.[8]

As usual, Langlois's propositions found an echo. Achille Bergevin, the member for Beauharnois, and one of Langlois's co-conspirators in the "coup", promptly congratulated his friend for his agitation in favour of educational reform. Even Gouin responded. On May 20, it was announced that provincial funding for new elementary schools would be increased by $50,000, double the amount spent previously. Still, the new Premier persisted in downplaying the significance of his cabinet's gestures. "We have no intention to hurt, destroy or overturn," said Gouin, "We only want to improve, strengthen and consolidate."[9]

Langlois never hid his displeasure with the church's role in Quebec's educational system, or indeed, with its fostering of what he considered to be an unhealthy conservatism. He did not attack the church directly, but never failed to chastise publicly its staunchest defenders and the institutions it managed. Of the most harassed was Charles Magnan, the Superintendent of Quebec's Catholic Schools, who in 1903 felt compelled to publish a defence of the school system in a book entitled *Honneur à la province de Québec*. Magnan rejected all Liberal progressive propositions for reform. "We cannot restrain ourselves in reproaching Mr. Magnan, and others, for hoodwinking our province," Langlois argued repeatedly.

> Every time a publicist, an orator, or a citizen demanded legitimate improvements in our school system, the same voice was always heard that we had the best schools and that those who demanded reform were enemies of the established order. It is that unfortunate tactic that has provoked all sorts of prejudice, that has stopped progress, but that permitted certain individuals to maintain their influence.[10]

Provoked by Magnan's claim that the educational system in Quebec was "the best in the world" (a declaration that could be heard still coming from Maurice Duplessis in the 1950s), *Le Canada* pressed for educational reform and pointed to the Third Republic as an example of what should be done, throughout the fall of 1905. Its scoffing at Vatican pronouncements angered Archbishop Bruchési. "That newspaper publishes regular dispatches on Rome and the Vatican that are always false, biased and written with an unfavourable tone towards the church," Bruchési complained to Senator Béique. "Does it not seem [...] that those items that deal with such delicate subjects should be controlled with greater care?

Should it continue, I would find myself obliged to publish a note so as to caution the faithful regarding those news stories. But I am convinced that a word on your part to *Le Canada*'s director will put an end to this sort of thing."[11]

The Archbishop's menacing words were ignored, and Langlois was not alone in persistently calling into question the church's institutions. Critiques by the old radical George Washington Stephens and William Alexander Weir in November 1905 found favour in *Le Canada*. "Must I conclude that we will have to resume the old battles that seemed resolved? I would regret this deeply," lamented Bruchési to Gouin.

> *Le Canada* has been playing a saddening role for some time. I know who manages it, but where he draws his inspirations, I don't know. But I see that those who have authority over him and who let him run their newspaper, approve of him, at least tacitly. What is said in the offices of that newspaper cannot be printed. It may appear imprudent and premature, but it is hoped that more vigilance will be shown. We have enemies there, men who will always be against us. The church can expect nothing from them. I am well informed, my friend, and I am keeping guard. I read *Le Canada* attentively every day and I am under no illusions as to the campaign it has undertaken. I know, with God's grace, how to be patient; but with God's grace also, I know how to fulfil my duties as first pastor, however painful it may be.[...] I am a pacifist by nature and I only make war when duty demands it; but if that newspaper wants war I am ready.[12]

The political authorities were thus warned again of the consequences of keeping Godfroy Langlois as director and editor at *Le Canada*. Bruchési's warnings, for now, would go unheeded, but his political message did carry clout. At a political gathering on December 9, 1905, Langlois added fuel to the fire when he demanded that a Royal Commission be established to examine the educational system. "There is no need to revolutionize," Langlois said (borrowing Gouin's rhetoric), "but we must achieve a better system than what exists today."[13] He was undoubtedly trying to influence Liberal opinion on the eve of the celebrated and much awaited banquet that was to be given in honour of Quebec's new Premier, and he was successful. Over 600 people gathered at the Windsor Hotel on December 11 to celebrate. The room was thick with cigar smoke when Rodolphe Latulippe, the President of the *Club Letellier* addressed Gouin and urged reform in education. Spurred by George Washington Stephens and Senator Joseph-Philippe Casgrain, Gouin responded. "Many people speak of creating a Ministry of Education," he told the partisan crowd. "That proposal is made in good faith, I have no doubt about that. But why resume the discussions and again give rise to the difficulties that would inevitably hamstring the efforts that men of good will are ready to devote so as to make education in this province progress?" "Education," he concluded to loud cheers, "has been made the primary objective of my administration, the first concern of my political life, the goal of my efforts."[14]

Bruchési's fear of witnessing the beginnings of educational change substantiated further in the winter of 1906. That February, Joseph-Edouard Caron, the member for L'Islet, proposed that religious institutions be taxed by municipalities. Caron then tabled in the Assembly an amendment to the Charter of the Town of St-Germain-de-Rimouski that put that resolution into practice. On February 15, most Liberals present voted to make the bill law. Langlois, Walsh, Stephens, Weir—even Gouin and Turgeon—voted in favour of the principle. It was passed by a vote of 38 to 15.[15] The bill made its way to the Legislative Council where it was amended in response to the Archbishop's intervention against the measure. Thomas Chapais, the same man who had defeated the Marchand educational reform bill in 1898, fought the principle tooth and nail, and cemeteries, hospitals and charities were exempted from taxes. Religious communities, moreover, would pay only a water tax, and a share of funding for sewers and fire protection, something most of

Town in the North East

them already paid.[16] The tax bill therefore did not set the precedent people like Bruchési feared, and reformers like Langlois hoped for. That same day, however, Langlois seconded George Washington Stephens's demand for more state support for schools.[17]

A month later, Stephens was again on the offensive. As president of the Canadian Rubber Company, he declared that he had found his French Canadian employees incapacitated by their poor education. In April he repeated his contention at a banquet of the *Club de Réforme* offered in his honour. At the same occasion, J.C. McCorkill, the provincial treasurer, declared himself in favour of mandatory school attendance.[18] Evidently, some of the ideas promoted by the progressive faction of the Liberal party were spreading again. "Does our public school system respond to the needs of our time and to the demands of evolution?" Langlois asked in his address to yet another Liberal banquet organized by Liberal progressives:

> It is ineffective. For three-quarters of a century, we have worked to produce men of professions. We have allowed them to distance themselves from the world of business, of industry, of agronomy, from the sphere of practical things. Today, we have the small jobs, the miserable and often humiliating positions, the small salaries. Anglophone people have the choice morsels. In the factories, the best positions go to strangers and immigrants.[19]

In the fall of 1907, Langlois wrote again that "we are headed to national ruin if we do not modify our educational system in a progressive direction." "The need is pressing, imminent," he warned. "If we do not want to educate the people today, what will we be tomorrow, in the presence of our competitors?"[20]

Langlois's campaign for better education and his quest to link directly the survival of French Quebec to a reformed educational system did not neglect the deplorable working conditions of the mostly female teachers. "Unfortunately [...]

we produce teachers who don't teach, because the career of a teacher is a career with no gratification, a humiliating career, a career of misery," he grumbled in 1904.[21] Time and again, he sought to make the government admit that it was permitting the impoverishment of teachers by asking pointed questions in the Assembly. "Which are the school boards, in the province of Quebec, whose teachers receive a salary of less than $100?" he asked as early as March 1908.[22] The answer was as depressing as it was horrific, as 25 school boards reported average annual salaries of less than $100, with some paying their teachers as little as $60 for a year's work.[23]

It was time, Langlois argued, for society's underprivileged to receive their due from the state. "Education today costs too much for the workers: ways must be found to reduce the sums poor people must pay to give their children the education they need," he told a crowd assembled for a banquet in his honour at the *Club de Réforme* in 1909.[24] To reduce the cost of education for the masses, Langlois proposed that books be standardized throughout the province. A family would thus have to buy one set of books, assured that their purchase could be reused by succeeding members of the family, or at least be sure of finding a future re-selling market. To this end, Langlois submitted a bill in the Legislative Assembly in March 1908, a bill that did not survive even its first reading.[25]

Langlois's call for educational improvements included improving the sanitary conditions of school houses. This was seen as another attack on the authority of the church leaders who increasingly grew hostile to Langlois's comments. In 1907, the General Report of the Minister of Public Works and Labour concluded that there remained much work to be done before all school children were safe in their own schools. Langlois did not fail to embarrass the government by highlighting the report's findings.[26] In 1909, he quoted numerous reports by school inspectors and told the Legislative Assembly that 1974 of the 8604 classrooms in the prov-

WHY WOULD THE CHURCH WERE MORE GODLY THAT OUT HOUSE THAN FLUSH TOILETS?

ince (22%) were poorly ventilated.[27] He also made the "radical" demand that more efforts be expended in making schoolhouses more fireproof. "We have the duty to do as much as the city of Toronto, whose school board voted a $30,000 subsidy to improve school buildings and these are the improvements: A greater number of exits, wider and more numerous stairways, an alarm bell, etc."[28]

Langlois's demands for more school inspections received some support. In 1906, the President of the Community Health Committee of Montreal's City Council, Alderman Dagenais, declared that the number of school inspectors in Montreal had to be increased from 21 to 50![29] "For certain sectarians," Langlois wistfully observed in 1907, "the medical inspection of schools is [...] an audacious, almost anti-religious initiative."[30] If Quebec was slow to appreciate Langlois's efforts for school inspections, better treatment for teachers, standardization of school books and mandatory attendance, France certainly was not. In 1907, Langlois was awarded the title of *Officier d'Académie* by the French Ministry of Public Instruction and Fine Arts.[31]

Langlois's victories in gathering support for his causes were small consolidations. Frustrated by his incapacity to sway the majority of the Liberal party, yet convinced of the masses' desire for educational reform, Langlois made the centralization and democratization of the school boards in Montreal his *cause célèbre*. It was undoubtedly the most controversial initiative of his political career.

In early May 1905, only a few weeks after the opening of the first post-Parent Legislature, Langlois proposed a bill to unite Montreal's school boards.[32] He argued that neighbourhood school commissions such as they existed in Montreal should be abolished. Instead, he suggested that all parents be called upon to vote for 15 of 18 commissioners (three seats he willingly reserved for the clergy), instead of the nine presently chosen to oversee operations by the provincial government. The concept of democratically-elected school trustees was not a new one in the Montreal area. Already, the parishioners of Ste-Cunégonde, St-Henri, St-Jean-Baptiste, Duvernay, St-Denis and Hochelaga elected their own school trustees. Nonetheless, Langlois's proposal met immediate hostility. His bill barely survived its first reading and disappeared in committee.

Not to be intimidated, Langlois took up his cause again a year later. Paul Martineau, a long-time supporter of school reform, spoke in his favour[33] as did J.A. Chauvet, A. Girard, J.A. Dupuis, Jérémie Décarie, Philippe Roy and D. Lacombe in the Legislative Assembly.[34] Protestants were also becoming increasingly impatient with the foot shuffling of the School Superintendent. In February 1906 they proposed that the Protestant Committee of Public Instruction, the institution that oversaw Protestant school boards in the province, be democratized. Montreal's representatives wielded too much clout, according to some, and could only be tamed by increasing the number of rural district members.[35] With Gouin's help, Langlois's bill was given a second reading.

Gouin's gesture, an acknowledgement of support for the bill's principles, sparked an angry reaction from Mgr Bruchési. "Langlois bill unacceptable," the Montreal Archbishop cabled the Premier, "would have deplorable consequences. Three priests could not sit on planned board [...]. In the real interest of our schools, I hope the bill will be rejected."[36] Bruchési objected to having priests sit on a committee in which they would have little influence and, as he wished, the bill did not go further than with a second reading. The session ending shortly thereafter, and the Langlois proposal died on the order paper. Still undaunted, Langlois proposed the same measure again, a year later, in 1907. This time, Bruchési implored Langlois personally not to reintroduce the bill. Langlois was unmoved. "I believe that it is our duty, as public figures, to find the ways to interest the father of the family in school issues," Langlois told Bruchési in a private letter from the capital:

Yet in Montreal, we have only encountered indifference from them. The taxpayers pay no more attention to the works and debates of the school board than they do to the debates of either the Senate or the Legislative Council; they feel no enthusiasm whatsoever for institutions that are not accountable to the public. An elected school board will surely draw their attention, will stimulate their zeal and will put to work their national pride and their devotions. I remain convinced that those who have children will make it their duty to choose trustees worthy of the patriotic mandate entrusted to them.[37]

Langlois insisted he would not withdraw the bill, as he considered it too important and too timely: "This bill only sanctifies a principle of liberty, a right that the struggles and sacrifices of our fathers made sacred and invaluable. I want to believe, Monsignor, that you will consider the higher motives that inspire me, the patriotic spirit that animates me and the sense of duty I seek to obey."[38]

"For thirty years we have asked for similar reforms," he declared a few days later, noting that in 1882 a Royal Commission had proposed such a plan and that since 1900, Montreal's Chamber of Commerce had done the same.[39] W.A. Weir, Langlois's old comrade-in-arms, supported the motion in that year, but counselled patience. He even promised Langlois that he would introduce a similar bill on behalf of the government in 1908. Opposition to the bill came from various sources. *La Presse*, Langlois's adversary on most political, economic and educational matters, vigorously rejected the proposal. "Establish popularly-elected trustees," its editor wrote in January 1907, "and you throw teaching into anarchy. The ambitious will throw themselves into the political arena to grab the rights to manage four or five thousand dollars a year: this is an open bargain for speculation."[40] Such voices prevailed, and Langlois's attempt to instill some notions of democracy in Montreal's school system again died its death in committee.

In 1908, Weir was unable to secure the cabinet approval for the bill he had promised Langlois the year before, so Langlois again reintroduced his bill for the fourth time. Once again, it was killed at its second reading. Undeterred by the negative reactions to Langlois's initiatives, Dr. John Finnie, member for St-Laurent, introduced a bill that aimed at making Protestant school commissions elected bodies in 1909. Langlois then proposed his own measure. "We are in an assembly with a Liberal majority that will not be scandalized, I would hope, by a liberal measure," he said optimistically.[41]

Henri Bourassa, elected to the Legislative Assembly in 1907, labelled Langlois's bill as "anti-democratic and anti-liberal." He charged that Langlois's allegations of poor administration were fabricated and argued that any increase in taxes resulting from reforms would be unacceptable. Reviewing Langlois's suggestion that school trustees be elected, Bourassa proposed that each parish elect members to its own local school board and that one representative of each commission sit at a central council.[42] Bourassa later argued that limiting the clergy's presence on the board to one sixth of total representation was insufficient to guarantee the catholic orthodoxy of present arrangements. Elected trustees, he added (contradicting what he had said earlier), would not likely be worthy of confidence when dealing with school responsibilities.[43] In a short speech, Langlois rejected Bourassa's charges. He took exception to the idea of electing parish school boards because it did not address the issue of administrative inefficiency, duplicated costs and, on a province-wide basis, the issue of inconsistent standards and results.[44] He further accused Bourassa of using tactics that only served to camouflage complacency about a totally inefficient system. Gouin then intervened to moderate a debate that grew increasingly bitter as two old foes once again locked horns. Gouin argued that both the Langlois and the Bourassa proposals had advantages and disadvantages, but suggested that the bill be given its second reading so as to enable a committee to examine it more closely and gauge public reactions.

Langlois's bill, like the others he had submitted earlier, seemed destined to die the same diplomatic death, but this time unexpectedly bore fruit: Eager to diffuse the issue before another Langlois-Bourassa conflict emerged, Gouin followed Langlois's earlier advice and ordered a provincial Royal Commission to examine the state of education in Montreal in August 1909, with the specific task of investigating the applicability of Langlois's many proposals. The Commission was composed of a priest, a senator and an unknown anglophone: The Senator was Raoul Dandurand, the priest would be abbé Philippe Perrier and the anglophone representative was T.J.C. Kennedy.

The immediate reactions of the Commission were encouraging to those who had advocated reform. Pushed by alderman Daniel Gallery, the Montreal Catholic School Commission adopted a resolution in May 1909 that school attendance be made mandatory.[45] A week later, Montreal's chamber of commerce proposed to the Commission that primary schools be made free and that attendance be made mandatory.[46] Simultaneously, J.A. Rodier of the Montreal Trades and Labour Council made the demand that schoolbooks be standardized throughout the province and that they be loaned to students free of charge.[47] In early January 1910, the members of the French-language section of the Canadian Socialist Party repeated the same refrain.[48] Evidently, the efforts of those who had demanded educational reform in Montreal were paying off as their ideas were gaining currency in widely differing circles.

Despite his success in at least influencing the establishment of a Royal Commission on the issue that had given so much bearing to his years in Parliament, Langlois was having more and more trouble with his own party. "We challenge the member for St-Louis to show us one letter, any note from Sir Wilfrid or from the hon. Prime Minister of the Province which approves of his campaign," pointedly asked *La Presse* in the course of a critique of Langlois's demands for educational reform.[49] Indeed, though he was supported in many circles, Langlois would have been hard pressed to find a leader to endorse his campaigns publicly. Evidently, his harsh criticisms of Quebec society, of the church and of the Council for Public Instruction alienated a great many of the Liberal progressive friends he had attracted to his causes at the turn of the century.

Since Langlois's entry to the Legislative Assembly in 1905, some members of the Liberal party had demanded that he be removed from the politically-sensitive job of editor of *Le Canada*. His assessment of education and the implications for the church of his criticisms angered his traditional adversaries and some of his closest allies. "I have noticed that many of our political friends who are part of the clergy are beginning to turn away from us and that the editor of the C[anada] is for them an enormous *bête noire* they will try to crush by any means," observed one Dr. Bachand in a letter to Sir Wilfrid. "I believe that there is only one way to remove the pain at its source, and that is to change the editor. This time, I think we should chose a more prudent man, of broader visions [...]. If you chose this strategy, the position [of the party] will be saved."[50]

A Liberal from St-Pascal reiterated similar fears. "The newspaper *Le Canada*, the organ of our party, is doing enormous harm to our party," one Hector Lachance wrote to Sir Wilfrid:

It is a source of suspicion for some, and a danger for others. [...] It is denounced from our catholic pulpits and with reason— that Godfroy Langlois is accused of being a Freemason [...] and the Liberal party, Monsieur Laurier, the party that you lead with such respect, is accused of concealing all sorts of anti-catholic principles [...]. Godfroy Langlois is ruining our party. Say a word and our priests will be happy to recognize that the words of Godfroy Langlois on certain matters are not yours [...]. Godfroy Langlois must disappear from our organ.[51]

Langlois continued to protest "against the legend that seeks to find revolutionaries where there are only honourable citizens, moderate progressives and convinced patriots," but the critics were unmoved.[52] Even Laurier's patience, tried especially hard since the coup against Parent, was now finally wearing thin. "It is high time to think of a reorganisation at *Le Canada*, concluded Laurier in March 1906 after Langlois published criticisms of the projected federal Lord's Day Act.[53] Senator Béique agreed, but the task would prove easier said than done. "The only remedy," Béique responded, "is to put in charge of the newspaper a person who enjoys your confidence."[54]

Few people had the stature to replace Langlois, and the latter still possessed a great deal of support in Montreal—obviously too much for Laurier to remove him without a very good reason. But the year 1907 saw friction increase between Mgr Bruchési and the Liberal daily as the Montreal Archbishop increased the rate of his reproaches to *Le Canada* for publishing "incorrect" stories regarding the church. One article which Langlois had borrowed from a Parisian newspaper in August 1907 particularly irked the prelate. The piece in question extolled Guiseppe Garibaldi's anticlericalism and republicanism, as well as the Italian rebel's capture of the Vatican in the early 1860s. "Why you published this article without any commentary, I do not know, but you will admit that it is highly unjust for the church and the papacy," raged Bruchési in a letter to Langlois:

> I will not suffer that a newspaper recognized as the organ of an important political party in Canada, and which is read by so many catholics, reproduces writings that are false and injurious towards the Holy See. I would ask therefore that you disavow immediately and formally that truly unfortunate article.
>
> I take advantage of this opportunity, Monsieur, to tell you that on many occasions I have regretted the publication and especially the reproduction of articles dealing with religious issues in your newspaper [...]. I have the duty to maintain the doctrine and morality in my diocese, and I cannot allow the diffusion of principles and doctrines that are erroneous and timorous.

> I will monitor closely *Le Canada* on this point and I hope that you will not put be in a situation where I will have to denounce it as I have had to do with other papers.[55]

Langlois never paid much attention to the *de facto* leader of the catholic church in Quebec. His personal faith was undoubtedly weak, making his treatment of church authorities all the more abrupt. A few months later, Bruchési asked Langlois to substitute the "Notes mondaines" and "Carnets mondains" titles of his weddings columns with a simple "Marriage" heading. "This small modification, easy to do, I think, would indicate that the subject is an august religious ceremony and a sacrament."[56] Langlois's acerbic reply betrayed his impatience. "I am really surprised to see the Archbishop trying to involve himself in what can be called the newspaper's kitchen," he responded to Bruchési. "The editing and the writing of the social columns are things that are best left to the judgment of the Editor's assistants, especially when they are inoffensive as in the case you bring to our attention. Suffer, Monsignor, that the coal porter be master in his own house."[57]

At a time when most Liberals were increasingly concerned with Henri Bourassa's criticism of the Gouin administration, party members seemed to close ranks. The election of 1908 was very different from the one held four years earlier. Whereas the 1904 contest had seen numerous Liberal rivalries, only eight ridings witnessed inter-Liberal battles in 1908, and no cabinet members saw their nominations challenged by members of the Liberal party in this lacklustre contest. The members of the Liberal progressive faction were also unassailed. W.A. Weir, Archille Bergevin, Maurice Perrault, J.E. Caron, J.C.Walsh and J.C. Kaine were opposed only by Conservatives or "nationalistes". The only "radicals" to be challenged were John Finnie and Godfroy Langlois, whose election was contested by none other that Henri-Benjamin Rainville. H.R. Bloomfield, listed in the press as either the "Jewish" or the "Israelite" candidate, also presented himself as an alternative to Langlois.

Langlois was prepared as he took very good care of his constituency association. A.P. Pigeon, editor of *Le Canard*, a satirical magazine and an early supporter, was made chairman of the riding association almost as soon as Langlois won his first election in 1904. In early 1908, in anticipation of the upcoming election, local riding headquarters were moved to a more spacious locale on Ste-Catherine street and the *Club Libéral du Quartier St- Louis* held its nominating convention on May 21, 1908. Langlois, acclaimed as the Liberal candidate, gave a short speech of thanks, then yielded his place to a litany of well-wishers. All lauded Langlois's patriotism and zeal for reform. Traditional supporters such as the Presidents of the *Club Letellier* and of the *Club de Réforme* addressed the crowd, as did the writer Pamphile du Tremblay. A few days later, Senator H.J. Cloran spoke in favour of Langlois, calling him one of the most brilliant members of the Legislative Assembly.[58] On June 4, a political gathering was organized on the corner of Roy and Sanguinet streets. Numerous people again volunteered to speak in favour of Langlois, not the least of which was his old friend Gonzalve Desaulniers, poet, Freemason and jurist.[59]

Election day was surprising in some of its results. Shaken by a downturn in the economy and devastating revelations of corruption among junior ministers, Liberals lost a considerable number of seats, and the Conservatives improved their standings in equal measure. In total, six Liberals were elected by acclamation, and 52 of them were elected at the polls, a drop of eight seats. No Conservatives were elected by acclamation, but 13 of them were elected on polling day, an increase of seven seats. Three "nationalistes" were also elected, but most surprising was the percentage of votes earned by the Liberals. It dropped from 87% in 1904 to 57% in 1908.[60]

Langlois trounced his opponents. Against his 1868 votes, Rainville received 963 and Bloomfield had 347. Langlois won all but two of the thirty polling stations, and both his opponents lost their $200 deposits.[61] Lomer Gouin was

I BELIEVE THAT AT DATE (1908) IT WAS PERMITTED + USED FREQUENTLY FOR THE LEADER TO RUN AT 2 LOCATIONS

reelected, but not resoundingly. In what was an unexpected defeat, the Premier was narrowly beaten in his traditional riding of St-Jacques by Henri Bourassa. Gouin was elected in another riding, however, and could afford to be philosophical. "The St-Jacques verdict does not affect me more than it should," he told Laurier, persisting in seeing a silver lining to the worst Liberal showing since 1897.[62]

If Langlois's positions were supported by the St-Louis electorate, church leaders were not cheering. His acrid denunciations of political inertia and church interference reaffirmed the belief of many in the Liberal party that Langlois was doing greater harm than good at the helm of *Le Canada*. Langlois's boss now lost patience. He told Langlois that he was not happy with the irreverent tone of the publication. *Le Canada*'s editor apparently replied that editing the newspaper was his job and that he should be left alone to do it. "The newspaper has ceased to be the organ of the party in Ottawa and in Quebec; it has become and becomes even more with every day that passes, the organ of Langlois," a now embittered Senator Béique told Laurier in 1909.

> He has alienated numerous friends we had among the clergy for a long time now, and the newspaper is now despised by a large number of Liberals. This situation has favoured the *Action Sociale* newspaper and will help Bourassa's newspaper. [...]
>
> For my part, I think the moment has come to take things out into the open with him,—by telling him that the paper has ceased to be that of the party, that he is turning it into his own mouthpiece, and that on many points we no longer share the same ideas. The situation grows more insufferable with every day, and it will be more difficult to act later than it would be now.[63]

Laurier similarly grew increasingly concerned. "I concur with your views," he immediately cabled Béique,[64] and expounded his views in a probing follow-up letter. "I have indeed spoken about *Le Canada*'s position with many friends and I informed them of my hesitations to break with the radical group of our party," he confided to the Senator.

> That notwithstanding, I note that it is time to take sides and that the time has come to act. Our friend Langlois has given to *Le Canada* a slant that, as you know, does not suit me. I had always hoped that he would eventually understand that it is not loyal on his part to substitute his personal ideas to those of the party, but since he now considers it to be his business, there is only one thing for us to do; and that is to make him understand that it is not his business, but ours.
> I am ready to do my part. I trust your judgment as to what should be done; just let me know what you expect me to do.[65]

Laurier entertained many ideas as to how to dispose of Langlois, but continued to hesitate. "I understand that you are perplexed by the possible effect Langlois's departure from *Le Canada* could have on his friends," Béique admitted. Others concurred. "It is not easy to simply abandon him," Thomas Côté, an editor at *La Presse* remarked to Gouin, "the secretariat of the International Commission on International Waters is being considered as a place to drown him."[66]

While Laurier was content to wait out the crisis and act on Béique's call, Bruchési grew impatient. The Montreal Archbishop was proud to have taken part in the opening ceremonies of the Oka Agricultural Institute, and expected (in vain) to see *Le Canada* carry a comprehensive story, but he was disappointed. In early February 1909, *Le Canada* again extolled the virtues of protestant education by celebrating McGill's McDonald College of Agriculture at a time when the preparations for the official inauguration of the Oka agricultural institute were in the works. Bruchési was angered and took up the matter with Senator Béique: "After all the sacrifices that have been made by the government and by the church to support an institution where our youth will find, in addition to serious agronomy studies, all the desirable national and religious guarantees, why seek to direct sympathies to another project?"[67] Bruchési, invoking a promise

made to him by Béique that Langlois would soon be removed, demanded that the Liberals do something to muzzle
their editor. "I'm waiting," he reminded Laurier and Béique,
"we are all waiting".[68] "I have done my duty, I ask that the
directors of *Le Canada* do theirs," he continued six weeks
later.[69] "This has been going on for years," the Archbishop
complained again the following day, when still nothing had
been done to remove Langlois.[70]

Bruchési's temper had already reached a boil when in
August 1909 Langlois again reprinted articles from the
French radical press. "This is surely not worthy of the organ
of the Liberal party," he told Senator Béique. "It is indeed a
scandal, and you have heard the protests made by other
journalists. *Le Canada* is the only paper in Montreal that
accepts such ads. I suppose it should be enough to draw your
attention to this fact. You should have noted, Monsieur le
Sénateur, that one of the French newspapers most often
borrowed from in *Le Canada* is *Le Journal de Paris,* an
antireligious and pornographic paper. I have done my duty;
I ask now that the directors of *Le Canada* do theirs."[71]

A week later, the Archbishop's ire was again provoked
when Langlois printed an article lauding the accomplishments of a French lycéé which had abolished religious studies
altogether and replaced them with dancing lessons. "I am not
saying that they are bad, but I find it strange that in a catholic
paper of our city, the writings of an antireligious and *pornographic* paper from France are cited," raged Bruchési to
Senator Béique in speaking of *Le Canada*'s latest excesses in
demanding school reforms. "All this demonstrates the spirit
and the tendencies of *Le Canada*."[72] To add weight to his
complaints about Liberal progressivism, Bruchési urged the
faithful of his diocese in September 1909 to boycott *La
Semaine*, a new weekly founded by Gustave Comte, poet and
Liberal radical since the early 1890s. The "rights of the
church" had been misrepresented, argued Bruchési:

> Insinuations and malicious accusations regarding people and
> things religious came through in many of its articles, and, in

its programme, it proclaimed itself independent of all things
[...].

On matters of teaching and the rights of the state, the same
errors were evident, as are all the reproaches, all the grievances against the clergy and the religious orders that have
been time and again refuted. The articles border on persiflage.
The clergy and our benevolent institutions are treated as
veritable enemies.

It is almost word for word the language of the worst
newspapers in Europe. It the same tactics, the same prophe-
cies of miseries.[73]

Sternly, Bruchési demanded action with regard to the
Liberal party's official publication, threatening that *Le Canada* would suffer the same fate imposed on *La Semaine* if
ideological positions were not rectified. "My repeated observations over the years will undoubtedly irritate the directors
of *Le Canada*," Bruchési told Senator Béique after proscribing
La Semaine. "A formal separation will probably have to
come," the Archbishop affirmed, "but it is not without some
sadness that I think of those who will suffer. [...] The cause
of this problem will not disappear, obviously, as long as the
cause is allowed to survive. It should be so easy to have a
morning newspaper that would be respectable and catholic
in Montreal!"[74] Bruchési's threats had to be taken seriously
now. An episcopal denunciation of a Liberal daily such as *Le
Canada* could have far-reaching consequences, and it made
no sense to endanger such a prosperous venture merely to
please Langlois. At the end of August, the Montreal Archbishop seemed ready to condemn *Le Canada* for the same
reasons he had placed *La Semaine* on the index.

Langlois's authority was seriously challenged. It was no
longer a few hundred students clamouring for his removal,
it was a threatening church leader and many Senators and
Members of Parliament. The Liberals who had grown tired
of this criticism of the church in matters of education needed
a pretext to get rid of Langlois, and the perennial issue of the
Masonic conspiracy provided a convenient lever to dispose

of him. The party leadership's resolve to remove Langlois was heightened a few weeks later on the revelation that Langlois was a leading member of the *Loge l'Emancipation*. This was nothing new, as the label had been fixed to Langlois since his earliest days in politics, and it was a difficult label to shed. Though the complexities of his beliefs eluded most people (he was married in the Catholic church and had his child baptized), Langlois never denied being a Freemason.[75] The party leadership, moreover, had conveniently ignored the matter for 15 years.

It was Raoul Dandurand, recently named President of the Royal Commission charged with investigating Montreal's educational system, who took on the job of convincing Langlois that for the sake of the party, it was time to go. "You have committed the imprudence of joining a lodge affiliated to the Grand Orient [the leading French Masonic lodge], who is the declared enemy of the church," Dandurand reproached Langlois:

> I say imprudence from the point of view of your position as director of the newspaper, for outside that consideration, your actions escape entirely my criticism. [...] Your presence at *Le Canada* hamstrings our newspaper during the battles where moderate liberalism should fight. We are hamstrung and the critics mock our impotence. [...] You are viewed as an adversary of the doctrine and we are handicapped and unable to broach the many other questions that should be within our reach.
>
> A debate could arise at any moment when it would be critically important that our sincerity and our collective orthodoxy could not be called into question. I ask you in all sincerity: Do you think that in these conditions we are not justified in asking of you a sacrifice in the interest of the party for which this newspaper was created to defend?[76]

It was replication of the same old debate, the same old internecine rivalries among Liberals that had robbed French Canadian radicalism of its consistency throughout most of the nineteenth century. Dandurand, who had tacitly encouraged Liberal progressive calls for massive educational reforms, for a removal of Préfontaine and Parent, and for regulation of utilities, was now finding Langlois's tactics to be counterproductive. He knew that his royal commission would support the reforms Langlois had advocated for almost twenty years and did not want to see his seemingly innocuous suggestions and recommendations made suspicious by the radical enthusiasm that would inevitably accompany the release of his report. "The clergy knows your most intimate thought and the influence you enjoy on a certain group and uses your name as a scarecrow to raise public opinion against every project you propose," Dandurand observed before accusing Langlois outright of deliberately hampering the Liberal progressive movement: "You serve [the clergy] as much as it wants and it uses you to eradicate the most sound movements, the most sensible—such as the uniformity of textbooks, which is demanded by everybody— As soon as a liberal idea is emitted by you [...] it is attacked by the clerical phalanges as emanating from Lucifer's direct and official representative."[77]

With those words, the Liberal party initiated negotiations aimed at securing Langlois's resignation. Dandurand met with the editor at the end of September 1909, but evidently reached no agreement. In November, a propitious opening was created in the Legislative Council by the death of a member, and Langlois was widely touted in the press as the candidate to replace him. Questioned by Laurier as to what was to be done with the vacancy, Gouin seemed evasive. "I really don't know who we can nominate to the Legislative Council," the Quebec Premier told Laurier. "You know enough about the embarrassments in which I find myself on this subject. In any case, you can rest assured that I will act in the best interest of the party."[78] Gouin was facing a difficult situation indeed. Langlois was now ardently campaigning to be named to the post, as was Achille Bergevin, a key player in the politics of Liberal progressivism for almost fifteen years. The Premier of Quebec stalled, and time was quickly running out for Langlois.

Langlois's demise was assured as the year ended, probably on Christmas eve of 1909 when Albert Lemieux, a reporter for *L'Action Sociale*, met with Laurier in the Prime Minister's office that afternoon and revealed directly to him whatever evidence he had pertaining to Langlois's relationship with the *Loge l'Emancipation*.[79] It is not clear what Lemieux revealed. It could have been details surrounding rumours that Langlois and others at the *Loge l'Emancipation* had discussed opposing Liberals in the upcoming municipal elections at their recent 10 December meeting. It is interesting to note that earlier that day, a certain Dr. P.S. Côté was buried in a civic ceremony in Montréal. Côté, apparently though not an official member of the *Loge l'Emancipation*, was considered a fellow-traveller. The unprecedented display of a parade of 400 friends and family escorting a civic funeral ceremony apparently caused quite a stir. It is not known if Langlois attended the funeral. Apparently, Gonsalve Desaulniers was a part of the parade, but hopped on a passing tramway to escape being seen. Did Lemieux see Langlois at the funeral that morning and report it in person to Laurier later that day?[80]

Regardless of its revelations, the evidence certainly proved difficult to deny and Langlois apparently could now do little to defend himself. On January 7, 1910, *Le Canada* quietly announced that the founding editor and director had accepted a federal government posting as Canadian secretary to the International Commission on Boundary Waters. Langlois reportedly had a long talk with Gouin a few days later, but little was divulged to the press.[81] "He was forced out of his position and the influence brought to bear upon him was none other than that of Sir Lomer Gouin," observed the editor of *Beck's Weekly* a few days later.

Sir Lomer personally offered to appoint Mr. Langlois to the Legislative Council if he would retire from his journalistic position. Mr. Langlois, knowing something of the value of political promises, demanded that the appointment be made at once. Sir Lomer demurred, pleading the exigencies of an election campaign then pending [In Montreal], but gave his "word of honour" that an appointment would be made and called upon the later Honourable Charles Devlin to bear witness to his promises. Mr. Langlois performed his part of the compact and then found there was great reluctance on the part of the Premier to perform his.[82]

Langlois, who clipped the *Beck's Weekly* commentary for his own scrapbook, had good reasons to be bitter. By the end of February 1910, there were three more positions opened in the Legislative Council. Langlois was still widely expected to be named,[83] but those hopes never materialized. On March 9, Gouin finally came to a decision and announced that Achille Bergevin would be named Legislative Councillor. The following week Dr. E. Choquette (Senator Philippe-Auguste Choquette's brother) was also nominated to the Upper House. Evidently, Gouin was willing to name progressive Liberals to the august upper chamber, but perceived Langlois's presence in the Legislative Council as dangerous to the interest of the party, and if he ever did make a deal with Langlois, certainly never upheld his part of the bargain. As the once optimistic Senator Choquette wrote years later, bitter that Gouin had also intervened against him in the 1910 Quebec City mayoral race, Gouin "was an ingrate to those who had brought him to power."[84]

Why did the Liberal party abandon Langlois in January 1910? Was it the revelation of his role in the *Loge l'Emancipation*? Was it the pressure from the Archbishop? Was he the victim of factional bullying within the party? Part of the answer can certainly be found in the first two variables, but its essence can be found in the increasingly difficult relationship Langlois maintained with his party over the contentious educational issues and the nature of urban reform. Langlois made things worse by using the issue of reform to call into question the church's role in society, and to castigate the nationalists.

The Gouin government did react in various degrees to Liberal progressive prodding. Many initiatives were taken to promote and regulate competition in the hydroelectricity industry and serious gains were made in educational reform. Provincial government contributions rose substantially in the first five fiscal years after the Gouin "coup" from $536,150 in 1905-06 to $908,391 in 1909-1910 (a 69.4% increase) and total moneys directed into the educational system increased from $4,338,552 in 1905 to $6,210.530 by the time Langlois was removed from *Le Canada* in January 1910, a 43% increase.[85] There were other notably progressives educational initiatives in these five years: the government sponsored an *Ecole Normale* for girls and numerous *Ecoles Techniques*. Perhaps the most welcome innovation was the establishment of the *Ecole des Hautes Etudes Commerciales* in Montreal, which Langlois identified as a landmark event signifying "the date when the Province of Quebec shook off its routine lethargy to take great strides in the direction of industrial and commercial progress and to rejoin those who have taken a lead on her in this field."[86] With time, however, as financing proved less generous than promised and as priests composed strong proportions of the teaching faculties, Langlois grew disappointed with the performance of the fledgling institutions. Langlois's pleas for an administrative overhaul of the educational system also prompted other politicians to at least consider investigating his views. In the summer of 1909, Gouin had formed a Royal Commission to investigate Langlois's proposals for centralizing Montreal's disparate school commissions. It commenced hearings as Langlois was forced out of his office, but heard testimony that only substantiated his views.

Through the 1890s and 1900s, Langlois had played a leadership role as a spokesman for the Liberal progressives, helping to unite individuals and focusing them on particular issues. As editor of *Le Canada*, he sought new inspirations, found them in Republican France and attempted to convince his colleagues that the solutions espoused by the *Radicaux* had validity on this side of the Atlantic. He continued to impress many friends and allies with his campaigns for active state involvement in regulating utilities and reforming education, but his rhetoric alienated those moderates who had gravitated around him in the early years. When in 1905 students demanded that he be removed, nothing could be done as he was still the undisputed leader of a potent faction of the party. Exactly four years later, the politics of Liberal progressivism had isolated him, leaving him surrounded by only a core of ardent supporters.

During his stay at *Le Canada*, Langlois manifested his frustrations with the Liberal party leadership, and never cringed at the thought of revealing some of the more scandalous aspects of the state of education and of the economy in the province. The issue was not whether Gouin was "progressive". Indeed, his administration was a vast improvement on that of his predecessor. To Langlois, however, it mattered that Gouin was not doing enough to fill Quebec's urgent economic and educational "retard". Through its clever compromises, the more moderate members of the Liberal party showed that there was a middle way in pressing for reform. In the process, they helped to isolate Langlois to the point where few members of the "generation of 1905" continued to follow the outspoken maverick.

Notes

1. Laurier Papers, C822, Choquette to Laurier, 5 may 1905.
2. Claude Larivière, *Albert Saint-Martin: Militant d'avant-garde* (Laval, 1979), p. 48.
3. *Ibidem*, p. 55. (The whole of chapter 4 is dedicated to this by-election).
4. *La Presse*, 2 avril 1905.
5. *Ibidem*.
6. *Ibidem*, 29 avril 1905.
7. *La Presse*, 19 mai 1905.
8. *Ibidem*, 12 mai 1905.
9. *Ibidem*, 22 mai 1905.
10. *Le Canada*, 29 mai 1905.

11. Archives de la Chancellerie de l'Archevêché de Montréal, Paul-Napoléon Bruchési Papers (RLBr), Newspaper Correspondence, Bruchési to Béique, 22 août 1905.

12. *Ibidem*, Political Correspondance, Bruchési to Gouin, 4 novembre 1905.

13. *La Presse*, 9 décembre 1905.

14. *Ibidem*, 12 décembre 1905.

15. *Ibidem*, 15 février 1906.

16. *Ibidem*, 28 février 1906.

17. *Ibidem*.

18. *Ibidem*, 2 avril 1906.

19. Speech reproduced in *Le Canada*, 11 décembre 1908.

20. *Ibidem*, editorial, 21 octobre 1907.

21. *Ibidem*, 6 avril 1904.

22. *JALQ*, Vol. XLII, 25 mars 1908, p. 145.

23. *Ibidem*.

24. *Le Canada*, 30 mars 1909.

25. See *La Presse*'s criticism of the Langlois motion, editorial, 25 mars 1908.

26. JALQ, Vol. XLI, 4 mars 1907, p. 237.

27. *Ibidem*, Vol. XLIII, 16 mars 1909, p. 101.

28. *Le Canada*, 6 avril 1904.

29. *La Presse*, 19 septembre 1906.

30. *Le Canada*, 27 août 1907.

31. Certificate is in Langlois Papers, Private Collection, File D, 1 mai 1907.

32. *La Presse*, 5 mai 1905.

33. *Le Canada*, 14 février 1906.

34. *La Presse*, 7 mars 1906.

35. *Ibidem*, 8 février 1906.

36. ACAM, Bruchési Papers, Political Correspondence, Bruchési to Gouin, n.d.

37. Langlois Papers, Private Collection, File B, Langlois to Bruchési, 6 février 1907. (Copy also in RLBr, 4, 249-50).

38. *Ibidem*.

39. *La Presse*, 13 mars 1907.

40. *Ibidem*, editorial, 28 janvier 1907.

41. *Ibidem*, 30 mars 1909.

42. *Ibidem*, 2 avril 1909. This tendency in French Canadian discourse, not different from American conservative rhertoric, is dissected in Ralph Heintzman, "The Political Culture of Quebec, 1840-1960", *CJPS*, XVI,I, 1983

43. *Le Canada,* 29 avril 1909. It is worth noting that even the conservative Bourassa did not fight the notion of democracy in the school system, or indeed fear the onslaught of politics in what should have been an "apolitical" field.

44. *La Presse,* 7 avril 1909.

45. *Ibidem,* 24 novembre 1909.

46. *Ibidem,* 2 décembre 1909.

47. *Ibidem,* 13 décembre 1909.

48. *Ibidem,* 11 janvier 1910.

49. *Ibidem,* editorial, 7 mars 1908.

50. Laurier Papers, C839, Bachand to Laurier, 31 octobre 1906.

51. *Ibidem,* Lachance to Laurier, 21 février 1907.

52. *Le Canada,* 22 décembre 1905.

53. Laurier Papers, C833, Laurier to Béique, 31 mars 1906.

54. *Ibidem,* Béique to Laurier, 2 avril 1906.

55. ACAM, Bruchési Papers (RLBr 4, 289-90), Newspaper Correspondence, Bruchési to "Le directeur du Canada", 18 août 1907. See also RLBr (4, 319-320) Bruchési to "Le directeur du Canada", 24 septembre 1907.

56. Langlois Papers, Private Collection, File B, Bruchési to Langlois, 6 novembre 1907.

57. *Ibidem,* Langlois to Bruchési, 7 novembre 1907.

58. *La Presse,* 2 juin 1908.

59. *Ibidem,* 5 juin 1908.

60. Jean Hamelin, Jacques Letarte and Marcel Hamelin, "Les élections provinciales dans le Québec," *CGQ,* 7, octobre 1959-mars 1960, figure XII.

61. *La Presse,* 9 juin 1908.

62. Laurier Papers, C863, Gouin to Laurier, 12 juin 1908.

63. Laurier Papers, C872, Béique to Laurier, 2 février 1909.

64. *Ibidem,* Telegram, Laurier to Béique, 4 février 1909.

65. *Ibidem,* Laurier to Béique, 4 février 1909.

66. PAC, Lomer Gouin Papers, Vol. 13, Côté to Gouin, 20 mars 1909.

67. Bruchési Papers, (RLBr, 5, 52), Bruchési to "Les Directeurs du Canada" 6 February 1909.

68. Laurier Papers, C873, Béique to Laurier, 22 février 1909.

69. Bruchési Papers, Newspaper Correspondence, Bruchési to Béique, 7 avril 1909.

70. Laurier Papers, C873, Bruchési to Laurier, 8 avril 1909.

71. Bruchési Papers (RLBr, 5, 180-181), Bruchési to Béique, 7 août 1909.

72. Bruchési Papers, Newspaper Correspondence, Bruchési to Béique, 14 août 1909.

73. *Le Canada*, 2 août 1909. See also *Mandements des évêques de Montréal*, tome 14, 313.

74. Bruchési Papers, Newspaper Correspondence, Bruchési to Béique, 14 août 1909.

75. Typically, Langlois would respond to such accusations by stating that he was as much a freemason as his accusers (whatever that meant).

76. Laurier Papers, C880, Dandurand to Langlois, 12 septembre 1909.

77. *Ibidem*.

78. Laurier Papers, C883, Gouin to Laurier, 22 novembre 1909.

79. *La Presse*, 15 juin 1910.

80. See Roger Le Moine, *Deux loges montréalaises du Grand Orient de France* (Ottawa, 1991), p. 61, p. 87.

81. *Ibidem*, 12 janvier 1910.

82. *Beck's Weekly*, clipping, n.d. (May 1914?) Langlois Papers, private collection, Scrapbook A, p. 33.

83. *La Presse*, 5 mars 1910.

84. Philippe-Auguste Choquette, *Un demi-siècle de vie politique* (Montreal, 1936), p. 177.

85. Province de Québec, *Annuaire statistique du Québec, 1916* (Québec, 1916), pp. 227-228.

86. *Le Canada*, editorial, 16 mars 1907.

CHAPTER XI

THE LAST REFUGE
OF THE OUTCASTS: LE PAYS

> *"What do you want? Here progress is
> decried. When in so many countries
> we see the most extraordinary efforts
> for intellectual progress, for reforms of
> all sorts, when all the peoples of the
> world spend enormous sums in the hope
> to arm themselves for the struggles of
> life, there remains a heroic country which,
> with each step of humanity, protects
> itself against any attempt at improvement.
> That record belongs to
> la belle province of Quebec."*
>
> —Le Pays, 1910[1]

> *"You are not one of us today."*
> —Mgr Bruchési to Langlois, 1912.[2]

U PON LEARNING OF HIS DISMISSAL, the grateful staff asked Langlois to pose for an oil portrait and eventually offered the beautiful painting to him in memory of his time at *Le Canada*. He was still posing for Ulric Lamarchewhen he officially assumed his government post in January 1910 after leaving *Le Canada*, but never fully exercised his new authority. In the fall of 1909, as Béique and Dandurand attempted to ease him out of his position, Langlois and a few friends had contemplated founding a new weekly designed to encourage the cause of educational reform. As Henri Bourassa launched *Le Devoir* in mid-January 1910, Langlois's *Le Pays* hit the stands. Named after the old *rouge* journal, it would set a precedent and be published on Sundays. Langlois resigned his public service position a few weeks after assuming it.[3]

Aided by a small coterie of people that included his nephew Roger Valois (a fellow member of the *Loge l'Emancipation* who followed him from *Le Canada*) Langlois doggedly pursued the radical course he had set for Liberal progressivism in *Le Canada*. It proved to be an uncompromising search for a new liberalism, a clear declaration on the routes that should be taken by Liberal progressivism. As in the past, many of Langlois's ideas were aimed at reforming City Hall, although the issues of state involvement in educational reform, utility regulation and conservative nationalism never disappeared. Perhaps the only real departure was its treatment of the Liberal party. *Le Pays*, while still professing its loyalty to Liberalism, proved to be a harsh critic indeed. That it survived and prospered in these trying years was an eloquent testimonial to the fact that *Le Pays* spoke for a considerable number of disgruntled progressives of the Liberal party.

Langlois launched the new publishing venture with all the panache expected. "*Le Pays* will defend the politics of intellectual and social progress against the coalitions of interest groups and the enterprises of the unscrupulous," he thundered in his opening editorial. It was clear from the beginning that *Le Pays* saw it as its mission to reorient Liberal thinking in Quebec. The task at hand was nothing less than to lead a social and intellectual revolution, and the Liberal party had to lead it:

> It is high time that we begin in this country to open the minds of the population to the new ideas of social progress, of intellectual independence and of egalitarian democracy. The task, the supreme task of Liberals in this country must be to achieve a greater sum of individual freedom and moral well-being through the diffusion of ideas, through the workings

of successive laws, and through an energetic struggle for the good of society.

The Liberal leaders can rest easy, we are not preaching sedition. We will remain content to remind our friends of the respect they owe to the ideas and the principles that have always been and that remain still the essence of Liberalism. This is why men of goodwill who have found refuge in their spirits of independence, in the properness of their convictions, believed it necessary to gather on common ground— the columns of *Le Pays*—to defend freely the principles of the Liberal party, the fundamental ideas that were the strength of our cause in years past and at the same time to fight and unmask those who repudiate everything to serve their greed, their rapacity, who sacrifice everything for their personal advancement, who enter politics only to leave it for big positions or who stay to fatten and stuff themselves and their families.[4]

Though his newspaper's circulation remained relatively small, Langlois maintained his audience. 4000 copies were published of the first edition. Four weeks later, that number had grown to 7000. Until 1911, it was published in a 4-page format but gradually grew to 12 pages. Advertising was plentiful. Its price, two cents, remained stable.

Le Pays was only one demonstration of the reaction against the Liberal party leadership. It will be remembered that Montreal politics had grown so corrupt by 1909 that a Royal Commission had been assigned to make recommendations on how best to reform the system. The Cannon Commission had suggested that a Board of Control be established. The Gouin government accepted the recommendation and in the 1910 municipal election, those board members were to be elected for the first time.

Cannon's revelations of political corruption also fuelled the launch of a new reformist crusade: The Citizens' Association. It was the brainchild of Hormisdas Laporte, who had been Mayor of Montreal from 1904 to 1906. Many Liberal progressives joined the new organization. *Le Canada*, now directed by Fernand Rinfret, supported it, as did its owner,

Senator Béique. As the election approached , the Citizens' Association began to search out its prospective candidates for Mayor and settled on Liberal James John Guerin, a fluently bilingual doctor.

Born in 1855 in Montreal, Guerin had graduated from the Collège de Montréal before studying medicine at McGill University. In 1895 he was elected in a provincial by-election and was later asked by Marchand to sit in cabinet as Minister without portfolio: Guerin kept his post until 1904. He was active in trying to curtail the rights of the Montreal Light, Heat, and Power Company when its charter was debated in 1901, but had never endeared himself to the Liberal progressive faction. During the 1904 provincial election, he was challenged by aldermen Gallery and J.C. Walsh, and the latter was elected to the Legislative Assembly on the same tide that carried Godfroy Langlois.

Guerin had not renounced his political career following this setback. In the summer of 1905, he decided to campaign for a Liberal nomination in the riding of St-Laurent. Four people presented themselves to run against him, including James Cochrane, former Mayor of Montreal, P. Smith and Dr. John Finnie. The debates were acrimonious. Finnie and Cochrane lambasted Guerin for his past inactions, but were defeated on the first two ballots. Only in the third round did Guerin receive a slim majority over Smith. Interestingly, it was Ucal Dandurand, the infamous protector of the Montreal Light, Heat, and Power Company who crowned Guerin the Liberal candidate.[5]

Guerin seemed a natural choice for what turned out to be a very conservatively-minded Citizens' Association. Many people shared the view that the Citizens' Association was nothing but a Conservative party plot to overthrow the Liberal domination in City Council.[6] It is important to highlight the importance of Conservative party affiliations in the Citizens' Association because it has been overlooked by historians who ascribed its ultimate failure as a reform organization to a sudden "resurfacing of conservatism."[7]

There was nothing sudden about the conservative nature of the Citizens' Association. Indeed, it was conservative from its very beginnings, regardless of party affiliations. Ucal Dandurand was considered one of its number, so was Henri-Benjamin Rainville. More surprising was the encouragement received from Raoul Dandurand and alderman Vallières, two men who had fought Rainville and Ucal Dandurand for years.[8]

The radicals did not stand by idly while the Dandurands, tentatively representing the reformist strain of the Liberal party, joined hands with proven conservative forces. If one report is to be believed, the resistance first took root in a meeting of the *Loge l'Emancipation*. A.J. Lemieux later recounted that Langlois, Gonzalve Desaulniers, T.D. Bouchard, Gaston Maillet, and Labour spokesman Gustave Francq discussed political strategies at a Masonic meeting held in early December 1909. It was resolved that the Citizens' Association be opposed. A consensus also dictated that Louis Payette be supported to fight Guerin and that Langlois, along with Joseph Ainey, a Labour candidate, be supported to run for a seat on the Board of Control.[9] Regardless of its possibly clandestine origins, the movement to oppose the Citizens' Association was officially born on January 10, 1910 when a public gathering of over 1000 people was held at the Monument National. Payette, the incumbent Mayor, who had atoned for his past sin of selling out to the Montreal Light, Heat and Power Company, was drafted as the candidate for the new association. Langlois was chosen as candidate for the Board of Control.

Yet, the still nameless association of progressive Liberals ran into trouble almost immediately. Payette decided to decline the invitation to renew his mandate, leaving the association without a candidate.[10] Upon hearing the news, Senator Joseph-Philippe Casgrain offered to run against Guerin. Casgrain had been a Liberal progressive since the earliest days. He had denounced Mercier in 1892, had fought the Préfontaine clique and had consistently supported radical causes through the years, and was a dear friend to Godfroy Langlois. The prospect of the nomination of such a high profile Liberal Senator to fight other Liberal senators like Dandurand and Béique, did not please Laurier. The Prime Minister urged Casgrain not to run.[11]

Casgrain took exception to Laurier's favouritism of Senators Dandurand and Béique and even criticized Laurent-Olivier David, the Clerk of Montreal's City Council: "Those three men are jealous of me because I have friends in Montreal [...] They want to have everything and run everything."[12] Casgrain misread David's part in the affair; the latter did not support Dandurand's association with what he perceived to be a Conservative-laden political association, and even urged Laurier to impress on *Le Canada*'s new management the need to remain neutral in this potentially divisive race for Liberals. He went so far as to predict a Casgrain landslide victory.[13]

On January 17, Casgrain finally made public his decision to run for Mayor. J.C. Walsh and Langlois publicly supported him, as did Louis Payette.[14] *Le Pays*, the new radical organ, established its opposition against the Citizen's Association in its first edition. Ten days later, Raoul Dandurand spoke out in favour of Guerin and Henri Bourassa rallied against Casgrain on account of the "Masonic plot".[15] Casgrain came to suspect Dandurand of using federal patronage to fight his candidacy and again complained to Laurier. "If Dandurand did not want to harm me, I am sure I would make Dr. Guerin lose his deposit," he told the Prime Minister.[16] The fight of Senators also sparked off other divisions in the ranks. One struggle took place in Langlois's own neighbourhood of St-Louis, when the incumbent, Dr. Gadbois, ran under the banner of the Citizens' Association. Gadbois had supported Langlois since 1906 and had distinguished himself as a reformist politician during the debates over the Payette deals with the Montreal Light, Heat, and Power Company. In 1909, however, the Cannon Commission had found him guilty of influence peddling, and Langlois ceased to support him. Instead, *Le Pays* endorsed an old friend and Freemason,

Dr. Gaston Maillet, a dentist, who had been instrumental in founding the secularly-managed St-Luc hospital.

Maillet immediately adopted much of Liberal progressivism's standard platform. Like Philippe Roy two years before, he promised to have Montreal's drinking water filtered, and pledged to reduce the cost of electricity. Langlois (who had withdrawn from the Board of Control race in favour of Labour candidate Joseph Ainey) immediately spoke in favour of Maillet and indeed never left his candidate's side. Bourassa's *Le Devoir* saw grave consequences in Maillet's candidacy and immediately launched a bitter attack on Langlois's protégé, insinuating that Maillet was nothing but an unrepentant Freemason (which he was). On January 24, 1910 Maillet and his lawyer Gonzalve Desaulniers (who was also a member of the *Loge L'Emancipation*) filed a libel suit against Bourassa seeking $10,000 in damages.[17] The case, however, was never pursued.

Langlois and the new *Le Pays* reacted in equally harsh tones. On January 22, one L.P. Dupré lashed out at Gadbois for allegedly ejecting a woman from the audience he was addressing. Dupré labelled Gadbois, a "brat" and cited Langlois's description of Gadbois: "Here is an individual [...] who compromised himself in a dirty affair in City Hall, who was caught in trafficking building permits, who was found guilty of perjury before the royal commission and who now tries to hide his turpitude behind religion and seeks refuge in the columns of *l'Action Sociale*. Mr. Gadbois also throws himself into the free-masonry conspiracy comedy and also wants to cut down the enemies of the church."[18]

Langlois raged against the Citizens' Association, comparing it to New York City's Tammany Hall. "What have Messrs. Laporte and Vallières done?" he asked an audience. "They went to the Bank of Montreal, to the Montreal Light, Heat, and Power Company, to the Montreal Street Railway to get some money, and with that money, they formed an association whose leaders will have only one goal: to have their candidates elected so that they can pull the strings of their puppets."[19] When the dust settled following the election of February 1, 1910, the results were devastating. Only ten incumbents survived the Montreal electorate's wrath against the City Council (only two were elected by acclamation) and all but two of the Citizens' Association candidates were triumphant. Guerin defeated Casgrain by an enormous 10,000 vote plurality. *La Presse* called it a revolution.[20]

Ironically most Liberal progressives were swept by this new tide of "reform". Turner, Sadler, and Bumbray decided they had had enough, and did not run for reelection. Gallery, Clearihue and Lavallée, three high profile members of the progressive rump were defeated. In St-Louis, both Gadbois and Maillet lost their deposits. Things could not be worse as Ucal Dandurand, the man who had never hidden the fact that he was working for the interests of the Montreal Light, Heat, and Power Company, finally won a seat in City Council by being elected as a Citizen's Association candidate! *Le Pays* perhaps best illustrated the results of the election when it published a cartoon on its front page depicting "mother tory" as she was crowned by Hormisdas Laporte and Raoul Dandurand.

It was clear that the Liberal progressive presence in City Council was now a thing of the past and the disillusionment of Langlois, now personally and politically defeated by Dandurand, with former Montreal Liberal progressives ran deep. *Le Pays* waxed increasingly acerbic in its criticisms of the party, denouncing it as a corrupt organization of self-serving lawyers. It accused the Liberal party of having lost the right to refer to itself as "Liberal" as it had completely lost the progressive impulse. It lamented the ideological compromises made by party leaders in order to please the clergy and demanded a democratization of the party structures.[21] "The municipal election of February was true disaster for us," wrote Alfred Marcil, the leader of the *Loge l'Emancipation*, to the *Grand Orient de France* in Paris. "Despite hard work, the luck we thought was with us until the last days of the campaign, abandoned us and we have recorded a horrific defeat. The elements against which we battled were formidable: the press had sold out to the clergy; the priests were going door-to-door with their cabals; intimidation, impersonations, money, everything was used by our enemies to fight us, and we were defeated, convincingly, in spite of the enthusiasm and support we had brought to the fight."[22] In the Legislative Assembly a month later, Langlois proposed regulations so as to control the amounts of money spent by candidates during elections. His motions, as usual far ahead of their time, fell on deaf ears.

Many Liberal progressives, even some of Langlois's closest friends, soon became alienated by Le Pays's harsh tone. According to Gonzalve Desaulniers, who helped found the publication, Le Pays's original aim was not to embarrass the party leadership: "But following circumstances you are aware of [the denial of a position in the Legislative Council] a few of its shareholders wanted to give it a more irreverent character," he wrote to Laurier.[23] "He [Langlois] has started on a road that is absolutely false and that will prejudice his own interests," said Desaulniers. "He should understand that at his age [43], one does not begin to walk backwards."[24] Laurier, for his part, was less surprised. "Those who are heading that newspaper are young radicals filled with the most acerbic prose of Parisian journalism," observed the Prime Minister, "and who understand neither the time nor the country in which they live. Our friend Langlois is at the helm of this movement and it is he who inspires the attacks that are more and more directed towards us. I had many discussions with Langlois regarding the direction he was giving Le Canada. I cannot say that my reproaches had the slightest influence on him. I regret that, but I cannot do anything about it."[25]

The freemasonry was going through difficult times as A.J. Lemieux stepped up his campaign publicly against it. Late in the evening of 23 April 1910, Lemieux and his brother assaulted Ludger Larose, the Loge l'Emancipation treasurer as he stepped off a tramway. Brandishing a gun to Larose's forehead, Lemieux demanded money and the documentation Larose was carrying, documentation which included the members list. A month later, Lemieux published *La Loge l'Emancipation*, a pamphlet that summarized all the meetings since early October 1909, and which included contrived tales of conspiracy, including one false accusation that the *Loge* members were conspiring to trick priests into visiting the brothels of de Bullion street during the upcoming International Eucharistic Congress. Lemieux's actions triggered an ugly witch-hunt that reached into the administration of the city of Montreal.[26]

Panic broke out. On the session of 13 June 1910, the *Loge l'Emancipation* decided to suspend all its activities, and to burn all its papers.[27] Langlois's activities in the lodge were unclear, but his enthusiasm for the freemasonry seemed to have waned. When a new lodge, *Force et Courage*, was created a few years later, he did not join. The leaders of *Force et Courage* were intent on not making the same mistakes of the *Loge l'Emancipation* which had allowed itself to become too lax, too willing to compromise, too willing to welcome individuals who were not genuinely committed to the ideals of French masonry. *Force et Courage* would not be "a political antichamber" but a genuine circle of philosophical studies."[28]

In the midst of this cruel witchhunt for Freemasons, Langlois felt personally betrayed by the party leadership, and his bitterness reflected itself in *Le Pays*. "For twenty years I struggled for my party," Langlois confided to a reporter in 1911 when asked if he would ever campaign again for Sir Wilfrid. "Since I was judged to be compromising and since I am today the same man I was yesterday and since I especially do not want to embarrass my party, it can be suffered that I will stay at home."[29] That did not mean that he was turning his back on the Liberal party or that he would retire from politics. After being snubbed repeatedly by Gouin for the Legislative Council seat, Langlois did consider retiring altogether, but decided against it. "I have resolved to stay in politics," he said to Laurier, "I will therefore continue to take my seat in the deputies' chamber because I am considered too liberal to be allowed to sit in the Legislative Council."[30]

Langlois complained bitterly of the treatment he received. "Those I believed my friends have not smothered me with recognition since my 'execution'," he told Laurier.[31] The Prime Minister was unimpressed by Langlois's lamentations. "Allow me to protest your use of expressions: that you were executed at *Le Canada*," Laurier responded. "This is a question on which we have both agreed to disagree: you persist in believing that it was an execution, I persist in believing it was a suicide."[32] "This was no ordinary suicide," retorted Langlois. "In order to commit it, the arms of the virtuous Senator Dandurand, the honest Mr. Béique, a highway robber currently before the courts [Arthur Ecrement, MP for Berthier] and a few other characters I will qualify later, were required. Suicides are pretty rare in our party."[33] Langlois wasted no time in "qualifying" his assailants. "You have presided over my execution with a rare brutality," Langlois told Dandurand in a vitriolic letter worth quoting at length as it summarized neatly the journalist's vision of the Liberal party potentates:

> I was treated as the lowest of house boys. No one remembered that for fifteen years, without ever disarming or weakening, I had done my duty towards my party. Indeed, for fifteen years I virtually wrote the party organ in Montreal by myself for a salary that averaged the same as that of young school mistress and to reward me, I was thrown on the pavement.
>
> It is you, my dear Senator, who directed that last ceremony. When one assassinates, one does not have the right to criticize the victim as undeserving of favours. You draw my attention on "more than one incident" in my career, but you know very well that what I repaid you in devotion and in supports of all kinds that exceeded the favours you did for me. But this is not the time to settle our accounts.
>
> I believed in the friendships of men like you, Dandurand, like Brodeur, like Gouin and others, I was naive.

Gouin, that heartless character, that monster of hypocrisy, completed your work by having torn to shreds by the bishops [the municipal election] in February [1910]. [...]
All the same, life is strange. If I had been slightly more devoted and joined hands with the likes of Ecrement and the merchants of the temple, I would probably be a Legislative Councillor right now, or a senator.

But because I did not want to be a hypocrite, for not trafficking, I have been reduced to a position as editor of a poor Sunday newspaper.

I have reconciled myself to my fate philosophically. I don't blame myself and I rather pity those who believed, in their generosity, that a secretariat position could be a reasonable compensation for a man who never practiced the methods of an Ecrement and who made himself a religion of staying loyal to an ideal and to principles you once knew.[34]

Langlois was not penniless after his "execution". He was, largely because of his wife's inheritance, independently wealthy. He pulled out his $800 investment in *Le Canada*, and although payment was slow in coming, he did recover this substantial sum.[35] His material comforts, however, did not soothe his bitterness. Langlois frequently harped on the fact that the party had become a creature of the legal profession and demanded that more French Canadian businessmen be invited to run for office.[36] In 1911, he went so far as to denounce all of Montreal's Liberal MPs as incompetent[37] and demanded their resignation.[38] Laurier publicly reproached Langlois for his newspaper's political and religious effronteries. "You know better than anyone that no word was ever spilled from my pen either against religion or against the clergy," retorted Langlois.

I have, in matters of religion, views and convictions that I do not traffic and which are not a part, I believe, of the ranks of unbelievers. But there are, it seems to me, enough "castors" who live to lynch me without having a man of your situation, mentality, and habitual correctness casting my reputation as a journalist with the most unjustifiable imputations.[39]

Still, it was Raoul Dandurand who bore the brunt of Langlois's criticisms. An old comrade of Langlois, Dandurand rapidly became the scapegoat for Langlois's criticisms of the party. "If it is Mr. Dandurand who is now the 'boss', we know hundreds and thousands of Liberals who refuse to serve under him," wrote *Le Pays* in August 1911. "It has now been twenty years since he began exploiting the party. Mr. Dandurand is now worth half a million, without ever having pleaded a case since 1876. He was as poor as a church rat until Mr. Laurier's arrival to power. [...] Guys like Senator Dandurand and others used the party to serve their own personal business, their unbounded ambitions, and their passions for honour and for money."[40] Dandurand was understandably angered by the criticism, and completely cut off relations with Langlois. "[He] has not forgiven me the manner in which I settled my accounts with him. My playful jabs obviously hurt him," Langlois wrote some eighteen years later.[41] Langlois, privately and publicly, did not hide his feeling for what he considered a minority of people taking advantage of the party. In June 1910, he accused some Liberals of using the party to get special favours and promotions and evidently touched a nerve. Brodeur, frequently criticized by Langlois in *Le Pays* as a source of corruption, urged Laurier to tell Fernand Rinfret, *Le Canada*'s new editor, to challenge *Le Pays* on its accusations.[42]

Numerous issues were taken up by *Le Pays* and measured against the record of Liberal accomplishments. Senate reform, for instance, a permanent fixture of Liberal electoral platforms on which Langlois himself had written extensively, now seemed to be a particular case in point. "We have been in power now for fifteen years," complained Langlois, "and we have continued to make of the senate what the Tories used to make of it: a titular shelter, a hospital of the politically-handicapped [...]. If that continues, we will be nothing more than disguised Tories."[43]

Langlois again pointed to political corruption in the Liberal Party when in the fall of 1910, what should have been a

NOTE: THE SENATE is A HOSPITAL FOR THE POLITICALLY - HANDICAPPED routine by-election, turned sour. The Drummond-Arthabaska by-election, in Laurier's old riding, was fought on the controversial Naval Bill. According to Langlois, nothing was done to counter Bourassa's offensive. "One would believe that our friends were afraid to confront their adversaries. They gave the impression of muted dogs," he wrote. Langlois perceived the by-election's result as the product of a faltering Liberal morale, the product of massive demoralization. "For fifteen years, the Liberal party has been the manipulation of a few men. It is when that little group of men is seen, men who sell jobs and promotions, who traffic in influence and believe that the supreme ambition of a man is to indulge in profitable politics, that one understands why so many people in our party are demoralized and disgusted."[44]

For these reasons, Langlois did not participate in the 1911 election. "*Le Pays*, it must be understood, will not renounce its own programme and its own tools of mobilization just because we are on the eve of general elections," he commented.[45] Perhaps Langlois's actions were symptomatic of what had gone wrong in Liberal party ranks. The defeat in the 1911 election did not rattle Langlois who had predicted a sharply reduced Liberal majority. Still, he saw a silver lining in that cloud. "The humiliating defeat that we have suffered attacks the Liberals far more than Liberalism," he observed.

> Since 1896, our party has removed itself bit by bit from its programmes and abandoned itself to the pleasures of power. It began to second guess the old doctrines and delivered the politics of expediency, and often it appeared to govern in order to stay in power and to prepare easy victories instead of realizing dreams and bringing life to ideas.[46]

Langlois's prescription for a Liberal return to health was not surprising. "Let us reorganize our management," he urged, "let us purge our ranks, let us realize our programmes, let us open the Liberal party to all men of good will, let us put Papineau and Dorion in the gallery of our great ancestors and let us march towards the future."[47] *Le Pays* accused Liberalism of having lost the progressive instincts and of its members having no other ambition than to be in power. Langlois's personal campaign, both in *Le Pays* and on the hustings lucidly illustrated the ideological gulf that now separated former progressives.

Langlois involved himself in Montreal's thorny problems for the last time in the winter of 1911. For years, Montreal's growing public transportation system had been bedeviled by a complex system of disjointed schedules, uneven prices, poor distribution of services and constant labour problems. Langlois called for the involvement of the Public Utilities Commission to settle a particularly disruptive strike "since it is the public and the workers who are affected the most."[48] The problem lay in the fact that many companies serviced the Montreal area and that problems in one firm inexorably affected all others. To rectify the dilemma a bill was drafted by the provincial Liberals. Though he said he did not agree with all the clauses in the proposed law, Langlois volunteered to pilot the bill through its readings on behalf of the government. The "Langlois bill", as it came to be known, quickly sparked debate. It called for all the companies in Montreal to merge, in return for a fifty year franchise. Lower prices, better service and strict accountability to the Public Utilities Commission would be the net result—something Langlois wanted to see.

Mayor Guerin denounced the bill and urged Gouin to suspend debate until Montreal's City Council made proper representations. To demonstrate its opposition, City Council debated the motion that Montreal separate from the province should the bill be passed! On March 1, 1911, a collection of some of Montreal's most influential personalities congregated in the Premier's office to protest the government's initiative. The Mayor, the Board of Control and several aldermen urged Gouin to withdraw the bill as it ignored Montreal's autonomy by sponsoring a private monopoly and by implicitly involving the provincial government in negotiations to set prices and lengths of contracts. J.C. Walsh's *Herald* also broke with Langlois on the issue. Indeed, Langlois was now being painted as the defender of a trust. He defended his unusual position by arguing that the monopoly already existed and that the issue was to control it. "Look at the situation objectively," he insisted. "The trust is already created: the tramway company and the companies it controls are masters of the field in Montreal and in certain suburbs and I cannot be held responsible for that situation. At least with this bill, we will be able to place the trust under the jurisdiction of the Public Utilities Commission and we will be able to pin it down."[49]

Langlois's position slowly gathered adherents and eventually a compromise solution was reached. While the consortium was formed, the bill was amended to allow the city to negotiate its own agreements and to award a contract of up to 42 years. The city thus kept its "autonomy" explicit, the new transit company was placed under the authority of the Public Utilities Commission and people could look forward to better public transit in Montreal. Despite his success, the tramways bill was Langlois's last attempt to reform the politics in Montreal. It was clear that few radical Liberals now wanted to get involved in municipal issues, and *Le Pays*'s pages reflected that disgust with Montreal's politics.

By that time, Langlois had come to the conclusion that change could only happen if it was radical: stop-gap measures, and piecemeal reforms only threatened real change, they did not encourage it. He ploughed his energies in his newspaper. As he was still sitting in the Quebec legislature, most of *Le Pays*'s editorials were written by Langlois under pseudonyms. "An ancient" or "Vindicator" were standard signatures. His style could also be recognized in the biting "Notebooks of an ignoramus," which he signed under the name Népomucène Hébardet. Of course, "Coups de plume" made the trek from *Le Canada* to *Le Pays*. As Langlois distanced himself from his time at *Le Canada*, *Le Pays*'s pages increasingly reflected an even greater desire for change. The limits of the Liberal left were sought by Langlois's own philosophical explorations in this publication. Speeches by renowned politicians were routinely reproduced. Roosevelt, = TEDDY Briand, Lloyd George and especially Jean Jaurès were regularly published in *Le Pays*.

Individualism continued to occupy an important place in *Le Pays*. As Langlois said in his first speech after being fired from *Le Canada*, "a country's worth can only be valued as the collection of the strength of its individuals, like a chain is measured by the resistance of its links. We have, it is true, a few individuals who throw splendour and spark on our country; but it is with peasants and workers that are better educated, more productive and more sober, it is with businessmen better equipped and harder working that we will definitely assure the greatness and the permanence of our race."[50]

Le Pays's obsession with individualism compelled it to intensify the anti-clerico-nationalist campaign Langlois had started in *Le Canada*. *Le Pays* took particular exception to Catholic Superintendent Charles Magnan's slogan that Quebec "was a leader in the world" in educational matters. It protested, moreover, the increasingly nationalist overtones of what was supposed to be a religious holiday, the St-Jean-Baptiste day. "By St-Jean-Baptisme, we mean that false mentality of our compatriots who sincerely believe that they are the most advanced people on earth and who proclaim it especially on that day," exclaimed "Villars" (Roger Valois).[51] Not surprisingly, *Le Pays* was revolted when it learned that Charles Magnan, chief defender of the educational *status quo*, would be re-appointed Quebec's Superintendent of Public Education, the top bureaucratic position in the province's educational structure. "He is one of the leaders of the reactionary school who has resisted for 25 years all the necessary reforms," fired Langlois under the pseudonym "Vindicator".[52] "St-Jean-Baptisme", "Bourassisme", and "Magnanisme" were all held to be synonyms of "Cretinism".

Perhaps what best illustrated *Le Pays*'s attitude towards nationalism was its reaction to a small event that took place in May 1911 in the village of Verchères, on the South Shore. The Post Office authorities had decided to display their sign in English only. In protest, a procession of schoolchildren, led by the local curé, carrying small flags and singing traditional French Canadian tunes, marched from the parish church to the local post office. Once they reached their destination, they heard their priest speak in favour of French signs and on the virtues of the French language. "But is this not the most ridiculous thing?" intoned "Villars", "Is this not St-Jean-Baptiste enough?" Roger Valois argued that numerous important issues such as public sanitation and educational reform deserved serious attention, and yet were ignored by the church authorities, while vain protestations on the issues of signs were voiced. "When all our energies are wasted on futilities of this sort, and when comes the time to seriously demand our rights or to affirm our aspirations and our hopes, we are like a flock of lambs." *Le Pays* was not against the principle of French signs in Verchères, it rather protested the importance with which the issue was invested and the political orientation of the church. If the purity of the French language was to be preserved in Quebec, it would be through better schools, not through French signs on post-offices. "I believe that in spite of French signs," mocked Valois, reflecting on the common usage of English words by French Quebeckers, "the brave people of Verchères will continue to go the 'post office' either to get their 'mail', or to buy their 'stamps'."[53]

Langlois's concern for individualism and for democratic equality compelled him to reconsider socialism. "We will applaud the demands of the workers' party," he declared in his opening editorial, "and we congratulate its leaders for their guidance, for their courage and for their concern for the public. We perceive in their demands a great breath of liberalism."[54] Langlois argued in the Legislative Assembly that workers be represented in Quebec's Technical Schools

Council and that farmers sit on the Council for Public Instruction.[55] In February 1912, he argued that the labouring classes be represented in the planned Montreal Metropolitan Parks Commission. "Before giving thought to the creation of great boulevards and carrying out embellishment plans, the commission should think of providing more welfare to the labouring class by working to find a solution to the problem of sanitary housing for the workers," he told the Legislative Assembly.[56]

Le Pays allowed Langlois the freedom to further develop his thoughts on the role of the state in the economy. "What must be done," *Le Pays* concluded in 1911, "is to replace the system by an economic planification that would not allow the corrupt, the men who lack a conscience, the egotistical speculators, to exploit the naive because they are clever or hypocritical or to exploit the weak because they are powerful in society."[57] Langlois's desire to see the individual remain supreme, however, meant that the success of any policy allowing the state more power would be measured by the degree to which individuals would be free as a result of the initiative.

But individual freedom was not simply an issue for the state to rectify. Society had to reform itself. "Our attitude towards the Jews is wrong," Langlois argued in January 1910. The Jew, Langlois argued, should be allowed to practise his religion freely. In the same vein, Langlois defended individual socialists. When W.A. Cotton, for example, wanted to campaign in the 1911 federal election in Montreal, Langlois supported him. City officials, with the tacit approval of the "reformist" Citizens' Association majority in City Hall, however, barred Cotton from speaking, or from addressing a crowd. It was only after long discussions with the authorities that the socialist was allowed to speak to a crowd on the street, but only as long as he did not mention socialism. Langlois and *Le Pays* fulminated at the injustice, "Why this restriction?" Langlois asked.

Socialism is a political and economic doctrine which is freely discussed, except in Russia and in the province of Quebec.

In Russia, admittedly, only servitude is practised. But here at home, under a democratic regime, one needs mediocre notions of freedom of expression and a fear of ideas to stop a man from explaining to his fellow citizens what socialism is.

In the province of Quebec, three quarters of the people imagine that socialism is a synonym of anarchy. By muzzling Mr. Cotton, do we hope to prolong this regime of ignorance?[58]

Langlois again cast a glance overseas to find inspiration. He had an unusual opportunity to witness personally the beginnings of the constitutional crises that rocked Great Britain in 1909. He made his visit to London as a member of the Canadian delegation to the Imperial Press Conference in June of that year. What he saw was a reinvigorated liberalism. The House of Lords had refused to ratify Prime Minister Asquith's "People's Budget." British Liberals countered by submitting a bill to the House of Commons aimed at reducing the Upper House's prerogatives. The Commons was dissolved twice in rapid succession over the question, and Liberalism emerged victorious.

The formulation of a democratic socialism as evolved by the Webbs, the vigour of the Labour party and the emergence of the suffragettes prompted Langlois to strike a note of optimism. "The era of silent generations has passed," happily reflected *Le Pays*'s editor. "The era of equitable social demands begins. It is high time that the double regime of excessive wealth and excessive poverty disappears from the lives of civilized peoples."[59] Regardless of his explorations and his vehement wishes for radical change, however, Langlois was never a genuine socialist. *Le Pays* explained the evolution of the Labour party as the upshot of the apathy of the upper classes and he demanded that legal measures be made to redress capitalism's more sordid aspects. The problem in industrial relations, was considered to be, not surprisingly, a lack of education. "The boss is often full of good will in trying to win the sympathies of his workers as he begins," Langlois contended, "he often does not succeed, he feels challenged from all sides, and becomes discouraged and often authoritarian: he does not know how to lead. Why? Because he was never taught."[60] Indeed, *Le Pays* never failed to defend capitalism and its captains. While Langlois harshly criticized the Liberal party for closing its doors to the working class movement, he also lambasted it for not opening its doors wider to the French Canadian businessman.

Langlois's vision of Liberal progressivism continued to evolve as *Le Pays* prospered. It continued to be anchored in the advocacy of educational reform, and Langlois could write about education in Serbia and then tackle a flattering interpretation of Maximilien Robespierre. But if *Le Pays* spoke on many subjects, its subjects relentlessly spoke of educational reform. A quantitative measure of the number of articles published regarding this question would not fully indicate the importance it held in the hearts of *Le Pays*'s editors.

In February 1911, the Dandurand Royal Commission on the state of schooling in Montreal that had been formed by Gouin in the spring of 1909 submitted its report to the Legislative Assembly. In a decision that could not help but bolster Langlois's credibility, the Dandurand Commission proposed that the 30-odd school boards on the island of Montreal be unified in a central body. The main reason, the commission argued, was financial. A centralization of administration and tax collection would allow a more equitable distribution of funds. Rich neighbourhoods would thus help subsidize the cost of educating the children of less fortunate quarters of the city. The cost of administering the system would also be reduced as less work would be duplicated.

The Dandurand Commission also proposed that the number of school commissioners on the expanded Montreal Board be increased from 9 to 12 and that they be *elected* simultaneously with aldermen. "This convocation to the polls will perhaps lead to a greater interest in educational issues on the part of the fathers, for whom these should be of primordial importance," the commissioners concluded in language that strongly recalled Langlois's own speeches between 1905 and 1909 and for which he paid so dearly. "The electors would find the opportunity to voice their opinions, to express their views on all sorts of questions that fall within the field of the school board."[61]

Gouin, who was never entirely hostile to the Langlois propositions, was greeted in his office the next day with petitions drafted by various union locals. They indicated that a three-pronged reform of the educational system was desirable and demanded the uniformity of books, free and mandatory education as well as the proposed fusion of the school boards on the island of Montreal.[62] Still, Gouin stalled. *Le Pays* published a "Worker's plea" as editorial a few weeks later and it reflected well Langlois's disillusionment. "In other days, Sir Lomer, you preached the creation of a Ministry of public education, the uniformity of textbooks, and school reform in all its aspects. Why did you renounce that program? [...] Why do you allow us to be exploited by the book merchants? [...] Can you tell us why the Liberal party did not maintain while in power the program that helped it win the elections in 1897?"[63] Langlois's harsh words concerning education and the church provoked the anger of Montreal's Archbishop again. "Permit me to tell you that I have been saddened by many of the articles published in 'Le Pays'," the Archbishop told Langlois. "I have, assuredly, no heresies to reproach it with. Nor have I read anything in it against sound morality. But the tone, the general spirit, leaves much to be desired. The editors do not seem to want to make this newspaper a friend of religion. I do not worry about purely political issues. But when a great number of issues touch catholic interests, you must admit that another language could be used in the paper."[64] Bruchési added a personal touch to his letter. "Why do you not prepare for Easter and frankly return to the faith of your youth?" asked the Archbishop.[65] Predictably, nothing was done to change the tone of *Le Pays*, and there is little doubt that Langlois continued to boycott the church on Sundays.

The backlash against Langlois over his numerous criticisms of Quebec's elite was manifested during the 1912 provincial election. Langlois had continued to run a tight ship in his riding by maintaining close relations with the federal representatives of the area and he was always closely linked with the local alderman. A *Club du Quartier St-Louis* was formed sometime during Langlois's stay at *Le Canada* and A.P. Pigeon was regularly re-elected its president. By 1913, it counted 400 members, something which prompted *La Presse* to identify Langlois's clique as one of the most prosperous of the Liberal "phalanx".[66]

Langlois was well prepared for the 1912 election. He probably expected Henri-Benjamin Rainville to run against him, but found that the Liberal challenge to his reign in St-Louis would come from elsewhere. Mendoza Langlois (no relation), a wealthy land speculator, decided to run on a Liberal Independent ticket. Opposition also came from the Conservative party and from a non-partisan independent. Langlois, for his part, clinched the Liberal nomination in a meeting of the local riding association presided by former Mayor Louis Payette. A.P. Pigeon proposed that Langlois be re-nominated, and the radical gladly accepted the honour once again. "I am an old Liberal," he told the assembly, "and I have been loyal to the flag of the old Liberal party. But I have always placed my country above my party and my ideas above men."[67] Langlois continued to enjoy substantial support from the 11,000 Jews of his riding (39.4 percent of Montreal's Jewish population lived in St-Louis by 1911—the greatest concentration in Montreal[68]). J.S. Miller, a community leader, promised to Langlois the Jewish vote during the convention. A few days later, a young Peter Bercovitch (future minister in Taschereau's cabinet) did the same.[69]

Two riding offices were opened this time, and each served as local party headquarters. Mendoza Langlois, strongly supported by Dr. Gadbois, provided Langlois with stiff competition. If elected, the challenger promised, "the St. Louis division will no longer suffer the humiliation of being called backward, ignorant, sheep and other inanities that are the main baggage of our deputy's discourse."[70] The St. Louis fight turned out to be the highlight of an otherwise lacklustre campaign. There was no concerted effort to reinforce the "radical" contingent of Liberals. Gouin, who had fulfilled his 1908 promise of retiring the provincial debt a few weeks before the election, campaigned on a programme of road and street improvement. In the end, with criticism of the government being drowned out by the horrific news of the Titanic's sinking, Liberalism maintained its majority in the Assembly. 65 seats were won by Liberals, 2 were taken by Labour candidates and 15 by Conservatives. Bourassa, who effectively retired from politics in early 1912, did not seek reelection in St. Hyacinthe. He was succeeded by a brash young radical, Théodore-Damien Bouchard. In St. Louis, Langlois trounced his adversaries again. Winning all but 8 of 49 polls (2 to the Conservative and 6 to the independent), Langlois collected 50 percent of the votes, costing all three of his opponents their $200 deposits. Strengthened by this show of popularity, Le Pays made its demands: " that Sir Lomer govern to erect, to consolidate, to improve and to expand," exhorted Langlois two days after the election, "that he apply liberalism!"[71]

As soon as the new Parliament convened in November 1912, radical ideas again made their mark on the political scene when Dr. John Finnie proposed that schooling for Protestant children be made mandatory. The bill was similar to that which Grosbois had submitted in March 1900, except that it would apply to Protestant children between the ages of 7 to 13 exclusively. Finnie defended his submission with the standard arguments regarding individual potential and the needs of the working class.

Langlois, of course, supported the bill in the Assembly, but another young defender of the bill made some impact:

T.D. Bouchard, a onetime member of the *Loge l'Emancipation*. "I am a Liberal," boasted Bouchard, "and that is why I believe it my duty to support this bill." Bouchard went further and argued for an extension of the law to all denominations, but seemed content to leave the bill with its present restrictions. "The protestant minority believes it is presently able to improve its situation by decreeing for itself mandatory schooling: As a Liberal, I am ready to vote in favour of this law, respecting the spirit of our constitution and thus supporting a measure that will improve the condition of the government to which it will apply."[72]

Le Pays mercilessly pestered the government to act. Angered by its accusations and innuendos, Gouin launched a personal attack on Langlois in the Legislative Assembly: "The member for St-Louis need not be shy: If he has something to say to me, he can say it from his place in the House, face to face, and not in *Le Pays* under the mask of 'Vindicator' or some other pseudonym."[73] Never shy, Langlois responded to Gouin's challenge on the morrow and urged the Assembly to vote in favour of the Finnie proposals. "If the catholics do not want mandatory schooling," he argued, "they do not have the right to refuse it to the protestants."[74] Gouin in turn disputed Langlois's arguments. Popular support did not manifest itself in favour of such a measure, the Premier noted. "Let us fight the good fight," he urged, "let us work to convince all the people, by words and by example, of the necessity of keeping our children in school. Let us pay, if need be, for those who are too poor to send their children to school. But until our population ends its goodwill in having its children educated, we should suspend such a rigorous measure."[75]

The debate was quickly ended with Gouin's stunning blows to the Finnie-Langlois arguments. When the votes were tabulated on the issue the next day, Finnie had reason to be disappointed. Even Bouchard, who had spoken so eloquently in his defence, voted against the measure because, he said, most of the protestants in the Assembly did not support the motion. Indeed, only six people did so, including Finnie and Langlois.[76] *Le Pays*'s editor was livid nevertheless at Gouin's intervention. "If it pleases French Canadians to immobilize themselves in fear and inaction, the English have to right to move ahead. This is the new doctrine Sir Lomer Gouin is promoting and against which we rebel," he wrote.[77]

Gouin, in the meantime, basked in the congratulations of the Catholic hierarchy. "You pulverized the member for St-Louis in your speech by the justness and the strength of your arguments," gingerly wrote one supporter.[78] "To make schooling mandatory for the protestants was assuredly to breach our educational system and to violate at the same time the natural right of parents, to whom the care of children was entrusted. It was also to give reason to those who have made it their mission to change our province and to present it as the home of ignorance," wrote Ste-Hyacinthe's Bishop.[79]

Despite the setback suffered over the Finnie bill, Langlois continued to raise the questions of reform in education and continued to meet with a measure of success. The notion that schoolbooks be provided free of charge to children, for example, was slowly winning sympathizers. In April 1912, longtime Liberal progressive alderman L.A. Lapointe, a member of the Montreal School Commission, wondered aloud if the time for such a measure had not arrived.[80] The question was examined by the School Board in 1913, and a study commissioned by the province concluded that books could be freely provided by the state for approximately $20,000. Nothing came of it. On another question, Montreal's school board again indicated a penchant for Langlois's ideas when it decreed in December 1912 that teachers without an "école normale" education would be dismissed; and that medical examinations would be required of all those teaching.[81]

Langlois won another small battle of sorts in 1913 when an old question resurfaced. The Legislative Assembly finally passed a bill forcing the City of Montreal to purchase a lot within two months in order to erect a municipal library. The issue had been debated since 1901 when Andrew Carnegie had offered the city a grant to match its investment in such a venture, but the Council had refused to submit a bid. The issue was significant and demonstrated that many shared in 1913 the ideas that were once considered heretical.[82]

Archbishop Bruchési persisted in exhorting Langlois to change the tone of his newspaper, but to no avail. On June 12, 1912, Montreal catholics were formally warned of *Le Pays*. "Catholic faith, it is clear, means little to them," Bruchési observed in his missive. "Their sympathies for the church's adversaries and for the things that are rejected by the church are obvious [...]. They do not have the respect that is due to religious authority and in the events they report, and in their interpretation of the facts, they show a preference to everything that could be against religion." In a confidential letter to Langlois, Bruchési reiterated his objections to *Le Pays*'s treatment of the school question. "It is true that you err on numerous points, that your statistics are wrong and it strikes me that you speak ill of our province too much," the Archbishop said. "But that is not the issue here. I have told you my grievances against your paper and you will have to agree that I have not exaggerated. It is not only direct attacks against dogma that can have a nefarious influence on the faith and the religious feelings of those who read you."[83] The prelate persisted in exhorting Langlois to personally return to the faith:

> You are not one of us today; I hope still that you will return to us, for there is nothing you can substitute to the faith of your youth that will fully satisfy your soul and your heart.[...] Do not resent me if I tell you that I pray for you with all my heart every day, so that God can bring you back to Him and to your first beliefs: it is to ask on your behalf for the purest and sweetest joys that can be tasted on this earth.[84]

Nothing changed. On September 29, 1913, Archbishop Bruchési officially barred catholics from reading *Le Pays* with little explanation except to say that Langlois's publication continued to "gravely hurt religious interests, and has created a real harm, especially among youth."[85] *Le Pays*'s response encapsulated the essence of Langlois's thought. Indeed, it was so comprehensive that it was reprinted, in English and in French, as a pamphlet. "Why this interdiction?" an infuriated Langlois wrote. "Is it because we have asked French Canadians to behave like men, to have pride, to grow in work and effort so that our race can grow, to practise the freedom of thought and speech?"[86] Langlois attacked the hegemony of clerico-nationalistic thinking, and mocking Bruchési's words, boldly continued to publish *Le Pays* unfettered by any clerical considerations.

Langlois probably expected Bruchési's condemnation of *Le Pays*. In his search for new ideas, he had gravely isolated himself from mainstream Liberalism and could no longer be protected by the Tartes and then the Béiques who had defended him time and again before the Archbishop. A few friends lingered around *Le Pays*'s editorial offices but little could be done to remedy Langlois's growing cynicism about politics in Quebec. *Le Pays* continued to advocate reforms of all sorts, but its tone was increasingly resigned and depressed. It grew tired of the Board of Control's extravagance, railed against Gouin's missed opportunities for reform and criticized the Liberal party continuously.

When in April 1914, Médéric Martin, a Liberal who had fought progressivism for a dozen years, was triumphantly elected to the Mayor's office in Montreal following a highly nationalistic campaign, Langlois lost all hope of ever affecting the course of his party. On May 5, 1914, Martin walked into his office and declared that he would now be responsible for many of the Board of Control's operations. He declared that he would personally oversee the hiring and firing of personnel, told the office of engineers to dismiss three foremen, placed the Roads Department under the surveillance of police detectives, and arbitrarily informed two aspiring firemen that no employment would be theirs until they could speak French.[87]

Finally, Martin's victory graphically illustrated to Langlois that his ideas were a spent force in Quebec. The Quebec government had decided to open an office in Brussels to encourage trade with the French-speaking countries and Langlois sought the opportunity to represent the province. On May 14, 1914, it was confirmed that Langlois would be named Quebec's Trade Representative in Brussels at a salary of $6000 per annum. On the Saturday evening of June 22, the *Club Canadien* offered a banquet to honour Langlois one last time. He was given a gold watch and chain. Indeed, the occasion marked Langlois's 25th year in Liberal politics. Langlois left Montreal with his family soon thereafter and boarded the "La France" steamer in New York.

Beaten, depressed, Langlois left Canada without remorse. Radical Liberalism seemed defeated; reforms that had been initiated, that had proven their popularity, had been sabotaged. *Le Pays* had been a last-ditch attempt to reaffirm principles most held to be lost. It proved to be both a continuation and a new departure for Liberal progressivism. *Le Canada*'s battles had been continued, but Langlois could not hide his disappointment with the cause. To him, the problem was not that Liberal progressivism was too radical. Quite the contrary, Langlois moved his understanding of radical Liberalism noticeably to the left in *Le Pays*. He embraced the trade union movement as never before and demanded open discussions of socialism. He rejected the authority of the church and denounced nationalism as an artificial fabrication of the reactionaries. He was not deaf to the suggestion that liberalism had much to learn from other ideologies and diligently applied himself and his readers to a study of the alternatives. His conclusions were, in the end, not unpredictable: To survive, Liberalism had to be radical. Still, ideologies, he realized, were useless if no one dared to put them into practice.

Langlois staunchly continued to press for reform. The controversy over the Finnie bill proved that his thoughts on educational reform still had currency, and his actions in trying to contain the strength of the public transportation companies proved his willingness to involve himself personally to affect change. Far more than Langlois's revenge for being fired from *Le Canada* and for being denied a Legislative Council position, *Le Pays* was the last refuge of the radical Liberal progressives. It was an entertaining little publication, one that regularly paraded Langlois's irrepressible wit. Few escaped his biting sarcasm, and, in turn, it was denounced from all sides as it ceaselessly provoked controversy. It represented one element of Liberal progressivism's battle to remain radical at a time when many friends seemed to withdraw into the same contradictions that had plagued nineteenth century radicalism in French Canada. Langlois, who had begun his political career after strolling the streets of Paris, would end it in the same way. His political career had paralleled that of France. He was as optimistic as she in 1889; he was as disillusioned when together they heard the roar of the guns of August 1914.

Notes

1. *Le Pays*, 26 novembre 1910.
2. Langlois Papers, File B, Bruchési to Langlois, 11 juin 1912.
3. PAC, G. Gibbons Papers, Vol. 7. See Langlois's correspondence with Gibbons. Langlois got into a dispute over payments. He billed the government for his services, although he never worked in Ottawa. Presumably, he was billing for preparatory work in Montreal, but the issue remains unclear.
4. *Le Pays*, front page editorial, 15 janvier 1910.
5. *La Presse*, 4 juillet 1905.
6. Laurier Papers, C881, Casgrain to Laurier, 28 décembre 1909.
7. See Francine Nagant, "Politique municipale à Montréal, 1910-1914: L'Echec des réformistes et le triomphe de Médéric Martin" (M.A. Thesis, Université de Montréal, 1982), p. 287.
8. *Ibidem.*
9. See A.J. Lemieux's graphic description of the meeting in *La Loge l'Emancipation* (Montreal, 1910).

10. *La Presse*, 12 janvier 1910.

11. Laurier Papers, C881, Laurier to Casgrain, 15 janvier 1910.

12. *Ibidem*, Casgrain to Laurier, 13 janvier 1910.

13. *Ibidem*, C885, David to Laurier, 15 janvier 1910. David reaffirmed his objections to Dandurand's actions in the 1910 Municipal election in his *Souvenirs et biographies* (Montreal, 1911), p. 222.

14. *La Presse*, 28 janvier 1910.

15. *Ibidem*, 27 janvier 1910.

16. Laurier Papers, C881, Casgrain to Laurier, n.d. [late January 1910?]

17. *La Presse*, 24 janvier 1910.

18. *Le Pays*, 22 janvier 1910.

19. *La Presse*, 29 janvier 1910.

20. *Ibidem*, 2 février 1910.

21. *Le Pays*, 19 avril 1913.

22. The letter is quoted in Roger Le Moine, p. 49. See alsop. 60.

23. Laurier Papers, C890, Desaulniers to Laurier, 3 mai 1910.

24. *Ibidem*, Desaulniers to Laurier, 9 mai 1910. Desaulniers was clearly having second thoughts about his relationship with Langlois (a relationship that went back over 15 years) and with the freemasonry. He was singled out as a coward and a thief by the leader of the Loge L'Emancipation. See Roger Le Moine, *Deux loges montréalaises du Grant Orient de France* (Ottawa, 1991), p. 86.

25. *Ibidem*, Laurier to Desaulniers, 5 mai 1910.

26. See Roger Le Moine, *Deux Loges montrealaise du Grand Orient de France* (Ottawa, 1991) p. 49-53. Le Moine provides a very good description of some of the hysteria around the masonry witch hunt of the summer of 1910.

27. *Ibidem*, p. 57.

28. See Roger Le Moine, *op. cit.*, p. 63 for letter from Albert Marcil to Vadécar. See also p. 57 for Marcil's diagnosis of what went wrong with *l'Emancipation*. Langlois is not mentioned by name in any documents, so we don't know if Marcil considered Langlois a part of the problem, or a genuine strength within the movement. I suspect the former rather than the latter, since Langlois did not adhere to *Force et Courage*.

29. *La Presse*, 1 août 1911.

30. Langlois Papers, File B, Langlois to Laurier, 9 mars [1910].

31. Laurier Papers, C884, Langlois to Laurier, n.d. [probably early september 1910]

32. *Ibidem*, Laurier to Langlois, 14 septembre 1910.

33. Langlois Papers, File B, Langlois to Laurier, 15 septembre 1910.

34. *Ibidem*, Langlois to Dandurand, 5 décembre 1910.

35. Laurier Papers, C884, Langlois to Laurier, n.d. [early Septembre 1910]

36. *Le Pays*, 15 octobre 1910.

37. *Ibidem*, 26 avril 1911

38. *Ibidem*, 16 avril 1911.

39. Laurier Papers, C903, Langlois to Laurier, 19 avril 1911.

40. *Le Pays*, 5 août 1911.

41. Langlois Papers, File C, Langlois to Ernest Lapointe, 6 février 1928.

42. Laurier Papers, C881, Brodeur to Laurier, 10 juin 1910. On Langlois's private criticisms, see Langlois Papers, File B, Langlois to Laurier, 15 septembre 1910 and 5 décembre 1910.

43. *Le Pays*, 26 mars 1910.

44. *Le Pays*, 6 novembre 1910. It is obviously very difficult to prove whether Langlois's assertion regarding the demoralization and disorganization of party workers was really valid. Certainly, Laurier was having difficulties of this sort in Ontario. Paul Stevens has chronicled the faltering Liberal organization in his "Laurier and the Liberal Party in Ontario, 1887-1911" (Ph.D. thesis, University of Toronto, 1966).

45. *Le Pays*, 5 août 1911.

46. *Ibidem*, 23 septembre 1911.

47. *Ibidem*.

48. Archives Nationales du Québec à Montréal, Fonds Godfroy Langlois, Memo, "L'intervention de la commission" (rough draft), 15 janvier 1911.

49. *Le Pays*, 4 mars 1911. The development of Montreal's public transit problems in this era are surveyed in C. Armstrong and H.V. Nelles "Suburban Street Railways in Montreal, Toronto and Vancouver, 1896-1930" in Gilbert A. Stetler and Alan F.J. Artibise (eds.) *Power and Place: Urban Development in the North American Context* (Vancouver, 1986).

50. *Ibidem*, 26 mars 1911.

51. *Ibidem*, 10 juin 1911.

52. *Ibidem*, 10 août 1912.

53. *Ibidem*, 20 mai 1911.

54. *Ibidem*, 19 janvier 1912.

55. *La Presse*, 19 janvier 1912.

56. *Ibidem*, 16 février 1912.

57. *Le Pays*, 11 février 1911.

58. *Ibidem*, 26 août 1911.

59. *Ibidem*, 23 mars 1912. On Langlois and Britain, see *Le Canada*, 26 mars 1909; 1 février 1909; 1 septembre 1909.

60. *Le Pays*, 15 octobre 1910.

61. The text is reprinted in *La Presse*, 10 février 1911. For an exhaustive exploration of the Commission's conclusion's, see Ruby Heap, "Urbanisation et Education: La centralisation scolaire à Montréal au début du XXe siècle" *HP*, 1985, pp. 137-145.

62. See Lomer Gouin Papers, Vol.2, Montreal Buildings Trades Council to Gouin, 10 February 1911; Union des Briquetiers de Montreal to Gouin, 14 février 1911; International Association of Bridge and Structural Iron Workers to Gouin, 16 February 1911; United Association of Journeymen Plumbers, Gas Fitters, Steam Fitters and Steam Fitters' Helpers to Gouin, 18 February 1911; Fraternité Unie des Charpentiers et Menuisiers d'Amérique, 26 février 1911. Such working class support for the mandatory education proposal lay to rest the notion that such measures were perceived by the proletariat as "capitalist intrustions". It also supports Thérèse Hamel's findings of agreement for such measures in the Quebec chapter of the T.L.C. See her "L'obligation scolaire au Québec: Enjeu pour le mouvement syndical et agricole" *L/LT*, 17, Spring 1986.

63. *Le Pays*, 31 décembre 1910.

64. Langlois Papers, File B, Bruchési to Langlois, 22 avril 1911.

65. *Ibidem*.

66. *La Presse*, 16 janvier 1913.

67. *Ibidem*, 26 avril 1912.

68. The 1911 census is cited in *La Presse*, 21mars 1914.

69. *Ibidem*,12 mai 1912.

70. *Ibidem*, 14 mai 1912.

71. *Le Pays*, 18 mai 1912.

72. *La Presse*, 27 novembre 1912.

73. *Résumé d'un discours prononcé par l'honorable Sir Lomer Gouin à l'Assemblée législative de Québec, 26 novembre 1912* (Quebec, 1913), p. 30.

74. *La Presse*, 28 novembre 1912.

75. *Ibidem*.

76. *La Presse*, 29 novembre 1912.

77. *Le Pays*, 23 novembre 1912.

78. Lomer Gouin Papers, Vol. 13, Charles Guay to Gouin, 28 novembre 1912.

79. *Ibidem*, "A.X. de Ste-Hyacinthe to Gouin, 2 décembre 1912; See also Paul Bruchési to Gouin, 30 novembre 1912; Emile Roy to Gouin, 28 décembre 1912; "Père Godfroy" to Gouin, n.d.

80. *La Presse*, 24 avril 1912.

81. *Ibidem*, 31 décembre 1912.

82. *Ibidem*, 12 novembre 1913.

83. Langlois Papers, File B, Bruchési to Langlois, 11 juin 1912.

84. *Ibidem.*

85. Reprinted in full in *Le Pays*, 4 octobre 1913. Published in English as *Still Standing* (Montreal, 1913), and in French as *Toujours Debout* (Montreal, 1913).

86. *Ibidem.*

87. *La Presse, 6 mai 1914.*

EPILOGUE

EXILE

*"Who will now lead the battle
for ideas in the province of Quebec?"*

--Le Pays, 1914[1]

I T WAS ALMOST NATURAL for Langlois's nomination as the first official representative of the Province of Quebec in a foreign country to be controversial.[2] To no one's surprise, the ultra conservative *l'Action Sociale* did not agree with the appointment to the extent of three columns under the heading "A National Shame." Still, not all took offence to Gouin's choice, and many Liberals probably breathed a sigh of relief upon learning that one of the party's fiercest critics and troublemakers would be silenced.

As Langlois sailed to his destination, Europe was slowly being engulfed in war. He visited his old friend Philippe Roy, who had been the Canadian Trade Commissioner to France since 1911, and awaited developments. It was soon obvious that there was little hope of reaching Brussels. Langlois made arrangements with the Quebec government to settle in Paris for a time. His daughter Marcelle was enrolled in the same school as the Roy daughters, and Langlois whiled the years in Paris devoted to his reading and exploring what was left of a free Europe.

Contacts between Langlois and Quebec were minimal in this period, at least until 1917. Putting old differences aside, Laurier asked Langlois in November of that year to act as the representative of the opposition in the monitoring of the Canadian election overseas.[3] Langlois agreed to bury the hatchet, and responded to his old boss's request. He left Paris on November 30 and headed for Boulogne. It was estimated that there were anywhere between 500 and 1000 polling

327

stations, and Langlois soon found it necessary to recruit assistants. Considering the anti-Liberal, anti-Quebec, atmosphere on the front, the job was delicate. "I am counting on my electoral flair to work things out," Langlois confidently told Laurier.[4]

Godfroy Langlois thus spent most of December 1917 in the mud of northern France. He visited polling stations in Boulogne, Calais, Etaples, Montreuil, Château-de-la-Haie and smaller stations. He crossed the now dormant battle fields of Caravey and Soudrez. "I saluted Vimy, whose craters will forever speak of the heroism of our troops," he wrote to Sir Wilfrid. "This whole region is of an indescribable desolation, of infinite sadness."[5] Langlois's work was soon hampered by an allied offensive that temporarily suspended his efforts. The election would take much longer in Europe than in Canada, where results had already given the Union government of Robert Borden an overwhelming mandate.

Langlois assumed his official functions as Quebec's General Commissioner in Brussels in 1919, opened an office on the boulevard Bischoffsheim, settled his family in an apartment on rue de Spa, and integrated rapidly into the Belgian capital's political and high-society circles. To propagate Canadian economic conditions(Langlois would never see his mandate as strictly for Quebec), he launched a small publication, *Belgique-Canada*, and it was also well received. In November 1920, he was named to the *Ordre de Léopold* and in December 1923 was named Officer of the Order of the Belgian Crown. Lomer Gouin, returning from a trip to Europe, told Sir George Foster, Borden's Minister of Commerce, that Langlois was *persona grata* among the Belgian cabinet and proved well connected with the Belgian financial and press communities.[6] Langlois toured Belgian manufacturing and financial centres, giving speeches not on the state of Liberalism, but on the merits of Quebec cheese, honey, butter, apples, canned fish, jams and tobacco, and acted as intermediary for Belgian businessmen considering investments in Canada.[7] Partaking in the activities of the Automobile Club of France, the *Cercle inter-alliés* of Paris and the *Cercle des sports de Bruxelles*, Langlois hosted numerous Canadian visitors to Belgium and took advantage of the available luxuries to indulge his gourmet appetite and his refined taste for antique furniture during numerous trips to various regions of France. One trip to the Bordeaux region was particularly memorable, it seems, for all the menus featuring pre-war vintages were carefully collected and preserved.[8]

Langlois's prestige in Belgium soon surpassed that of the Canadian Trade Commissioner, and his successes compelled him to ask that the two offices be integrated under his supervision and that he receive (of course) the two salaries. French-Canadians, he often argued, were inadequately represented in Europe,[9] and besides, the Quebec Government Commission was now receiving 95% of Canadian requests for information, he told Gouin.[10]

The Canadian government was unimpressed even though Canada's trade relations with Belgium certainly prospered during the first years of Langlois's stay. In 1916, Canada's exports to war-torn Belgium had totalled only $334,762. By 1920, exports to the rebuilding country had grown to $28,463,855 and reached a record high of $40,252,487 in 1921, only to drop by 50 percent over the next seven years.[11] It is difficult to say what part Langlois played in encouraging Canadian exports to a Belgium that was restoring its economy. But clearly, governments both in Ottawa and Quebec City were in the process of reevaluating the usefulness of maintaining offices in Belgium while Langlois anxiously made requests for an increase in salary. Oblivious to the realities of Belgium's growing reluctance to import Canadian products, Langlois nonetheless demanded in 1925 that his $6000 salary be raised by a third to match that of the Quebec representative in London.[12] His request was not granted.

When Langlois returned to Canada for the first time in 1921, it seemed as though the bitterness that had clouded the years before his departure had dissipated. He was deeply touched by a banquet given in his honour in Montreal. "I appreciate the value of your esteem and I am infinitely grateful that you have chosen to forget that in the past I was a combative man, sometimes even after the battles, to only remember that I was always and that I remain a man of good will," he told the crowd of assembled politicians and journalists. "We have the satisfaction of living in a time when friendship is not an empty word: your presence tonight gives me that assurance [...]. All the past I lived with you now appears as a smile to me, and I bless the hour that brings us together."[13]

Despite the warm welcome, Langlois could not resist harking back to the mistreatment he had lived a dozen years before. Poking criticism at Quebec Liberalism's unwillingness to accommodate new ideas, he extolled the efforts of Belgian catholics, Liberals and Socialists as they tried to piece together their country after four years of German occupation. "The three parties live together without denying their essential doctrines and agree to compromise in the short term so as to restore the Belgian fatherland. I have seen up close some of those public figures and I feel it is my duty to pay them homage for their altruism and for their genuinely national courage."[14] Langlois thereafter rarely returned to Quebec—not even to witness his daughter's wedding in 1924 to Dr. Albéric Marin, a distinguished war hero and Montreal dermatologist.

From his side of the Atlantic, Langlois continued to observe the political events of the world. Trade disputes forced him to reconsider his early views. Time had proven his early free-trade impulses wrong, he recognized. "In my days of candour I believed in 'Cobdenism' and lulled my young journalist's illusions with the music of free-trade," he wrote to Lomer Gouin while in Belgium. "I have turned my back on that chimera. A country like ours must be protectionist if it wants to ensure the survival of its national industries and pursue a sound development of its economic strengths."[15] If Langlois reaffirmed his rejection of nineteenth century radical *rougisme* he grew increasingly dissatisfied with the evolution of that other font of his inspiration, French Radicalism. Despairing over the worsening economic and social climate of Europe in the 1920s, he despised Edouard Herriot's Radical government for applying what he considered unnecessarily harsh remedies. "My liberalism and my common sense are revolted by that sectarianism which is cross-bred with intolerance, revolutionary socialism and antipatriotism, and by the politics of failure and capitulations," he confided to Lomer Gouin. "Don't think I am exaggerating. I would be tempted to be a conservative, at this hour, if I was French."[16]

Godfroy Langlois became ill shortly after escorting the illustrious Montreal academic Edouard Montpetit on an eminently successful lecture tour in Belgium and northern France at the end of 1927, and rapidly lost weight. Doctors had difficulty in diagnosing the illness, and Langlois gradually came to suspect there was more at work than the "bad cold" to which his physicians alluded.[17] Things went from bad to worse in March. The once obese and energetic Langlois was now thin and lethargic, unable to get out of bed. He died of a liver cirrhosis in his apartment on rue de Spa in Brussels on April 6, 1928, at the age of 61. "Another of my friends is gone!" Gouin moaned in his diary upon hearing the news.[18] A year earlier, Langlois had revised his will and reaffirmed his renunciation of catholicism by asking to be cremated.[19] His wish was not granted. Putting herself through much trouble in her time of grief, his widow arranged to have the remains transported back to the shores of the St. Lawrence. A funeral mass was sung in St. Scholastique church and Langlois was buried in a catholic cemetery on July 28, 1928, not far from the house where he was born.[20] Father Jules Graton, his old teacher at St. Thérèse, signed the official funeral documents.[21]

The Quebec office in Brussels was closed six months later.

Notes

1. *Le Pays*, 27 juin 1914.

2. Langlois Papers, File B, Cherrier to Langlois, 14 mai 1914.

3. Laurier Papers, C915, Telegram, Laurier to Langlois, n.d. [November 17, 1917?]

4. *Ibidem*, Langlois to Laurier, 23 novembre 1917.

5. *Ibidem*, Langlois to Laurier, 7 décembre 1917.

6. Lomer Gouin Papers, Vol. 32, Gouin to George Foster, June 12, 1920. See also anonymous letter to Gouin, November 4, 1922.

7. Langlois Papers, File C, Langlois to Taschereau, 11 décembre 1924.

8. See Langlois Papers, File G.

9. See Gouin Papers, Vol. 32, Langlois to Gouin, 24 mai 1922.

10. *Ibidem*, memo, Langlois to Gouin, n.d.

11. *Canada Year Book, 1930* (Ottawa, 1931).

12. Langlois Papers, File C, Langlois to J.L. Perron, 23 janvier 1925.

13. *Ibidem*, File G, speech notes, 1921.

14. *Ibidem*.

15. Gouin Papers, Vol. 32, Langlois to Gouin, 4 juin 1924.

16. *Ibidem*, Langlois to Gouin, 16 décembre 1924.

17. Langlois Papers, File C, Langlois to L.J. Lemieux, 27 février 1928.

18. Gouin Papers, Diary, 7 avril 1928.

19. Langlois Papers, File I, Testament Olographe, 19 février 1927. Cremation continued to be contentious among catholics. In 1886 the Holy See officially forbade cremation for catholics, in reaction to a resurgence in its practice in the mid-nineteenth century, when some groups and individuals chose cremation as a public denial of the Christian belief in the resurrection of the body. This rule was further emphasized in the 1917 church law, which was only revised and liberalized in 1983.

20. The documents are in the Langlois Papers, File H.

21. Graton would be one of the witnesses to sign the certificate of Langlois's inhumation. See Extrait du registre des sépultures, 28 juillet 1928, Langlois Papers, File H.

CONCLUSION

THE LIBERAL PROGRESSIVE TRADITION

> *"... And yet I cannot help admiring the tenacity of the small group of men who set out to infuse some democratic blood into the veins of a party that has never been more than a syndicate of private interests."*
>
> *-P.E. Trudeau, 1956.*[1]

"A FIGURE WHICH FLASHED VIVIDLY across the political life of Quebec during a number of years died early yesterday morning," commented *The Gazette* upon reporting Langlois's death in April 1928.[2] It was an admirable description of this newsman's career, but it could also be extended to describe the movement he exemplified.

Rescued from oblivion by the timely rise of a new generation, radical *rougisme* had not disappeared at Confederation nor was it completely hushed out of the Liberal party by Laurier and Mercier. Indeed, the *rouges*, under different guises, reemerged to become a vibrant force in Wilfrid Laurier's Liberal party in Quebec which affected not only policy, but leadership as well. Shaped by the evolution of a new generation, the French Canadian radicalism of the nineteenth century became a vital aspect of Quebec's experience of "progressivism" at the turn of the century.

Modern times, modern problems demanded modern solutions. The new generation of Liberal radicals that grew around Honoré Beaugrand and *La Patrie* in the 1890s saw educational reform as primordial in assuring not only French

Quebec's survival but also in preparing individuals to face life's struggles. This was in itself a great departure. Nineteenth century radicalism had paid lip service to educational reforms of sorts, but their efforts were never as concerted nor as convincing as the campaign led by the regenerated *rouges* to pressure Félix-Gabriel Marchand into action.

Langlois and the many people who founded *Le Signal* and later *Le Pays*, never ceased to be inspired by the myths of old radicals—men like Rodolphe Laflamme, Honoré Beaugrand and Joseph Doutre. Many of them, Langlois included, had personal ties with nineteenth century radicalism. Nonetheless, men like Joseph-Philippe Casgrain, P.A. Choquette, G.W. Stephens, H.J. Cloran, F.L. Béique, Lomer Gouin, Raoul Dandurand, J.C. Walsh and the litany of organizers, club activists and journalists who gravitated around them, were indelibly affected by the world in which they matured. They inherited many of the traits worn by their predecessors, including an irreverence towards the church and a respect for the revolutionary ideals of 1789, 1837 and 1848, but they were not afraid to modernize their loose doctrines to fit a new, transformed world. Most were vehemently devoted to the idea that the state should involve itself in economic life so as to give French Canadians a chance in the struggle for life and thus reach parity with the anglophone majority in an industrial world. They were adverse to the concepts of monopoly, be it a monopoly of ideas, of educational control, or of the distribution of electricity, and they fought any hegemony that in any way imperiled the perceived liberties of individuals. They gave a new, broader meaning to the concept of democracy. That meaning now had to go beyond mere political freedoms and extend to social and economic realities. This ideological impulse distinguished them from their party confreres who remained wedded to a classic liberalism that favoured unbridled, *laissez-faire* liberalism.

What most prompted the distancing of the new radicals, or the new Liberal progressives, as I chose to label them in light of their secure anchors in liberal ideology, from their nineteenth century roots was the rise of urbanization and industrialization. The perceptible result of the brutal nature of capitalism at the time, a new class of potentially alienated people was growing in Montreal and it was obvious to the new *rouges* that the *status quo*, in order to survive, had to legitimize its existence. Their rhetoric was vastly different from that spoken by their ideological forefathers. The Liberal party, they argued, was ideally suited to the task of bridging the gap between the classes, as long as it adopted progressive policies and ceased to be the label of corrupt, self-serving politicians whose thinly veiled support of particular business interests could only damage the party.

The Liberal progressives were distinct from their nineteenth century radical predecessors in three ways. First, they were sensitive to the potential alienation of the masses and the political impact of corruption on the legitimacy of the *status quo*. Secondly, they were deeply committed to the reform of urban conditions. Industrialization had been uncompromising in its treatment of the urban proletariat, and the Liberal progressive felt the need to repair that potential crucible of discontent. Their call for active state involvement in numerous areas of the economy was not an attempt to curtail the powers of business, nor was it an attempt to help business, but a move designed to remedy the growing suspicion that government, despite its pretensions, did little to protect the ideals of democracy. Finally, they rejected the nationalism of their day, dismissing it as a screen erected by conservative forces designed to hide harsh realities that needed urgent tending.

The fight for "justice" that took shape against the Raymond Préfontaine clique in Montreal and against Simon-Napoléon Parent affirmed the strong urban reform movement that existed within the Liberal party. Campaigns at the municipal level and at the provincial level to rid the party of its label of corruption brought together a consistent membership. The line dividing the radicals from the conservative Liberals was never as sharply focused as on this turf. In Quebec, the most vital campaigns for urban progressivism were not fought along non-partisan lines nor merely in the interest of business. The politics of progressivism were fought within the Liberal party, for very real ideological and political reasons. The Liberal party thus continued to be a coalition of at least two dominant factions, one conservative and the other, radical.

It was also partly out of the concern for the legitimation of the bourgeois-capitalist system and the purification of the party that many came to argue that the state had to play a greater role in redistributing social benefits. Langlois and *Le Canada* perhaps went further than most by repeatedly calling for municipalisation of utilities and for government-sponsored social welfare programs. In Montreal, they fought for a system of elected school trustees, and an elected Board of Control in order to render credibility to the "democratic" rule that was alleged to exist. As W.D. Lighthall, onetime Mayor of Westmount and Liberal-progressive sympathizer, told a reporter in the spring of 1905, "the safety of capitalism lies in justice."[3]

The Liberal progressives fought many adversaries, some of which have come to be seen by historians as "progressive." In their own party, they faced the hostility of those who feared the social, economic and political consequences of Langlois's use of the Liberal label. *La Presse*, the business press and many publications in Quebec certainly adhered to a sort of "liberal" ideology that on a theoretical plane had commonalities with the views given expression by progressive Liberals. Philosophical liberals valued individual rights, the right to ownership and social harmony, but there were marked differences, indeed critically important differences on issues of strategy and tactics required to reach those liberal goals. *La Presse*'s liberalism, for example, proved it was different in a number of ways: it defended the Préfontaine clique, supported the Payette team, and fought all Liberal progressive attempts to reform education, to make school boards accountable to the people, and even opposed the establishment of the Board of Control for a time. Liberalism cannot be seen, therefore, as a consistent package on which there reigned a particular consensus. A distinction must be made between those who argued for a slowly-paced pattern of reform and the Liberal progressives, who by their very nature argued that change would not happen until "radical" solutions were found to "radical", root problems.

Similarly, it is striking to see how the rising nationalists fought all progressive proposals. Surely, some of them (Olivar Asselin comes to mind) came to see the desirability of public ownership of utilities, but they were singularly slow in recognizing its merits. The nationalists, most of whom were deeply conservative long before they appropriated their new label, were most antagonistic to Liberal progressive proposals for educational reform. "As a young member of the *Association catholique de la jeunesse canadienne* we were taught that the Ministry of Public Education and the concepts of free and mandatory schooling, dear to Godfroy Langlois, were strategies whereby the Masonry would take control of our educational system," remembered one of Langlois's arch-critics, A.J. Lemieux.[4] It was the nationalists who fought educational reform as the *Ligue de l'Enseignement* was formed, it was they who opposed Langlois's bill to centralize the administration of schooling in Montreal and Liberal progressivism's call for free and mandatory schooling, and schoolbook standardization. In the fight against the corruption of Montreal politics, and against the Montreal Light, Heat and Power Company, they were absent (Asselin, again, was the exception).

The Liberal progressives constituted a minority, but a vibrant, demanding faction of the Liberal party. Their membership was small, and their adherents often changed. Like their French counterparts, some people moved in and out of the weakly organized clique as the strategies and tactics of the day appealed to them. Lomer Gouin, who had supported so many of Langlois's ventures both in urban and provincial affairs, maintained his distance when he captured power, but never renounced Liberal progressivism. What his government accomplished in educational reform and utility regulation had been conceived by Liberal progressivism. The major disagreement was over the timing of reform, not the nature. Similarly, Raoul Dandurand, a man who considered himself a *rouge*, often fought radicalism in the party but rallied behind *La Patrie* and later *Le Canada*'s call for urban reform. By 1909, even though he had been instrumental in Liberal progressivism's successes, Dandurand had also distanced himself from Langlois's evolving and uncompromising definitions of Liberal progressivism. Langlois was proving too radical, too impetuous in his demands. Like Gouin, Dandurand represented a growing body of opinion within the Liberal party that accepted Liberal progressive values and proposals for reform. Yet they were too unsure of their political capital to attempt risky investments in policy-making. Perhaps the best example of fluctuating membership was Louis Payette. A friend of Langlois's until 1905, he entrenched the monopoly of the Montreal Light, Heat and Power company but rejoined Langlois in 1909 with his calls for state ownership of the electrical utilities and fought the spurious "reform" politicians of the Citizens' Association led by Dandurand.

In light of the shifting coalitions within Liberal progressivism, the role of Godfroy Langlois must be highlighted. Though Liberal progressives held in common many ideals, Godfroy Langlois's life experience sheds much light on the dynamics and the vicissitudes of an often confused movement. He was eager to draw the outlines of Liberal progressivism, he gave it colour, devised its aims and spearheaded many of its campaigns. He played the key role in the search for the means to modernizing the obsolete nineteenth-century radicalism he had inherited. Borrowing heavily from the radical liberalism of the early politicians of the French Third Republic and then from Léon Bourgeois's concepts of *solidarism*, Langlois and his coterie sought to convince Quebec's society of the necessity of giving the state greater powers and the individuals a chance to access greater freedoms. By drafting extensive lists of the ills that hampered Quebec's modernization, Langlois fought for an adaptation of liberalism to a new urbanized and industrialized society. He challenged the church authorities, the trusts, many self-styled nationalists, and above all, provoked Liberal party authorities in reassessing their own politics. His sense of urgency even compelled him to attack the slow moving adaptations of Liberal progressivism in Montreal and Quebec City. At stake was nothing less than the future of Quebec, and of the individuals who composed it.

Unfortunately, Langlois's hopes of a Quebec that would eagerly follow the French Third Republic's example remained nothing more than pipe dreams. His desire to emulate French radicalism in all its aspects alienated a great many potential allies especially as his interpretation of Liberal progressivism waxed increasingly radical after 1905. Certainly, the vehemently anti-catholic, anti-nationalistic flavour he gave Liberal progressivism was unpalatable to many. "We recognize that we have not advanced as fast as you have," he said while toasting France on Bastille day, 1911:

> We are still at a stage of infancy in certain freedoms. Our resolve has lost a part of its vigour and primitive impulse, but the tricolour flag continues to fly in our winds as it does in those of France. After fighting off the assaults of a few men who wanted to change flags, the tricolour has even resisted the church of St-Jean-Baptisme. I am of those who believe that the province of Quebec is not the most advanced nation on earth. The old tree is more vigorous and greener than the offshoot. Our schools languish while they await decisive action and once in a while you will hear voices telling French Canadians to follow the example of France in taking the road to progress. We have to develop and accumulate our intellectual strengths.[5]

The sense of time was ultimately the philosophical feature that differentiated Liberal progressives from those in the mainstream of liberalism. The sense that time was running out, that Quebec was "suspended in time" by the policies of an old-style *laissez-faire* liberalism espoused by the government, gave Liberal progressivism its tone and its impetuous-ness. Conservative forces in the Liberal party were not hostile to its objectives, as long as they stayed in the planning stages. With the element of time removed, Liberal ideologies can appear to be similar. It was the concern for time, for time running out, that made Langlois brook compromise, that compelled Liberal progressives to action and that gave shape to their politics.

Were the Liberal progressives successful? While it is evident that their record on the local scene was largely a failure, Liberal progressive efforts were not all in vain, for they did develop some of those "intellectual strengths" in Quebec that Langlois was hoping for. The presentation of the Marchand bill for educational reform, the demise of the Préfontaine clique, the rise of Langlois to the top ideological position in the French Liberal party press, the Gouin "coup", the establishment of a Board of Control and the reforms in utility policies were all attributable to the tangible pressures exerted by Liberal progressives.

School reform was given a boost. While Langlois sat in the Quebec legislature, numerous trade schools, including a business school, were sponsored by the Gouin government. Total spending in the field of education rose 127.8 percent between 1906 and 1914 in Quebec, with the Gouin government increasing its contributions from a paltry $536,150 in 1905-1906 to $1,724,110 in 1914, a 221.6 percent increase.[6] The Gouin government's decision in 1916 finally to act on what Liberal progressivism had advocated for ten years and unify Montreal's disparate school boards prompted Raoul Dandurand to now demand publicly that school attendance be made mandatory.[7] Dandurand even met with Archbishop Bruchési and several people in the *Conseil de l'Instruction publique,* but was no more successful than Langlois ever was.[8]

It was Théodore Damien Bouchard, far more than Dandurand, who projected Liberal progressive opinions into the world of Louis-Alexandre Taschereau, and later, Adélard Godbout. Considering himself "an intellectual son" of the *vieux rouges,*[9] Bouchard was convinced early by Liberal progressive calls for the public ownership of utilities. In his memoirs, he recounted listening to Albert Saint-Martin's (then a quasi-Liberal) economic discourse in 1901 and remembered being impressed. "Without subscribing to all his opinions in matters of political economy," he recalled, "I believed in the public regulation of essentials of life, and in the intervention of the state against monopolies."[10] Like the Liberal progressives in Montreal and Quebec City, Bouchard began his political life fighting the "trusts" on the municipal scene of his native Ste-Hyacinthe. He also reflected Liberal progressive impulses in his demands for educational reform, including mandatory attendance and schoolbooks standardization. He was, for a time, a member of the *Loge l'Emancipation*. His motions in the Legislative Assembly in 1919, designed to parallel Dandurand's pleas, were as controversial as anything proposed by Joseph Robidoux, Tancrède de Grosbois, Godfroy Langlois or J.T. Finnie.

Bouchard applied much of his political career to curbing the potential disaffection of the working class. He "infiltrated" workers' clubs and sought to address the workers in his newspapers, which explained much of his political success. In that respect, he was also very close to Langlois. For all of Bouchard's efforts, the Premier of Quebec in 1944, Adélard Godbout, finally made school attendance mandatory in 1941. Godbout also named Bouchard as chairman of the "nationalized" Montreal, Light, Heat and Power Company in 1944. Those gestures, which I would consider the first cannon shots of the quiet revolution that marked Quebec in the second half of the century, would have made Langlois smile.

Notwithstanding the longer-term successes that indicated that Liberal progressives were simply avant-garde thinkers frustrated by the slow evolution of thinking in Quebec, the fact remains that in their day, Langlois and the Liberal progressives who gravitated around him had reason to be frustrated with their lack of progress. The chief reason for that lack of success must be the unsustained leadership. If

Langlois was successful in consistently formulating and giving voice to an ideology, there were persistent difficulties in realizing those political goals. Many a mayoral race was decided because of poor candidates emerging from Liberal progressive ranks, men like Henry Ekers, James Cochrane, and Arsène Lavallée. The campaigns of Philippe Roy in 1908 and Senator Casgrain in 1910, were unable to ride the strong tides of reform. Here Langlois must share part of the blame. As one later admirer recognized, "his play was always interesting and often really brilliant, but it was sometimes lacking in discussion [...] his fiery criticism seemed at times to lack the constructive aim and persuasive tone."[11] Perhaps there was also modesty at play. Langlois probably could have been elected to the mayoralty had he sought the post in either 1906 or 1908. That he did not seek the post in those trying years for Liberal progressivism defies explanation, and that failure ultimately weakened the movement severely.

In light of the time, perhaps the greatest accomplishment of the Liberal progressives was to have survived at all. Indeed, they were more than only "vivid flashes," to use *The Gazette*'s phrase: they launched a new movement in French Canadian political, economic and social thought. Marcel Trudel argued that the Voltairian tradition was one of the most enduring in French Canadian thought,[12] but it could be argued that it was not lost by 1900 as he concluded. Voltaire's irreverence and search for a positive role for the state lived in the words and actions of the Liberal progressives.[13] Men like T.D. Bouchard, Adélard Godbout, J.C. Harvey at *Le Jour* and later *Cité Libre*; men who often thought they invented a new philosophy, merely continued to ask the questions posed by the first generation of Liberal progressives and imitated Langlois's calls for strict control of utilities, improved education and the ensurance of the legitimacy of the state. With these views, and with a similar perception of the evolution of French Canadian nationalism, they guaranteed the survival of the Liberal progressive tradition. Godfroy Langlois gave birth to many of the ideas that became common currency since the 1960s: because his activism was political as well as philosophical, I would call him the intellectual father of modern Quebec.

He borrowed some of his ideas from the burgeoning American urban reform movements, but his ideological sources consistently flowed from France, particularly from French Radicalism, at a time when France was undergoing a thorough secularization.[14] He was, it goes without saying, the *bête noire* of conservative thinkers in Quebec. Langlois and his allies, like all philosophical Liberals, held tightly to the ideals of economic and intellectual freedom, but were not content to give it a simple meaning. The ideals of equality, of liberty and of freedom were cherished and in their day of great transformations, the Liberal progressives sought the help of the state to guarantee at least a partial realization of their dreams. Democracy was not a term taken lightly. The search to make that term meaningful gave cardinal directions to the Liberal progressives. Godfroy Langlois came to the conclusion that democracy could not be fulfilled without a commitment to help society's disadvantaged. Free speech was a high ideal, but society's ability to digest free speech was equally critical. Liberal progressives were dedicated to the notion that an educated society was the best defence of democracy. For French Canada, the state's ability to defend the down-trodden was even more important. Survival, so critical to conservative thought, played a major role in driving Liberal progressive thought. Like their French cousins, they sometimes disagreed over the means required to achieve the end they all cherished.

Historians looking for consistency in Quebec's Liberal progressives will be disappointed. As they sought practical solutions to complex problems, consensus was never easy to achieve. As in all politics, certainty was far more obvious in rhetoric than in practice. Liberal progressives knew that there were no easy answers, but they had greater ambitions than to limit themselves to declarations of easy slogans. In his desire to propose concrete solutions to concrete problems, and to buck compromises, Langlois, in particular, became a lightning rod for the accusations of those who were unwilling to go beyond the pious canting of empty rhetoric.

If it is true, as Lionel Trilling wrote forty years ago that liberalism was "a large tendency rather than a concise body of doctrine,"[15] the same is true of Liberal progressivism in Quebec at the turn of the century. At times, Liberal progressives distinguished themselves in the tone they used, and in the sentiments they expressed. As Trilling noted, "certain sentiments consort only with certain ideas, and not with others", and certainly the same can be said about the Liberal progressives. It is in this light that the study of liberal thought and of its offshoots must be undertaken. Indeed, it is because liberalism is so vague an ideology that its politics—the political *actions* of those who say they are liberal—must be closely scrutinized. Only then does a liberalism take on a measurable form, and this has certainly been the conclusion of American historians examining the record of turn of the century "progressives" in the United States. Quebec's Liberal progressivism's intrinsically amorphous nature does not make it unique. The noted French historian Theodore Zeldin once wrote that the "radicalism" of the early Third Republic of France, a liberalism also, was scarcely more consistent. "It was [...] an extremely contradictory, many sided and complicated force," he remarked, "they [liberals] are exceptionally difficult to characterize precisely."[16]

The people who invented the strains of Liberal progressivism must be approached with this prejudice. They agreed on a variety of public policy issues, they used a certain tone that indicated their impatience for change. Many times, there were disagreements. Some left the fold for untold reasons. Some made outrageous contradictions in the heat of battle when philosophy is sometimes temporarily cast aside to advance personality and personal ambition. That's politics. Still, they stood together often enough, and were considered by their Liberal friends and enemies as a radical faction too often not to be labelled as such. The character of the Liberal party under Félix-Gabriel Marchand, Simon-Napoléon Parent and Lomer Gouin would have been much different if the Liberal progressive faction had not existed.

Liberal progressivism was thus an attempt to redirect nineteenth century laissez-faire liberalism as interpreted by the radical *rouges* into a modern, democratic, state-oriented philosophy. The liberal goal of making the individual the master of his or her own fate endured, only the means of guaranteeing that freedom suffered a revision. In its deliberations, Liberal progressivism established itself as an important, if now forgotten, part of Quebec's political culture. Kenneth Minogue, an observer and critic of liberalism, once illustrated this ideology as a moving train, "likely to transpose its carriage at any moment, and stopping periodically to allow people to get on and off."[17] Godfroy Langlois got on the train after the old nineteenth century radicals had fallen off in the late 1880s, wrestled with the conductor, and with the help of many friends tried to steer the train onto a more progressive track. They were successful, but only until the conservative Liberals and the progressives in the train who disagreed with Langlois's search for a trajectory banded together to wrestle back control of the engines. The uncompromising radical Liberals were brutally pushed back and there were enough bumps and bruises endured to remind them for a long time of this drama's bitter failures. Together they formed *Le Pays*, a publication nostalgically named after the old *rouge* journal. Radical Liberalism had thus come full circle. It has risen above many of the contradictions that had plagued it in the mid-nineteenth century and had reoriented itself to address pressing problems of modernity. It gathered strength at the turn of the century and overthrew many of those who had opposed its evolution. Unfortunately, the problems of defining the role of the temporal in Quebec society divided the Liberal progressives as it evolved after 1905. Radicalism was once again hopelessly split, with some finding inspiration in Sarah Bernhardt's France while others stubbornly refused to take the bold steps necessary to advance democracy.

The vision of those jolly boaters who for a fleeting moment had gathered to smile before the photographer's camera; those men who eventually formed a Masonic lodge, who fought Liberal "machine" politicians, who ran for office municipally and provincially, who controlled newspapers, who demanded education reform, who battled "trusts" as much as the church's influence, who fought the good fight while remaining members of Sir Wilfrid's party; would take some sixty years before becoming a reality.

Notes

1. *Vrai*, 3 novembre 1956. Cited in Gérard Bergeron "Political Parties in Quebec" *UTQ*, Vol XXVII, 1957-58.
2. *The Gazette*, April 9, 1926.
3. W.D. Lighthall Papers, Vol. 1, Memo, 5 April 1905.
4. A.J. Lemieux, *Les réformes scolaires et la franc-maçonnerie* (Roxton Falls, 1940), p. 5.
5. *La Presse*, 14 juillet 1911.
6. Province de Quebec, *Annuaire statistique du Québec, 1916* (Quebec, 1916), pp. 227-228.
7. See *Des écoles primaires et l'enseignement obligatoire: texte de la conférence donné au Club de réforme par l'honorable Sénateur Dandurand* (Montreal, 1919).
8. See Marcel Hamelin (ed.) *Les mémoires du Sénateur Dandurand* (Ottawa, 1966), pp. 246-248.
9. T.D. Bouchard, *Mémoires, Vol. 1* (Montreal, 1960), p. 25.
10. *Ibidem.* p. 15. See also p. 42, 45, 49.
11. Irving Orrin Vincent, *The Right Track* (Toronto, 1920), p. 60.
12. Marcel Trudel, *L'influence de Voltaire au Canada Français, Tome II* (Ottawa, 1945), p. 257.
13. On Voltaire's ideas regarding state intervention, see Constance Rowe, *Voltaire and the State* (New York, 1968).
14. On the impact of Europe's evolving meaning of liberalism in American, see Arthur Ekirch, *Progressivism in America* (New York, 1974) and Louis Hartz, *The Liberal Tradition in America* (New York, 1955).
15. Lionel Trilling, *The Liberal Imagination*, (New York, 1951), p. viii.
16. Theodore Zeldin, *France, 1848-1945* (London, 1973). p. 683. On the inconsistencies of radicalism in France, see also Jacques Kayser, *Les grandes batailles du radicalisme, 1820-1901* (Paris, 1962), p. 2.
17. Kenneth Minogue, *The Liberal Mind* (New York, 1968), p. 17.

ABBREVIATIONS

AJES:	American Journal of Economics and Sociology
AHR:	American Historical Review
AQ:	American Quarterly
ARCS:	American Review of Canadian Studies
ASLH:	American Journal of Legal History
ASR:	American Sociological Review
CD:	Cahiers des Dix
CGQ:	Cahiers de géographie du Québec
CHAR:	Canadian Historical Association Report
CHR:	Canadian Historical Review
CJEPS:	Canadian Journal of Economics and Political Science
CJPS:	Canadian Journal of Political Science
FHS:	French Historical Studies
HP:	Historical Papers
HS/SH:	Histoire Sociale/Social History
IRSH:	International Review of Social History
JALQ:	Journaux du conseil législatif de la province de Québec
JCH:	Journal of Contemporary History
JCS:	Journal of Canadian Studies
JMH:	Journal of Modern History
JP:	Journal of Politics
L/LT:	Labour/Le Travail
MS:	Mouvement Social
MVHR:	Mississipi Valley Historical Review
PNQ:	Pacific Northwest Quarterly
PS:	Political Studies
RHAF:	Revue d'histoire de l'amérique française
RHES:	Revue d'histoire économique et sociale
RHLQCF:	Revue d'histoire littéraire du Québec et du Canada français
RS:	Recherches sociographiques
UTQ:	University of Toronto Quarterly

BIBLIOGRAPHY

I: PRIMARY SOURCES

1: Manuscripts

Public Archives of Canada (PAC)

Treflé Berthiaume Papers
Henri Bourassa Papers
Adolphe Caron Papers
Philippe-Auguste Choquette Papers
Raoul Dandurand-Félix-Gabriel Marchand Papers
Alphonse Desjardins Papers
Laurent-Olivier David Papers
Charles Fitzpatrick Papers
Louis-Honoré Fréchette Papers
Henri Joly de Lotbinière Papers
Némèse Garneau Papers
George C. Gibbons Papers
Lomer Gouin Papers
Philippe Landry Papers
Wilfrid Laurier Papers
Rodolphe Lemieux Papers
Henri Morgan Papers
Ernest Pacaud Papers
Israël Tarte Papers
J.S. Willison Papers

Archives Nationales du Québec à Québec (ANQQ)

Arthur Buies Papers

Félix-Gabriel Marchand Papers
Simon-Napoléon Parent Papers

Archives Nationales du Québec à Montreal

Document Godfroy Langlois

Archives de la Chancellerie de l'Archevêché de Montreal (ACAM)

Paul-Napoléon Bruchési Papers
Charles-Edouard Fabre Papers

McGill University Archives

Herbert Ames Papers

College Lionel-Groulx, Ste-Thérèse-de-Blainville, Quebec

Les Annales Térésiennes, 1881-1884.

Private Archives:

Henri Bourassa Papers (In the possession of Mlle. Anne Bourassa,
    Outremont, Quebec)
Godfroy Langlois Papers (In the possession of Mr. Godfroy Marin,
    Westmount, Quebec)

II: Newspapers

La Bataille, 1897.
Le Canada, 1903-1910.
Le Clairon, 1889-1890.
Les Débats, 1898-1900.
L'Echo des Deux-Montagnes, 1890-1892.
L'Evénement, selections.
The Montreal Gazette, selections.
Le Glaneur, 1890.
The Monteal Herald, selections.
La Liberté, 1892-1895.
Le Monde, 1893-1895.

La Patrie, 1890-1902.
Le Pays, 1910-1914.
La Presse, 1890-1914.
Le Soleil, selections.
Le Signal, 1896-1899.
The Witness, selections.

III: Official Sources

Canada Year Book. Ottawa, 1930.
Desjardins, Joseph. *Guide Parlementaire*. Ottawa, 1905.
Journaux du Conseil Législatif du Québec, 1897-1914.
Province de Quebec, *Annuaire statistique du Quebec, 1916*. Quebec, 1916.
St-Pierre, Jocelyn. *Débats de l'Assemblée législative du Québec, 9ieme législature, Premiere Session, 1897-1898*. Quebec, 1981.

IV: Memoirs and Biographies

Béique, Caroline. *Quatre-vingts ans de souvenirs*. Montreal, 1939.
Bernhardt, Sarah. *Memories of my life*. Grosse Pointe, Michigan, 1968 (reprint).
Bouchard, T.D. *Mémoires, Tome 1, Tome 2*. Montreal, 1960.
Buies, Arthur. *Chroniques canadiennes*. Montreal, 1978. (reprint)
___. *Reminiscences. Les jeunes barbares*. Quebec, 1892.
Choquette, P.A. *Un demi-siècle de vie politique*. Montreal 1936.
Cartwright, Richard. *Reminiscences*. Toronto, 1912.
David, Laurent-Olivier. *Mes contemporains*. Montreal, 1894.
___. *Souvenirs et biographies*. Montreal, 1911.
___. *Mélanges historiques et littéraires*. Montreal, 1917.
___. *Au soir de la vie*. Montreal, 1924.
Dunn, Oscar. *Dix ans de journalisme*. Montreal, 1876.
Fournier, Jules. *Mon encrier*. Montreal, 1922.
Fréchette, Louis-Honoré. *Mémoires intimes*. Montreal, 1977. (reprint)
Hamelin, Marcel (ed.) *Les mémoires du Sénateur Raoul Dandurand*. Ottawa, 1967.
Pacaud, Lucien. *Sir Wilfrid Laurier: Lettres à mon père*. Ottawa, 1966.

Langelier, Charles. *Souvenirs politiques, Volume I: 1878-1890.* Quebec, 1909. *Volume II: 1890-1896.* Quebec, 1912.

Liassais-Tassé, Henriette. *La vie humoristique d'Hector Berthelot.* Montreal, 1934.

Marchand, Félix-Gabriel. *Mélanges politiques et littéraires.* St-Jean, 1899.

Piquefort, Jean. "Portraits et pastels litteraires" *Guêpes canadiennes, Volume 1.* Montreal, 1881.

Roy, Pierre-George. *La dixième législature de Quebec.* Lévis, 1901.

Tremblay, Remi. *Pierre qui roule.* Montreal, 1924.

Vieux-Rouges. *Les Contemporains.* Montreal, 1898.

V: Contemporary Pamphlets (in chronological order)

Conférence de C. Beausoleil au Club National de Montreal, vendredi le 6 février 1891. Montreal, 1891.

M. Mercier jugé par les libéraux. Montreal, 1891.

Les libéraux honnêtes répudient M. Mercier. Montreal, 1892.

Buies, Arthur. *Quebec en 1900.* Quebec, 1893.

Mercier, Honoré. *L'Avenir du Canada.* Montreal, 1893.

David, L.O. *Le clergé canadien, son oeuvre, sa mission.* Montreal, 1895.

Un message de paix: la motion Marchand. n.p. 1895.

Un manifeste libéral: L.O. David et le clergé. Quebec, 1896.

Langlois, Godfroy. *La république de 1848.* Montreal, 1897.

___. Sus au Sénat. Montreal, 1898.

The Provincial Election of 1897: A Redeeming Policy. n.p.,n.d..

Chapais, l'Hon. Thomas. *Discours sur la loi de l'instruction publique, 10 janvier 1898.* Quebec, 1898.

La Ligue de l'Enseignement. Montreal, 1903.

La Ligue de l'Enseignement. *La question de l'instruction publique dans la province de Québec.* Montreal, 1903.

Magnan, C. *Honneur à la province de Québec.* Quebec, 1903.

Discours prononcé par l'hon. Lomer Gouin, ministre de la colonization et des travaux publics, 24 mars 1904. Montreal, 1904.

Discours-programme prononcé par l'hon. Lomer Gouin à l'ecole Montcalm, Montreal, 5 avril 1905. Quebec, 1905.

Politique provinciale: Trois discours de l'hon. Lomer Gouin. Quebec, 1908.

Discours sur l'instruction publique prononcé à l'assemblée législative de Québec par l'hon. Rodolphe Roy. Quebec, 1906.

Lemieux, A.J. *La loge l'emancipation.* Montreal, 1910.

Résumé d'un discours prononcé par l'hon. Sir Lomer Gouin à l'assemblée législative de Québec, le 26 novembre 1912. Quebec, 1913.

Toujours debout: le mandement de Mgr Bruchési et la réponse du "Pays". Montreal, 1913.

Les écoles primaires et l'enseignement obligatoire: texte de la conférence donnée au club de réforme par l'honorable Senateur Dandurand. Montreal, 1919.

Lemieux, A.J. *Autrefois... Les réformes scolaires et la franc-maconnerie.* Roxton Falls, 1940.

VI: Interviews

M. Godfroy Marin (Grandson of Godfroy Langlois) 5 October 1986.

Mme. Corinne Maillet (Family friend of Godfroy Langlois) 5 October 1896.

II: SECONDARY SOURCES

I: Theses

Bance, Pierre. "Beaugrand et son temps" Ph.D. thesis, University of Ottawa, 1964.

Cahill, Elizabeth. "The Legislative Council of Quebec: Attempts to abolish or reform, 1867-1965" M.A. thesis, McGill University, 1966.

Caya, Marcel. "La formation du Parti Libéral au Quebec: 1867-1887" Ph.D. thesis, York University, 1981.

Charbonneau, Jean-Claude. "The Lay School Movement in Quebec since 1840" M.A. thesis, McGill University, 1971.

Dirks, Patricia Grace. "The Origins of the Union Nationale" Ph.D. thesis, University of Toronto, 1974.

Gauvin, Michel. "The Municipal Reform Movement in Montreal 1886-1914" M.A. thesis, University of Ottawa, 1972.

Genest, Jean-Guy. "Vie et oeuvre d'Adélard Godbout, 1892-1956" D es L thesis, Universite Laval, 1977.

Germain, Anne. "Mouvements sociaux de réforme urbaine à Montreal, de 1880 a 1920" Ph.D. thesis, Université de Montreal, 1980.

Heintzman, Ralph. "The Struggle for Life: The French Daily Press of Montreal and the Problem of Economic Growth in the Age of Laurier, 1896-1911" Ph.D. thesis, York University, 1977.

Jackson, Eric. "Organization of the Canadian Liberal Party, 1867-1896" M.A. thesis, University of Toronto, 1962.

Landry, Pierre. "L'idéologie du journal Le Canada, 1903-1907" M.A. thesis, Universite Laval, 1970.

Lapierre, Laurier. "Politics, Race and Religion in French-Canada: Joseph-Israèl Tarte" Ph.D. thesis, University of Toronto, 1962.

Laurin, Luc. "Le nationalisme et le radicalisme du journal La Patrie, 1879-1897" M.A. thesis, McGill University, 1973.

Lessard, Victrice. "L'instruction obligatoire dans la province de Québec de 1875 à 1943" Ph.D. thesis, University of Ottawa, 1962.

Lovink, J.A.A. "The Politics of Quebec: Provincial Political Parties, 1897-1936" Ph.D. thesis, Duke University, 1967.

Macleod, J.T. "The Political Thought of Sir Wilfrid Laurier: A Study in Canadian Party Leadership" Ph.D. thesis, University of Toronto, 1965.

Nagant, Francine. "Politique municipale à Montreal, 1910-1914: L'échec des réformistes et le triomphe de Médéric Martin" M.A. thesis, Université de Montreal, 1982.

Oliver, Frank. "Political and Social Ideas of French Canadian Nationalists" Ph.D. thesis, McGill University, 1956.

Piette-Samson, Christine. "Louis-Antoine Dessaulles, rédacteur du Pays, journaliste libéral doctrinaire" D.E.S. thesis, Universite Laval, 1968.

Rioux, J.P. "L'institut Canadien, les debuts de l'institut canadien et du journal l'Avenir, 1844-1849" D.E.S. thesis, Université Laval, 1967.

Robertson, N.S. "The Institut Canadien: An essay in Cultural history" M.A. thesis, University of Western Ontario, 1965.

Russell, Daniel J. "H.B. Ames as Municipal Reformer" M.A. thesis, McGill University, 1971.

Stevens, Paul. "Laurier and the Liberal Party of Ontario, 1887-1911" Ph.D. thesis, University of Toronto, 1966.

Trepanier, Pierre. "Le Ministère Joly" M.A. thesis, University of Ottawa, 1972.

Zoltvany, Yves. "Les Libéraux du Québec, leur parti et leur pensée, 1867-1875" M.A. thesis, Université de Montreal, 1961.

II: Books

Ames, H.B. *The City Below the Hill*. Montreal, 1972. (reprint)

Anderson, R.D. *France 1870-1914: Politics and Society*. London, 1977.

Armstrong, Christopher and H.V. Nelles. *Monopoly's Moment: The Organization and Regulation of Canadian Utilities, 1830-1930*. Philadelphia, 1986.

Augenot, Marc. *1889: Un état du discours social*. Montreal, 1989.

Angers, F.A. *La Pensée d'Henri Bourassa*. Montreal, 1954.

Auspitz, Katherine. *The Radical Bourgeoisie*. New York, 1982.

Bardonnet, Daniel. *Evolution de la structure du parti radical*. Paris, 1960.

Barthe, Ulric. *Wilfrid Laurier on the Platform*. Quebec, 1890.

Beaulieu, Andre and Hamelin, Jean. *La presse québécoise des origines à nos jours. Vols II,III,IV*. Quebec, 1979.

Behiels, Michael. *Prelude to the Quiet Revolution*. Kingston and Montreal, 1985.

Belanger, Réal. *L'impossible défi: Albert Sevigny et les conservateurs fédéraux, 1902-1918*. Quebec, 1983.

Bernard, André, and Laporte, Denis. *La Législation électorale au Québec, 1790-1967*. Montreal, 1969.

Bernard, Jean-Paul. *Les idéologies québécoises au XIXe siècle*. Montreal, 1973.

____. *Les rouges: libéralisme, nationalisme et anticléricalisme au milieu du XIXe siecle*. Montreal, 1971.

Bliss, Michael. *Plague: A Story of Smallpox in Montreal*. Toronto, 1991.

Boisonneault, Charles Marie. *Histoire de la province de Québec 1867-1920*. Montreal, 1936.

Bramstead, E.K. and K.J. Melhuish (ed.). *Western Liberalism: A History in Documents from Locke to Croce*. London, 1978.

Brown, R.C. and Cook, R. *Canada 1896-1921: A Nation Transformed*. Toronto, 1914.

Brunet, Michel. *La présence anglaise et les canadiens*. Montreal, 1958.

Buenker, J.D. *Urban Liberalism and Progressive Reform*. New York, 1973.

Careless, J.M.S. *The Union of the Canadas*. Toronto, 1967.

Chalmers, David Mark. *The Social and Political Ideas of the Muckrackers*. New York, 1964.

Charbonneau, Jean. *L'école littéraire de Montreal*. Montreal, 1935.

____. *Des influences françaises au Canada, Tome I*. Montreal, 1917. *Tome II*, Montreal, 1918.

Charbonneau, Pierre. *Le projet québécois d'Honoré Mercier*. St-Jean, 1980.

Choko, Marc H. *Les grandes place publiques de Montréal*. Montreal, 1987.

Clark, Lovell C. *The Guibord Affair*. Toronto, 1971.

Cloutier, E. and Latouche, D. *Le système politique québécois*. Montreal, 1979.

Colombier, Marie. *Le voyage de Sarah Bernhardt en Amérique*. Paris, 1881.

Cooper, J.I. *A Short History of Montreal*. Montreal, 1968.

Copp, T. *The Anatomy of Poverty*. Toronto, 1974.

Cornell, Paul. *The Alignment of Political Groups in Canada, 1841-1867*. Toronto, 1962.

Costisella, Joseph. *L'Esprit révolutionnaire dans la littérature canadienne-française de 1837 à la fin du XIXe siècle*. Montreal, 1968.

Crunican, Paul. *Priests and Politicians*. Toronto, 1974.

Dafoe, J.W. *Sir Wilfrid Laurier*. Toronto, 1974. (reprint)

Dangerfield, George. *The Strange Death of Liberal England*. New York, 1961.

Dales, J. *Hydroelectricity and Industrial Development in Quebec, 1898-1940*. Toronto, 1957.

David, L.O. *Laurier, Sa vie, son oeuvre*. Beauceville, 1899.

Denis, Roch. *Luttes de classes et question nationale au Québec, 1940-1968*. Montreal, 1979.

D'Erbree, Jean. *La maçonnerie canadienne-française*. Montreal, n.d.

Dion, Leon. *Nationalismes et politiques*. Montreal, 1975.

de Bonville, Jean. *Jean-Baptiste Gagnepetit: Les travailleurs montrealais à la fin du XIXe siecle*. Montreal, 1975.

de Bonville, Jean. *La presse québécoise de 1884 à 1914: genèse d'un media de masse*. Quebec, 1988.

d'Ormesson, Jean. *Grand Hotel: The Golden Age of Palace Hotels and Architectural and Social History*. London, 1984.

Dorsett, Lyle. *The Pendergast Machine*. New York, 1976.

Dumont, Fernand (ed.). *Idéologies au Canada francais, 1850-1900*. Quebec, 1971.

_____. *Idéologies au Canada francais, 1900-1929*. Quebec, 1974.

Dussault, Gabriel. *Le curé Labelle*. Montreal, 1983.

Duverger, Maurice. *Political Parties*. New York, 1954.

Ehrenberg, Lewis. *Steppin' Out*. Westport, 1981.

Eid, Nadia. *Le clergé et le pouvoir politique au Quebec*. Montreal, 1976.

Ekirch, Arthur. *Progressivism in America*. New York, 1974.

Ellis, J.D. *The Early Life of Georges Clemenceau, 1841-1893*. Lawrence, 1980.

Elwitt, Sanford. *Making of the Third Republic*. Baton Rouge, 1975.

Felteau, Cyrille. *Histoire de La Presse, Tome I: Le livre du peuple, 1884-1916*. Montreal, 1983.

Filler, Louis. *Crusaders for American Liberalism*. Yellow Springs, 1939.

Forcey, Charles. *Crossroads of Liberalism*. New York, 1961.

Fortin, Lionel. *F.G. Marchand*. St-Jean, 1979.

Gagnon, Marcel A. *Le ciel et l'enfer d'Arthur Buies*. Montreal, 1965.

_____. *La vie orageuse d'Olivar Asselin*. (Montreal, 1962)

_____. *Jean-Charles Harvey: Précurseur de la révolution tranquille*. Montreal, 1970.

Galarneau, Claude. *Les collèges classiques au Canada français*. Montreal, 1978.

Girvetz, Harry K. *Evolution of Liberalism*. New York, 1950.

Godin, Pierre. *L'information-opium: Une histoire politique du journal La Presse*. Montreal, 1972.

Hamelin, Jean and Hamelin, Marcel. *Les moeurs électorales dans le Quebec de 1791 à nos jours*. Montreal, 1962.

Hamelin, Jean and Huot, John and Hamelin, Marcel. *Aperçu de la politique canadienne au XIXe siecle*. Quebec, 1965.

Hare, A.P. Borgatha, E.F. Bales, R.F. *Small groups*. New York, 1967.

Hartz, Louis. *The Liberal Tradition in America*. New York, 1955.

_____. *The Founding of New Societies*. New York, 1964.

Hobhouse, L.T. *Liberalism*. London, 1934.

Hoststadter, R. *The Age of Reform*. New York, 1955.

Hogue, C., Bolduc, A., Larouche, D. *Quebec: Un siecle d'electricité*. Montreal, 1979.

Hopkins, Castell (ed.) *Canadian Annual Review*. Toronto, 1902-1915.

Hughes, H.S. *Consciousness and Society*. New York, 1958.

Huthmaker, J.J.. *Senator Robert F. Wagner and the Rise of Urban Liberalism*. New York, 1968.

Kayser, Jacques. *Les grandes batailles du radicalisme, 1820-1901*. Paris, 1962.

Kesterton, W. *A History of Journalism in Canada*. Toronto, 1967.

Kolko, G. *The Triumph of Conservatism*. New York, 1963.

Lamonde, Yvan et Raymond Montpetit. *Le Parc Sohmer de Montreal 1889-1919. Un lieu populaire de culture urbaine*. Quebec, 1986.

Lamontagne, Leopold. *Arthur Buies, homme de lettres*. Quebec, 1957.

Larkin, Maurice. *Church and State after the Dreyfus Affair*. New York, 1974.

Lariviere, C. *Albert Saint-Martin, militant d'avant garde*. Montreal, 1979.

Laski, Harold. *The Rise of European Liberalism*. London, 1936.

Lefranc, Georges. *Les gauches en France*. Paris, 1973.

Lemieux, V. (ed.). *Personnel et partis politiques au Quebec*. Montreal, 1982.

Le Moine, Roger. *Deux Loges montréalaises du Grant Orient de France*. Ottawa, 1991.

Levitt, J. *Henri Bourassa and the Golden Calf*. Ottawa, 1969.

Levy, David W. *Herbert Croly of the New Republic*. Princeton, 1985.

Linteau, Paul-André, René Durocher and Jean-Claude Robert. *Histoire du Quebec Contemporain: De la Confédération à la crise (1867-1929)*. Montreal, 1979.

Linteau, Paul-Andre. Maisonneuve.

Loubere, Leo A. *Radicalism in Meditteranean France*. Albany, 1974.

Mailhot, Laurent (ed.) *Anthologies d'Arthur Buies*. Montreal, 1978.

Marion, Seraphin. *Les lettres canadiennes d'autrefois. Tome VIII*. Hull, 1954.

_____. *Les lettres canadiennes d'autrefois, Tome IX*. Hull, 1958.

Milbourne, A.J.S. *Freemasonry in the Province of Quebec*. Montreal, 1960.

Miller, Carman. *Painting the Map Red: Canada and the Boer War*. Montreal, 1993.

Miller, Zane. *Boss Cox's Cincinnati*. New York, 1975.

Minville, Esdras. *Syndicalisme, legislation ouvriere et regime social au Quebec avant 1940*. Montreal, 1986. (reprint)

Moniere, Denis. *Le développement des idéologies au Quebec*. Montreal, 1977.

Monet, Jacques. *The Last Cannon Shot*. Toronto, 1969.

Neatby, H.B. *Laurier and a Liberal Quebec*. Toronto, 1963.

Nicolet, Claude. *Le radicalisme*. Paris, 1967.

Nordmann, Jean-Thomas. *Histoire des radicaux*. Paris, 1974.

_____. *La France radicale*. Paris, 1977.

Orban, E. *Le Conseil legislatif au Quebec, 1867-1967*. Montreal, 1967.

Owram, Doug. *The Government Generation*. Toronto, 1986.

Partin, Malcolm O. *Waldeck Rousseau, Combes and the Church: The Politics of Anti-Clericalism, 1899-1905*. Durham, 1969.

Pelletier, R. (ed.) *Partis politiques au Quebec*. Montreal, 1976.

Perrin, Roberto. *Rome in Canada: The Vatican and Canadian Affairs in the Late Victorian Age* . Toronto, 1990.

Pipes, Richard. *Struve: Liberal on the Left, 1870-1905*. Cambridge, 1970.

Rearick, Charles. *Pleasures of The Belle Epoque* . New Haven, 1985.

Regenstreif, Peter. *The Liberal Party of Canada*. Toronto, 1970.

Regier, C.C.. *The Era of the Muckracker*. Gloucester, Mass., 1932.

Rivet, L.A. *Honoré Mercier: Patriote et homme d'état*. Montreal, n.d.

Rowe, Constance. *Voltaire and the State*. New York, 1968.

Roy, Fernande. *Progrès, harmonie, liberté: Le libéralisme des milieux d'affaires francophones à Montreal au tournant du siecle*. Montreal, 1988.

Rudorf, Raymond. *Belle Epoque*. London, 1972.

Ruggiero, Guido de. *History of European Liberalism*. Boston, 1966 (reprint)

Rumilly, Robert. *Histoire de la province de Quebec, Vols 7-13*, Montreal, 1942.

_____. *Histoire de Montreal, Vol. 3*. Montreal, 1972.

_____. *Honoré Mercier et son temps, Vols I & II*. Montreal, 1936.

Rutherford, P. *The Making of the Canadian Media*. Toronto, 1968.

Ryan, W.F. *The Clergy and Economic Growth in Quebec, 1896-1914*. Quebec, 1966.

Savard, Pierre. *Jules-Paul Tardivel, La France et les Etats-Unis, 1851-1905*. Quebec, 1967.

Saywell, J.T. *The Office of Lieutenant-Governor*. Toronto, 1957.

Seideman, David. *The New Republic: A Voice of Modern Liberalism.* Wesport, 1986.

Shattuck, Roger. *The Banquet Years.* New York, 1968.

Sheehan, James J. *German Liberalism in the nineteenth century.* Chicago, 1978.

Simpson, Jeffrey. *Spoils of Power: The Politics of Patronage.* Toronto, 1988.

Skelton, O.D. *Life and Letters of Sir Wilfrid Laurier, 2 Vols.* Toronto, 1921.

Siegfried, A. *Le Canada: Les deux races.* Montreal, 1906.

Silver, A. *The French Canadian Idea of Confederation, 1866-1900.* Toronto, 1982.

Stearns, Peter N. *Priest and Revolutionary.* New York, 1967.

____. *The Revolutions of 1848.* London, 1974.

Steele, Ronald. *Walter Lippman and the American Century.* New York, 1980.

Swados, Harvey (ed.) *Years of Conscience.* New York, 1952.

Teboul, Victor. *Le Jour: Emergence du Libéralisme moderne au Quebec.* Montreal, 1984.

Therio, A. *Jules Fournier.* Montreal, 1954.

Thurston, Robert. *Liberal City, Conservative State: Moscow and Russia's Urban Crisis, 1906-1914.*

Trilling, Lionel. *The Liberal Imagination.* London, 1951.

Trudel, M. *L'Influence de Voltaire au Canada, Tome II.* Montreal, 1945.

Turcotte, G. *Le Conseil Legislatif de Quebec, 1774-1933.* Beauceville, 1933.

Underhill, F. *In Search of Canadian Liberalism.* Toronto, 1960.

Underhill, Frank and Fox, P.W. *The Radical Tradition: A Second View* of Canadian History. (Script of "Explorations", CBC Television, June 8 and 15, 1960.

Vachet, André. *L'idéologie libérale, l'individu et sa propriété.* Paris, 1988.

Vigod, Bernard. *Quebec before Duplessis: The Political Career of Louis-Alexandre Taschereau.* Kingston, 1986.

Vincent, Irving O. *The Right Track.* Toronto, 1920.

Weinstein, J. *The Corporate Ideal in the Liberal State, 1900-1918.* Boston, 1968.

Weibe, R. *The Search for Order.* New York, 1967.

____. *Businessmen and Reform*. New York, 1962.

Weiler, Georgette. *Sarah Bernhardt et le Canada*. Quebec, 1973.

Weinberg, Arthur and Lila. *The Muckrackers*. New York, 1961.

Willison, J.S. *Sir Wilfrid Laurier and the Liberal Party*. Toronto, 1903.

Wilson, T. *The Downfall of the Liberal Party*. Ithaca, 1966.

Wyczynski, Paul (ed.) *L'école littéraire de Montreal*. Montreal, 1963.

____. *Emile Nelligan*. Montreal, 1988.

Young, Brian. *Promoters and Politicians*. Toronto, 1978.

Zeldin, Theodore. *France 1848-1945*. London, 1973.

II: Articles

Armstrong, C. Nelles, V. "The Rise of Civic Populism in Toronto, 1870-1920" in Russell, Victor. *Forging a Consensus*. Toronto, 1984.

____. "Contrasting Development of the Hydro-Electric Industry in the Montreal and Toronto Regions, 1900-1930" *JCS*. Spring 1983.

____. "Suburban Street Railway Strategies in Montreal, Toronto, and Vancouver, 1896-1930" in Stetler, Gilbert A. and Alan F.J. Artibise (eds.) *Power and Place: Urban Development in the North American Context*. Vancouver, 1986.

Audet, Louis-Philippe. "La Querelle de l'Instruction obligatoire" *CD*. 1959.

Ayearst, M. "The Parti Rouge and the Clergy" *CHR*, Vol 9, NO. 4. 1934.

Baumer, Franklin. "Intellectual History and its problems" *JMH*, September 1949.

Beaudin, Francois. "L'influence de La Mennais sur Mgr. Lartigue, premier évêque de Montréal" *RHAF*, Vol. 25, No.2, septembre 1971.

Bélanger, André and Lemieux, Vincent. "Le nationalisme et les partis politiques" *RHAF*, Mars 1969.

Bernard, Jean-Paul. "Définition du libéralisme et de l'ultramontan-isme commes idéologies" *RHAF*, septembre 1971.

____. "Les idéologies québécoises et américaines au XIXe siècle" in Claude Savary (ed.) *Les rapports culturels entre le Quebec et les Etats-Unis*. Quebec, 1984.

Bergeron, Gerard. "Political parties in Quebec" *UTQ*, Vol. XXVII, 1957-58.

Berube, Renald. "Jules Fournier: Trouver le mot de la situation" in Wyczynski, Paul. *Archvies des lettres canadiennes, vol. VI: L'essai et la prose d'idees au Quebec*. Montreal, 1985.

Bonenfant. J.C. "L'Evolution du statut de l'homme politique canadien-français" *RS*, 1966.

____. "Le Bicaméralisme dans le Quebec" *CJEPS*, 1964.

Bouchard, Gerard. "Apogée et déclin de l'idéologie ultramontaine à travers le journal *Le Nouveau Monde*" *RS*, mai-decembre 1969.

Bourassa, Guy. "Les élites politiques de Montreal: de l'aristocracie à la démocratie" *CJEPS*, 1965.

____. "La structure du pouvoir à Montréal: Le domaine de l'éducation" *RS*, 1967.

Blais, André. "Third Parties in Canadian Provincial Politics" *CJPS*, September 1973.

Burke, T.A. "Mackenzie and his Cabinet, 1873-1878" *CHR*, Vol. XLI, No.2, 1960.

Citron, Suzanne. "Enseignement secondaire et idéologie élitiste entre 1880 et 1914" MS, juillet-septembre 1976.

Chevrier, B. "Le ministère de Félix-Gabriel Marchand" *RHAF*, juin 1968.

Condemine, Odette. "Louis Fréchette, un admirateur de François-Xavier Garneau" *RHLQCF*, Vol.7, hiver-printemps 1984.

Corrigan, P., and Bruce Curtis, "Education Inspection and State formation: A preliminary statement" *HP*, 1985.

Darnton, Robert. "The symbolic Element in History" *JMH*, Vol. 58., No.1, March 1986.

de Bonville, Jean. "La liberte de presse à la fin du XIXe siecle: Le cas de *Canada-Revue*" *RHAF*, Mars 1978.

Dion, Leon. "The concept of Political Leadership" *CJPS*, March 1968.

Falardeau, J.C. "L'origine et l'ascension des hommes d'affaires dans la société canadienne-française" *RS*, 1965.

Friedrich, C.J. "Political leadership and the problem of Charismatic Power" *JP*, February 1961.

Gaudreau, Guy, "L'exploitation des forêts publiques au Québec (1874-1905): Transition et nouvel essor" *RHAF*, Vol. 42, No. 1, été 1988.

Gow, J.I. "L'administration québécoise de 1867 à 1900: Un état en formation" *CJPS*, 1979.

Graham, W.R. "Liberal nationalism in the 1870s" *CHAR*, 1946.

Guitard, Michelle. "Pour une histoire de l'Institut Canadien de Montreal" *RHAF*, Vol.27, No. 3, decembre 1973.

Hamel, T. "L'obligation scolaire au Québec" *L/LT*, Vol 17, Spring 1986.

Hamelin, Jean and Beaudoin, Louise. "Les cabinets provinciaux 1867-1967" *RS, 1967.*

Hamelin, Jean, Letarte, Jacques, Hamelin, Marcel."Les élections provinciales dans le Québec" *CGQ,* octobre 1959-mars 1960.

Hardy, René. "Libéralisme Québécois et ultramontanisme à Québec: Eléments de redifinition" *RHAF*, septembre 1971.

Hathorn, Ramon. "Sarah Bernhardt et l'acceuil montréalais" *RHLQCF*, Vol. 5, 1983.

Hathorn, Ramon. "Sarah Bernhardt and the Bishops of Montreal and Quebec" Canadian Catholic History Association *Historical Studies*, Vol. 53, (1986)

Hays, S.P. "The Politics of Reform in Municipal Government int he Progressive Era" *PNQ,* October 1964.

Hayward, J.E.S. "Solidarity: The social history of an idea in nineteenth century France" *IRSH*, Vol IX, 1959.

_____. "The Official Social Philosophy of the French Third Republic: Leon Bourgeois and Solidarism" *IRSH*, Vol. VI, 1961.

_____. "Educational Pressure Groups and the Indoctrination of the RAdical Ideology of Solidarism, 1895-1914" *IRSH*, Vol VIII, 1963, part 1.

Heap, R. "La Ligue de l'enseignement, 1902-1904: Héritage du passé et nouveaux défis" *RHAF*, decembre 1982.

_____. "Urbanization et education: la centralisation scolaire à Montreal au début du XXe siècle" *HP*, 1985.

Jaumain, Serge. "Paris devant l'opinion canadienne-francaise: Les récits de voyages entre 1820 et 1914" *RHAF*, 38, 4, printemps 1985.

Knopff, Rainer. "Quebec's 'Holy War' as 'Regime' politics: Reflections on the Guibord Case" *CJPS*, 1979.

Lamonde, Yvan. "Le membership d'une association au XIXe siècle: Le cas de l'Institut Canadien de Longueil" *RS*, 1975.

Laporte, P.L. "La nouvelle europééne et la presse québécoise d'expression francaise (1866-1871)" *RHAF*, mars 1975.

Lederle, J. "The Liberal Convention of 1892" *CJEPS*, 1950.

Lemieux, Vincent. "Les partis et le pouvoir politique" *RS*, 1966.

Levitt, Joseph. "Images of Bourassa" *JCS*, 13, 1978.

Linteau, P.A. "Quelques reflexions autour de la bourgeoisie québécoise, 1850-1914" *RHAF*, Vol. 30, No. 1, juin 1976.

_____. "Rapport de pouvoir et émergence d'une nouvelle élite canadienne-francaise à Montreal, 1886-1914" *JCS*, December 1986.

Loubere, Léo. "French Left-Wing Radicals: Their views on Trade Unionism, 1870-1898" *IRSH*, Vol. 7, 1962.

_____. "Left-Wing Radicals, Strikes and the Military, 1880-1907" *FHS*, Vol 3, Spring 1963.

_____. "French Left-Wing Radicals and the Law as a Social Force, 1870-1900" *AJLH*, Vol.8, January 1964.

_____. "Les radicaux d'extrème-gauche en France et les rapports entre patrons et ouvriers (1871-1900)" *RHES*, Vol. 42, 1964.

_____. "French Left-Wing Radicals: Their Economic and Social Program since 1870" *AJES*, 26, April 1967.

MacMillan, C. Micheal. "The Character of Henri Bourassa's Political Philosophy" *ARCS*, Spring 1982.

Matheson, Thomas. "La Mennais et l'éducation au Bas-Canada" *RHAF*, XIII, 4, mars 1960.

McCormick, R.L. "The Discovery that Business Corrupts Politics: A Reappraisal of the Origins of Progressivism" *AHR*, April, 1981.

Morin, Leo. "Historique du college de St-Laurent" *Enseignement Secondaire au Canada*, Vol XIII, Janvier 1934.

Mowry, G.E. "The California Progressive and his Rationale: A Study in Middle Class Politics" *MVHR*, September 1949.

Neatby, H.B. and John Saywell, "Chapleau and the Conservative Party in Quebec" *CHR*, March 1956.

Nelles, H.V. "Public Ownership of Electrical Utilities in Manitoba and Ontario, 1906-1930" *CHR*, 1976.

Orban, Edmond. "Bicaméralisme quebecois: rétrospective comparative" *RHAF*, septembre 1971.

Pelletier, Jean-Guy. "La presse canadienne et la guerre des Boers" *RS*, 1963.

Pouliot, Leon. "L'institut Canadien de Montréal et l'Institut National" *RHAF*, septembre 1971.

____. "Le cas de conscience de Gonzalve Doutre" *RHAF*, decembre 1969.

Rambaud, A. "Quebec et la guerre Franco-allemande de 1870" *RHAF*, decembre 1952.

Rayside, David. "Federalism and the Party System: Provincial and Federal Liberals in the province of Quebec" *CJPS*, 1978.

Ratnam, K.J. "Charisma and Political Leadership" *PS*, october 1964.

Rudin, R. "Regional Complexity and Political Behaviour in a Quebec County, 1867-1886" *HS/SH*, 1976.

Rutherford, Paul. "Tommorow's Metropolis: The Urban Reform Movement in Canada, 1880-1920" *HP*, 1971.

Savard, Pierre. "Le catholicisme canadien-francais au XIXe siecle" *HS/SH*, 1971.

Saywell, J.T. "The Cabinet of 1896" in F.W. Gibson (ed.) *Cabinet Formation and Bicultural Relations*. Ottawa, 1970.

Shils, E. "Charisma, Order and Status" *ASR*, April 1965.

Silver, A.I. "Some Quebec Attitudes in an Age of Imperialism and Ideological Conflict" *CHR*, 1976.

Snell, J.G. "Canadian Emigrant Elites: The Rouges and Confederation" HS/SH, 1973.

Sorcoran, J.I.W. "Henri Bourassa et la guerre sud-africaine" *RHAF*, decembre 1964, juin, 1865, septembre 1965, decembre 1965.

Stevens, Paul. "Wilfrid Laurier: Politician" in Hamelin, Jean (ed.) *Les idées politiques des premiers minstres*. Ottawa, 1969.

Stewart, Gordon T. "Political Patronage under Macdonald and Laurier, 1878-1911" *ARCS*, Spring 1980.

Sylvain, Philippe. "Libéralisme et ultramontanisme au Canada français: affrontement idéologique et doctrinal" in Morton, W.L. (ed.) *Shield of Achilles/Bouclier d'Achille*. Toronto, 1968.

Thério, Adrien. "Louis-Antoine Dessaulles: sous le signe de la liberté et de la justice" in Wyczynski, Paul (ed.). *Archives des lettres canadiennes, Vol. VI: L'Essai et la prose d'idees au Quebec*. Montreal, 1985.

Trofimenkoff, Susan Mann. "Henri Bourassa and the Woman Question" *JCS*, 10, 1975.

Vachet, André. "Post-scriptum à Jean-Paul Bernard: Libéralisme ou pas..." in Claude Savary (ed.) *Les rapports culturels entre le Quebec et les Etats-Unis*. Quebec, 1984.

____. "L'idéologie libérale et la pensée sociale au Quebec" in C. Panaccio et P.A. Quintin. *Philosophie au Quebec*. Montreal, 1976.

Ward. P.C. "Infant Birth Weight and Nutrition in Industrializing Montreal" *AHR*, April 1984.

Weaver, J.C. "Tomorrow's Metropolis Revisited: A Critical Assessment of Urban Reform in Canada, 1890-1920" in Artibise. A.J. (ed.) *The Canadian City*. Toronto, 1977.

Weilbrenner, Bernard. "Les idées politiques de Lomer Gouin" *CHAR*, 1965.

Zimmermann, Moshe. "A Road not Taken: Friedrich Naumann's Attempt at a Modern German Nationalism" *JCH*, 17, 1982.

Index

Marcil, Dr. Charles: 85, 243
Marin, Albéric:
Marin, Godfroy: 9
McCorkill, J.C.: 174, 209, 211, 269
Meunier, Léger: 17, 77
Mercier, Honoré: 10, 26, 27, 28, 29, 36, 37, 38, 45, 46, 55, 57, 59, 65, 66, 67, 72, 73, 74, 83, 84, 88, 95, 96, 98, 109, 132, 136, 138, 139, 140, 142, 153, 155, 193, 226, 233, 297, 333
Mercier, Wilfrid: 79
Merchants Light, Heat and Power: 234, 238
Miville-Dechêne, François G.M.: 74, 83, 84, 85, 88, 96, 97, 99, 117, 152, 155, 158
Monet, Dominique: 21, 207, 210, 213, 214
Montreal Light Heat and Power: 184, 185, 186, 187, 191, 192, 193, 198, 199, 200, 201, 202, 204, 208, 214, 218, 220, 221, 222, 223, 224, 225, 226, 227, 228, 229, 230, 232, 233, 237, 238, 255, 258, 262, 296, 297, 299, 300, 337, 338, 341

Nantel, Alphonse: 79
Nelligan, Emile: 56, 162

Pacaud, Ernest: 36, 37, 59, 65, 81, 113, 116, 153, 179, 181, 194, 201
Papineau, Louis-Joseph: 10, 25, 26, 29, 61, 306
Parent, Simon-Napoléon: 10, 97, 99, 100, 152, 153, 154, 155, 156, 157, 158, 166, 167, 170, 174, 178, 187, 190, 191, 193, 194, 196, 197, 198, 200, 201, 202, 203, 204, 205, 206, 207, 208, 209, 210, 211, 212, 213, 214, 215, 218, 219, 220, 222, 238, 242, 263, 270, 277, 285, 335, 345
Payette, Louis: 197, 221, 222, 225, 226, 227, 228, 229, 230, 231, 233, 236, 237, 297, 298, 315, 336, 338
Pelletier, Sen. Alphonse: 78, 152, 206
Perrault, Maurice: 157, 226, 230, 278
Piché, Camille: 79, 164, 177, 210, 213, 214
Pigeon, A.P.: 164
Préfontaine, Raymond: 33, 34, 37, 38, 55, 131, 136, 137, 138, 139, 140, 141, 142, 143, 145, 146, 147, 152, 170, 172, 175, 176, 177, 178, 179, 180, 182, 188, 196, 198, 201, 207, 208, 210, 221, 224, 225, 238, 258, 263, 285, 297, 335, 336, 340
Prince, Lorenzo: 78

Walsh, J.C.: 138, 178, 201, 203, 214, 221, 225, 229, 230, 235, 278, 296, 298, 307, 334

Weir, William Alexander: 88, 97, 158, 159, 173, 177, 208, 214, 267, 268, 273, 278

Wilson-Smith, Richard: 176, 177

WITHDRAWN

PRINTED IN CANADA